HEARTS TURN

HEARTS TURN

Sinners, Seekers, Saints
& the Road to Redemption

MICHAEL SUGICH

TELLTALE TEXTS

ISBN 978-0-9893640-0-3

Cover designed by Mukhtar Sanders
Cover art by Maaida Noor

For Moulay Hachem al-Belghiti
who took me by the hand and turned my heart

And dedicated to the memory of
the poet Daniel Abdal Hayy Moore
&
the teacher Shaykh Yusuf Da Costa

CONTENTS

Contents

Contents

AUTHOR'S NOTE

I have made considerable effort to be true to every narrative related on the following pages, to capture the voice of the protagonist and give context to the story being told. There were those who, for personal or professional reasons, asked to remain anonymous. Their stories are no less true, but their names have been changed.

In a certain sense this book has been inspired by the ancient biographies (*tabaqat*) and hagiographies of the saints, many of whom led less than exemplary lives before turning to God and taking the Path. I have included a number of stories from the ancient texts, which are identified by the symbol:

Know that knowledge is life, wisdom is a mirror, contentment a protective wall, hope a mediator and intercessor, remembrance [of God] a remedy, and repentance a cure.

Repentance is the signpost on the path, the leader of the kingdom, the key to the treasure, the intermediary that assists you to become united with God, the condition for being accepted to the Divine presence, and the secret of all happiness.[1]

ABDULLAH ANSĀRĪ OF HERAT

1   From The One Hundred Fields (*Sad Maydan*) translated by Nahid Angha in 'Stations of the Sufi Path'

INTRODUCTION

WE ARE LIVING in dark, uncertain times, full of distraction, turmoil and violence that are either upon us, or impending. We see this turmoil every day on television, in movies, in the headlines, online. We cannot escape it. And, as Muslims, we are drifting, as if in a riptide, away out into an open notional sea of uncertainty, far from the heart of our belief. I have watched this trend, sometimes in the midst of it but mostly from the sidelines, and I have seen its impact on the hearts of believers. This book is a small attempt to ameliorate this insidious drift.

Since 'Signs on the Horizons' was first published I have made several book tours that have put me in direct contact with many wonderful Muslims, with beautiful hearts and the best of intentions. They fill me with hope. Yet I have been astonished by a deep and prevailing insecurity and lack of confidence I hear from many. The influence of a stark and rigid, and frankly heretical, form of Islam, which focuses on externalities and equates sin with unbelief, has had a pervasive and dispiriting influence on the hearts and minds of Muslims around the world whether they subscribe to these doctrines or not. At the same time, many have been raised with a distorted understanding of their faith, or no understanding at all.

The late author Hassan (Gai) Eaton, may God have mercy on him, once told me that when he was working as an advisor at the Regent's Park Mosque in London, he befriended a sincere and pious young Pakistani-British Muslim. The young man came to him in a terrible state. He said to him gravely, "Sidi Hassan, I've come here to tell you that I have to leave Islam and enter *kufr* (unbelief)." Sidi Hassan was taken aback, to say the least. "Why?" he asked. The young man said, "You see I grew up and was educated here in England. I have an advanced degree and a good job. But my parents have insisted that I marry a girl from their village back in Pakistan. She is an uneducated peasant girl. She can't even read or write. I simply can't marry her. And so I have to leave Islam."

"Why on earth do you think you have to leave Islam?" asked Sidi Hassan.

"But of course I have to leave Islam because I have disobeyed my parents. This is unbelief so I have become an unbeliever."

To say that this is taking filial piety to extremes is putting it mildly but what I find more disturbing than the young man's inherited misunderstanding is that he seems to have divorced basic human intelligence and common sense from his faith.

On a visit to Birmingham in the U.K. a friend of mine told me that he had attended a discourse in a local mosque where the imam told his congregation that whoever does not bend their toe while in the sitting position of the prayer, their prayer is not acceptable to God. This idiot has no place lecturing a congregation in a mosque, but I'm afraid that this kind of gross ignorance and willful stupidity is more prevalent than any of us would like to believe.

I have spoken to many young people, particularly young Muslims who were born into the faith, who have (quite naturally) fallen prey to many of the temptations of modern life, or who have learned an ethnocentric interpretation of Islam that takes no account of the time and place we live in. For those who enter Islam from another faith or from no faith at all, exposure to a dysfunctional mainstream can have an unsettling impact on their new faith and practice and propel them to deviant versions of Islam that provide simplistic answers to subtle questions.

Today young Muslims read books about the perfection of the Messenger of God, peace be upon him, his Family and Companions and the ancient saints of Islam (the *awwaleen*), may God be well pleased with them all, and feel, by comparison, doomed to perdition or, at best, inadequate to the spiritual path of *Ihsan* that forms the very heart of our faith. Most young people have lost touch with traditional teaching. They pick up where their parents left off, for better or for worse, or they are stuck with very, and sometimes grotesquely, imperfect teaching. They feel weak and unworthy, as if they've stepped beyond the pale. Somehow in the process they've lost sight of, or never understood, the fact that the purification of the heart is a process of continuous turning.

In English, 'repentance' is a forbidding word that suggests a puritanical finality. But in Arabic the term *tawba* is dynamic, meaning to turn or return. *Al-Tawwab* is one of the Names of God, the Oft-Returning. It is an active constant, an ongoing reality that renews every moment we are alive.

The saint Sahl ibn 'Abdullah al-Tustari, may God be well pleased with him, wrote, "*Tawba* is a duty incumbent upon a human being every moment whether of the elect or common folk, whether obedient to God or disobedient."[2] *Tawba* is, therefore, our default setting. Everyone sins, even saints, but the sins of a saint are of a different order. For an ordinary mortal, a sin is usually gross. For a saint, forgetting God for a single instant is a sin requiring a return to God. When someone asked Dhu'l-Nun al-Misri, may God be well pleased with him, about repentance he answered that the common people repent from sins, whereas the Elect repent from forgetfulness.[3]

According to the master Abu 'Ali al-Daqqaq, may God be well pleased with him, "Repentance consists of three parts. Its beginning is *tawba* (repentance), its middle part is *inaba* (turning to God), and its end is *awba* (returning to God)." And Imam al-Qushayri, may God be well pleased with him, comments on this saying, "Whoever repents out of fear of [divine] punishment acquires a repentance (*tawba*). Whoever repents out of desire of [Divine] reward acquires turning to God (*inaba*). And whoever repents out of compliance with [divine] command, not out of desire of reward, nor out of fear of punishment (*awba*), acquires return to God.[4]

The saint Rabi'a al-'Adawiyya prayed:

> O God, if I worship You for fear of Hell, burn me in Hell,
> And if I worship You in hope of Paradise,
> Exclude me from Paradise.
> But if I worship You for Your Own sake,
> Grudge me not Your everlasting Beauty.

Of the saints, our master Sidi Muhammad ibn Al-Habib wrote:

> *So their Tawba is ongoing, for God and by God;*

---

2   From the *Tadhkirat al-Awliya* (Memorial of the Saints), translated by A.J. Arberry
3   *Al-Risala Al-Qushayriyya fi'ilm Al-Tasawwuf*, Translated by Alexander D. Knysh
4   Ibid

Their fear is veneration of His mightiness and awe.[5]

This book is a declaration of mercy and certainty. Formed of a collection of stories I've experienced, read or heard, it is about how malleable the human heart can be and how wrongdoing, remorse, need, and yearning intersect with Divine Compassion, Forgiveness and Guidance. It is also about the sudden transitions from confusion to clarity, from sin to virtue, from sleep to wakefulness, from ignorance to knowledge, from foolishness to wisdom. And finally it is about the path of our lives, which leads us gradually, and for those whom God favors, inexorably to salvation.

Inevitably my own story comes into play. If I am going to retell the lives of others then it is only fair that I should come clean about myself, and the turning of my own heart.

May God forgive me and have mercy upon me, and make my turning sincere and constant and bless all those who turn to Him constantly and struggle on the Way.

> *Though my sins may surely weigh heavy upon me*
> *still I trust in Your goodness to mend my brokenness.*
> *Favor us, O Most-Forgiving Lord, with repentance*
> *that effaces the mistakes which were made in times past.*
> *And increase us in blessings, and light, and unveilings,*
> *and enable us to guide with permission and the secret.*
> *Support us in what we say and do,*
> *and make easy our provision from a place we do not know.*
> *Here we stand at the door of benevolence*
> *awaiting without hardship the kindness of the Friend.*[6]
> SIDI MUHAMMAD IBN AL-HABIB

---

5   The Diwan, *Qasida* 'If you would ascend the Path of Lovers', translated by Fouad Aresmouk, Michael Fitzgerald and Moulay Abdel Kebir Belghiti
6   Ibid *Qasida* 'Praise'

If you sinned until it reached the heaven, then repented,
surely God would turn unto you.[7]
THE PROPHET MUHAMMAD

You must know that repentance (*tawba*) is the first station of
pilgrims on the way to the truth, just as purification (*tahara*) is
the first step of those who desire to serve God[8]
'ALI IBN 'UTHMAN AL-HUJWIRI

7 *Musnad Ahmad* III 238: Ibn Majah 37:30 related in The Book of Repentance
8 *Kashf al-Mahjub*, translated by Reynold A. Nicholson

Part One

GOD FINDS YOU WHEREVER YOU ARE

There are so many things in my story that are profane and worldly, but that's where I was: I was very worldly and very profane. I truly believe that God finds you wherever you are.

'ABDALLAH SCHLEIFER

Beauty

Now I lay me down to sleep
I pray the Lord my soul to keep.
If I should die before I wake
I pray the Lord my soul to take.

THIS WAS THE only prayer Marc David Schleifer ever learned as a child. His mother taught it to him. When he was two or three years old he would kneel by his bedside, put his palms together and make this prayer. This was the only time in his childhood that he talked to God. This was his only religious experience growing up. It is a 17th century Protestant prayer from The New England Primer. For centuries it was common for children to recite this prayer before sleep. In Marc Schleifer's case it was uncommon. He was a Jew.

His grandparents were Jewish immigrants who had fled from pogroms in Hungary and Russia but his parents were not observant Jews. "My parents were very good people, very kind, very compassionate, very decent." But they were not religious at all. "I think they were, like many people whose parents were very religious, living on the spiritual and ethical capital they had inherited.

"When I was a teenager in 1948 I was thrilled when New York Yankee slugger Joe DiMaggio hit his 39th home run for the season and ran to my maternal grandfather, who was not so religious but had a strong sense of his heritage, to tell him the news. He took this in, thought for a minute and then asked, 'Is it good for the Jews?'

"My grandfather on my father's side was deeply religious. He was an immigrant from Hungary. I went off to spend a few weeks with him. He would officiate at the Passover. He wore this wonderful hat, which was like a Central Asian hat. He would go every morning to the synagogue and I would accompany him. He'd pray the morning prayer. He performed the afternoon and evening prayers at home religiously. I was impressed by his personal piety. There was something very striking about this: to get up early in the morning, to go to the synagogue and pray. But, in reality, it had no religious impact on me.

"I remember coming home that summer and saying to my mother, 'I was really impressed being with grandfather Schleifer and I think when I grow up I want to be a Rabbi.' My mother said, 'You realize that if you become a Rabbi you won't be able to eat bacon, lettuce and tomato sandwiches anymore.' I said, 'Really?' She said, 'Yes.' I said, 'Oh, well forget that!' It was, I suppose, an outrageous spiritual betrayal, to sell out for a BLT. Worse than selling out for thirty pieces of silver."

Throughout his youth and young adulthood he was "either indifferent and not thinking about belief in God or indifferent and thinking about it." Apart from being *Bar Mitzvah'ed* when he was thirteen, Marc had no spiritual relationship to the religion of his birth, but he was acutely conscious of the social implications of being Jewish.

Born in New York in the 1930s Marc left home to attend the University of Pennsylvania in 1952. "If you wanted to pledge a fraternity at Penn in the 1950s, there was an ironclad rule: there were Jewish fraternities and there were Christian fraternities. Jews were prohibited from pledging by a Christian fraternity unless they had converted. I became obsessed with my Jewish identity in a White Anglo-Saxon Protestant (WASP) world. This was the Eisenhower era, the Last Hurrah of American WASPism."

While at Penn Marc was introduced to the music of Bach, Palestrina and Vivaldi. "My family listened to classical music but they never listened to Baroque or Pre-Baroque music. They were listening to the Romantics, like Rachmaninoff and Tchaikovsky. It took me a while to figure out why. I realized that two-thirds of Bach's compositions were in one way or another sacred liturgical music, either masses or saint's day celebrations, like the St. Matthew's Passion; more so with Vivaldi and even more with Palestrina. It dawned on me that the culture I inherited from my parents had passed through a secular Jewish filter with no Christian element in it. This disturbed me because I considered myself to be a Western man and I had been deprived of a full exposure to Western culture because of my Jewish background.

"I wasn't religious but I wasn't an atheist out of conviction. To be a convinced atheist is a form of faith. It's a belief. You believe there's no God. That's as much a belief as believing there is a God. I was what I would call an 'Existential Atheist.' I said, 'Well maybe there is a God but who cares? What does it have to do with me?' I inhabited an atheist world without necessarily believing in atheism. I didn't deny the possibility.

3

And I wasn't an agnostic either. I wasn't troubled over whether there is or isn't a God."

Worth a Mass

So Marc was an existential atheist, a profane intellectual and collegiate Casanova. In his sophomore year at Penn he decided to date nurses because he figured that it would be easier to get them into bed. "This was the 1950s and college girls wouldn't sleep with their boyfriends until they were engaged but nurses were working girls who were also familiar with the human body. I figured that they had a more casual attitude toward sex." There was a school of nursing at Penn. The girls lived in dormitories. Marc met an Irish-American nursing student and took her out on a date. The date went well. She asked him if he would take her to the nursing school's prom. Her invitation was his cue. "I said to her, 'Well, you know proms usually run very late and your dormitory closes at midnight. We'll want to stay up and have an early morning breakfast, which is a tradition. Here at Penn everybody makes reservations at the Sansom Hotel on campus.'" And then he made his move. 'I'll make the reservation in the name of Mr. and Mrs. Schleifer.' But then she made her own move. She agreed on one condition: (the prom was on Saturday night) that on Sunday morning he went to Catholic Mass with her. He agreed.

In the 1590s King Henry of Navarre laid siege to Paris but was unable to take the French capital. The Catholic nobles held out against Henry's army for years but finally agreed to surrender the city on one condition: that King Henry would renounce his Protestant faith and convert to Catholicism. And King Henry acceded with the famous response: "Paris is worth a Mass."

"If I had known this story at the time I would have said 'the Irish Catholic nurse is worth a Mass.'"

Up to that point in his life Marc had only experienced Conservative Jewish prayers – the Friday night prayers and High Holidays. "Conservative Judaism is very much like the Protestant church without the cross. At best, for me it was a bore. I never experienced any sense of the sacred."

So he went with his Irish Catholic conquest to attend Mass. That was the deal and he upheld his part of the bargain. This was before Vatican II 'modernized' the liturgy. The mass was in Latin. He was deeply moved.

"The least you can say of the Catholic mass is that it's sacred theater. Its ritual and gesture is very beautiful, a different type of beauty from Muslim prayer because in Muslim prayer we're all priests. We're all doing it, simultaneously or by ourselves. But in the mass there's a different relationship between priests and laity. I was stunned by its beauty and I sensed that what was going on was a kind of sacred drama. My first spiritual awakening was at that moment, witnessing the Catholic mass."

Throughout his time at Penn Marc became increasingly attracted to a bohemian lifestyle. On visits to New York he would hang out in Greenwich Village at the fabled Cedar Tavern, frequented by abstract expressionist painters like Jackson Pollock, Franz Kline and William de Kooning. And, touched by his experience of the Mass, he stumbled onto Anglo-Catholicism.

"Anglo-Catholicism is a branch of the Church of England. It is even higher than High Church and is dedicated to restoring the Catholic dimension to the Church of England. So they would perform the Mass. It was in English but the English was beautiful, the language of the King James Bible and the Book of Common Prayer. In fact Anglo-Catholicism was, after Vatican II, more Catholic than the Catholic Church. Lots of incense, lots of genuflection. I found it extraordinarily beautiful. I would simply suspend my disbelief and sit at the services to witness these beautiful rituals.

"I didn't believe in the Trinity. If someone asked me what do you think of the Trinity I would have had a Jewish reaction: I would have said, 'I don't believe in God but if there is a God certainly He's not three.' But it wasn't doctrine that attracted me. It was plain and simply the ritual, the beautiful liturgy."

Marc was baptized and became an Anglo-Catholic.

"I didn't find any conflict with my Jewish background because I was in flight from Judaism. I'm going to university in the 1950s and I'm this Jewish kid from Forest Hills, the suburbs of New York City, and suddenly I'm in this Ivy League environment and I understood very quickly what it's all about. My parents simply wanted their son to go to an Ivy League school because they're the best schools. Presidents went to Ivy League schools. They didn't realize that the Ivy League was the sanctuary of WASP power. When I realized this, I said to myself, 'Whoah! This is where it's at!' I wanted to join the WASP elite."

So Anglo-Catholicism fit right into Marc's agenda. "On the one hand there is the liturgy and ritual of Catholicism but also technically speaking I was now a Protestant because Anglo-Catholicism is a segment of what in America is known as the Episcopal Church. I had the best of both worlds." He was now an honorary Protestant who could also attend the Mass.

But Marc had a deeper problem:

"I couldn't comprehend God."

After converting, Marc took Confession.

'Forgive me, Father, for I have sinned,' he told his Confessor.

'Tell me how you have sinned, my son,' said the priest.

'Well to start off, I don't believe in God.'

Marc was being provocative, a smart aleck, to get a rise out of the priest, but at the same time what he told him was the truth. "Then he said something that took me completely by surprise.

"The priest replied, 'Would you like to believe in God?'

"I thought for a moment and said, 'Yeah, that would be wonderful if I could believe wholeheartedly in God, because I love the Church. I think it's beautiful. I just don't believe in God. Right now I suspend my disbelief and enjoy the ritual.'

"The priest said, 'Try to pray to God to give you faith.'

"What he was saying to me in his own way was that I had submitted but I didn't have belief."

Many years later he discovered the parallel to the priest's counsel in the Holy Qur'an:

> The Bedouin say, 'We believe.' Say, "You believe not. Rather say, 'We
> have submitted,' for belief has not yet entered your hearts.
> Yet if you obey God and His Messenger, He will not diminish for you
> aught of your deeds.
> Truly God is Forgiving, Merciful.[9]

---

9   Holy Qur'an, *Sura al-Hujurat* 49:14

Marc prayed half-heartedly for faith a few times. He continued to savor the beauty of the Anglo-Catholic liturgy. He made the sign of the cross with fervor. But eventually "it just didn't make sense to me. Here I am doing all these things and I don't believe in them. I had to suspend my disbelief every time I attended mass. I'm practicing a religion but I don't believe in God. I began to find my situation ridiculous" and after a couple of years as an Anglo-Catholic, he drifted away from the Church.

"I say to myself, 'I'm just a wandering Jew,' whatever that meant. And one afternoon I'm wandering in the Lower East Side in New York, where I'd come to live after graduating from Penn and I hear the sound of a Jewish chant coming from a basement. I walk toward the sound. I say to myself, 'These are my roots. I've got to go back to my roots.' I walk into the basement and sit in the back of a small gathering with barely a *minyan* of ten old men. I didn't realize it but it was Yom Kippur and they were performing the *Kol Nidrei* prayer."

The old men were all rocking back and forth at their own speed, holding up books and reciting prayers. "They were reading from books even if they had these prayers memorized for seventy years. They really were 'People of the Book.'"

There was an altar in this basement synagogue, and a tabernacle where the sacred Torah was contained. "The man I thought was the Rabbi, who turned out to be the Cantor, approached the Tabernacle. And then he did something extraordinary. He lifted up his hands, palms out and touched his ears. Then he made a full prostration. This made a powerful impression on me. I sensed that this was a profoundly spiritual act. For the first time in my life I see a submission to God. Much later I realized that gesture was identical to the *takbir* that begins the Muslim prayer. Then the cantor was lifted up from prostration. That gesture, that movement, I recognized it was from God."

But apart from that one sacred New York minute, Marc's life was headed in another, altogether more profane, direction.

His first job after graduating from Penn was in an advertising agency in New York. But he quickly got bored with the job "so I started writing on the side for the Village Voice," the alternative leftist news tabloid that had just been started. His editor knew that Marc was an aspiring poet so he assigned him to interview the Beat poet Allen Ginsberg, famed for his controversial epic *Howl*. Marc became enthralled with both Ginsberg and the Beat movement.

Marching to a New Beat

The Beat generation was composed of writers and poets who rejected mainstream American literary, moral, social and political values. They celebrated jazz, sexual liberation and black culture, contemplated the meaning of life, and embraced heavy drug use. They claimed to seek spiritual meaning in life instead of going along with America's post-war affluence and materialism. According to historian Allen Matusow, "Beats had deviant tastes in literature, music, language, drugs and religion. They were alienated from American values because they rejected materialism, hygiene, sexual repression and lived in voluntary poverty."[10] Norman Mailer wrote that the prospect of nuclear holocaust, compounded by the fear of a slow death of the spirit by conforming to American materialist values, impelled the Beats to seek out extreme life experiences and then write about them.

"I quit my job at Young and Rubicam, hung my gray flannel suit in the closet and started hanging out with Allen Ginsberg and everybody around him." Marc joined the Beat Generation.

Cuba Libre

At the same time, he became heavily involved in radical leftist politics. The Beats who were politically inclined romanticized Fidel Castro's Cuban Revolution. Castro's guerilla uprising against the U.S.-backed dictator Fulgencio Battista triumphed in 1959. When Fidel set up a socialist state ninety miles off the coast of Florida, the American government imposed an embargo, which exists to the present day.

Marc became a member of the Fair Play for Cuba Committee, which was set up in 1960 by leftist intellectuals to support the Cuban Revolution from attacks by the U.S. government. He wrote poems glorifying Fidel and violated the U.S. ban on travel to Cuba to journey to Havana and join a revolutionary militia.

"I was deeply involved in the Cuban Revolution and made two illegal

---

10   Allen J. Matusow, The Unraveling of America: A History of Liberalism in the 1960s, New York: Harper & Row Publishers, 1984), 283.

trips to Cuba, spending over a year and a half there." In Cuba he took up arms with the Fidelistas against counter-revolutionaries. During this period, Castro turned the revolution over to the Cuban communist party. "I understand why he did it. The American embargo really hurt. Ninety per cent of everything they had was from America. The U.S. forced Castro into the Soviet orbit. Fidel was a social revolutionary, not a Marxist." But his need for Soviet support drove Fidel to communism and Marc became, for a time, a passionate anarcho-syndicalist. He was also a passionate womanizer and in Cuba he combined his two passions, attracting the romantic attentions of a beautiful Cuban commissar.

"She came to inspect my militia unit. She asked them about me. My duty was to be stationed on a rooftop with a Czech-made submachine gun to guard factories and the newspaper offices of La Prensa and Revolución against counter-revolutionaries who would try to climb the fence and hurl firebombs. She came to me and said, 'I talked to your *compañeros* and they told me the reason they put you up on the roof is that you're the one man in the unit they are absolutely certain will shoot to kill.' She said this with incredible passion and I could tell she was falling for me because she was convinced that I'd kill for the revolution. I didn't stop and say, 'That's pretty weird, babe.' I went off with her. But that really troubled me; the inhumaneness of it—that a man who had no compunction about taking a human life for the sake of a revolution would make a woman fall in love with him. I mean, she was a commissar, the revolutionary ideal."

Disillusion

"Before my eyes, I watched the Stalinization of Cuba. I had read books like 'Darkness at Noon' by Arthur Koestler who was a disillusioned ex-communist. And I'd read 'The God that Failed,' written by British and French ex-communists who accused communism of being a false religion. I realized that what they were writing about was exactly what I was witnessing and that communism was a false religion. It shook me to the core."

Nearly six decades later he sees the parallels between his communist conversion and the conversion of young people to radical Islamist ideology. "Young Westerners who are not Muslim or nominal Muslims trawl through social media and watch ISIS convoys driving through villages, flying their black flags, shooting guns and executing Shia soldiers. That turns them on and they convert, not because they want to be part of Islam. They want to be part of ISIS. To be part of ISIS you have to be a Muslim so they learn the ISIS version of Islam. Even those who come from Muslim families are for the most part not religious; some have been in gangs or prison. They get their religion from ISIS.

"I think people of my generation in the '60s, whether they were going to Havana or Latin America or joining the Baader-Meinhof gang or the Red Brigade in Europe, or the Weather Underground in the U.S., that in all cases, it wasn't so much that armed struggle was the means to an end. It was the other way around; that the socialist revolution gave us the *raison d'être* for taking up guns and violence – the attraction of being an armed rebel, a hero. I'm suggesting that this has nothing to do with true religious conversion. It's about guns and violence."

Marc wanted to get out of Cuba. "I had traveled to Cuba illegally and had to figure out how I was going to get back to the U.S. without losing my passport. So I spoke to the Cubans and they put me on what was called a 'Watermelon Plane'. They loaded up a plane every day with watermelons, flew it to Toronto and offloaded the watermelons. They were trying to get a chicken industry started in Havana so they accepted payment in baby chicks. I flew in the jump seat next to the pilot and co-pilot. The rest of the plane was full of watermelons. We landed in Toronto and I jumped out and ran across the tarmac into the woods to meet two Trotskyites I'd met in Canada who drove me across the border into the U.S."

He settled back into his hedonistic bohemian life in Greenwich Village for a year but his illegal sojourns in Cuba forced him to leave the U.S. again. "I made an enquiry and learned that the State Department was not going to renew my passport unless I came in and talked to them about my illegal travels to Cuba. I had to get out before my passport expired."

At the time San Francisco, Mexico City and Tangier were the Beat sanctuaries. "I decided to travel to Tangier to join my Beat compatriots. I wasn't going out of an interest in Arabs or Islam, but I had stopped off in Morocco for two or three days in the 1950s and was stunned by the beauty of the country. Morocco in the 1950s was extraordinary. Everyone was in traditional dress - all the colors and lights. Back then I stopped off to see the writer Paul Bowles to ask him to write for a literary magazine I was planning to publish. And also, the finest hashish in the world came from the Katami province in Morocco, which was another reason I passed through.

Parallels

"I booked passage to Tangier on the *Jugolinija*, a Yugoslav freighter that had been modified to take passengers. In those days, if you were a beatnik or hipster you sailed on the *Jugolinija*. We first arrived in Casablanca where they had to unload their freight. I was stoned on hashish and got down on the dock to walk around. Suddenly I hear this exquisitely beautiful call to prayer. It was dark. I see dockworkers forming prayer lines. In front of them is the man who's going to lead them. Obviously, he's the priest or something. I didn't know anything about Islam. All of a sudden, the imam takes his hands and touches his ears in *takbir* and prays and then goes into full prostration and the image of the cantor prostrating in Yom Kippur comes back to me. They all do this prayer. This might offend Muslims but I'm saying to myself, *'These guys are more Jewish than the Jews!'* In fact, this would happen over and over again. I would see the traditional dress. It was Biblical dress. The Jews had abandoned this but the Muslims had retained it. It was very beautiful.

"I was really knocked over in my very first moments in Morocco, and through the year things like this kept happening.

"When I finally arrived in Tangiers, Paul Bowles was still presiding, William Burroughs was there, and Allen Ginsberg and Gregory Corso were in and out. I was traveling with Irving Rosenthal, who was sort of the Proust of the Beat Generation."

Marc settled in a beautiful Moroccan house in the old city of Tangiers, near Bowles and Burroughs. He plunged in to the unbridled Beat lifestyle – stoned, promiscuous and debauched. "Whatever I was afraid of I did. I followed the principle of experimentation, 'disordering the senses,' as Rimbaud said. I did anything that was semi-criminal, short of murder." Stealing, lying, rampant sexuality, drugs.

"I'm in my house and I hear a commotion. I look out and see knives and blood in the streets." At first he was frightened. "Did they realize that most of the Beats were depraved infidels? Were they slaughtering them in the streets?" As he looked on he realized what they were doing. "They were sacrificing sheep on *Eid al-Adha*. And then I saw something else. I saw that many of those making the sacrifice would put their hands in the blood and press it on a door. It was, I learned, the 'Hand of Fatima.'

"This reminded me of the liturgy of the Jewish Passover, when the People of Israel are told to sacrifice sheep for God and put their hands in the blood and then place their hands on their doors so that the Angel of Death would pass over their homes. This was because Pharaoh decreed that the first-born male child in each household must die.

"Everywhere I went in Morocco I saw the Hand of Fatima and couldn't help but associate the Muslim tradition with the Jewish tradition. But whereas it was something from the past in modern Judaism, it was alive in Morocco."

All around him he was beginning to see so many parallels.

"For example from the beginning I would hear Muslims say *insha'Allah* (God willing). My great-grandmother, whenever she was talking about the future would say, 'God willing.' She was an orthodox, practicing Jew. And the Catholics say *'Deo Volente'*, if God wills it.

God Finds You Wherever You Are
"People ask me where I learned about Islam and I have to say it was through my hash connection. In the evening I would sit in the café with Muhammad. He knew broken English and Spanish. He was a Muslim. He was a believer and he would always amaze me. For instance, we had this thing together about not being grown up. (He was in his twenties. I was around thirty.) I would say to Muhammad, 'what do you want to be when you grow up?' And he would say, 'I want to get married.' I said, 'What? You want to get *married*?' 'Yeah, I want to get married and have a family.' A big part of Beat philosophy romanticized criminals. You find this idea of the sanctity or heroism of the criminal, the ultimate nonconformist and rebel.Suddenly this drug pusher who in an American context would be considered a criminal, is telling me he wants to get married and have a family.

"On another occasion I noticed Muhammad had a scar on his face.

I asked him, 'How did you get that scar?' He said, 'One day my father was angry with me and threw a plate at me and it cut my head.' I said something like, 'Oh fathers are a drag.' He said, 'Please don't speak that way. You shouldn't be speaking that way about your father, much less my father.' That threw me. Here is someone I thought was super hip and liberated, yet his idea of a great future is to settle down, get married, have kids and to respect his parents, which I saw as bourgeois.

"One day, we're sitting in the *Socco Chico* in Tangier, which is a small central square full of coffee shops. We're having a coffee and a funeral procession enters the square headed toward the Great Mosque. The deceased is in a shroud on a wooden pallet and men in the crowd are taking turns carrying the pallet. Suddenly everyone in the square stands up. Muhammad stands up. I stand up and watch them. They were chanting *La ilaha illa 'Llah*, rhythmically.

"When the funeral procession passed we sat down and I said to Muhammad, 'This person must have been some incredible dude. Who is he?' Muhammad said, 'I have no idea. I've never seen these people before. They must be from a village.' I asked, 'Then what are we standing for?' He said, 'We're standing out of respect for death and out of respect for a human soul who has been taken by death. We would do the same for you hippies. If one of you died we'd stand for you.' This knocked me over. If I died, they would stand for me even though I wasn't a Muslim?

"Another time Muhammad said, 'You hippies probably think you're cleaner than we are because you have new clothes and we have old clothes.' It was true. I noticed that Moroccans could have old tattered clothes but they would be very clean. You would see someone wearing a *djellaba* with twenty patches but it was spotless.

"He said, 'You think you're cleaner than we are but actually we're cleaner than you.'

"'What do you mean?'

"'Have a look at your underwear, it's stained.' And I realized he was right.

"'Ours isn't.'

"I asked why. He said, 'Because we wash ourselves with water. Water washes away impurities.'

"This really got to me. It made absolute sense. This may be disappointing for Muslim readers who are expecting that I might have had a vision on the road to Damascus rather than a scatological awakening but this is where I was. God finds you where you are. 'Wow!' I said to myself. 'I'm going to try this,' and I did. So before I was a Muslim I was washing myself like a Muslim.

"The Beats in Tangiers were highly promiscuous. Everyone was sleeping with everyone else. As a result crabs and other venereal diseases were common. I'm sure that Muhammad had taken people to the drugstore to buy medicine to get rid of their pubic lice. He said to me, 'We don't have that problem.' I asked him why. He said, 'We shave our pubic hair and under our arms. This is part of our religion.' Again, it made absolute sense. I started to practice this and I felt really clean.

"Whenever I'd asked him about anything he would say, 'This is what the Prophet did. This is what the Prophet said. This is from the Holy Qur'an.'

"I'd be walking down the street and I see a man pushing a wagon loaded with wood up a hill. He'd pass a café and two guys would jump up and help him push the wagon. You still see this, to this day, in Cairo. You could be crossing a bridge and someone's car stops and a young man will jump out of his car and help. So I see that and I mention this to Muhammad.

"'That's amazing that they left their table and helped this guy push his wagon up the hill.' Many people would say, 'That's what are our parents did. Those are our customs.' But Muhammad would invariably say, 'This is in our religion.' And if I pressed him he might say it was in the Qur'an or that's what the Prophet said or did.

"I saw a father and son, four or five years old. They were obviously prosperous. An old man approaches them. He was obviously poor, wearing a patched *djellaba*. The father greets the old man. The father introduces the son. The son takes the old man's hand and kisses it. I came from a culture where youth is what matters, not old age and here's this young child showing respect. In America everyone shows respect for the young. They want to dance like the young, watch movies like the young, carry on like the young. If you're old you're finished, you're sent off to the old people's home. 'What? Kissing the hand of an old man?'

"So again, I go back to Muhammad. And, again, he tells me this is

14

part of Islam. I was really getting a complex about this, the logic of it, the way to live. Everything made sense and everything originated from God, through the Qur'an and the teachings of the Prophet. It was so logical. In the house I was living in, if I opened the door nobody could look in because behind me was a blank wall, so the privacy of the family is not violated. Everything I encountered was like this. I was deeply moved by the beauty of it all, by the organic composition of the traditional city and the beauty of Islamic architecture and traditional costume. In those years, all the men in the old city wore the *djellaba* and the women wore the *djellaba* with a face veil that was very dainty. It was incredibly beautiful.

"I became really troubled by all this. The way one lives, the clothes one wears, the manners and courtesies, even the gestures, were so beautiful.

"About this time I had stopped drinking and was observing the purifications that I learned from Muhammad but I was still using drugs. One night I was out on the street completely stoned and see a group of traditionally dressed men in a procession, chanting. I could see a light coming from this gathering. They were illuminated. I followed them. They arrived at a mosque. They went into the mosque and the mosque was blazing with light. It wasn't just the electric light. It was utterly luminous. From the street I gazed at this overpowering light."

For Marc, the perception of light formed a stark contrast to the sinister darkness of the life he was leading.

Evil

"A writer had come to Tangiers and we learned that he was going to do a story about the Beat community. It was still a small circle. We realized that a story about us could unleash a flood of hippies into Tangiers. So we had an informal meeting in the house where I was living. Someone suggested that we should murder him. It was agreed."

In the warped Beat world the notion of murder wasn't far-fetched. The Beats embraced Albert Camus's French Algerian anti-hero Mersault in his existentialist novel 'The Stranger', who kills an Arab Algerian for no particular reason. The novelist Norman Mailer stabbed and nearly killed his second wife and then bragged about it. Marc's Tangiers neighbor William Burroughs, the author of 'The Naked Lunch', who had been a heroin addict, infamously shot and killed his own wife while playing a game of William Tell, in which he placed an apple on her head and missed.

"Someone suggested that we draw straws. We used matchsticks and one was broken. Everyone drew a matchstick and the one who drew the broken matchstick was the one who had to murder this reporter. I drew the broken matchstick. Up until then, whatever I was afraid of I did without question. I had always held to this principle but this time I just couldn't bring myself to do it. Perversely, I was wracked with guilt, feeling that I was betraying my principles. I was violating the code of the existential hero. But I just couldn't do it. I felt very guilty about not killing somebody."

That night was the *Moussem* of Sidi Bouarrakia.

"I ate this jam loaded with hashish and a cocktail of other hallucinatory drugs. So on the way to the *moussem* I was completely stoned. I had taken up with a British girl and we went to the *moussem* together. I was so wracked with guilt and so stoned, that I started to think that in recompense for not killing the journalist I should kill my British girlfriend but I didn't want to kill her either. So now I was doubly wracked with guilt."

Marc and his girlfriend joined the *moussem*.

"What is so extraordinary about traditional Islam is that nobody is an outcast. There's a perception of value. There were circles of heaven and circles of hell. The center of the circle was where the *hadra* happened. You could hear the chanting. And then around them were those that appreciated the *hadra* but weren't in it. And around them were the worldly people, like pious merchants, working people and housewives. In Morocco at that time everyone loved the *awliya*, the saints of Islam. You didn't have to be in a Sufi order to love the *awliya*.

"At the edge of the circle were thieves and prostitutes and the outermost circle was for the non-believers who would show up. We were all there. This is a sign of traditional religion; there were no outcasts. There are sinners and there are saints and those in between but nobody is an outcast. If nobody is an outcast then everybody has the possibility of redemption. That doesn't mean that people ignore who you are. You're a sinner, a prostitute, a gambler, a thief, a non-believer. But you're here in this community so you too have a place. That place recognizes the fact that you are what you are so the possibility of repentance and redemption is clear. You're not locked out. This is important. As I looked around the circle I was struck by this realization.

"By the end of the *moussem* I'd completely collapsed. I could see the sun rising and I could see that they had finished the dawn prayer. The saint's tomb was on the waterside and a lot of people were in the sea with their clothes on. The sun is coming up and I'm being carried back to the house.

Hell

"And back home I went straight to Hell.

"I was on fire. I didn't see flames but I was on fire. I couldn't sleep. William Burroughs sent over two apomorphine pills that are so powerful they can break a heroin addiction. It is what he used to break his addiction. You don't get high but it fulfills the craving until you get over it. I took them. Nothing happened.

"I didn't believe in hell. I was not conditioned to believe in hell. My parents never talked about hell. I never read anything about hell or hellfire or punishment but I recognized the symptoms of hell. I would go to the mirror to see if horns were growing. I knew it was psychotic but I believed that at any moment horns were going to come out as punishment for not killing the girl. This condition lasted for two weeks. At the beginning it was drug-induced. But the drugs wore off and the state persisted. The drugs took me to hell and left me there. I truly believed that I was going to be in hell forever.

"I didn't eat. I didn't sleep. I was on fire. I thought I would never sleep again. People in the house looked after me. They washed me. I saw that everybody was looking after me but actually that we were all in Hell together. They were my friends but we were all devils. I was on fire endlessly. I was in agony. If you feel like you're on fire all the time, then you're in the fire.

"I'm lying on this bed, trying to sleep and I see all my one-night stands – women I'd had sex with once appeared to me. These were very promiscuous times – after the pill and before AIDS. That period of time was ultra-promiscuous for the young and Beats were pioneers of promiscuity. We saw it as a virtue. Make love everywhere.

"I'm lying there in this state and out of the wall come phantoms – all the women I had one-night stands with. You sleep with them. You don't call them back. They're hurt. I hurt them. So these hurt souls came out of the wall like phantoms. They would come at me, one after another. I was half-crazed, hallucinating.

"After two weeks hell subsided but I was catastrophically shaken. I didn't know about heaven but I knew now with certainty that hell exists. I wore sunglasses day and night because I thought I might have the evil eye and I didn't want to give it to anyone.

"My English girlfriend was going to Paris and offered to drive me. She never knew about my homicidal urges and I was way over thinking about killing her."

Marc had made a deal with the U.S. government after he tricked a consular officer in Tangier into renewing his passport. The deal was that he would never visit Cuba again illegally but only as an accredited journalist, which was legal. They accepted. He had a complicated ticket taking him to Havana and then to New York.

"I had a ticket from Paris to Prague to Havana and then to New York. I flew into Havana and after a month there I made my way back to the U.S. By the time I got back to America, I was saying to myself, 'There is an alternative to all this,' and that was what I experienced of the people of Morocco. The alternative was Islam. By the time I reached the U.S. I decided that I was a Muslim.

"The first day I'm back in New York I get on a crowded bus. Everyone's squashed together. Nobody is talking to each other. Nobody looks at one another. Everyone is completely alone in the crowd. It's very depressing. It's just the opposite of Morocco. When I was on a bus in Morocco, I would see a Moroccan getting on and saying, 'As-Salaam Alaykum'. The bus driver would return his greeting and he'd sit down next to the bus driver. Then another passenger would greet the driver and they all acknowledged each other. It was, again, obviously social behavior that came out of their religion. Suddenly I'm back in New York. I'm on the bus and the guy next to me is reading a newspaper. I glance at it and he gives me a dirty look. There's something inhuman about it all. Then the woman standing next to me starts talking to me. She says, 'How are you doing sonny?' Another human being is talking to me! I say, 'I'm doing fine ma'am. I just got back to America but I'm doing fine.' And she says, 'Well be careful because at 5:30 tonight *the Martians are coming to take over the city*.' And I'm thinking, 'The only human being on this bus is insane!'

"My heart was pierced with agony. I'd been to hell. Now I was out of hell but this was another kind of hell, not the hell of my destiny, but the hell of life. It was grim, lonely and miserable. There was no beauty in the way people were living. And the only person I met that day who behaved like a normal human being was insane. It was devastating.

Comprehension

"I retreated to my apartment in the Lower East Side. I had brought back the Name of God from Fez, printed on card. In those days these cards were everywhere in Morocco. I knew that Islam was the way to live. But I still couldn't comprehend God. I was in great inner conflict. The way the Moroccans lived was so beautiful. And I knew enough to know that there is a connection between God and beauty.

"It's Islam. But I can't comprehend God. These things that I admire are from God and His Prophet but I can't comprehend God. It would be great if I could but I can't. He is beyond comprehension.

"I know the truth is in Islam but I can't comprehend God. It's all based on God and I can't comprehend God." Marc was on the verge of despair.

"I take out a translation of the Qur'an I was reading. This time I treat it like the *I Ching*[11]. I close my eyes and flip the pages and put my finger on a passage. In the particular Qur'an I was using it was translated this way:

> *He is above all comprehension, yet comprehends all things.*[12]

"I read this verse and it says God is beyond comprehension. I raised my eyes to heaven and said, '*I can believe in a God Who tells me that He is beyond my comprehension.*' At that moment I became a Muslim. I hadn't said the *shahada* (the Muslim declaration of faith) but in my heart I said, 'this is it.'

---

11   An ancient Chinese manual of divination
12   Holy Qur'an, Sura *al-An`am* 6:103

Marc went to Brooklyn and knocked on the door of the State Street Mosque. The Imam was Shaykh Daoud Ahmad Faisal, may God have mercy on him, who was a prominent figure in 20th century Islam in America. Born in Grenada, Shaykh Daoud immigrated to the United States after the First World War and became a leading activist in the Harlem Renaissance movement before embracing Islam. He was a founding member of the International Muslim Society and then established the Islamic Mission of America at his home in Brooklyn. He was also a *muqaddam* (deputy) of the Algerian gnostic shaykh Sidi Ahmad Mustafa al-'Alawi, may God be well pleased with him.

"Shaykh Daoud opens the door. He's dressed like a Moroccan, wearing a Moroccan *djellaba* and turban with prayer beads around his neck! I say, '*Salaam Alaykum*', and he says, '*Salaam Alaykum*. Are you a Muslim?' I say, 'I want to be.' He says, 'Come with me.' He has me do the ritual ablution (*wudhu*). He says, 'First of all if you're going to become a Muslim it must be witnessed.' He calls people over. I said, 'Wait a minute, I don't know anything about Islam.' I'm assuming that like in Christianity you have to study the Catechism to convert. In Judaism they have to say no to you three times. Here he's ready to give me *shahada*.

"I said, 'I don't know anything about Islam.'

"He said, 'You have your whole lifetime to study Islam. What matters is that you submit to God now.'

"Then he and the congregation witnessed my entry into Islam. He gave me the name 'Abdallah.

"He said, 'We're going to pray now.'

"I said, 'I don't know how to pray.'

"He said, 'Now you're going to pray with me.'

"I said, 'But I don't know how to pray.'

"He said, 'Afterwards we'll go upstairs and I'll teach you the prayer but for now just say '*Allah*' and pray as I do.

"Then he said to me, '*When you pray, pray as beautifully as you can for surely you cannot see God but God can see you.*'"

I have known 'Abdallah Schleifer for over forty years. In all that time I had never seen him cry. But when he came to this part of his story, fifty years after the fact, he broke down and wept.

"He repeated another version of the very words that brought me to him.

Vision comprehendeth Him not, but He comprehendeth (all) vision.
He is the Subtle, the Aware.[13]

"And we prayed together."

'Abdallah Schleifer and his new wife, 'Aliyya, who embraced Islam at the same time, emigrated to Jerusalem where he embarked on a distinguished career as a journalist. He lived in the wall of the al-Aqsa Mosque and in 1967 witnessed the defeat of the Arab armies and the Israeli occupation of the sacred city. He wrote an acclaimed (and controversial) book, *The Fall of Jerusalem*, about the historic event. He was a courageous war correspondent covering the Lebanese Civil War as Middle East Bureau Chief of NBC News. Throughout this period he wrote prolifically on politics and Islam. He retired from journalism in 1980 and joined the American University at Cairo (AUC) as Distinguished Professor of Mass Communications. At AUC he established the Kamal Adham School of Television Journalism, which was the first institution of its kind in the Middle East and has trained generations of leading Arab journalists. He retired from AUC in 2005 and has continued as an incisive and wise commentator on Arab politics and Islam. He was one of the signatories of The Common Word message to Pope Benedict and a member of the delegation of Muslim scholars to the Vatican. He has written extensively on politics, Islam and interfaith dialogue. He follows a spiritual path of prayer and remembrance.

Now in his ninth decade, he has for a half century been an eyewitness to the escalating conflict, turmoil, tribulations and entropy afflicting the Muslim world – the Great *Fitna*.

"I'll tell you. The way things are going in this world, sometimes I think that I remain a Muslim for two reasons: the prayer, because I feel utterly at home in the prayer – I only feel at home in the *salat* – and the *dhikr*, the remembrance of God. What Islam has become in my lifetime is so horrendous. Without the *salat* and the *dhikr* I would leave Islam as it is being practiced and understood. But it is prayer and remembrance that keep me within this beautiful, beautiful religion."

---

13   Ibid

Well Past High Time

AL-FUDAYL IBN 'IYAD al-Talaqani was a dangerous criminal. He led a gang of ruthless highwaymen on the road between Merv and Bavard during the late 8th century (2nd century of Hijrah). The gang beset caravans and hapless travelers, robbed them, beat them and sometimes even killed them. Al-Fudayl masqueraded as a dervish, wearing sackcloth, a woolen cap and a rosary (*tasbih*) around his neck, but pious disguise notwithstanding, he was a hardened scoundrel who ruled his gang with an iron fist, keeping inventory and dividing the loot.

Yet he had within him the seeds of piety. He was, by nature, dignified and possessed a sense of chivalry. He refused to rob women or penurious travelers and he would always leave his victims with a portion of their belongings to carry on with their travels. He had a romantic streak and, it was said, was madly in love with a woman to whom he gave his share of the swag.

Al-Fudayl's gang caught wind of an approaching caravan and readied themselves to attack. A traveler with the caravan carrying a bag of gold had been forewarned of Al-Fudayl's highwaymen and when the caravan approached this treacherous stretch of road he took off to find a place to hide his cache. He came upon a tent and entered to find an ascetic dervish. He asked the dervish if he could leave his bag for safekeeping with him. The ascetic instructed him to place the bag in one corner of the tent, which he did.

The traveler returned to the caravan to find that it had been attacked and robbed by bandits who left the travelers fettered, hand and foot. He loosened their restraints and the ransacked caravan moved on. The traveler stayed behind to retrieve his bag of gold but when he approached the ascetic's tent he saw the dervish among the bandits, squatting in a circle and dividing plunder.

"*Ahhh, I've left my gold to a thief!*" he thought to himself and made to slip away. But Al-Fudayl caught sight of him and called him over. He approached the band of highwaymen fearfully.

"What do you want from me?" he asked.

"Take your bag from where you left it in my tent," said al-Fudayl.

With a mixture of relief and bewilderment the traveler retrieved his bag and took to the road to catch up with the caravan.

Al-Fudayl's gang was outraged. "How could you let him leave? The entire caravan didn't yield even one dhirham in cash and yet you let him leave with a bag of gold!"

Al-Fudayl replied, "This man had a good opinion of me, and I have always had a good opinion of God and the hopes that He will one day accept my repentance. I justified the traveler's good opinion of me so that God might justify my good opinion of Him."

The following day the gang attacked another caravan. After the event, a traveler from the caravan approached the circle of bandits, who were taking their lunch.

"Who is your leader?" he asked the group.

"He is on the other side of that tree by the river bank. He's praying."

The traveler was confused, "But it isn't the time for prayer."

"He is performing supererogatory prayers," he was told.

"Why is he not eating with you?" asked the traveler.

"He's fasting."

"But it isn't Ramadan," said the traveler.

"He is performing a supererogatory fast," said the thieves.

The flabbergasted traveler approached Al-Fudayl, who was praying with great concentration. When the bandit had finished his prayers, the traveler addressed him.

"How can you fast and pray and at the same time rob and murder Muslims?"

Al-Fudayl turned to him and asked, "Do you know the Qur'an?"

The traveler replied in the affirmative.

"Well then, does not God, Who is exalted say: *And others have confessed their sins; they have mixed a righteous deed with another evil?*" leaving the traveler dumbfounded.

His life continued in this strange dissociative way, mixing crime and piety, until one night, as he was atop a wall, on the lookout for more plunder, a caravan passed and Al-Fudayl heard a traveler reciting from the Qur'an:

*Is it not time that the hearts of those who believe should be humbled
to the remembrance of God?*[14]

Al-Fudayl was thunderstruck, his heart pierced to the core, and he
cried out, "*It is high time indeed! Nay, it is well past high time!*"

And with that Al-Fudayl fled in shame to a ruin. There he found an
encampment of travelers, who assumed he had come to rob them. They
made to flee but one from the group said, "We can't leave. Al-Fudayl is
on the road.

"Good news!" cried Al-Fudayl. "He has repented!"

Al-Fudayl tracked down every one of his victims, restored the wealth
he had stolen and sought their forgiveness.

For thirty years no one ever saw him smile, except on the day when
his son died. Only then did he smile. When he was asked by a disciple
why he smiled he replied, "I realized that God was pleased that my son
should die and I smiled to accord with God's pleasure."

He became one of the greatest saints of his age. May God be well
pleased with him and may we be inspired by his repentance.

> *"My Lord have mercy! For You know my repentance;*
> *And do not punish me, for You have power over me.*
> *O God, You keep me hungry and You keep my children hungry.*
> *You keep me naked and You keep my children naked.*
> *You do this to Your Friends.*
> *By what spiritual station has Al-Fudayl earned this great blessing from*
> *You?"*[15]

AL-FUDAYL IBN 'IYAD

---

14 Holy Qur'an, *Sura Al-Hadid* 57:16
15 Retold from the *Tadhkirat al-Awilya* (Memorial of the Saints) of Faridud'din Attar,
translated by A.J. Arberry

24

Forgiveness

MARTIN ASKEW WAS a violent East London racketeer, hailing from gangster royalty. His cousin and mentor was Lenny McLean, 'The Guv'nor,' a bare-knuckle fighter, bouncer, criminal and prisoner, bodyguard and enforcer, who was known as 'the hardest man in Britain.' Martin's father was a criminal and his mother had been the girlfriend of one of the gang that pulled the notorious £7 million Bank of America robbery in Mayfair in 1976. The father of his stepfather, Tommy Welch, was godfather to the nefarious Kray brothers. The world he grew up in was the world of the Krays, Ronnie Biggs and Charles Bronson.

"While people were earning twenty-five quid, they was pulling up in Lamborghinis, on the way to St. Tropez. In the East End, they was the best dressed, the most charismatic," said Martin. "The downside was that the violence was extreme. It was a vendetta culture and lives were lost because of it. These families were the ones that run the 'manors' and my 'manor,' Hoxton, was one of the toughest 'manors.' In Victorian London they said if you put a net over Hoxton you got half the world's criminals. In Wilmer Gardens they put a copper [a policeman] down a drain. They put his hat on the drain. It was infamous."

As a teenager Martin loved driving, but he was underage. An older guy in the neighborhood had a flash car. "I was only fourteen but he let me be the chauffeur. He said, 'Make yourself look a bit older and you can drive me around.' So I did." Martin would drive his older friend from place to place. He would pull up outside these places and his friend would walk slowly into the premises and then come out running and jump into the backseat. He'd say to Martin, 'Okay go! Not too fast, not too fast!' "I didn't figure it out until he got nicked. He was doing armed robberies and I was his getaway driver."

Heir Apparent

Martin was an heir-apparent, 'one of the chaps.' "No one would come near me. I was a big one then, fifteen and a half stone. I was eating. I was training three times a day. I was pumping. All Armani suits, expensive shoes. Always like beautifully turned out. Always clean-shaven, never straggly. I was one of the chaps. I was one of the boys. I didn't give up to get in clubs. I was living the same way you see in the movie 'Goodfellas.' I was dangerous and extremely volatile.

"My mates, my age group, were like 'Wow, he's one of the chaps.' People used to come up to me and say 'you're one of the chaps, now ain't you boy.' They'd massage my ego. You're standing outside in your area. You had nice cars. So what I'm saying is that there's the lineage, and I was taught that etiquette and how to hold myself and be that sort of man, but it wasn't for me in the end.

"It was a business, a family business. It was a business that I thought I could excel in. I wanted to be like my father, my cousin Lenny and my uncles. I always believed in God but I thought, 'You can still be a criminal and be a good guy at the same time. You could be a good guy in a bad world.' It was a cultural thing, like the Arabs during the *Jahiliyya* period. It was a brutal, macho culture but there were good people.

The Law of the Street
"My cousin Lenny McLean used to say, 'If you don't fight in the East End you're nothing and no one.' So you had to be tough to put that barrier between you and others who could step on you because there was a lot of tough people. If you got that notoriety, you was one of the boys, one of the chaps. And as long as you're in the club you become like a Guv'nor, a Capo. You become someone who can move freely and do business. Otherwise you ain't made your bones, you can't live freely 'cause people are going to step on you. It's the same in most of those urban environments, whether you are in New York or Marseilles or London – the law of the street. But there is also a real honour.

"If you gave your word you had to live and die by it. It was like the Arabs in the *Jahiliyya*. When I read the Qur'an and *hadith* and I saw these rules and regulations, I understood that. I could live by rules and regulations. We had these. Like you mustn't be a 'grass,' an informant. When I was only seven years old, I was standing outside my door and the Flying

Squad[16] came around asked me if so-and-so was in my house. Even then I wouldn't tell them. I learned all these codes and rules, what was right and wrong in my environment."

Martin was different. He was highly intelligent, a voracious reader, and he was searching. "I was reading Nietzsche. I tried to be a Christian but I had a big, big problem with the Trinity. It didn't sit right." But he found simple faith in Hoxton wherever he turned.

"I'm a street guy and in the East End people say 'God bless you son. Could I have a fifty, Charlie, you old boy?' and they'd go 'God bless you.' They'd make a prayer! They was really just ordinary people and they believed in God."

Curiously it was his cousin Lenny McLean, 'The Guv'nor', who tried to steer him away from the family business. "He was my idol. He was the toughest man in Britain. And he was the man who guided me away from that path. He saw that I was writing and he said, 'You're good at this son. You can go another way.' He said, 'How old are you?' I said 'I'm twenty.' He said, 'You want to be stabbed at twenty-two? You want to be shot at twenty-six? You want to be looking over your shoulder? You want to be lying on your bed unable to sleep?' He put it into terms I understood and this stayed in my head. I could see he wanted a way out and he ended up becoming a professional actor and then writing a bestselling book. He looked at his life and saw that his reputation as a gangster was so big that he couldn't escape from it. I was terrified that would happen to me. And at that point it don't matter if you become something else. You'll always be known as that and it will stick.

Mortality
Murder and tragedy was the turning point for Martin. "I was with my best mate Paul and my mate Joseph, a young black guy who I took under my wing. The East End wasn't multicultural in the way it is now. It was a racist area. I looked after Joseph. And he used to love being with me because I was like one of the chaps. We was walking round the neighborhood and these Scottish geezers called out to Joseph, 'you black this, you black that' and I said, 'Oi! Don't talk to him like that!' And they said,

---

16   A branch of the Serious and Organised Crime Command within London's Metropolitan Police Service

'What you going to do about it?' So I said to Joseph, 'Get back, son,' and I turn to the Scottish, 'Come on then let's have a straightener.' That's the East End. People would just stand there and have a fag and watch a fight. To them it was brutal but honourable. The loser would say, 'All right, you done me.'

"But the Scottish pulled out blades and I realized they were going to try to kill me. So I move behind a skip with my mates, and said, 'Let's get tooled up.' We went back at the Scottish and my mate Paul was stabbed. He died at the back of a bin, Joseph holding him as life left him.

"On the way to Paul's funeral, I'm driving, following my other best mate. He takes a wrong turn, so I double back beneath an underpass to catch up with him and I run into a traffic jam. And just when I'm about to try to turn around I see a helicopter landing up ahead. So I'm stuck in this slow moving traffic and we pass a horrific accident. I'm looking at all this carnage. Body parts. Decapitations. And as I pass I look into the rearview mirror and realize my best mate's car is turned over. It was my friends. They were all dead. One murder and four deaths."

Martin had a breakdown and had to be hospitalized. "All this in my small circle and I thought, 'It's me, I'm next.' I had no control. I had to be treated for post-traumatic stress disorder. I went into hospital with Falklands vets. It was the mortality. I was terrified of dying like that. I was terrified that one-second you're here and the next second you're not, and it brought it home to me. I started contemplating my own mortality at an early age.

"I was not mentally fit to do anything else so I slowly drifted back in to crime because I was terrified.

Ways of Escape
"I threw myself into drugs and drink and partying, ecstasy, the rave scene and trying many different ways to escape, to cope, but none of it filled the hole until I started looking into literature, the arts and spirituality. Many times I tried to become a born-again Christian but it didn't work. It felt soulless. I'd go to Bible meetings. I'd go up to blocks of flats with friends who'd become Christians. I went to Narcotics Anonymous. I went to AA [Alcoholics Anonymous]. I started reading Zen. I was searching for a way to connect with God.

"I always believed in God but I never had a way to connect. Even as a criminal I was always helping people. There were occasions when I saved lives. I'd stop things from happening. I always went to extremes but I didn't want to go over the edge, where someone's life could be lost. I knew there was accountability.

"There were many other events on the way. I lost a lot of other friends in horrific circumstances – ODs, murders. There's always something terrible and tragic going on in that world. And you think, 'Am I gonna be a statistic?' Also my own violence was becoming extreme. I kept re-lapsing. I would go to the gym. I would train. I would get myself healthy, but I wasn't training myself not to react.

"I was trying to get into acting. I had a part on TV. I was trying many different ways to escape and then I'd revert and burst out in violence somewhere and go back to my old habits, to the extent where I was beginning to self-destruct. I went into an abyss. I had a severe cocaine habit for six months and nearly overdosed a couple of times on crack cocaine. I was rushed to hospitals. I didn't want to die in this state."

Rage

Martin was smoldering with rage. He couldn't control his arrogance and anger.

"I started a fight outside a club in King's Cross because they wouldn't let me in. I said, 'Who do you think you are?' I'd done a couple of these bouncers. I just smashed them and walked away. But they radioed through to the gate – it was a massive nightclub – three bouncers were waiting for me. They were smashing and smashing and I'm lying on the pavement, completely overpowered. Completely lost. They snapped me arm. They were beating me to death. I cried out in my heart, *'Please God don't let me die like this'*, and then, a blue flashing light come and touched me to the core.

"I was in the hospital recovering. I had met a Muslim woman in a nightclub who later became my wife. I ended up having a child with her, but we later divorced. She was not a devout Muslim, but when I come out of hospital she said, 'Listen you've got to read the Qur'an.'

"I said, 'What are you talking about?'

"She said, 'The Qur'an is the Muslim's bible.'

"I said, 'I'm a Christian. Leave me alone.'

"She said, 'You're a Christian? What sort of Christian are you?'

The Complete Truth

"I didn't want to be a Muslim, I wanted to go back to my religion, which was crime. I was dealing drugs. I was stealing. I knew that all the money I was making had to stop coming because I knew it was wrong. You got to remember, the older generation they all knew that what they were doing was wrong but it was what they did. It was their profession.

"One day I walked into a bookshop and the first book I saw was the Qur'an, in the religion section. I bought that book and when I opened it, it really started to change things in my life. It was like complete truth. And I thought, 'I can't do this because all this is against what I'm doing.' But slowly and surely I started doing bits of it because I really believed in it."

Anger Management

Martin began reading from a translation of the Qur'an and then about the life of the Prophet Muhammad, peace and blessings be upon him. In his readings he came upon a hadith:

> A man said to the Prophet (peace be upon him): "Counsel me."
> The Prophet (peace be upon him) said: "Do not get angry." The man repeated his request many times, but the Prophet (peace be upon him) kept saying: "Do not get angry."[17]

"This one sentence changed my life. I was driven by anger all my adult life. I thought, 'But how can you not get angry?' The Prophet kept repeating 'Do not get angry' until they thought he was never going to stop.

"I suffered from terrible anxiety. Terrible fears in my own self, which I couldn't really talk about, so when I got angry and aggressive it changed the way I felt. I wasn't feeling under threat. I wasn't feeling insecure. I was actually in the moment, in the now. It was almost a spiritual event. Before I loved it when there was a twelve-man brawl. It was being alive, in the moment. It was addictive. But in the end someone would have walked up behind me and shot me or I would have done the same to them.

17   Related by Abu Hurayra in Sahih al-Bukhari

"So I understood that hadith completely. I always thought about my anger the night my friend was killed. I thought to myself, 'If only I'd known this hadith then. If only I'd not reacted.' I got angry because these people upset me in my own area. *They don't know who I am!'* My ego was inflated. I was under the influence of alcohol and other substances. I was arrogant. I had to let 'em know that they couldn't offend me because that was the rules. If I'd have known that hadith then I wouldn't have got angry.

"And then I tried *not* getting angry and everything changed. I thought that this was for me. That hadith alone gave me that mercy and changed the way I felt. So I changed this destructive addiction into a constructive addiction. I became addicted to not getting angry."

Repentance

Martin began reading from the *hadith* literature. What he discovered was the transformative power of Islam. He read how, before Islam, the great Companion and second Caliph of Islam 'Umar ibn al-Khattab, may God be well pleased with him, had buried his daughter alive. "I read that he wept remembering when he was burying his daughter, she was rubbing sand off his face. This was how ignorant the people of Makkah were before Islam. They had done so many bad things and yet through Islam and the door of repentance, they became such beautiful people."

Martin went into a mosque on Barking Road and asked to be accepted into Islam. He entered Islam and was given the name Muhammad Saleh. "I wanted to make *dhikr*. When I began to do *dhikr* that became an addiction. When I started the prayer that became an addiction. I changed all my negative addictions into positive addictions. And yet, one can still do all that and it can be soulless. As a Muslim one can let the anger take over. You know anger is one of the most dangerous things and I realize now why the Prophet said what he said. A lot of Muslims don't understand how important that hadith is.

"What I loved about Islam was that I could cut out the middleman and go straight to the Source. I didn't need anyone. I was told I could be as worthy as anyone. That struck a chord. I had saved people's lives, my friend got stabbed to death, I'd chased murderers down the road and they'd run like cowards, I nearly lost my life on numerous occasions by people trying to hurt me. But I was protected somehow.

"I had a really deep belief in God but I didn't know how to get that connection. And when I started learning about Islam, it all fit into place. But Allah has been there from Day One and He is closer to me than my jugular vein. I realized I had been on a learning curve to understand and have this connection. My life is still a life of learning. I realize that I don't know who is truly pious and who is not. I can only know myself really. I knew my capacity for violence; at one stage of my life I was very, very violent.

A Reunion

"I was praying in the mosque one day. I felt someone behind me. I turn to him and say, 'Are you okay?'

"He's a big black guy. He's looking at me. He says, 'Can I talk to you brother?' I sensed the street vibe. And I say, 'I've got to do my *Sunna* prayers.' I'm getting a little edgy, you know, me old self coming back. I went to the back of the mosque and I'm thinking, 'Not in the mosque. I don't want any problem in the mosque. Get it out of the mosque.' I've got a bit of trouble there. He's a right big lump.

"He comes up and says to me, 'Are you that guy?'

"'What guy?'

"'Are you that guy who used to wear the black Burberry mac and stand on the street there?'

"'Yeah, that's me. I'm a Muslim now. I said, '*Allahu Akbar!*' and he began to cry. And I remembered.

"I had been in my room one day. I had a nice car outside and he and two or three of his mates was about to break into my car and try to nick me stereo. I saw them and shouted, '*Oi!*' And they went, 'Who are you talking to?' And I went 'Wait there!' I was highly volatile and I said, wait there you.... and made some racial slur. They went, 'What'd you say?' I said, 'Wait there!' And I went into me zone. I got me self up. I was gonna do 'im. And I chased him down with a big knife. Chased him down the road. He was really fast and he got away.

"And now he was the Imam of the mosque. I thought, '*Allah Subhan-ahu wa ta'ala* can make anything happen.'

Self Control

"After I became a Muslim I was walking down the street wearing a Muslim hat on my head, and someone who I would have considered an inferior in my world made fun of my appearance. In the past I would probably have left him in a pool of blood. I was insulted but I was making *dhikr* and I let it go and walked away through an understanding from the hadith that if you don't react the Angels defend you. So I was thinking about Angels and the Next World and the way the Prophet smiled and walked on. He was now my hero. My heroes had always been my uncles and my cousins but now I was following the Prophet. So I was bringing these ancient teachings into my urban environment and they was steering me clear of all the problems. It was the ideal place to be, the inner city.

"My friend asked me, 'When you leave your house do you got a weapon on you?' And I would say no. He was dumbfounded and said, 'You mean you don't carry nothing no more?' I said, 'I leave with God in peace and I go home in peace and I keep good intentions.' I've got the Greatest Protector. I don't need a piece of metal. And that was transformative for someone like me; to change the patterns I'd had instilled in me. I was going to the mosque for every prayer. I mean outside I was an ascetic. I was cocooned, in a bubble, reading Qur'an and hadith. I had to be extreme in my religion to get to the stage where I could then practice it in that setting. I hadn't moved away from Hoxton.

"My son was born in the East End and I was trying to practice Islam but every time I left the house, they was there and they wanted me back. All I wanted to do was come out of the house, go to the mosque and go home. It became a nightmare. I just couldn't continue like that.

"Finally I prayed '*Allah please get me out of this place.*' And Allah made it easy for me and I escaped to a better environment, which gave me some peace without people knocking on my door with the old histrionics I was entrenched in. I would never have got free of it if I didn't practice my faith."

Atonement

Before he left Hoxton Martin began revisiting people he had harmed.

"I was making *tawba* to people I'd see in the street. I'd say, 'What I done to you, I want you to forgive me.' I remember I saw a guy who had done a terrible crime. It was a horrific thing he'd done. He crossed the line. He had raped someone in a block of flats and was arrested and went to prison. When he got out he had left the area but had the audacity to come back. It was unforgiveable what he'd done, so I done a terrible thing to him. I smashed him to pieces and left him in a bad way. Years later I see him at a bus stop with his daughter and I walked up to him. He was shocked. He was terrified I was going to attack him. I walked up to him and said, 'It's all right', I said, 'I'm not going to do nothing. I just want to ask you if you can forgive me.' And he started crying. I said, 'I'm a Muslim now. I want you to forgive me for what I've done.' He did. He wept. So I witnessed the power of this faith, if you're willing to change."

O child of Adam, as long as you beseech Me and hope for Me, I shall forgive you whatever you have done, without minding in the slightest. O child of Adam, were your sins to reach up to the clouds of Heaven and then you asked forgiveness of Me, I should forgive you, without minding in the slightest.

O child of Adam, even if you were to bring Me enough sins to fill the earth, but then you met Me without associating anything with Me, I should bring to you the selfsame measure of forgiveness.[18]

HADITH QUDSI

---

18   Related by Anas ibn Malik, included in The *Mishkat al-Anwar* of Ibn 'Arabi, translated by Stephen Hirtenstein and Martin Notcutt

The Beginner

A SAUDI INDUSTRIALIST I knew called me up out of the blue. He sounded troubled and his call in itself was unusual in that I rarely heard from him. He asked me if I could come to his factory immediately. His factory was in the old industrial area of Jeddah and I was at home in Makkah at the time. The journey took over an hour and I used to try to minimize my travel, but his call intrigued me and I was, to be honest, a little flattered that he seemed to need to see me.

When I arrived I found him in his office. He was uncharacteristically subdued. Before he was able to tell me what it was he wanted to see me about, a short, stocky, slightly funny-looking foreigner wearing a goatee and spectacles charged through the door. He had a paper in his hand, which he slammed on the desk. "Did you write this?" he shouted. "How could you write this to me? At least speak to me face-to-face!" The fellow was extremely agitated and my industrialist friend, who was in his late fifties and very conservative, just couldn't cope with this outburst. He waved his hands, palms out, in front of him as if to repel this fellow's emotional energy and said, "Please go out. Go out. I can't accept this!" or something to that effect.

After the intruder stormed out, the industrialist turned to me and said, "This is why I asked you to come here." I asked him who he was and he told me his story. He was a British engineer who'd been hired as Plant Manager (the factory produced PVC pipe). He was evidently a troubled soul. He had debts and a bad marriage back in England. The industrialist was a very religious man and dedicated to proselytizing Islam. He was also generous. As a Christmas gift he paid off the engineer's debts, which amounted to something like £16,000 (nice Christmas present!). When the man's wife threatened to leave him, he resigned and was sent home. Then he changed his mind and asked to have his old job back. In Saudi Arabia this was a complicated, red-tape-ridden process, but the industrialist gave him his old job back. All the while he was talking to him about Islam and, in the end, the engineer converted.

This is when the trouble started. The new convert began to act strangely. He became overfamiliar and started to treat his boss like a father. He would come over to his employer's house and get involved in his personal affairs. Saudis tend to be very private, very family-oriented people. They rarely fling their doors open the way Muslims from other cultures do. They may be friendly and hospitable but tend to keep outsiders at arm's length. So when this fellow started turning up at his boss's house unannounced and involving himself in his benefactor's charities, he became very uneasy.

"Last Friday I came into my kitchen and found him having tea with my maid," he said, perplexed. "I simply can't have this!" He didn't know what to do. So he wrote him a stiff note (the one just thrown on his desk) ordering the new convert to cease and desist.

The upshot was that he wanted me, as a western Muslim who at least appeared to be normal (I was never as normal as he imagined), to have a talk with him.

I tracked the engineer down. He was ready for me. We went into a small meeting room off the shop floor. He struck me as weird. He was a tough, hard-looking blue-collar character; hardly your garden-variety western Muslim convert. He wore a gray work shirt and an incongruous Palestinian *keffiyeh*, which made him appear eccentric. We sat down face-to-face. He said he knew why I was here. I began trying to explain his boss's position. I said something like, "Look, you have to understand that Saudis aren't used to the kind of emotional familiarity westerners are. You've got to let up." But before I had the chance to say much he interrupted me. "Before you go on, I think I'd better tell you something about me." He then began to tell me one of the strangest stories I've ever heard. To this day I have no idea whether any of it was true but, for reasons I'll explain later, I think it was. He told his story in intricate, wild, graphic detail and his tale lasted for about two hours, maybe more.

The gist of it was this: He was a mercenary assassin working for MI6. He was a genuine chemical engineer (an expert in explosives) but his real assignment was as a deep cover operative, or sleeper, embedded in Saudi Arabia as part of a contingency plan to assassinate Israeli Prime Minister Menachem Begin. (I'm not making this up.) According to my

36

new troubled convert friend, if he were activated he would travel across the Saudi border to Jordan and then into Israel to assassinate the then Prime Minister. If he was caught, the Saudis could be blamed for the action.

But this was only part of the story – the bizarre opener. He told me that his path to Islam began back in 1967, when he was a mercenary with an extralegal British unit fighting the communist insurgency in Yemen. He told me that during an operation where his unit wiped out almost an entire Yemeni village he was wounded and left by his comrades to die. He told me that as he was bleeding out he pulled a cyanide capsule from his pocket, which he and his comrades in arms were ordered to take if they were compromised in any way. He was looking at the capsule, debating whether to end his life then and there, when a Yemeni from the village they'd just attacked, kicked the capsule out of his hand, dragged him into his house and nursed him back to health.

After he'd related this part of the story he opened his wallet and fished out a torn fragment of a Yemeni Rial note stained with what looked like a thumbprint of blood, laminated in plastic. "This is the note that I offered the Yemeni in payment for saving me. He refused. I have never forgotten what he did for me. This is where my journey began."

He ennumerated his troubles. He'd been through a painful divorce and diagnosed with cancer. He claimed that when he embraced Islam he went to his MI6 control in Jeddah and told him that he had become a Muslim and wanted out. The control said, "There is no out. The only way out is death. You will be killed." He was a nervous wreck.

He then began recounting, in some detail, his various exploits as a mercenary assassin. I only remember one. He described with what seemed to be grim satisfaction garroting some hapless adversary under a bridge.

Finally, after about an hour of lurid detail, I said to him, "Look, I kind of like reading about espionage and the sort of thing you're talking about in novels, but, really, what you're describing is disgusting. It doesn't impress me. It sickens me. You know what impresses me? When I hear of someone who can stay up all night in prayer. I am awestruck by that because I can't do it. That is really hard."

I continued, "Your fate, your destiny is in the hands of God. If God wants you to die, then you can seal yourself in a vault, take every precaution and you will not escape death. And if God doesn't want you to die, your control can detonate a nuclear device under your bed and you will not die."

At this, he shook his head, saying, "*You're far out.*"

What I was hearing was so far-fetched, so ridiculously melodramatic, that I didn't know what to make of it. My new ex-assassin friend took me to his flat near the factory. When he entered the flat, he checked to see if a hair he had stuck on the doorjamb had been dislodged. It had. He went over to his coffee table and found a tiny thin metal plate on the floor. He said, "They've been in here. This plate should have been in this book." It was like a scene out of a bad spy movie. I began to have real doubts. We sat down in his parlor and talked some more.

He was very high strung. "I don't know anything," he said. "I'm like a baby as a Muslim. When I go to the prayer the other workers are helping me. I always stand in the last prayer line in the mosque because I'm not worthy of being in the first line."

Up to this point I really thought I was listening to a psychotic fantasist. But then he said something that changed my mind.

He said with great agitation, "*I'm freakin' out here!* I never believed in God before. I never had any religion. And now I believe in God! I never prayed before. And then I started praying. And, you see, I wanted a cat. I just had this feeling that I wanted a cat. So I asked God for a cat. And then, THIS CAT CAME! I found a cat! And I'm thinkin' I'm goin' crazy. I got this cat! But is this real, from God? Or am I going crazy? I'm really freakin' out!"

And with that, I believed him. The way he said it, his logic, his wonder, was just too real. I had heard similar comments from other converts who had experienced God's responsiveness for the first time. This could never have been fabricated. It rang true. I said, "For those of us who remember God, this is something normal. God is Present. God hears our prayers. God is the Most Generous of the Generous, the Most Merciful of the Merciful. He is our Provider. Of course the cat came. And of course this is a gift from God and a signal to enhance your faith. Have no doubt about it."

He began to calm down. I said to him, "Look, your boss is a kind and generous man, but he's not your father. He's not someone you can become too familiar with. You're making him uncomfortable. You need to relax. Leave him alone. Get on with your life. Enjoy your faith."

We parted company. About two or three hours had passed. I returned to my industrialist friend's office. I said, "Has he told you his story?"

He said, "Yes, but I don't believe it."

I shook my head, saying, "You'd better hope he's telling the truth because if he's lying, *he's the most insane person I have ever met* and you need to get him out of the country immediately."

I continued, "But I think he's telling the truth. He's someone who's had a very sordid and depressing life who has been rescued. However, if he keeps on recounting his squalid exploits, trying to impress, you need to send him out of the country as fast as you can because, if he persists after what I told him, he's psychotic and he could get you into serious trouble. I gave him some good, commonsense advice. If he heeds it, he won't cause you any more problems and this will be a sign that he is telling the truth and has genuinely converted to Islam and is, *insha'a llah*, on the road to salvation."

And this is what happened. The mercenary settled down, stopped bothering his boss, and got on with his life.

I met him two more times. The first time, I visited the factory and he took me into the little office off the shop floor. He told me happily that his troubles were over. He had had a biopsy and his cancer was in remission. As for the death threat he faced, he told me that he went to his control and said, "Okay, if you're going to kill me, let's get it over with." They took him to a remote beach far north of Jeddah. They got out of the car and held the traitor at gunpoint. He said, "Before you do whatever you do, I want to say my prayers." His control nodded his head and said to go ahead. The Mercenary was a peculiar-looking fellow in his Palestinian *keffiyeh*. They watched this oddball bobbing up and down performing *salat* on the sand. When he finished he came back to his assailants to face his destiny. His control looked at him in disgust. "You're crazy," he said. He threw his car keys into the Red Sea, walked back to his own car and drove away.

The last time I saw him was in front of a supermarket in Jeddah. He introduced me to a Korean nurse who had become his fiancé. He seemed happy and level-headed. May God protect him wherever he is and increase his faith and guide him on the Straight Path and may God bless his goodhearted and generous benefactor and have Mercy on his kind soul.

The Blacksmith's Heart

ABU HAFS 'AMR BIN SALIM[19] lived in Nishapur in the 9th century (3rd century of Hijra). He was an illiterate workingman, a blacksmith by trade, which gave him his last name al-Haddad ('The Blacksmith'). As a young man he was consumed by desire for a serving girl. He lusted after her. He was desperate to have her. His friends told him about a Jewish magician living on the outskirts of the city who could cast a spell on her.

The practice of magic (*sihr*) is utterly forbidden (*haram*) in Islam. At the same time Abu Hafs lived, the Hanafi jurist Ibn Humam stated categorically that magic is forbidden and that the act of holding it permissible was an act of disbelief or *kufr*.[20]

So Abu Hafs walked headlong into the *haram* to satisfy his lust. The magician told him, "To begin with you must not mention God's Name on your tongue, or have any good intentions whatsoever for forty days. Then I will prescribe a talisman that will fulfill your desire."

Abu Hafs followed the magician's instructions. This meant that he had to abandon prayer, invocation and good thoughts, intentions and actions for forty days. For a Muslim to abandon his obligatory prayers and even good intentions to satisfy his lusts through black magic is utterly monstrous. Abu Hafs was on the road to perdition.

When he returned, the magician created a talisman so that the woman would succumb to his charms. The talisman failed. Abu Hafs returned frustrated.

"There is no doubt that during the forty days some good was manifested in you," said the magician, "otherwise I am absolutely certain that you would have achieved your desire."

Abu Hafs protested. "I have done nothing." He cast about in his memory to see if there was anything at all that he had done to undermine the spell. He had meticulously followed the magician's instructions. "The

---

19   Retold from *Tadhkirat Al Awliya*, translated by A.J. Arberry.
20   Related by Ustadh Faraz Rabbani from the *Fath Al-Qadir* of al-Hafiz al-Kamal Ibn al-Humam al-Hanafi.

only thing I can think of is that on my way to receive the talisman I kicked a stone out of the road so that no one would trip on it."

When he heard this, the magician was shaken to the depths of his being. He had seen the reality of God's vast omniscience and immense generosity. "You should never offend a God who has not let such an insignificant act be wasted even though you willfully neglected His commands for forty days!" He recognized God's Compassion and Power and at that moment the Jewish magician accepted Islam. Seeing the magician's sudden change of heart Abu Hafs turned to God and changed his life.

Abu Hafs continued to practice his trade, keeping the miracle he experienced to himself. Every day he earned one dinar. At night he gave his earnings to the poor and secretly left money for widows. After the night prayers he would then set out to beg for his sustenance. When he was overwhelmed with hunger he would go to the public basin where women washed vegetables and pick over the leavings. He continued in this way for some time until one day a blind man passed through the market reciting:

> Were those who work evil to possess all that is on the earth and the like of it besides, they would seek to ransom themselves with it from the terrible punishment on the Day of Resurrection. And there would appear unto them from God that they had not reckoned.[21]

This verse overpowered the blacksmith's heart and he fainted dead away. When he revived, he returned to his work but was so distracted that, instead of pulling iron from the fire with his tongs, he reached into the furnace with his hand and pulled out the white hot iron, laying it on the anvil for his apprentices to hammer. When they saw Abu Hafs turning the iron with his bare hands they cried out. "Strike," he shouted. "Master, where shall we strike?" they asked. "The iron is clean."

At this Abu Hafs came to his senses, seeing the iron in his hand, and flung the metal away. At that moment, he left his trade, never to return.

"I long desired to deliberately give up this work and failed until this event came upon me and forcibly wrested me from myself. Though I

---

21   Holy Qur'an, *Sura al-Zumar* 39:48, translation from the Study Qur'an

kept trying to abandon this work, all was to no purpose until the work abandoned me."

Abu Hafs al-Haddad exchanged his trade for the Path to God, struggling against his lower self in a life of solitude and contemplation. He kept company with Imam Abu'l-Qasim al-Junayd, the saint Abu Bakr Shibli and other great men of the Way, may God be well pleased with them.

He had great tenderness of heart and loved the poor. When he arrived in Makkah al-Mukarrama to perform the Pilgrimage, he saw a crowd of destitute pilgrims. He conceived an aching desire to relieve their poverty but he had nothing to give. He was so overcome by his longing to give to the poor that he picked up a stone from the earth and in his heart cried out to God, "By Your Majesty, if You do not give me something to give I will break all the lamps in the Haram!" He then began his circumambulation of God's House. In his first circuit a man approached him and handed him a purse of gold, which he spent on the impoverished pilgrims.

> Sins are messengers of unbelief in the same way as fever is a messenger of death.[22]
>
> ABU HAFS 'AMR BIN SALIM

22   *Al-Risala al-qushayriyya fi 'ilm al-tasawwuf* (Epistle on Sufism), translated by Alexander D. Knysh

It is recounted that a man asked Ibn Mas'ud about a sin he had committed: did he have a chance of repentance? Ibn Mas'ud turned away from him, then turned back and saw tears flowing from his eyes. Ibn Mas'ud said to the man: *'Indeed Paradise has eight gates which open and close, but the gate of repentance, guarded by a special Angel, does not close; do [repent], and do not despair.'*[23]

IMAM AL-GHAZALI

---

23   Al-Ghazali on Repentance, translated by S.M. Stern

Identity

"MY FATHER WAS in the Navy. I would see these pictures of him in a sea of white. White is what they were wearing and white is what the people were." This image haunted young Zachary Jackson because his father was black.

Zachary was the youngest of seven children. "My dad was in the Navy for thirty years. Everybody in my family was born in a different place: Puerto Rico, San Francisco. I was born in New York in 1963." Living an itinerant life in a military bubble, race was never an issue. "We never were taught anything about racism."

Which is extraordinary. America was, and to a distressing extent still is, a deeply racist country. Lynching African-Americans was common throughout the South up to the 1960s and the last recorded lynching of an African-American was as late as 1981. Even today, hangman's nooses are being left in public places across the U.S. as threats or reminders of the barbaric practice. The Ku Klux Klan still exists. Under Trump white supremacy has made a comeback. When Zachary was born the Civil Rights Movement was sweeping the country, led by the Reverend Dr. Martin Luther King. Under King's spiritual guidance, the Civil Rights Movement embraced non-violence and civil disobedience inspired by the teachings and political activism of Mahatma Gandhi. In 1964 King won the Nobel Peace Prize for his work, the ultimate accolade of the white liberal establishment. Yet there were many African-American activists who disagreed with his notions of non-violent change and integration with white society.

Black Power

When Dr. King was assassinated in 1968, many disillusioned African-Americans turned to disengagement and the militancy and implicit violence of Black Power movements.

I witnessed this change first hand as a white student at UCLA. After

King's assassination our African-American friends at university turned cold and distant overnight. I remember in 1969 attending a screening of the film version of LeRoi Jones's play 'The Dutchman' about a white prostitute who taunts a well-dressed, well-behaved black man, minding his own business on a New York subway until he explodes in rage. The climax is what has been called 'the Charlie Parker[24] speech':

> Charlie Parker? Charlie Parker. All the hip white boys scream for Bird. And Bird saying, 'Up your ass, feeble-minded ofay! Up your ass.' And they sit there talking about the tortured genius of Charlie Parker. Bird would've played not a note of music if he just walked up to East 67th Street and killed the first ten white people he saw. Not a note! And I'm the great would-be poet. Yes. That's right! Poet. Some kind of bastard literature...all it needs is a simple knife thrust. Just let me bleed you, you loud whore, and one poem vanished. A whole people of neurotics, struggling to keep from being sane. And the only thing that would cure the neurosis would be your murder. Simple as that. I mean if I murdered you, then other white people would begin to understand me. You understand? No I guess not. If Bessie Smith had killed some white people she wouldn't have needed that music. She could have talked very straight and plain about the world. No metaphors. No grunts. No wiggles in the dark of her soul. Just straight two and two are four. Money. Power. Luxury. Like that. All of them. Crazy niggers turning their backs on sanity. When all it needs is that simple act. Murder. Just murder! Would make us all sane.

I was sitting in Royce Hall auditorium, one of the few whites in attendance in a full house. At the end of this speech the audience exploded in a roar of approval. These were well dressed, well behaved and well educated African-Americans—my fellow students. This was how they felt. But of course they did. As a cossetted white boy, I was stunned. I slipped out of the auditorium wishing, more than usual, that

---

24   Charlie 'Yardbird' Parker (1920-1955) was an African-American saxophonist and one of the most influential musicians in the history of jazz.

I was invisible.

The most notorious African-American militant group at the time was the Black Panther Party, which evolved into a Marxist revolutionary group that fought police brutality and called for the arming of all African-Americans, among other radical proposals. In California, the 'US' Organization initially worked with the Black Panther Party. Led by Ron 'Maulana' Kerenga, it differed from the Panthers in its focus on promoting African-American unity through the creation of an African cultural identity, with a focus on East African Swahili heritage. Kerenga's most memorable contribution to African-American culture may be his invention of the *Kwanzaa* Festival, a weeklong celebration of African culture in the African-American experience, mirroring the white culture's Christmas festivities.

A few days after watching 'The Dutchman', I attended a talk by playwright Leroi Jones (who later took the name Amiri Baraka) and Ron Kerenga. They were flanked by large, menacing bodyguards and were cold as ice. For white people their presence was overtly threatening. I commented on this to Jones and he replied that white people *should* feel threatened. A few days later I was on my way to class and found that the university had been shut down. A rivalry had developed between the Panthers and 'US' over which organization's representatives would head the Afro-American Studies Center at the University of California at Los Angeles, which ended in a gun battle on the UCLA campus that left two Panthers dead and led to a series of revenge killings, signaling an end to the 'We Shall Overcome' optimism of the early civil rights protests.

By this time Zachary's father had been stationed in San Diego and the family settled down to what became a permanent home. "Our neighborhood was mixed and there was a strong sense of community. There was no racism in the community. Everybody was united based on poverty. Nobody had a lot of wealth. It was mixed. People were poor whites, poor Latinos, poor Asians." Nevertheless, Zachary's older siblings became involved with the 'US' Organization. "Everything was black pride, black attitude, *Kwanzaa*. But this expression of blackness for us wasn't an expression of anti-whiteness. It was an expression of who we were." It was one way of coping with being black in a white-dominated and still overtly racist society. "As a child of about seven or eight years old I said to myself, 'Wow, is this what I'm going to be up against when I get older?'" In 1971 Ron Kerenga's own violence caught up with him when he was convicted of felony assault and sent to prison for four years. When he was released he came to stay with Zachary's family for a time. Zachary was twelve years old. Kerenga "gave me a Swahili name, *Imara. Imara* means strong and that immediately did something to me.

"I immediately started to act out on the definitions of this name. I started to embrace more cultural things. I started to study Swahili as a kid. We found that all these Swahili names had meaning to them. We found out that people would name their children after the attributes they displayed as infants. So I started working out, doing push-ups. They had me in front of two hundred men showing them how to do push-ups."

Zachary was too young to be touched by the pent-up rage, bitterness and militancy the King assassination unleashed in the African-American community. By the time he did get involved the initial fury had passed. "I was learning about history. I wasn't on the front lines. I knew that there were soldiers. They had different lines of defense. There were members with black belts in karate but I saw this more as a definition of manhood. Protection. Protecting the community. Protecting the sisters. If the brothers got out of line, they would go and visit them."

The Change

As he got older he witnessed a change in the movement and in his society. "Where it used to be all about community—all about uplifting the brotherhood—now it was every man for himself. We grew up watching Blaxploitation films like 'SuperFly'. We wanted to be rich with all the trappings we'd see in these movies: long hair, long jacket, big hat, big bankroll of course, but no callouses on your hands. You don't work. This was what attracted us all. We grew up with that. I witnessed the change. You started to see people becoming pimps, players and drug dealers."

In his adolescence Zachary was trying to "establish some sort of identity". In his world "you were either an athlete or some sort of entertainer and you went on to do something. School was never introduced to me as some sort of vehicle to take me to great things. No one ever said to me, 'have you ever thought of being a physician?' It wasn't really confirmed that you could do this. For me it wasn't in education. I wasn't an athlete."

After thirty years of marriage, Zachary's parents divorced. "When they divorced I was about 13 years old. That took me in another direction. I didn't understand it at the time, but without a father around oh, man! He didn't disappear. He was on the other side of town. I would see him once a week. He was a good dad. But the fact that he wasn't there—oh my god, I had it my way." His mom spoiled him. "She was compensating. And it backfired."

Getting Down to Business

For Zachary junior high school was a pivotal time. "Two friends and I wanted to become 'businessmen'. We would come to junior high school dressed in suits carrying briefcases. We were like that all the way through high school. One girl approached us and asked, 'what do you guys know about selling something?' and I remember bragging to her, 'I can sell ice to an Eskimo.'" So she came back the next day with a drug Zachary had never seen before. She drops it on a towel and says, 'Can you sell this?' 'This' was PCP (Phencyclidine), also known as 'angel dust'. Angel dust has been described as a dissociative drug that distorts perceptions of sight and sound and produces feelings of detachment from the surrounding environment and the self. It has also been called 'the scariest of all drugs', making users extremely violent and self-destructive.

"During the 'US' period we didn't see drugs but there were drugs in the community. I wasn't into drugs but I was smoking weed (marijuana) and selling weed. It was a cool thing to do because everybody was smoking weed. My older brothers were smoking weed and selling it. So naturally I did what I saw them do. As I said, the influence we got was from the movies that glorified this life." It turned out that the girl's father was a major drug dealer in San Diego. She took the angel dust pills to Zack and his friends. "We sold the PCP and we made a lot of money." The school didn't know what hit them. Part of the student body flipped out on angel dust and school had to be shut down.

Winner

"After this the girl kept bringing the angel dust, and we sold it and she kept giving us more. She just gave it to us. I found out later she was taking it from her father. I was only about fourteen at the time and I was making a lot of money. People saw us with all this money and gave us a lot of love because of it. America is a society that loves winners. As long as you appear to be succeeding, nobody's going to say anything to you."

But too many people wigged out from PCP, so after his initial wave of success Zack took his angel dust earnings and developed his teenage business niche selling marijuana. Then, when he was a junior in high school he met a beautiful white girl who was a year younger than he was. "She liked me. We had some kind of connection." She disappeared for a year and turned up mysteriously just before Zack was ready to graduate. She had been in Los Angeles and invited him to come with her to L.A. "I really didn't want to. I had just bought a fresh quarter pound of weed to sell over the weekend." But she was persistent and Zachary gave in.

Easy Money
"We drive up Highway 5 to the 101 and get off on Sunset. When we hit Beverly Hills she gives me directions. I'm nervous. I've got these ten bags of dope with me. 'Is she trying to set me up?' We're driving down Sunset, a black man and a white girl, which was in those days enough to go to jail. I had no idea where we were going. She tells me she has an apartment. So I thought this was just going to be a sex run." On the way to the girl's apartment Zack sees dozens of streetwalkers. "On every other corner there were as many as fifteen hoes. They're working. We're not talking about women who looked like they were on drugs or beat up. These were like they stepped out of a magazine. She's giving me directions. We hit Roxbury Avenue in Beverly Hills. She says, 'turn here.'"

They stop and go up to the girl's apartment. "She says 'I'm going to get dressed.' I figure she's going to go into the bedroom and come out in a negligee. All of a sudden she comes out transformed. And she looks like one of them! Dressed like a model; blonde, white, green eyes." Zachary was way out of his depth. He didn't know what was going on or what he was doing but he tried to keep his cool and look hip.

"She says, 'Do you know what's up?' I said, 'Yeah, yeah, yeah I know what's up.' She says, 'Come on.' We get in the car and we ride." Zachary drops the girl off on Sunset. She tells him to pick her up at the same place at 11 pm. He cruises Sunset Strip for hours. "I had my weed with me. I could have ended up in jail so many different ways.

"I go back to where I dropped her off. She's cool. She's walking down a side street. She gets in the car. And she reaches down in her stockings, pulls out a roll like this, says 'here' and gives it to me. I almost fell out of my seat. 'I'm going to jail for sure. It's gotta be a set up. How's somebody gonna give me a roll of money like this?' I'm just holding this roll of money. I don't know what to do or say. If I say too much I'll let on that I don't know anything. I don't want to let her know that she knows more than me. So we're riding. It's 11:30 and a lot of people are still out on the streets. What do I do? So she says, 'I have a question for you.' So here it was. She said, 'Do you think you could get me some weed?'" She didn't know Zack was carrying his stash. "So I said, 'Oh yeah, hold on one second.' I get out and go down to these apartments out of her sight. I pulled out my own supply I come back and drop it on the seat. She says, 'You know where the weed is?' I said, 'I know where everything is.'

"She says, 'Cool. Won't you take me back out? The night is still young.' So I take her back. This is not counterfeit money. This is real money. So I go somewhere and I count it. It's like four hundred dollars. I said to myself, 'I wouldn't make four hundred dollars selling weed. This is better. If I'm going to do anything, this is the thing to do.'" Zack was looking for his street identity. "Everybody else was selling weed or a little cocaine. I couldn't do what everybody else did. This was perfect for me. This is something that nobody's doing. So I take the money, I go back. I get her. And she's got another five hundred dollars. *Nine hundred dollars.* This is like spinning straw into gold! There's got to be a catch to this. There's got to be a catch.

"I knew what she was doing. And actually even that is a felony. If you know that the person is going out and deriving funds from sex and you participate, this is pandering. Pimping is receiving the money. So having knowledge of this is a crime and taking money for it, that's a crime. For the woman, prostitution is a misdemeanor. They go to jail, the pimp gets them out and they carry on. I was like in shock the whole time. So much so that the next morning I couldn't wait to go back to San Diego, just to tell my friends what happened. I mean, I'm 17 years old, I'm in high school and I have to go back to class."

Back in San Diego in high school Zack thought his wild L.A. weekend was a one-off. But on Thursday the girl called him to tell him someone wanted to talk to him. "I thought that she was setting me up and that it was the police that wanted to talk to me. I knew about what she was doing and participated (pandering) and took the money (pimping). She's got me." Zachary was convinced he was headed for jail. But instead the girl introduced him to the man who had gotten her into the game.

'You're the one—the dude from San Diego! The girl been talking about you.' The pimp picked Zack up in a Rolls Royce. "He was cool. He was well known. He was a character out of SuperFly or Shaft. I wanted to be like that. I wanted to be a hustler. I wanted to make money without having to work. He says, 'the girl, she was stuffin' on me (holding back money). At first I was gonna crack on her (rough her up) but she told me about you and I wanted to meet you. Now I see you I want to have a hand in saying I helped turn you out.' I spent about two hours with him. He fed me. He gave me the girl's clothes and handed me twenty public nuisance tickets she had for prostitution. He told me the people to watch out for. He gave me a lot of instruction. I couldn't have done it without him."

So at age 17 young Zack Jackson became a pimp. He was still in high school. He felt like a winner. "I went back to school. I said to myself, 'I can't be in school and be a pimp, no way.' We had this class on Friday. The teacher would get everybody in a circle and we would drop these notes in a box. And one note asked, 'Is Zack going to the prom.' Another note said, 'graduation is upon us. What's Zack going to do?' When they read out the notes I said, 'I'm going pimping.' And everybody just laughed. Like it was a joke." But it was no joke.

"At that point it was about money but at the same time it was about establishing an identity. I have pictures of me in high school. I've got a big Borsalino hat and I've got the look. I wanted to be a hustler. I wanted to make money without having to work. I wanted to say, 'I did this.'"

Flash

When Zack graduated he left San Diego for L.A. and started pimping full-time. He had a three-year run. He was making big money. "I was more SuperFly than SuperFly. I drove a white Mercedes Benz. I had a tailor who made me snakeskin suits. I would pull up at stoplights and girls would drop their numbers into my sunroof. I felt like royalty but deep down I knew that I was nothing, that I didn't deserve that kind of attention. I knew that it was just the flash."

All the flash started to get him into trouble. "A friend of mine, another pimp, and I went out one night in L.A. to eat at a steak restaurant. We took a big table. We're very flamboyant. I had on about forty-thousand dollars worth of jewelry." Zack's friend had picked up a girl and brought her with them. When she was out of earshot, Zack said to him, 'Do you know this girl?' "He said, 'Don't worry about it. She's fine. She's good.' I said, 'You need to be careful. I've seen her before. I'm not sure where but it wasn't good.'" His friend ignored his warnings. Suddenly a gangbanger comes in to the restaurant, walks up to their table and says, 'I'm Batman.' 'Hm. Okay... how's it going?' "He was looking us over. He leaves. We order. And the next thing we know someone rushes into the restaurant and says, 'Everybody drop to the ground. Somebody's got a gun.'

"I'm on the ground, I'm taking my jewelry off and stuffing it in my pockets. I'm thinking I'm going to have to make a dash for it. We slip outside and get into the car. I said, 'Let's get out of here.' My friend said, 'I'm waiting for the girl.' 'Forget the girl! There's something she knows that we don't know. This is her part of town.' But we waited and the girl finally leaves the restaurant." Zack's friend insisted on following the girl in her car. "I said, 'You could be getting us set up.' I didn't know for sure what I was saying was true. I just felt it. We went around the corner. The girl pulls up into some driveway. On each side of the street three guys drop down from trees. They all had black ninja masks. It was like in a movie. They came to the car and pointed Uzis. They said, 'You know what this is.' I'm thinking, 'Oh my God! Is this how it's gonna end for me? No, this can't happen. This can't happen.' So I tell them I understand completely what they were there for." I still had this expensive jewelry I'd taken off in the restaurant in my pocket. One Ninja looks at me and says, 'Where's the necklace?' I said, 'Okay here it is.' The Ninja hits the driver in the head with his Uzi. "He said, 'I'm gonna smoke this fool.' I said, 'Please I'm going to make this the easiest robbery ever.'" Zachary gave him everything, even the money in his sock. "And they let us go."

As they rode off Zack had a very bad feeling that it wasn't over and on instinct he dropped to the floor of the back seat. "They lit up the whole back of the car. The guy driving got hit in the back of the ear. So he's driving straight on this long, long block. I'm telling him, 'Turn, turn!' He finally turns. I take the wheel trying to drive him to the hospital. We run into police officers with an ambulance that had stopped for some emergency. We tell them what happened and what we lost. The officer looks at me and says, 'You had that much jewelry? What were you doing with all that?' It hit me that this was going to be hard to explain. I'm not working. I don't have a business. What was I doing with forty-thousand dollars worth of jewelry anyway? He says, 'You take us back over and show us where it happened.' I said, 'Naw, forget it.'

The next day Zack drove back to San Diego to attend the funeral of a friend he knew from the hood. "As I walked through the door of the church the pastor was delivering the eulogy. He said, 'You know, we all have appointments in life, maybe the dentist or school, but this is one appointment that you won't miss, the one you won't be late for. This is your appointment with death.' I thought, 'Wow! 'Is he talking to me?' I felt like I died the night before. The street in me died. It could have gone another way. The eulogist was talking about the guy lying there in the casket. But he's talking to me. I said to myself, 'I don't want to meet my appointment in that state, doing what I'm doing.' So I started to disengage from that life at that point."

But disengaging wasn't so easy. Zack had started his career with the single girl he knew from high school but as he became more successful he became more ambitious. He wanted more money, more snakeskin suits, more cars, more jewelry and this meant more girls. He picked up two 15-year-old runaway girls from New York hitchhiking up the coast and tried to turn them. He took the two girls to San Diego and had one of his girls teach them. "It was cool for a couple of months but they got caught because they were underage runaways. The police showed them my picture. 'Do you know this guy?' 'Yeah, we know him.' The police said, 'We know him too and we know what you're doing.' So they told their story of what was happening and they arrested the girl I had who actually taught them. So I thought I was clear."

Not really. Zack's girl called him from jail to tell him that the vice squad was still after him. He didn't take her seriously. He drove downtown one night and was arrested. "They took me down to the precinct and questioned me all about these girls. I said, 'I don't know what you're talking about. I don't know these girls.' They said, 'We know you. You're gonna get ten years.' I bailed out and had my girl bailed out. I was really afraid. 'What am I gonna do? What's going to happen? We went to Hawaii.'"

In Hawaii the first person he runs into is the pimp who schooled him in the business. "I told him they have this case against me. They're charging me with pimping and pandering but I'm out on bail. He said, 'Pimping and pandering? Man, have they got the girls?' I said, 'Yeah.' He said, 'Don't go back. If you go back you're going to prison.'" So Zack was faced with a stark choice: become a fugitive or face the charges stacked up against him.

"My mom was sick in hospital. I wanted to see her. I didn't want to be on the run. At this point I started to think about giving it all up but too much had happened." His patron warned him, 'If you see these girls in the courtroom and they take the stand, that's it. If they ask the girls if you did it and they say yes, you're gonna get ten years.'"

Zack had just turned twenty-one. He was in shock. His meticulously manufactured image, his SuperFly lifestyle was falling apart. "Everybody was telling me, hey, you should run. Don't go to court. I'm thinking, you know, I want to go to jail because if I go to jail I'll come out on parole and I won't be able to go back to this life.'"

But at the preliminary hearing the girls put all the blame on Zack's girl. "They said, 'She did it. She taught us everything, what to charge, how to do it. Everything.' I was as guilty as could be but I thought I was gonna get away with this." The prosecutors didn't believe the preliminary testimony and bound Zachary's case over for trial. At trial, the girls flipped and testified against Zachary on all counts. He was convicted of two counts of pimping and two counts of pandering and sentenced to six years in prison.

Zachary was released on an appeal bond. "I stayed out for three more years, doing the same thing, pimping." One day in 1987 in Long Beach he sees a beautiful woman standing on a street corner. "Something seemed suspicious about her but I pulled up to her anyway and say, 'I seen you before.' She's looking at me. I say, 'Maybe I could meet up with you' and I give her the name of my hotel. She comes and meets me at the hotel. She's saying, 'Tell me more about...' and I felt that this could be a set-up but I said, 'Nah, what can they do? I'm just talking.' I thought I was untouchable." So against his own instincts Zack tried to turn the young woman. "I start to get nervous. I felt it. She goes into the bathroom. She's police and she's wired and she calls them in. She comes out of the bathroom. They come full force. They've got guns on me."

Hard Time

Zack was busted for the second time. With his previous conviction on appeal, his bail was revoked and he was sentenced to the full six years plus an additional two years for the Long Beach bust, eight years in all. He began serving time at the California Institution for Men at Chino in 1987, was transferred to Richard J. Donovan Correctional Institution in San Diego, and eventually to the California Rehabilitation Center (CRC) in Norco. Chino was for hardened criminals. CRC was set up, as its name suggests, to help offenders rehabilitate. Whichever way you cut it, Zack was doing hard time with some very scary criminals. "I'm thinking, 'Is this what my life is going to be like? I'm not going to make it through this.'

Education

"In order to get out on parole in four years I had to work. Every day worked was a day plus. But I didn't want to work, so I went to school instead. And being in school was just amazing. I made the Dean's list. I found out that I could be smart."

Zack also found out that his education could be useful on the inside. One inmate approached him to write a '602' administrative appeal citing misconduct by a prison officer. He did and the prisoner's appeal was granted. "He loved me for this. Another guy came by who was trying to write to his girl. He said, 'I been writin' but she ain't writin' me back. Could you help me put some words down?' So I flowered it up and she wrote back. And he loves me. The biggest man in the yard couldn't write. This guy had all this money on the streets but he couldn't write. They all came to me because they saw me going to school and they made me the rep for the African-Americans. So it became this thing where knowledge became valuable." Through education Zack had found his way of surviving the bleak, humiliating grind of prison life. "School is a place where they give you your dignity."

So he settled into full-time prison academics, racking up college credits, building up goodwill among his fellow inmates and generally behaving himself in hopes of getting out of there early. Even with parole he faced a grim four years. "Inwardly it was a sad place. Four years of Disneyland would have driven me crazy. Anywhere for four years is a long time."

One of his classmates in lockup was from Long Beach, the city of Zachary's downfall. His name was Larry. Zack told Larry about his fateful bust there and they formed a jailhouse bond. He and his friend would talk. "He was enamored with my pimp lifestyle. He said, 'When you get out, would you go back to that?' I said, 'Man, it's kind of hard to say. At first, I'd say yeah, but now I don't know.'"

Islam

It was during this period that Zack was tricked into his first exposure to Islam. "I watch this guy making the Muslim prayer (*salat*). What is he doing?" When the Muslim finished his prayers he approached Zack and invited him to come to the chapel to listen to Louis Farrakhan, the leader of the Nation of Islam. "Farrakhan was like a catchword. Everybody was in love with Farrakhan." Louis Farrakhan is the iconic leader of the Nation of Islam and, at that time, a virulent opponent of orthodox Islam, and had been implicated in the assassination of Malcolm X.

"I was not interested in Islam at all. I was interested in getting out of my cell. I just wanted some sort of entertainment, some sort of relief. So I went up to the chapel and there was no Farrakhan, there were no tapes. Nothing. I said, 'Where's Farrakhan?' He said, 'Just listen.' And the Muslim explained the orthodox religion of Islam to the young inmate in stark, simple terms. "He said that people give their lives over to all these material things and that all these things were like objects of worship. But they find out in the end that there's really only God. What he said struck a chord. It rang true and as he spoke I was saying to myself, 'Yeah he's right about that.' What he was saying was simple but it just made sense, so much so that I was afraid to go back.

"Then he said, 'I just wanted to let you know that Ramadan is coming up and you can fast if you want to.' I said, 'Fast? What are you talking about? Nah, nah, nah, I don't want to do that.' At that point my head was still in the streets." But this simple talk haunted Zack. He felt that what he heard was true. "I felt like, 'Okay now you heard something true, you can't pretend to be ignorant.' The Muslim group invited Zack to come to another meeting. When he turned up Larry was there. After the meeting Larry said, 'What do you think about Islam?' I said, 'I don't know.' He said, 'I don't know either but man can you imagine some of the people they become Muslim and they go back to the community. Can you imagine what sort of impact you'd have if you went back as a Muslim?' He made me think.

"Then, out of the blue Larry said, 'I'm thinking we should fast. Okay? You down?' Zack surprised himself and said, 'I'm down.' "The two of us started fasting together. The very next day we were in class. Larry was complaining of a headache. He laid his head down on the desk and didn't pick it up again. When class was over he went to the doctor. He came up that night to break the fast and he looked like he didn't even know where he was. I said, 'Dude are you all right?' The Muslims told him, 'Brother, you don't have to fast if you're sick.' He said, 'Allah will take care of me.' I said to myself, 'What is he talking about? How does he know about Allah taking care of him? I mean, we're not even Muslims.' We're just starting to fast."

The next day Larry died from spinal meningitis.

Zack was stunned.

"After Larry died, I started thinking about all the things we talked about. I knew that at least I had to finish fasting Ramadan." But Zack's relationship with Islam didn't end there. "I started to think about my life and the things that I'd done. I started thinking I should repent. One thing led to another and I started learning about the Qur'an, a little Arabic here and there. Once I became Muslim and I found out that there was a God that would forgive all of the stuff that I did. I prayed, 'If You get me outta this, just get me out of here in one piece, I will call people to Islam.' I promised to go back to the community and try to do everything I could to uplift my people because they need this. I kept asking. Of course, most people forget their supplications when they get out on parole. I couldn't."

Parole

Zachary did his time, started learning about Islam and stayed in school. He was paroled after four years and he kept his part of the bargain with God. "Islam flourished for me when I got out." Zack became active in the San Diego Muslim community. "I went with a group of brothers to Donovan to talk to people and tell them about Islam. I tell the brothers in prison, 'I know what you're going through because I was here.' The brothers said, 'No, you were not on this yard.' I say, 'I was in this yard.'

"I see what doing wrong did to me. Hearing the statistics on the recidivism rate, how many people go back to prison, really scared me. I could have been a career criminal. Once I got out I was so afraid. I remember first getting out and walking across the street and the stoplight blinking, 'Don't Walk, Don't Walk.' I said, 'I'm going back.' I don't want to disobey anything. Because if I go back what that means is that I could be a career criminal. They could get me back on anything."

Academics

Still trying to avoid work at all costs, Zack enrolled in San Diego City College. "I was only going there to get an AA degree but one of the counselors at SDCC says to me, 'you have 72 credits. Where did you get all these credits?' I said, 'In prison.' He said, 'Man you could transfer to a university.' I was like, 'No, I just want to get this AA so I can get a better job.' But he said, 'The classes are not much different than you have here and you could get more money from financial aid.' More money? He was right. I received ten thousand dollars a semester. I invested the money in buying cars. I got my business license and started a successful business selling used cars that helped me get through school.

"I received my Bachelor's Degree and thought I'd made it. In the process I discovered I wanted to teach. But I was told, 'They ain't going to let you anywhere near a school. Not with that felony.' That was a blow. I was this close to going back to my old life. But then my sister said, 'You should really go get a masters degree. There's this multi-cultural counseling program.' I said, 'They're not going to accept me into that program. I got this felony.' But she insisted that I give it a try. At the interview at San Diego State they asked me some of the things that happened to me that were unique. So I told them I'd been to prison. I told them about my history. They said, 'We want you in the program *because* of your background.' I earned my masters degree in education on multi-cultural counseling. I thought I was set."

Zachary took a series of administrative, counseling and lecturing positions at San Diego State. "I got a job teaching at San Diego State only because I was an alumnus. If I had applied through regular channels I would have been rejected because of my felony conviction." During this period a representative from the University of Southern California (USC) came to Zachary with an offer to apply for a PhD program in multicultural studies. He turned the offer down. He'd had enough school for the time being. But the rep pressed him and offered to extend the deadline for submission of an application. Zachary filled out the application in a way that he was sure would disqualify him, focusing on the unfair treatment of ex-convicts. And, again, he was accepted into USC's doctoral program precisely *because* of his response and background.

When he entered the program at first "I felt like I was out of my element. I didn't have anything to say to these people. I'm just listening, listening. And then it got to the point where I finally said, 'You know, a lot of what I'm hearing is just speculation, just talking about things that you've read or things that you've heard from people you interviewed. I lived some of this.' They wanted to know more about how I saw things." Zachary kept his doctoral studies close to home and excelled. He made the USC Rossier School of Education Dean's List and his doctoral thesis on 'Early Academic Experiences of Incarcerated Males' was nominated for dissertation of the year.

But then his past caught up with him again. He was offered a teaching position at USC. "I taught for one day and they came back and said, 'We've got your prints back and we understand that you have a felony.' I said, 'I told you I had a felony.'" Zachary was dismissed. He could take his doctorate there but he couldn't take on a teaching position.

"This is my biggest problem now. As I'm trying to establish myself professionally, and apply for positions they ask have I ever been convicted of a felony and I have to say yes. And they say, 'What was it?' When I relate my story the reaction is: 'You did what? How did you get a woman to do that? How did you get somebody to do that and then give the money to you?' It's hard to understand so it's hard to forgive. If you don't understand a crime how can you determine that somebody has been rehabilitated?"

Unable to find a teaching position in the U.S. because of his prison record, Zachary accepted a position as Assistant Professor teaching multicultural studies at a prestigious university in a Muslim country.

Remorse

"I have done things that were so foul. I realized that Allah could very easily have taken me in that state. He spared me. I think about some of the women who didn't straighten out. There are some that are still out there. I see them sometimes. I think, 'What can I do? How can I help someone that I misled?' After I became a Muslim I saw the first girl who went to school with me and I felt so bad. I should be giving everything I have to correct her life. I think about the things that I have done every day. Allah is the Most Merciful to let me survive. I know that I hurt people. I think that I should have done something good with the money that I made but I never came away with anything. When I came out of prison, the only way I knew to repent was to change. So I went to school and have tried to live a straight life."

Zachary is now happily married with three children. He is on a straight path, teaching, counseling and working with young people. "Now when people call on me to help I feel like it's my duty. I go to the streets and talk to people about the life I led, because I know that many young people still glamorize it.

"I have a second chance. I would not be Muslim, I would not be Muslim, I would not be Muslim had I not taken the path I took. I became a Muslim in prison. If I hadn't gone to prison I probably would have been a wannabe thug or maybe something else, but I wouldn't have become a Muslim. I think sometimes you need to sin because that's what's going to make you repent.

"For me, if I wasn't Muslim, I would not be anything. There's no other way. There are too many other ways that I could find loopholes. If I see a loophole or weakness I'm going to exploit it. Without Islam, to be honest, I might still be pimping. Half of the guys I knew back then who were pimping considered themselves to be Christians and wore diamond-studded crucifixes. They even said grace before they ate. But Islam doesn't have those loopholes. If you practice Islam, you can't hold hands with *Jahiliyya*. You gotta let go.

"True Islam is real. It transforms people. It is about knowledge. It says that you should learn. For me, this was a revelation, coming from a culture where the African-American joke is 'if you want to hide something from a black person, put it in a book.' We're fighting that kind of stereotype. For me Islam represents honor, dignity and respect, not based on race, ethnicity or color but based on piety. Allah gives everyone a chance. If He can forgive me for all the stuff that I did just by becoming a Muslim, why can't we learn to forgive one another?"

If you did not sin, God would destroy you and replace you by another people who would commit sins, ask for God's forgiveness and He would forgive them.[25]

THE PROPHET MUHAMMAD

---

25   Narrated by Abu Ayub al-Ansari and Abu Hurayra. Collected by Muslim (English trans., Vol. 4, pp.1436-7, nos. 6620-2).

Hospitality

IN THE DARK of night a cat burglar silently crept across the rooftops of Meknes until he came to a door ajar. He gingerly pried open the wooden door and carefully descended the uneven steps until he came to an opening. He entered a room. It was pitch black. He began to feel his way along the walls until he came upon a cabinet. He crouched down and began to silently sift through the contents of the cabinet to see if he could find anything precious. He fingered piece by piece, hoping for money or jewelry, anything of value he could steal.

"Please take anything you think of value." He froze.

"The only favor I would ask is that you allow me to keep my books and manuscripts. They are of no worldly value but I use them and they mean very much to me."

The voice was sweet, rich and serene. A light came on.

An elderly man was sitting on a bed, wide-awake, swathed in a *burnoose* against the cold, holding a set of prayer beads. "Please carry on. Take whatever you like."

Every night, all night Sidi Muhammad ibn Al-Habib kept vigil, repeating the Name of God, '*Allah*' twenty-four thousand times.

The thief, speechless, stopped his foraging, paralyzed with fear and shame.

In the darkness, the Shaykh had pressed a button beside his bed, which was a signal to bring tea. Suddenly one of his wives entered the room with a tea tray and poured tea for the thief. All the while the Shaykh spoke with great kindness to the intruder, welcoming him, insisting that he drink tea, invoking Allah's forgiveness and mercy.

The tea was replaced by a midnight meal, overseen by the Shaykh.

The thief burst into tears, weeping for a very long time.

In a few decisive moments he changed. He turned away from a life of crime and took the Path of God.

He who repents of sin is like one who has never sinned.[26]
THE PROPHET MUHAMMAD

"You must know that repentance (*tawba*) is the first station of pilgrims on the way to the truth, just as purification (*tahara*) is the first step of those who desire to serve God"[27]
'ALI 'UTHMAN AL-HUJWIRI

In my view, no one can become a Muslim just once. He becomes a Muslim, then he becomes an unbeliever, then again he becomes a Muslim, and each time something comes out of him. So it goes until he becomes perfect.[28]
SHEMS-I TABRIZI

26   *Musnad of Ahmad*, related in Al-Ghazzali on Repentance (*Kitab al-Tawba*) , translated by S.M. Stern.
27   *Kashf al-Mahjub*, translated by Reynold A. Nicholson
28   *The Maqalat*, translated by William C. Chittick

Part Two

TURNING POINTS

*Truly, God loves those who repent,
and He loves those who cleanse themselves.*[29]

The Big Picture

ISMAIL HAKKI ÇIMEN was born in 1959 in a small mountain village in in the province of Erzurum in Eastern Anatolia near the Iranian border. About one hundred families lived there the way people lived three or four hundred years ago. There was no electricity, no running water and no paved roads. They didn't need paved roads anyway because there were no cars. There may have been a school but Ismail can't remember because he never went to school. He never went to school because he was born blind.

Ismail's father died when he was five years old. He lost his mother when he was seven. His older brothers raised him. When he was seven they put him to work as a shepherd. A blind brother, even a blind brother who herds sheep, must surely have been a burden to Ismail's orphaned siblings. So when Ismail was nine his elder brother took him to Erzorum to an eye doctor in hopes that they could "open my eyes". They could not. Giving Ismail sight was, the doctor informed them, impossible.

In those days there were no hotels, inns, or restaurants in Erzurum. Visitors would stay in private homes. Ismail and his brother put up in the home of an old man who made coal-burning stoves. There were no gas heaters in those years.

"He took me to his workshop. I was just listening and watching him and he was telling me what he was doing." Ismail 'watched' the stove-maker intently. "He took more than one whole day, sometimes two days, to make a single stove. I was just listening and watching how he did things. I said, 'What are you doing? Why don't you be more practical? You are cutting one piece at a time. Why don't you cut five pieces all at once and you can save three or four hours that way.' He wasn't being efficient. He was surprised. He said, 'Nobody ever told me this until now. I've been doing this for forty years. Many people have visited me and nobody even thought about it. Not even the person I learned from.' And from the advice I gave him he was able to make two stoves in one day."

Before Ismail and his brother left Erzurum the stove-maker ordered his brother to make his ablution (*wudhu*), which the boy did. Then the old man brought out a Qur'an and ordered his brother to put his hand on the Holy Book, saying, "I want you to promise me something and before you make this promise I want you to swear on this Qur'an that if you do not fulfill your promise that God will punish you with Hellfire from which you will never be released." Ismail's brother protested, "But I don't know what I'm going to promise you." The stove-maker said, "Swear on the Qur'an first and then I will tell you." Fearfully, Ismail's brother put his hand on the Qur'an and swore. The stove maker then said, "When you go back to your village, find someone to teach your brother Qur'an so that he becomes *Hafiz*[30]. He has to learn Qur'an." Ismail's brother said, "Are you kidding? That's impossible. For any normal person it takes three or four or five years. It is impossible." The stove-maker said, "But you swore on the Qur'an and if you don't do this, you know what's going to happen to you. You will never come out of the hellfire."

The people of the village had simple faith. "They had strong religious belief but it wasn't an educated belief," Ismail remembers. "Whatever they heard from their parents that's what they believed." So Ismail's brother was terrified of not fulfilling his promise and going to hellfire for eternity, and when they returned to the village he went straight to the imam of the village mosque with the proposition. The imam said, "I don't know. I'm one hundred per cent sure he's not going to succeed but we can try."

They had arrived fifteen minutes before the noon prayer. The villagers were already entering the mosque. The imam began to go over the last ten chapters of the Qur'an. "He would recite each *sura* two or three times," remembers Ismail, "and I would follow him and within fifteen minutes I had memorized all ten *suras*." When the imam witnessed this, he said, 'I think this will happen.'

"So that's how I started. Normally when you are a child someone has to force you to do something. But no one was forcing me. I decided to memorize the Qur'an and within ten months I managed to do just that."

While he was memorizing the Qur'an, Ismail would listen to Qur'an recitations on a little battery-powered transistor radio. Broadcasts were

---

30   One who has memorized the entire Qur'an

from Istanbul and he realized that the recitations were completely different from what he was learning in the village. "The recitations from Istanbul were much more refined. They had nothing to do with the recitations I was learning in the village. I was told that Istanbul was the best place to learn Qur'an. So, after I had memorized the Qur'an, when I was ten years old, I decided that I was going to go to Istanbul and learn proper recitation so I could come back to the village and teach.

His brothers would not hear of it. "They said, 'it's impossible. Even we can't go and stay in Istanbul because it's a very different city. How can you do it?' I tried to run away twice and they caught me and brought me back to the village." So Ismail devised an elaborate escape plan. "I planned it so that they wouldn't discover I was gone until I was already half way to Istanbul.

"To begin with, from where we lived there was no direct way to get to Erzorum. There was a neighboring village about eight kilometers from our village. From that village a truck would leave three times a week and take passengers to Erzurum, which was about ninety kilometers away, or about fifty or sixty miles. That journey would take eight to nine hours by truck because there was nothing but a rough dirt track and the truck couldn't go more than about five to ten kilometers an hour. That was the only way to get to the town. If you missed the truck you had to wait for two more days for the next truck to get to the village.

"But even to get to the neighboring village was very dangerous because the area was infested with bears and wolves. Nobody would ever take this road alone. They would travel in groups of at least two or three people by day and they carried guns with them. I decided to make the trip alone in the middle of the night.

"I slept in a shed outside the house. I had a long pillow. I put that pillow on the bed as if it was me and I took the sheepskin we used as a prayer mat and bunched it up to be like my head. I covered the pillow and sheepskin with a blanket. There was an ox yoke in the shed so I dropped it behind the door as I left so that the door was blocked from inside. If they tried to open the door and found it blocked, they would look through the window and find me asleep in my bed.

"I left at two in the morning. I walked the eight kilometers until I came to the village but I couldn't enter. I had to wait until eight o'clock.

Of course in a small place everybody knows everybody and the first thing the driver asks me is, 'are you running away?' So I had to convince the driver that my sister was sick in Erzurum. I didn't have money to pay. I had to convince him that I would pay him when I came back. That's how I came to Erzurum.

"At the bus station in Erzurum they asked me if I had any money. At that time the ticket was about eighty or ninety Turkish Lira and I didn't have anything so they refused to give me a ticket. 'No money, no honey,' hah!"

Ismail went to the mayor's office and concocted a wild sob story. "I told the mayor that I lived in Istanbul already but came back because my mother had died. I had permission to come back for only four days to attend her funeral and return to school. I was on my way to the bus station and a thief came and took my money, and if I didn't get back to Istanbul I would lose my place in school." The mayor bought Ismail's fish story hook, line and sinker and gave the boy a free ticket to the capital.

The bus trip from Erzurum to Istanbul took twenty-seven hours. When the ten-year old arrived he had no particular place to go so he went straight to the Mosque of Sultan Ahmet, the Blue Mosque, and from there, with high hopes he set about finding someone who could teach him how to recite the Qur'an. He imagined that schools and teachers would welcome him with open arms, impressed with his achievement and full of compassion for his disability. He was to be sorely disappointed. "I applied to almost one hundred schools in Istanbul and was rejected by every single one of them. I was told, 'We are not able to handle even normal people. We have no place for a blind person. There is no room for you.'"

Ismail's hopes were dashed. Abandoned and embittered, he found himself alone in the city, an illiterate village boy of ten, sightless, penniless and homeless. He set about surviving. He discarded his aspirations to learn, he left his religion altogether and for the next four years lived on the streets of Istanbul. "I came with a dream. That was the reason I came to Istanbul to learn more and then go back to teach Qur'an in my village. But then nothing happened. I was shocked and angry. I didn't want any part of learning and religion.

"My life changed completely. I was selling cold water, chewing gum, balloons, whatever I could to survive." He lived among the people of the streets. "These were not people of the mosques and religious schools. They were runaways, orphans and other misfits. They all had different stories. They all had something that had happened to them. Some were using drugs. Most of them were older than I was - fifteen, sixteen seventeen years old." Life on the streets was transient. "It wasn't as if you have a permanent set of friends. On the streets you'd have a new set of friends every ten days or so."

Amazingly, Ismail never saw himself as unfortunate or deprived. "I was ten years old. No matter what the circumstances I never became sad or worried. I never said to myself, 'this is unbearable'. I was surviving. I was a free kid on the streets. I didn't have to go to school. I didn't have to go to the mosque. But I was learning. What was really good was that I was free. There was nobody to say, 'No, you can't sit here. You can't do this. This is what you should do. This is what you shouldn't do'. There was nobody to control me. I didn't have the notion that life was difficult or bad. There was no past and no future. It was the present moment. It was a very interesting experience."

Ismail's life on the streets of Istanbul was full. He would go with his friends to bars and restaurants where people drink and they would play musical instruments and sing. He was busy surviving and learning about life. He never gave a thought to returning to his village. "I didn't have another life to go back to. My life in Istanbul, even on the streets, was much better than it was in the village. In the village there was no future for me. I didn't feel I could survive in that place. My brothers were harsh. Life was harsh. In comparison with my life in the village, my life in Istanbul was much, much better."

He lived this way for four years. He was happy but he had this nagging sense that he needed to get his life together. "Something inside was telling me that this wasn't a good direction to take." When he was fourteen years old, he decided to make another stab at studying the Qur'an.

"I was told that there was this imam at the Blue Mosque, Gulen Mehmet Efendi. They told me that he was a kind man who helped many people all over Turkey and that he was a very important and influential person. Some of the street people had gone to Mehmet Efendi and they told me he gave them money. So one day I went to the Blue Mosque and after the afternoon prayer I managed to speak with him. I told him my story. I explained to him that I came to Istanbul to study Qur'an but it didn't work and that I wanted to go back and learn to recite the Qur'an. He asked me to recite some verses. Even after abandoning the Qur'an for four years it was still in my memory. When he heard my recitation he promised to find a place for me in a Qur'an school. He told me, 'Until I find a place for you in a school, you will be a guest in the Blue Mosque.' He gave me a small room to live in within the mosque.

"Through the summer, autumn and winter in 1974 I lived in the Blue Mosque. During the day I took walks among all the foreigners who would come to see the mosque. And at night, when the mosque was empty, I would retire to my room to sleep. The Blue Mosque was my home for eight months."

Toward the end of the year Mehmet Efendi found a place for Ismail to study beside the Fatih Mosque. He spent more than one year living in an apartment building with other students. "We shared a bath but everybody had their own rooms. We each received ten liras per week for living expenses, which was big money at the time. "

But it wasn't as if Ismail had found religion and embarked on a path of piety. It was a career move. "For me, it was like learning a profession." And as in any profession he was looking for career progression. He wanted a better situation. "Where I was I still had to cook for myself, do laundry and other things. There were Qur'an schools where you didn't have to do anything but study and teach the Qur'an."

An opportunity presented itself when Hafiz Ismail was invited to join a Qur'an school as an auditor, to listen to the students and correct their recitation. It was an unpaid position but he was given room and board and other benefits. It was a comparatively cushy job. The downside for Ismail was that the owner of the school was a strict *Salafi*. "I had to grow a beard and wear a hat, large *shalwar* trousers and a *jilbab*, a robe worn by imams. Nobody was allowed to listen to music on the radio. I had to turn off radios and tell students that music was *haram* (forbidden). For a free spirit like Hafiz Ismail this rigidity was almost unbearable. "I didn't believe any of it." But at 15 years old he was on a career path and he stayed around, all the while looking out for another opportunity.

"In all these years everything was good. I was sort of practicing religion. I would go through the motions, but it was external. It was like you go and practice certain things but you are not into it.

"Then one night I went out with some friends to a place to smoke the *nargileh* (water pipe). When we went to pay, the proprietor said, 'Your bill is taken care of.' We asked who paid. He said, 'The person that paid is not here but he'll come back tomorrow.' And I said, 'When he's there, let me know. I would like to thank him.'"

Ismail came back to the *nargileh* café the next night and tracked down the mysterious benefactor to thank him. This is how he met the sage who would become his teacher.

"From that time I would frequent the *nargileh* just to listen to the conversations this wise man had with his companions. I was hearing things I had never heard before."

Up until that time Ismail's understanding of Islam was of the hellfire and brimstone variety. It was self-righteous and reproachful. "Everything was forbidden (*haram*). If you do something wrong you will be doomed to burn in hellfire and if you do something right you are saved from hellfire." Suddenly he was learning in a completely different way. "This wise man would tell a funny story and everyone would be laughing and then he would say something that touched the heart. He spoke about what was inside us. He made me feel that if I made mistakes or did something wrong that there was always hope. These sessions weren't really about religion but they attracted me and I kept returning."

After a year or two working at the *Salafi* school an opportunity for a new job came his way. "There was a chance that I could become a *mu'adhdhin* (one who gives the *adhan* to call worshippers to prayer)." In Turkey, the job of *mu'adhdhin* was an official government position and there had been a longstanding law disqualifying blind people from holding official positions. In 1976 the law was changed but the minimum age requirement for official employees was eighteen years old. Ismail faced another hurdle. He had never been to regular school. He had no school certificates. He had to travel to the capital, Ankara, to convince government officials to waive the requirements and allow him to work in government. Ismail talked his way into a job as *mu'adhdhin* of the Bayezid Mosque. Underage and undereducated, he was now a government employee. "I had an official job. My salary was three thousand Turkish lira, which was very good money in those days."

What Ismail didn't know at the time was that the sage had also once been *mu'adhdhin* of the Bayezid Mosque and that he owned a bookshop in *Sahhaflar Çarşısı* (Old Book Market) adjacent to the mosque. Once he settled in to his new job, Ismail began to visit the bookshop, participate in the conversations and keep company with his teacher.

The wise man was one of Turkey's great metaphysicians, deeply versed in the sacred sciences and the doctrines of *Tasawwuf,* and yet he was down to earth, with a *joie de vivre* and rollicking sense of humor. "The way he taught was very effective, very interesting, constantly shifting from something profound to something that made you laugh, and yet you were always learning. Just being in his company had a great impact on me. He didn't teach me but I learned."

It was a casual relationship that, over eleven years, transformed Ismail's understanding of his faith and of life itself. He had come from a small mountain village where simple people practiced a basic, unsophisticated form of Islam. When he migrated to Istanbul his experience in the Qur'anic schools was unbending and sanctimonious, full of rules and regulations "you have to follow whether you like them or not or you are doomed."

For the first time in his life Ismail witnessed another form of faith, celebrating life, suffused with wisdom, tolerant of human frailty and full of hope. "It was completely different from what I had experienced before." For the first time in his life, he felt that practicing religion could be normal and that there was always the possibility of forgiveness and redemption. "Okay, if you made a mistake it's not good but that doesn't mean you should give up and that's it. And that was the turning point for me. He told me many things. He showed me whatever good comes to me that I should take it. He made me understand that I was not the one programming my life; that everything had already been programmed for me, that whatever happens in my life happens, and that whatever doesn't happen doesn't happen. 'Don't blame yourself' He told me. 'Nothing happens because of you.'"

Hafiz Ismail kept company with his teacher until his death in 1985 and yet he never became a dervish. He remained an outsider. With the passing of his teacher, he was at a crossroads. "My teacher's successor did not come to Bayezid Mosque and I felt if I wanted to continue I needed to become a dervish." It took Hafiz Ismail another decade to fully commit himself to that path. Making the pilgrimage in 1990 was an important step. "It was the first time I had ever traveled out of Turkey." He experienced the grace, serenity and good cheer in the company of dervishes, who observed the exquisite courtesies of *Tasawwuf*, remembered God in all conditions and performed the rituals of *Hajj* with sobriety and illumined hearts. He witnessed the stark contrast to the chaos and turmoil of so many thousands of Muslims bereft of guidance, panicking, pushing, shoving and shouting around him. He saw so many pilgrims overcome with anxiety and stress. "What I experienced was completely different. I was really enjoying the pilgrimage and I said to myself 'thank God I'm not trapped in that illusion. If I was not here in this company, I could be like these people'. This feeling stayed with me beyond the Pilgrimage."

All through this time, Ismail's world was opening up. "In the beginning, when I first arrived in Istanbul my only thought was to study Qur'an and return to my village." Then he ended up homeless on the streets of the city. The religion he had been exposed to all his life was closed-off and intolerant. Non-Muslims were infidels, doomed to hellfire. "I thought that if someone wasn't a believer then I should shun them." Living in Istanbul changed him. "I started learning languages. I was able to talk to foreigners. My attitude toward foreigners changed. I began to realize that each person has his or her own destiny. My attitude toward many things changed."

Over the years Ismail had picked up English and had begun to help foreign visitors to Istanbul overcome the language barrier and guide them through the city. "I was meeting many people in the Bayezid. A group of Brazilians paid a visit in 1991 and I accompanied them to Konya and *Şeb-i Arus*[31]. Three years later the same organizer brought another group of ten people and I acted as a translator for them. Our teacher was traveling to Kastamonu, a city in the Black Sea region, which was far from Istanbul, and he asked us to take the group there. My future

---

31   Literally, 'Wedding Day', an annual celebration of Jalalud'din Rumi's death held on December 17th in Konya. based on Rumi's declaration: "The day I die is my wedding day."

wife was part of the group and that's how we met. We went there and we ended up marrying and I ended up going to Brazil."

Over the arc of two decades Hafiz Ismail kept company with men of God. From the streets to the Beyazid to the sacred precincts of Makkah al-Mukarrama and al-Madinah al-Munawwara to the company of dervishes, his life transformed. "It took me time to realize why I was doing this because I never had anyone force me to do anything. I wasn't brought up with a family who told me what to do. Even after I came to Istanbul there was no one to tell me what to do. Nothing. I was on my own. When I was around thirty years old I realized why I did what I was doing, I was taking the Path because I loved it."

Throughout his life he never considered himself as disabled or disadvantaged. "On the contrary, sometimes I feel that I was advantaged. I feel that everything is not a matter of seeing; everything is a matter of understanding. There are many people who see things but they don't understand what they see. For me understanding is the most important thing. Sometimes there are things you don't see but you understand. There are things you understand but you don't see. For example, we understand we have a stomach, a liver and a kidney in our bodies. We don't see them but we understand they are there. We don't have to see them because we know they are there. I had no difficulties to understand things.

"I always liked living. I never went into a big depression. 'How could this have happened to me? Why?' It never happened. If you perceive that life is good then it is good. Your life is what you feel about it. Happiness doesn't really depend on material things. It is how you see it and how you accept it.

"I had come to a point where I had to make a decision and I decided that this was what I wanted. It was a big change." The alternative was the old perfunctory practice of Islam he had been raised on where "if you do this and don't do this you are going to hell. If I had stayed with that I would have been a very different person than I am now. I might have even left the mosque and religion altogether. That was a real possibility."

What Hafiz Ismail learned from his life and his teachers, above all, was that "everything is managed by Him. Nothing is managed by us. Everything is taken care of by Him. I see the Big Picture. Instead of saying, 'I've learned enough', I say, 'I have a lot to learn. I have a long way to go.'"

So, what has happened to 'we are satisfied with God's decree and destiny'? You must be satisfied. He created Shuaib blind, and he was satisfied. He did not see the faces of his dear ones though he did see their meaning. The outer aspect would have been sweet too. But it was not there, so he was satisfied. Satisfaction *is that* you be still and you not lose your intellect in the suffering...[32]

SHEMS-I-TABRIZ

---

[32]   *The Maqalat*, translated by William C. Chittick ('Me & Rumi')

A Love Story

LUCIANA BITTAR WAS born in Brazil. She hails from a heterogeneous immigrant lineage. Her maternal grandmother was Spanish. Her maternal grandfather was Italian. On her father's side grandma was Syrian and grandpa, Lebanese.

"My father is an atheist. He and my mother had this agreement that my mother was the one to take care of our religious, spiritual life. I was very close to my maternal grandmother. She left me a treasury of memories about how life was, how she felt. She believed in God and prayed to Jesus all the time. She would pray in front of this huge picture of Jesus with the beard and the blue eyes and bleeding heart but I don't think she was a Catholic. She would take me to the African circles where they would kill chickens and dance. She would go to spiritualists who believed in reincarnation. You were always a king or a queen in a past life. Even when I was small I used to wonder why nobody is ever poor or a beggar in a past life. Brazilians are a mixed culture and they accept everything but if you follow an established religion, you are considered to be stupid because you believe in dogma.

"I could never believe that Jesus is the Son of God but I would attend Mass. When I was a teenager I went to spiritual retreats. My younger sister was always making fun of me because she thought I was trying to play the good girl. I wasn't. I wanted to believe."

Luciana met her future husband at the age of seventeen. "He was a very handsome German and my mother very much approved of him." They were married when she was twenty. They had two children together. Luciana earned a law degree and began practicing as a corporate lawyer. Over the nine years her marriage lasted she and her husband gradually drifted apart. "I married too early. I was trying to find out who I was. I always had these interests. I wanted to travel. I wanted to work. I was reading. I gave my husband books to read. I wanted to discuss things with him but he wasn't interested.

"I had abandoned organized religion because I didn't think it was true. I believed that there was a Creator of all things but that man messed up religion." Luciana's disaffection from mainstream religion and her longing for a spiritual path led her to the teachings of the early 20th-century Greek-Armenian mystic George Ivanovich Gurdjieff.

Author Fritz Peters wrote that Gurdjieff 'dismissed all existing religions, philosophies and other systems of thought—as practiced—as being worthless.'[33] In the late 19th century and the first decade of the 20th Gurdjieff reputedly traveled throughout Central Asia, Turkey, Persia, India, Egypt and Tibet, visiting dervishes, rabbis, shamen, monks, magi, magicians and yogis. From all of these experiences he synthesized a mélange of mystical and occult traditions into a methodology he called 'The Work.' Gurdjieffian teachings were predicated on the notion that human beings are asleep and could be awakened by the disciplines he amalgamated from multiple sources. Gurdjieff claimed to have gained access 'to the so-called holy-of-holies of nearly all hermetic and mystic societies, congregations, parties, unions etc., which were inaccessible to the ordinary man, and of discussing and exchanging views with innumerable people who, in comparison with others, are real authorities.'[34] Beginning in Russia in 1912, he gradually attracted an international following of prominent intellectuals. His 'Work' consisted of a variety of physical exercises and psychological practices aimed at raising consciousness. He died in France in 1949 at the age of seventy-seven and left a controversial legacy that attracts adherents to this day.

Luciana's younger sister's boyfriend introduced her to a local Gurdjieff group he attended. She went with him and dragged her husband along to the meetings. "The Gurdjieff work made so much sense to me at the time. I became very serious about it and stayed in 'The Work' for ten years." She eventually joined a breakaway Gurdjieff group that offered studies in the Kabbala, Sufism (without Islam) and Shamanism.

"My marriage was not going anywhere. My husband didn't participate in my life. He would come in late. He didn't want to be with the children. He was only interested in his business." She finally asked for a divorce.

Luciana re-built her life as a single working mother and moonlighting

33   Attributed to G.I. Gurdjieff in 'Gurdjieff in the Light of Tradition' by Whitall N. Perry
34   Ibid

Gurdjieffian seeker. "I had two sides: the peace-and-love hippy and the corporate executive. I never fooled anyone. The executives considered me a hippy and the hippies thought I was an executive. I never fitted in.

Then she began having a series of dreams. In one dream,

"I was in the hallway of my house and there was a group of big men. They were big not only in size, they were important. They wore big hats. They were masters. They were walking in my hallway and they were all silver. Everything was silver. They approached chanting 'Love' but the word 'Love' was coming from another space. It wasn't a man's voice. All of them were chanting this word but not from their mouths. It was coming from them."

In another dream,

"I was lying down reciting La ilaha illa 'Llah and other invocations. In the dream I was asleep. Something woke me up. I couldn't move or get out of bed. Then this little creature came sliding up to me. I couldn't see his face. He wore a black robe with a pointy hat. He came over by my bedside and stopped. He said, 'I'm here to take care of you.'

"In 1994 I was invited to join my Gurdjieff group on a visit to Turkey. I was told that there was a master there. Our leader had already visited him in Istanbul and taken hand with him." The master was a saintly teacher of traditional Islam. Although the leader professed to be following the teacher's guidance, when he returned to Brazil he continued to make up his own pastiche of teachings and practices that had nothing to do with the spiritual traditions of Islam. He had been to America and met a group of the teacher's students in the U.S. The leader told Luciana to steer clear of them. "As a woman you will hate the whole thing because they make all the women cover their heads! It's ridiculous!"

But when she arrived in Turkey and had to cover her head on her first visit to the gathering, "I found it was such a beautiful thing, the scarf." It was a Monday night when music is played and the Mevlevi dervishes turn. "I was on another planet. The air coming from the skirt of the dervishes had something in it I can't explain. It hit me very deeply. And I am not the type to be affected by these things.

"I didn't prepare myself for this trip. I didn't read. I just came. I was open. I had a book on how to make the Muslim prayer and I had read a book by a Chishti master that described the Prophet, which touched me deeply. It was something so beautiful. The supreme beauty! The perfection.

"That night I dreamt that *I was a scroll of beautiful, rolling transparent illuminated calligraphy with flowers and vegetal patterns.*

"The next day we went to the Blue Mosque (*Sultanahmet Camii*). It was May 2nd, 1994. When I entered the mosque, my knees gave way. I couldn't stand. I started to cry. I was in crisis. I told everybody to leave me and go on. I didn't know what was happening to me. As I left the mosque I saw men making ablutions in the courtyard. I paid close attention to what they were doing. I had read about *wudhu* but I hadn't experienced it. I thought it was beautiful to wash in this way, so every couple of days I was washing myself in the manner I saw them washing. I didn't know when to do the ablution. I didn't understand anything about the timings of prayer, but I would attend the mosque and follow the ladies who were praying. We attended a Qur'anic recitation in the afternoon. It was so beautiful. I was taking it all in. We had one week in Istanbul and one week touring the country. The trip was prepared for our group. They were going to perform *dhikr* in Kastamonu. We traveled there by van and then to Konya and Pamukkale."

For the tour the teacher assigned Hafiz Ismail Hakki Çimen, the short blind *mu'adhdhin* of Beyazid Mosque to translate from Turkish to English. Luciana was the group's designated translator from English to Portuguese. So the glamorous well-heeled Brazilian lawyer and the humble Turkish *mu'adhdhin* were thrown together for the tour. "The food would come and nobody was taking care of Ismail so I took care of him. I gave him water, cut his meat. We started to talk. He was so open. He said to me, 'I think you're wasting your time with this group.' We were walking at one o'clock in the morning. It was quiet and Isma'il talked and talked. He was explaining life to me. He was so correct and always in a good mood. In his company I was discovering that I already was a Muslim.

"In Kastamonu we visited a mosque with cells on the upper level of the mosque for retreat (*khalwa*)." Luciana entered one of the cells to meditate. "I couldn't see the prayer below so I left the door open and followed the congregation. After this I came to the leader and said, 'I really want to take *shahada*.' The leader panicked. 'Oh, do you know what that means?' I said, 'Yes. I am at ease with this.' He said, 'In that case, when we return to Brazil you cannot participate in the women's group or any of our functions.'"

The journey to Turkey revealed to Luciana that the leader of her Gurdjieff group was a hypocrite. "He could lie to your face. It was very strange. He ordered the group not to drink alcohol on the journey. 'The people there [the dervishes] don't drink and if they find us drinking it will be a problem.' In Pamukkale we stayed near the ruin of an amphitheater. The leader announced they we were going to perform a shamanic ceremony there but we had to hide this from Ismail. I said, 'Ismail has been with us everywhere. Why can't we tell him?' The leader said, 'This is shamanic, it is out of the question that we tell him.' So we performed a shamanic ceremony calling for the Superior Intelligence to fix the world and suddenly there was a downpour. I was wearing a very expensive leather coat and didn't want it ruined in the rain so I excused myself. In truth, though, I just wanted to see Ismail.

"The rain had stopped by the time I arrived at the hotel. There was this mist. I was walking through a rose garden toward the rooms. I am walking through this mist. And I see him. He is wearing a suit because he thought we were going somewhere. He was proudly wearing that suit and he was happy. I call his name, '*Ismail.*' And he says, '*Oh, you are here!*' And I see him and I see love. I see whatever you can see. I don't know how to explain. It wasn't romantic. But what I saw said so much. The atmosphere was soft, like a marshmallow, a heavy mist. I didn't follow the footpath. I cut through roses to meet him. He was so luminous. He was illuminated—I saw him walking and it was indescribable. He stopped by a huge cabbage-like flower—his face and the white flower. He said, '*Oh! It's so good you are here!*' and I could see he really loved me. I could see love. 'This man, he loves me. He's in love with me.' And then this white butterfly landed on the white flower. In the night! After the rain! This man was in love with me. I could feel that. I didn't know what to do. There was a day when he was not together with us and I was trying to feel his smell. I wanted that smell. And then I went to bed and I woke up with the morning call to prayer, and I thought he was reciting for me. It was like the recitation of his love.

"I didn't want to remain single. I wanted to get married again, for me and for my sons. So I was always repeating, 'I met a man. This man is my president. This man loves me.' I was trying to attract that reality. In Konya I went to bed and fell asleep repeating this phrase and in a dream state someone was taking my words from my mouth.

They were repeating. 'I met a man. This man is my president. This man loves me.' Two men entered. They were so tall. Their heads were so long that they touched the ceiling but there was no ceiling. They were repeating, 'you have met your president, you have met your president'.

"I related the dream to Ismail. Ismail said that he had also had a dream. Then he said, 'I really love you.' Then I said something so stupid. I said, 'I don't love you as a man. I love you as a friend.' But he said something beautiful, 'What I meant is that I want to be your friend.'"

When she returned to Istanbul Luciana formally entered Islam and took the hand of the shaykh. Everything was happening so fast. She was overwhelmed by emotion and confused. She didn't want to make a mistake. She didn't see how a marriage to the blind *mu'adhdhin* would work. She told herself that it wasn't romantic. What would happen when she returned to Brazil? "I thought to myself, 'This is totally out of the question. We are from different worlds.'" So Luciana left. "At the airport I wrote that I was the canvas and he was the thread. I didn't know how it was going to be, the canvas without the thread. Somehow I knew it would be hard without him.

"I came back home. The first thing I did when I arrived was to call him. We talked every day. We were dating over the phone." The teacher told Ismail that they were already married in the Unseen. "I felt that this was true. I felt it from within myself. It was so clear. I had to marry Ismail. So I said, 'Okay you have to come here. You have to ask my father for my hand in marriage. You need to meet my children.'" A little more than a month later Ismail arrived in Brazil. "He came with his cheap little red bag on wheels from the bazaar. He was very happy. I was so excited. I sent my kids to my mother so we could spend the weekend together. It was wonderful. It was like a normal life. We were inseparable." Still Luciana harbored misgivings. "I said to myself, 'This man comes from Turkey. What if he doesn't like Japanese food?' This was my test. I took him to my favorite Sushi restaurant. I didn't say anything or prepare him in any way. I didn't say, 'Oh this is going to be raw fish.' I was sure that in Bayezid there was nothing like that. I just ordered Sushi, Sashimi, all these delicious things to eat. And he loved it! He passed my test!

"When my children came home after the weekend, they loved Ismail and started teaching him Portuguese. We couldn't live in Turkey because I had a career, money and everything in Brazil, so Ismail would have to retire. He met my dad and they discussed Palestine. Palestine was a huge thing for my father. He talked about Palestine all the time. Ismail knew even more about Palestine than my father did. Everything was easy." Ismail asked Luciana's father for her hand. Despite his misgivings "my father gave me the red flowers (signifying his acceptance of the marriage proposal). Ismail returned to Turkey and arranged to retire from his position as *mu'adhdhin* of Beyazit Camii. Six months later I came to Turkey to marry him. Our teacher married us in his home. I returned to Brazil. Ismail followed me in December and we had a civil wedding in Brazil on the 13th of December. After we were married, I learned that the 13th of December is the Day of Santa Lucia, the saint of the blind.

"In the beginning I didn't really appreciate much of what Ismail brought with him. I didn't appreciate half of what he was. He is a treasure. Only in hindsight have I seen."

Almost as an afterthought, as we walked away from their beautiful home in Uskudar, toward a taxi stand, Luciana shared a recent anecdote that illustrates her husband's singular quality and gives a deeper meaning to his saying: "There are many people who see things but they don't understand what they see. For me understanding is the most important thing. Sometimes there are things you don't see but you understand. There are many things you understand but you don't see them."

Luciana was undergoing color therapy treatments. The first step in the therapy process is for the 'patient' to choose three colored bottles to give the therapist a notion of what colors the subject responds to. Luciana brought Ismail to one of the sessions and for fun the therapist asked Ismail to choose three bottles from the wall of colored bottles in the clinic. Ismail approached the wall, reached over and picked out a bottle and put it down on the table. The bottle was lavender colored. The therapist asked Ismail to pick out a second bottle. He returned to the wall, reached for another bottle and carried it to the table. The second bottle was lavender colored. The therapist, with rising wonder, asked Ismail to pick a third bottle. He returned to the wall, reached for another bottle and put it on the table.

The bottle was lavender colored.

The Recalcitrant Shrink

TOWARD THE END of the 1970s I lived briefly in Tucson, Arizona with my wife and baby daughter, sharing a spacious Moorish ranch-style home on Speedway Avenue with an eminent Spanish neuropsychiatrist who had just converted to Islam. Dr. Mansur Escudero was a close protégé of the celebrated Spanish neuropsychiatrist Dr. Carlos Castilla del Pino, and was a pioneer in introducing gestalt and group dynamics therapies to Spain. As with many of us from the West, he had been attracted to Islam through a study of spirituality, which led him to the Sufi Path and Islam. He had come across a translation of a manuscript by the great Moroccan Sufi master Sidi 'Ali al-Jamal, the spiritual master of Moulay al-'Arabi al-Darqawi. After reading from the book, he had a dream. In the dream Moulay al-'Arabi al-Darqawi cut his head off! After decapitating the psychiatrist, he faced him and announced, "Your name is Mansur."

Before entering Islam he had studied Buddhism and was still reading books on the subject when we were sharing the house in Tucson. Notwithstanding his startling, and I would say auspicious, introduction to Sufism and although he had wholeheartedly dedicated himself to the practice of Islam to the extent that he left his medical career in Spain and relocated to the U.S. to live as part of a Muslim community, he was having a hard time accepting the *Sunna*. What I mean by this was that he considered all the outward rules and regulations (and restrictions) of the *Sunna*, the traditional practice of the Prophet Muhammad, peace and blessings be upon him, as related in the Hadith literature to be irrelevant.

The *Sunna* covered every aspect of life – eating, sleeping, dress, greeting, deportment, taking care of guests, praying, fasting, giving, and so on – in great detail. Steeped in Buddhist thought and psychiatry, he could see no reason for all the fuss about externalities. The Path, he reasoned, should be about inner knowledge. He scoffed at the need to establish an outward practice. I could understand this attitude in a non-Muslim but was baffled by someone obviously so committed to Islam yet who was just as obviously reluctant to accept any but the most basic aspects of its practice.

I spent hours talking to Mansur about the importance of the *Sunna* and the reasons for various practices, prohibitions and injunctions. I went on and on (I did go on in those days) to absolutely no effect. Mansur listened the same way that a psychiatrist would listen to a really disturbed patient, with a kind of silent, deadpan detachment. He made me feel as if I had an obsessive-compulsive disorder with a mad fixation on this thing called '*The Sunna*'. He betrayed a hint of amusement behind his poker face, as if what I was telling him was ludicrous. At the end of each of my futile sessions, he just shook his head and got on with things. We liked each other and the good doctor seemed to respect me but I was making no headway on the *Sunna* front. Then two things happened.

One day two African-American Muslims came all the way from Los Angeles to visit us in Tucson. I didn't know them but did know members of their community. They were interested in Sufism and had heard that we knew something about the Sufi Path. We welcomed them and invited them to stay with us. I was working at the time and was away all day on the first day of their visit. I came back and found Dr. Mansur in a state of bewildered wonder.

"Haroon," he said, slowly shaking his head, "you are not going to believe what happened today!"

"What happened?"

"He died."

"WHO died?"

"Our guest."

"*What are you talking about?*"

Mansur had been having coffee with our two visitors when one of them suddenly keeled over. Mansur took his pulse. Nothing. He was dead as a doornail. He immediately called an ambulance and rode to the hospital with the corpse.

"I swear to you, Haroon, he was clinically dead. He had no pulse, no heartbeat, no discernible brain activity, no vital signs." The paramedics transferred the body to a gurney and rolled the corpse into the emergency receiving, DOA.

Then the dead guest came back to life.

Had anyone else told me this tale I would have assumed that they were both confused and wildly melodramatic. But this was not some clueless claim from a hysterical bystander. This was a cold diagnosis of a medical doctor and distinguished neurologist.

We went into the room where our two guests were staying. Both were sitting together quietly. Our recently deceased visitor looked incredibly spaced out. We sat down in front of the two gentlemen. I asked the guest who hadn't died whether this had ever happened to his friend before and he said that it had once or twice. Seriously? I wasn't sure I believed him.

I then turned to our resurrected guest and asked him what happened.

He was in a daze. "I don't know. I don't remember anything."

So I asked him what he was doing when he blacked out.

"Nothing."

"Nothing? You must have been doing something."

"I wasn't doing anything, just *dhikru 'Llah.*"

"*Dhikru'Llah*? What *dhikru 'Llah* were you doing?"

"I was reciting '*Qul Huwa 'Llahu Ahad*' (*Sura Ikhlas*)."

Sura Ikhlas is the 112th Chapter of the Holy Qur'an. According to a tradition (*hadith*) of the Prophet Muhammad, peace and blessings be upon him, *Sura Ikhlas* is equivalent to one third of the entire Qur'an.

> Abu Darda reported God's Messenger as saying, "Is there anyone of you incapable of reciting a third of the Qur'an in a night?" On being asked how they could recite a third of the Qur'an he replied, "*Qul Huwa 'Llahu Ahad* (Say, He is God, One) [*Sura Ikhlas*], is equivalent to a third of the Qur'an."[35]

"Okay. How many times did you recite it?"

"Oh, I was reciting it all day, everyday."

"All day, everyday? How many days did you do that?"

"Oh, I guess for about three weeks."

---

35   Muslim transmitted it, and Bukhari transmitted from Abu Sa'id.

"THREE WEEKS? STOP! *Sura Ikhlas* represents one third of the Qur'an. It is an incredibly heavy invocation. Who told you to recite it like this?"

"No one."

"*Well don't do that ever again.* You nearly killed yourself."

Mansur watched the exchange with his usual alert detachment but it was clear that the episode made an impression on him.

A day or two later, after our guests had departed back to Los Angeles, I mentioned the incident and said, "Our understanding of that situation comes directly from the *hadith* literature, which forms the *Sunna*. Without the *Sunna*, we have no way of understanding our spiritual limits and, out of ignorance we can find ourselves in danger. The *Sunna* exists to protect us."

It seemed to be the first time that my talk about the *Sunna* made any sense to the recalcitrant shrink.

While in Tucson I'd run into an old acquaintance who had been a high-ranking member of a hippy-like 'Sufi' group (which bore no relation at all to authentic Sufi orders) in California, composed mostly of 'flower children' who had been followers of a strange, eccentric New Age guru named Samuel L. Lewis. Lewis claimed to be a Zen Roshi, Hindu Guru and Sufi Master all rolled up into one and created what he called 'Dances of Universal Peace', inspired by the dances of the early 20th century choreographer Ruth St. Denis. He claimed to be a shaykh of the Chishtiyya Sufi Order and became known as 'Sufi Sam.' His dances involved folk dancing movements accompanied by the recitation of invocations from many religions that became erroneously known as 'Sufi Dancing.' Sufi Sam's great contribution was purportedly that he managed to get a lot of young hippies off drugs and into a 'spiritual' life.

My old acquaintance was the only member of this group that ever demonstrated any serious interest in Islam and, when we met up, he started practicing orthodox Islam. We became good friends and in his enthusiasm for his new orthodox faith, he talked me into making a trip to San Francisco to spread the word among his fellow 'Sufis' about the real Sufism, which was the complete practice of Islam. So five of us, including Dr. Mansur, an African-American Muslim who followed a Libyan Sufi shaykh, my young friend Yasin Schleicher and I piled into

Yasin's VW bus to head for the coast.

In San Francisco we made the rounds of my friend's fellow-'Sufis.' Every single one of these generally nice people seemed to be, in middle-age, shipwrecked and rudderless, yet, to my friend's great disappointment, curiously unreceptive to Islam. It was almost as if they had all been inoculated against the Real Thing. All the while Dr. Mansur watched and listened, processing every exchange.

Our journey culminated in a visit to one of Sufi Sam's 'Sheikhs' or spiritual masters. The 'Sheikh' was having what they called '*Darshan*,' a Hindi word for what the Turks would call '*Sohbet*' and the Arabs would call '*Ders*' or discourse. We parked our VW bus near his house in a quiet neighborhood somewhere in the Bay Area. The 'Sheikh' was sitting cross-legged with his disciples facing him. We introduced ourselves and joined the disciples. The 'Sheikh,' it turns out, had just dropped a tab of Lysergic Acid (LSD), kind of nullifying the claim that Sufi Sam got his disciples off drugs.

So here we were, six stone-cold sober orthodox Muslims trying to have a conversation about Islam with a 'Sufi Sheikh' who was starting to hallucinate on acid. The longer we faced him, the more freaked-out he got. He started eating voraciously, everything that was put in front of him, cookies, cakes, fruit, chips. It was very disturbing. He became visibly agitated. His hand movements became erratic. His face was flushed. He began to sweat. His wife, poor lady, was standing by helplessly while her husband descended (or maybe ascended?) into some hypertrophic plane that rendered him all but incoherent. It got so bad that I started to feel sorry for the fellow. I have no idea what his disciples were making of this spectacle but clearly we were giving this hallucinating pseudo-Sufi a bad trip. I finally, said to him (perversely, I have to admit), "I'm sorry but you seem agitated. Are we making you uneasy?" He said, like a man being swallowed up by an unseen beast, *"Man, I'm tripping!"* We sat for a while longer as our host increasingly zoned out, and then made our excuses. Once we hit the street on the way back to the van, Mansur stopped, turned to me and said, *"Haroon, that did more for me than twenty of your talks!"* And with that, the good doctor accepted the importance of the *Sunna*.

Dr. Mansur Abdel Salam Escudero returned to Spain and became a pillar of the Spanish Muslim community, working tirelessly as President of the Islamic Council of Spain, to secure government acceptance and recognition of Muslim rights, establishing mosques, cultural centers and clinics, and calling many of his countrymen and women to Islam. He set up 'Verde Islam', the most influential Muslim website in Spain, and was instrumental in convincing Spain's educational authorities to recognize Muslim education in a staunchly Catholic country.

Mansur Escudero died in 2010 at the age of 62 while in the act of remembrance during the last third of the night. His final moment in life was a sign of the greatness of a man who his friend Sidi Emin Alzueta described as "The Light of Islam in Spain". May God cover him with Mercy and be well pleased with him.

Sincerity in Action

MALIK IBN DINAR was born in the 8th century, the son of a Persian slave from Kabul. He was, himself, free from bondage and made his way in the world. As so often happens with one born into poverty and deprivation, Malik was intensely ambitious and obsessed with acquiring status and worldly possessions. He was a handsome, clever young man and achieved great success and wealth in the world. He settled in Damascus and frequented the city's Great Mosque, which had been richly endowed by the Umayyad Caliph.

Malik decided that he wanted the prestige of being appointed the superintendent of the Great Mosque. To this end, for an entire year he made a great show of his piety, attending every prayer and taking a place in a prominent corner of the mosque to perform supererogatory acts of worship for all to see. In this way he calculated that the congregation would elect him as the most deserving of this position

He knew what he was doing was wrong. "*What a hypocrite I am!*" he would reprimand himself. But he couldn't stop. He craved the recognition.

In the evenings he would leave the mosque and indulge in worldly pleasures. He played the lute and would entertain his cronies late into the night. One night, as he was playing his lute, his audience had all dozed off. In the silence the lute spoke to him: "*Malik, what is wrong with you that you do not turn away from your sins?*" Malik dropped the lute in shock and ran to the mosque, bewildered and afraid. He said to himself: "For one year I have worshipped God to show off my piety. Isn't it better for me to worship God for His sake?"

Malik was filled with shame. He had coveted an appointment to take charge of the Great Mosque and made a display of piety to achieve his ambition. He now decided that if asked, he would refuse. He made sincere *tawba*. That night he spent alone in the Great Mosque, and prayed to God with a sincere heart.

The next day, the congregation assembled. One of the members pointed out that there were cracks in the mosque. "A superintendent should be appointed to oversee the care for the mosque." The congregation unanimously agreed that the best person for this position was Malik. He was, after all, a man of wealth and accomplishment and, most importantly, he was obviously pious.

Malik was in his corner, at prayer. Representatives from the congregation approached him and waited while he finished his cycle of prayer. They then asked him to accept the position of superintendent.

Malik cried out, "Oh God, I worshipped You hypocritically for an entire year to achieve this position and no one paid any attention to me. Now that I have given my heart to You and have firmly resolved not to accept this appointment, You have sent twenty men to me to give me this responsibility. *Subhanaka*, I don't want it!"

Malik ran from the mosque and dedicated the rest of his life to the purification of his heart, abstinence from the world, worship and remembrance of God. He became a disciple of al-Hasan al-Basri and achieved great stations of knowledge of God. May God be well pleased with him.[36]

Malik ibn Dinar was reported to have said, "The deed that I love best is sincerity in action." al-Hujwiri explained Malik's statement this way:

> Sincerity bears the same relation to an action as the spirit to the body; as the body without the spirit is a lifeless thing, so an action without sincerity is utterly insubstantial... Although a man should keep his heart sincere for a thousand years, it is not sincerity until his sincerity is combined with action; and although he should perform external actions for a thousand years, his actions do not become acts of devotions until they are combined with sincerity.[37]

36   Retold from *Tadhkirat al-Awliya* (Memorial of the Saints), by Attar, translated by A.J. Arberry

37   *Kashf al-Mahjoub* translated by A.J. Arberry

The Only Real Brahmin

KRISHNA JOSHI WAS born in England. His family was Hindu Brahmin but they weren't particularly religious. "Most Hindus in general, their religion is very strong as an identity but not necessarily strong in terms of the tradition and the way it's passed down. I didn't have any core belief structures as a child. We ate Big Macs and celebrated *Diwali* and the saga of the *Ramayana*. It was a kind of secular religiosity. My grandfather was a diplomat at the Indian Embassy in London. As he aged he assumed the role of a *Pandit* and performed rituals for death and other ceremonies in the community. He would tell me stories from the *Ramayana* and other mythologies but I never was taught the symbolism of those stories. I didn't have a strong identity of belief."

Krishna lived the life of a fairly typical upper middle class British Indian schoolboy with the occasional reminder of his heritage, until a total immersion into his inherited faith rocked his world.

Loss
Krishna's father had moved back to India when he was five years old and the boy lived with his aunt and uncle from the time he was very young. His uncle became a surrogate father to Krishna and he was the son his uncle never had. They had a very close relationship, even after his uncle emigrated to Australia. Krishna then moved to live with another aunt and uncle within his extended family. When he was fifteen years old his uncle in Australia committed suicide after his wife left him for another man. The shock of the tragedy was compounded by an alien sacred duty.

In the Hindu tradition, the eldest son must perform funeral rights for the father, but Krishna's uncle had no sons. So at age fifteen he was sent from Britain to Benares to perform the *Antyesti*, the Hindu funeral ceremony. Suddenly the young secular British Indian schoolboy found himself at the epicenter of Hindu faith, sitting cross-legged beside the Ganges, watching corpse after corpse incinerated on the *Ghat*. "For three days I had to perform all these rights and throw oil into a fire and recite Sanskrit *lokas* and verses for my uncle. As I was performing those rites the stark reality of the temporality of life became very apparent. I see bodies reduced to ashes. I see my own uncle incinerated. I put his ashes into the Ganges. I was faced with death."

The Search

When he returned to England after this sad and sobering experience he was changed. "The images I saw at Benares were very moving. We hide death in the Western world. Confronting death is a kind of growing up. To know that it is a certainty and that it is close. At the same time, I was living away from my parents. I felt quite lonely, not being with my family. I came back with a desire to know what life is about and what the Afterlife is. I longed for meaning."

At first Krishna looked to his own tradition. He joined the Hare Krishna Movement (ISKCON). "I would go to the temple in Watford and I would recite *mantras*. I read the *Gitas* and the big thing that would come up was Karma and the idea of rebirth. And so I had this kind of understanding that, yes, there is a human trajectory. There is a cycle. We are meant to get somewhere. There was an idea of the actualization of God within that. And that gave me a kind of framework to try and understand the world."

Krishna never formally joined the Krishna Movement. "It was spiritual but it didn't answer my question as to what life was about. It did give me a spiritual identity for the first time in my life. But as I was exploring my spiritual identity I became interested in the religious expression of other people. I was interested in general in the idea of the Afterlife. My philosophy at the time was there were different religions and everyone goes to God in the end. It was a kind of Beatles 'All You Need is Love' philosophy. I started looking at other religions. I explored Christianity, Judaism and Buddhism and, with the exception of Judeo-Christian ideas, they all claimed to be separate from the others, mutually exclusive, of different parts.

Islam

"At about this time, two of my school friends started practicing Islam and my class teacher actually took *shahada* and converted. That triggered an interest in Islam and I'd often debate them about women's rights and violence, claiming that Hindu non-violence was superior. They would respond to my arguments and give me things to read. I would win the debates in my mind but ultimately lose the argument because when I reflected, what struck me was that Islam didn't appear to me as just another religion out of other religions. Islam didn't fit my preconceptions of what religion was supposed to be.

"In my thinking Islam should have been a fourteen-hundred-year-old Arabic religion, coming from Arabia for Arabs. Instead, it challenged my idea that religions were fundamentally different and separate and presented a new framework: that all religions are the same, from One God and that there is actually one path revealed throughout time through all the Messengers sent by God and that path for all intents and purposes is and has always been Islam. The essence of the message of this one path is the Oneness of God and seeing that Oneness of God in everything. And Messengers have been sent to every nation. Mary is in the Qur'an. Moses is in the Qur'an.

"I kept reading and I reached the point where I actually started believing. I realized the fact that this message that came to the Prophet Muhammad just made sense. It was an intuitive realization. I reached the point where I had to ask myself, 'what does this entail?' This was not what I had planned to happen. I spent six months wrestling with this realization and the seeming impossibility of someone like me from a Hindu Brahmin background actually converting to Islam. This confusion remained until I spoke to a West Indian friend of mine who had converted to Islam. I had recognized the impact of his *tawba*, the change in his character, which made a strong impression on me. He said, 'you have to make a decision because you don't know how long you're going to be in this world. You don't really know if you're going to be alive tomorrow. You've been convinced and your heart is telling you this is true. It is time you affirm what you know and try your best to live by it and let God take care of the rest.'"

So at age 16 Krishna Joshi took what for him was a giant leap of faith.

"I was revising for my GCSE exams and I remember walking back and forth when, suddenly I turned, I spun around. At that moment I made the intention that I had to formally become a Muslim. At that moment in time I literally had that physical sensation of turning and I felt this expansion and I said, 'That's it.' Even before I formally declared it, at that moment, I felt, 'That's it!'

The moment I made that choice that this was what I was going to do, the whole veil of all the 'what ifs?' just left me. And I remember taking the *shahada* the next day with my friends. And in my first prayer, the *sajda*, the prostration, was like coming home. It was so familiar. I said to myself, 'I've done this before.'"

And then...

"My family freaked out."

Family Ties

"They freaked out to the point that they thought that there was a girl involved, or that I was on drugs. My parents were already living in India so they didn't find out until a month after I'd become a Muslim."

When his parents did find out they decided that the only way to save their son was to bring him to India.

He was thrown into turmoil. On the one hand, he was a faithful son, but on the other hand he was brand new in Islam. By that time Krishna, who had taken the Muslim name of Abdullah, had become part of a supportive Muslim community, particularly one family. He went to his surrogate Muslim family for advice.

"What they said was, 'You've just become Muslim and as a new Muslim you need company. You need to be grounded in your Islam more.' They suggested that I come and stay with them."

Curiously, one of his uncles gave him another very alarming reason to stay put in England. "He said, 'If you've converted to Islam and you go back to India, we stone people who do that.'"

Flight

But Krishna's parents prevailed and booked a flight for him to join them in Hindu India. The night of his flight he decided to escape. "I tried to climb out from the upstairs window but that didn't work. So I walked out through the front door when everybody was sleeping. They had this burglar alarm. I disarmed it and slipped out with a rucksack with some of my clothes and headed for my friend's house.

"I was literally running away from home. My heart was pounding. I was about 6'1" even in those days, dressed all in black and running. A police van passed me. They saw me running and pulled up beside me. It was obvious that something was happening. So they said, 'Who are you and where are you going?' I could have ended up in custody but Allah inspired me to blurt out, 'There's a party and I don't want to be late!' They laughed and replied, 'Ah, you don't want to be late for the booze!' and they let me go."

But when he arrived at his friend's house he was overcome with doubts. "What had I just done? What's going to happen next? I had always been part of a very loving family. What will this do to them?"

To calm him his friend played a recording of the legendary Qur'an reciter (*Qari*) 'Abdul Baset 'Abdul Samad. "A stillness descended."

This was the lull before the storm.

The Storm

The next morning Krishna's uncle discovered his nephew was missing and the family mobilized. "My parents came from India and my aunt and uncle came from America. My mother was very, very upset. She thought that I was rejecting them. 'We're your parents. Why would you choose someone else over us?'"

But Krishna held his ground. He stayed with his Muslim friend for several weeks against increasingly intense pressure from his family, who were on the verge of involving the police. Krishna's school found out that he had run away from home. "It became a huge thing in the school. They said, 'Okay you can leave home but you have to stay with a Muslim family we trust.'" What that really meant was that they trusted a Muslim family that was not religious. During this interim period with the Muslim family, Krishna/Abdullah had the chance to meet with Yusuf Islam, who counseled him to make supplications to God for help, but in the end his family prevailed. They pulled him out of school and shipped him off to California to live with an aunt and uncle and gain some work experience.

From India, his family did everything they could to lure him to the mother country. "My sister was still in India and my family convinced me that I should just come over for a visit." But when he landed his family confiscated his passport and kept him in India, doing everything they could to cut off him off from all contact with Muslims.

Hindustani Hoosegow

"I was in what was for me a foreign land. My education had come to a halt. This was before the Internet so I had no access to anyone except through the post. There was a constant emotional bombardment. I was only sixteen. It was suffocating. It was so intense. My father was very upset. It reached the point where he physically started beating me. He couldn't contain himself. He was cursing Islam, cursing Allah. It was very traumatic. As a young convert I'd read all these stories about the Companions of the Prophet resisting their parents. I was idealistic and I said if that's what it takes… but, looking back, I think I was emotionally immature. At one point I went to the British Embassy. I told the consular officers, 'Look, you have to help me get out of here,' but they said, 'The most we can do is to provide you travel documents if you don't have a passport but you need to raise the money yourself to travel.' I was stuck and I was lapsing." Just as things were reaching a crisis point, Krishna found a measure of relief.

Social life for India's upper middle class revolves around the club, a legacy of the British Raj. All the major metropolitan cities have clubs where members play squash, golf and tennis, swim, watch movies, meet, eat and drink. Krishna would go to the club to play squash. Under so much family pressure he'd given up praying. One day while at the club on impulse he went out and found a nearby mosque. He joined the prayer and, in prostration, "it all came back to me." Then something extraordinary happened. After the prayer he caught the attention of a member of the congregation. It turned out that this man had also converted to Islam from Hindusim. Even better, he worked at the club. He threw the struggling teenage convert a lifeline to Islam. He said, "India is not like England. If you were to broadcast your conversion here, there could be riots." He encouraged Krishna/Abdullah to keep coming to the club for company and promised to put him in touch with someone who could be his friend. "Your parents won't realize it, but this will be your support." That new friend Krishna was introduced to was a bodybuilder by the name of Firoz.

For one year Krishna/Abdullah would go to the club on the pretext that he was playing squash, but in fact, to meet Firoz. They would go walking on the track or jogging. "Our conversations, talking about Allah, sustained me for a year." At the same time, his family continued putting on pressure, watching his every move and doing everything possible to discourage him from practicing Islam. "It came to the point where Firoz said, 'Look, you need to get some space here. You need to tell your family you've left Islam if they ask you. You're never going to get space otherwise. What you do is eat vegetarian food so you don't have to eat *haram* food. If you're ever pulled into a gathering where there are idols, don't worship them, don't bow down. Know in your heart that these are not God and keep up your prayers in secret.' Emotionally and psychologically, if I look back, I think I needed that because I was close to breakdown."

Krishna told his parents that he had decided to leave Islam and set about hiding his practice. "I tried to find secret places to pray, which inevitably tended to be bathrooms. These were the only places I could keep praying without worrying that someone was going to come in. That was where most of my *Salat* was done for several months. I had to go to the sacred thread ceremony where my cousins and brothers were inducted into being Brahmins. I had to carry out Hindu rituals and visit Hindu shrines and all the while I'm secretly a Muslim.

"This went on for a period of months until I finally won the trust of my wider family and my grandfather. They were cognizant of the fact that my education had come to a standstill so they allowed me to resume my studies. Because they assumed I would eventually return to England, my father allowed me to go to Calcutta to an international school that was conducting A-Levels. We lived in a place called Jamshedpur, which was in Bihar, now in the state of Jharkhand.

"Calcutta was about three hours by train. I was nearly 17. One year of my life had been lost in this confrontation. And as they started to trust me they allowed me to move to Calcutta to study. They arranged for me to stay in Kalighat, which is an intensely Hindu neighborhood in South Kolkata, site of the famous Kalighat temple. There was a lot of slaughtering in that place, blood everywhere, and a lot of poverty.

"In Kalighat I was put amongst a group of five Hindus and had to continue to hide my Islam. Eventually I moved out and managed to find a place for myself in Central Calcutta and was able to start exploring my Muslim identity. I would pray in local mosques and had spiritual support from members of the *Tablighi Jamaat*[38]. There would be people coming from across the world and they'd speak to me and I was getting support from Muslims on their missionary work. This lasted for about a year until my parents trusted me enough to send me back to England.

Once he was back in England and had resumed his education he told his family that he had lied to them. "I told them 'I was always a Muslim. I never really left Islam.'" And to Krisha's surprise they told him they knew. "They said that they were hoping that would gradually die and then they realized that it would never die and then through time, *Alhamdulillah*, I now have a very good relationship with my parents and they're very supportive and understanding of that."

Taking the Path

So Krishna became, once and for all, Abdullah and began his journey as a Muslim, which eventually led him to the path of *Tassawwuf*. He submitted to the guidance of a teaching shaykh who told him, "This path is all about *Tawba*. The deeper *Tawba* is discovering who you really are and who Allah really is."

"And so as I took the path I came to a point where I entered a spiritual retreat (*khalwa*) under the guidance of my shaykh." After three days he experienced a profound insight. "I understood that Allah is with me and that He is closer than my jugular vein, that He is closer than my own sense of being. I understood that my sense of 'I am' is a delusion because it is through Him that I am. I understood the meaning of a couplet from one of the *qasa'id*:

> 'I am the Lover and I am the Beloved.
> Love for Me from Me is a wondrous thing!'
> ('ana huwa l'Mahbub ana l'Habib.
> al hubbu li minni shay'un 'ajeeb!)"[39]

---

[38]   *Tablighi Jamaat* is a global movement first established in India in 1927 to encourage Muslims to return to the basic principles and practices of Islam.

[39]   Abu al-Hasan al-Shushtari from his poem 'Love had annihilated me" adapted by Sidi Abdul Rahman Shaghouri

In the aftermath of Abdullah's *khalwa* he had to return to the life of duality and the constant struggle to realize that "He is with you wherever you are" (*wa Huwa ma'akum ayna ma kuntum*).

"I feel there's a long path to this realization, a journey of deepening tawba, knowing that the battle with the ego goes on. What is so beautiful is that when that realization dawns, then one leaves the Islam of identity and discovers the Islam of Reality. Yes, we converted. Yes Allah has helped us there but it has been a stepping-stone to realizing what we're asked to accept is what already is the pattern of existence. Everything has already submitted to God.

"I aspire to the asking forgiveness (*istighfar*) of the Knowers of God (*'arifin*). The *'Arif* says:

> *I confess to You Your blessing upon me, the blessing of existence*
> *and I confess to You my sin, the sin of thinking that I exist through myself.*[40]

"The negation of idolatry all has to come back to the negation of the ego, because that's the big idol. So *alhamdulillah*, that is the path that I am on."

Abdullah Joshi relocated to a Muslim country to study Islamic jurisprudence and the sciences of *Tassawuf*. And, as a young Muslim scholar he has also studied the scriptures of his Hindu heritage: the Vedanta, the Upanishads and the Yoga Sutras of Pathanjali. "When I read the Upanishads I was blown away. It all finally made sense. I told my parents, 'it took me becoming a Muslim to understand what the Vedas were about.' A Brahmin is someone who is devoted to Brahma, which is Absolute Reality. So I tell my parents, 'I'm the only real Brahmin in the family.' I had to become a Muslim to understand that."

---

40   Commentary on *Sayyid al-Istighfar*

> Like all music, the figured bass should have no other end and
> aim than the glory of God and the recreation of the soul; where
> this is not kept in mind there is no true music, but only an
> infernal clamor and ranting.
>
> JOHANN SEBASTIAN BACH

Bass Line

DANNY THOMPSON WAS a war baby. Born in in Teignmouth in South Devon in the spring of 1939. On September 3rd Britain and France declared war on Germany and Danny's father, who came from a Northumbrian family of miners, volunteered for the Royal Navy Submarine Service, which offered more pay than the infantry. He died in combat early in the war.

"My mother was devastated. There was no welfare in those days. She was a war widow with an infant and she was very lonely." Eventually his mother remarried a sergeant in the army and, toward the end of the war had a baby daghter who died suddenly from convulsions when Danny was five. After this her marriage fell apart and she moved with Danny to London to find work. They settled in a small flat on Wandsworth Common.

Britain had been devastated by the war. Bombed out, exhausted, bankrupt, millions of homes destroyed, unemployment soaring, austerity, acute shortages and rationing of everything, life in England was grim. "Growing up my father was always a hero to me because he had been killed in the war but, really, when I think about it now, my mother was a hero with what she had to face alone with no support in those terrible days."

Danny went to Catholic schools where there was a fervent belief in corporal punishment and where caning students was common practice. He also had a hard time understanding and accepting Catholic theology. When he reached his teens Danny was admitted to a prestigious college in Battersea but by this time he was becoming thoroughly disillusioned with Catholicism and with religion altogether. "I was an angry boy. At college things got really difficult and I started to have a go at the priests for whacking me." England was still very much a class society and Danny was a clever working class boy in a posh grammar school. "The music teacher would say, 'Today we're going to study Mozart. Forget this Thompson, this is above you.' They told me that Mozart was beyond me because his music was 'sophisticated.'"

Ironically, while he was being precluded from music in school, Danny was entering the world of music through the backdoor when he joined a Jug Band, or in 1950s British parlance, a 'skiffle' group. Skiffle was an early twentieth-century African-American makeshift musical form that used instruments like washboards, jugs, musical saws, kazoos, cigar box fiddles and wash-tub and tea-chest basses. Although Jug Bands had pretty much disappeared in America by the 1940s, the music had a big revival in post-war Britain in the form of skiffle.

"I tried mandolin and guitar but they hurt my fingers. I tried playing trumpet but you have to push a valve to get a note. With the double bass all you have to do is find the note and I found that happy." So Danny made a tea-chest bass out of a box, a piece of wire and a broom handle. "It went *'Doing, Doing, Doing.'"*

For Danny it was love at first sound. "I'd go to college and we'd sit around talking about what we were going to do when we grew up. You had blokes saying, 'I want to be a doctor.' 'I'm going to be a policeman.' 'I'm going to be a printer.' 'I'm going to be an artist.' 'I'm going to be a train driver.' I said, 'I'm going to be a bass player.' They go, 'Wha?' I was in love. I was going to be a bass player. That was it. I was 13 years old.

"Music gave me something to devote myself to. It became a religion for me. It allowed me to become."

So at the age of 13 Danny started gigging with a skiffle group. "We were doing pubs and I figured out a way to take this box apart. I dismantled it into five square pieces and I got little brackets so I would get to a pub and put it together with these brackets and get my broom handle and rolled up wire so I could get on a bus with the five bits and broom handle."

As he was forming a lifelong relationship with the string bass, Danny's relationship with Catholicism and college steadily deteriorated. After a confrontation with an abusive teacher he was called into the headmaster's office. The headmaster told him, 'We're obviously no good to you and you're obviously no good to us, so we're going to let you go early.' He left school that day and never came back. He was fifteen years old.

Danny wanted to study at Guildhall School of Music. "But you had to have five O levels and I didn't even have a spirit level. All I had was music."

Victoria

"My granddad's got one of them silly big violin things," said a girl in a youth club. And he wanted to sell it. Danny overheard her and instantly got granddad's address and tracked him down. "He was sitting there smoking a pipe by a coal fire and the double bass was in the corner of the room. I'd been playing with a box and broom handle for over a year and suddenly here's the real thing. What are the chances? I said, 'Mister, how much do you want for it?' He said, 'Five pounds.' I said, 'Can I give you five shillings a week?' He said, 'Okay.'

"So that was it. That afternoon I come back with a borrowed car and we loaded the bass on the top, wrapped in a curtain." They took it to a gig at a pub on Wandsworth Bridge Road. It was raining and Danny's new bass got drenched. "We go into the pub and I unwrapped the bass and started wiping the rain off her and all the black coal soot and grime wiped away and this beautiful varnish came through."

The next day Danny took his new instrument to Foote's Music Store on Brewer Street in Soho. It turned out that he had acquired a Gand, a French swell-back bass violin made by the celebrated luthier Charles Nicolas Eugene Gand circa 1860. They offered him £130 on the spot, a considerable sum back in 1954. Rather than cashing in on his windfall or gleefully carrying it off, Danny took the upright bass back to the old man and told him what he'd been offered for it. The old man said, 'That's all right old son. If you want it and you're going to play it, pay me a fiver.' Danny named her 'Victoria' and she has been his True Love for over sixty years. "She is beautiful."

So this fifteen year-old working class school dropout starts gigging with his fine double bass. "Because I owned a bass, I was in demand. I heard about this rehearsal band that played Glenn Miller stuff. I used to go down there a couple of times a week and play, which was teaching me how to read music. One day I'm walking back up St. John's Hill to my little place and a big American car, a Studebaker, pulls up and the driver says, 'You're obviously a bass player.' I said, 'Yeah.' So he said, 'I do American air bases and I'm looking for a bass player. I'll come and audition you.'" The next day Danny did a crude audition and was hired on the spot. He was taken to an American airbase. "We go into the PX and they say, 'Would you like something to eat with the band?' There are hamburgers! There's milk! *Milk!* Sweets! This stuff was on ration in England. I couldn't believe it. Then we did the gig and they were dancing. I thought, 'This is it! Fantastic! This is the life.'"

At that time Danny was working as a trainee window dresser at Barkers in Kensington and showed promise. "At only 16 years of age I had two of my windows on the cover of Display magazine." He walked in to the head of display and told him he was packing it in. "He said, 'You're making a terrible mistake. Don't you realize that one day you could be sitting here?' I thought, 'In twenty years time I could be sitting in his chair,' and that did it!" Danny quit the working world once and for all and set out, with Victoria, as an itinerant bass player.

"I did three or four gigs a week with this band. Then the same year I was offered a job in a Soho strip club, The Spider's Web, on Meard Street. I'd play for strippers until one o'clock in the morning. When the dirty-mac brigade would file out at closing, the club would be invaded by all these great jazz musicians, like Tubby Hayes, who would jam until seven or eight in the morning. So after hours I'd be amongst legends. Tubby Hayes was probably the greatest jazz musician we've ever had. I remember him saying to me, "Here, son, some of the notes you play hurt my eyes! But,' he said, 'you can always learn and you've got great time and great rhythm. You're going to make it.'"

After two years in the strip club Danny got a job with an 18-piece band that played at dance ballrooms around the UK until the young bassist was drafted into national service and sent to Malaya. He spent two years in Penang, playing for Radio Malaya and the Voice of America, and, against orders from the brass, fraternizing with the locals. When he was de-mobbed from the army in 1963 Danny returned to London and the first job he was offered was to play bass guitar for Roy Orbison. "I said, 'I don't play bass guitar.' They said, 'You don't have to really, it's easy.' I said, 'I haven't even got one.' They said, 'We'll get you one. You'll be brilliant.'" They offered Danny forty pounds sterling a week to play bass guitar and he took it.

The Big O

Roy Orbison, 'the Big O', who Elvis Presley once called "the greatest singer in the world", was a huge superstar in the 1960s. He headlined the tour, which included Gerry and the Pacemakers and, as the opening act, a fast-rising band called The Beatles. "Everybody used to do about 20 minutes of their hits and there used to be thousands of girls (because of the Beatles), screaming. The Beatles did the first half followed by Gerry and the Pacemakers. Roy Orbison would finish.

"He was a lovely man. Roy refused to ride in a limousine and insisted on riding on the bus with the boys. We headed to Scotland and I said to the bus driver, 'When we get to the border, pull over in a layby.' So we pull in at a layby and I say, 'Roy, you ever been to Scotland before?' He said, 'No.' I said, 'If you haven't then you've got to kiss the stone of Kelly Macradah.' And this bus full of rock stars are all looking at each other wondering what I'm up to. One of my mates pulled me aside and whispered, *'What are you doing?'* And I whispered back, *'There's got to be a stone in that field en't it?'* So I led Roy Orbison out of the bus. We climbed over a wooden fence and we're walking across this meadow and sure enough there's this great big rock covered in lichen and I get Roy Orbison down on his knees, kissing this stone and repeating after me: 'I promise to uphold the traditions of Scotland' and on like that. We go back and everybody's saying to me 'How could you do that to this icon?'

"We did a six-week tour with Orbison and the Beatles and on the last night of the tour the custom was for everyone to play jokes on everybody else. But someone from the management says, 'No one messes with 'The Big O.' So I said, 'If we don't do something, he's going to think that we think he can't take a joke, that he's not part of the gang. We've got to do something.' He used to walk on stage and people would give him the guitar and he would start singing. So I tuned the guitar up a semitone. Roy Orbison walks on to a sell-out crowd of three thousand screaming teenagers, gets his guitar and he goes, *dum, da, da, da, dum* and he used to finish on a high falsetto note. Half way through the song, he realized that he was never, ever going to make it. Of course, he thought it was fantastic and at the end of the tour he gave me a gold key. I gave my son 'The Big O's' key when he was 18."

Musicianship

After the tour Danny was invited to join Alexis Korner's Blues Incorporated, an immensely influential blues group that attracted some of the greatest musicians of the era. Danny did three years with Blues Incorporated and played with other jazz groups around London. He had become a seriously accomplished musician.

"There is a saying, 'If you want to be a great musician then make it a religion'. As you would a religion, practice every day. Devote your entire life to it. During that period music was my religion. So that's what I did. I wrote 'PRACTICE' above the wall of my flat. So I couldn't get out of my room without seeing 'PRACTICE'. I didn't have any prejudices about music. I'd play anything because it was all a good learning experience."

In 1967 Danny was playing at Ronnie Scott's, the legendary Soho jazz club, with some of the greatest jazz musicians in the world when he was invited by popular folk artists John Renbourn and Bert Jansch to form a new group with traditional singer Jaqui McShee. Danny introduced the group to jazz drummer Terry Cox and the seminal folk-jazz band The Pentangle was launched. For its time, The Pentangle was radically innovative.

"We didn't intend to be innovative. It just happened. I brought a jazz thing into John's folk thing. They were playing traditional music. But I was putting basslines they had never heard of. Terry and I brought improvisation. So it became innovative but it wasn't like we got together and said, 'We're going to make an innovative group'. It was just the love of doing what we were doing."

The band was an instant success. Their first public appearance was a sold-out concert at London's Royal Festival Hall and their first two albums were bestsellers. They toured the UK, Europe and the US, playing Carnegie Hall. They were making money. They were celebrities. And the grind began to take its toll. "It was do an album, do a tour to promote the album, do another album, do a tour to promote the other album and in the end it became 'Let's do this song, let's do that song'. It became a recipe. I remember being in New Orleans and Terry Cox turned to me and said, 'You gotta admit it is boring but it's great money'. And I realized that was the reason I was having such a hard time playing."

Going to Extremes

So in 1972 Danny walked away from The Pentangle and partnered with British singer/songwriter John Martyn, who was described by The London Times as "an electrifying guitarist and singer whose music blurred the boundaries between folk, jazz, rock and blues."

John Martyn and Danny shared "the same freedom and the same honesty. I wanted to be free and have a good time." Danny fell in with one of the most gifted and galvanic musicians in Britain and the duo worked together throughout the 1970s and on and off until Martyn's death in 2009, in a rich creative collaboration. During the 1970s the two musicians took the freedom and good times to extremes that, by the end of the decade, proved mutually self-destructive. Both men were hell raisers and heavy drinkers. "Alcohol, the worst drug; readily available, socially acceptable. We'd do a gig and then go out and get drunk or be drunk to do a gig. People would say, 'How could you play so amazingly that drunk?' I'd say, 'because I practice that drunk.'" Eventually drunkenness was no longer fun. "Alcohol became like a medicine. I drank in order to be able to function. I was a professional drinker." Danny had become a full-blown alcoholic.

By 1977 he hit bottom. The collaboration with Martyn foundered and the founder of The Pentangle, the master musician, was homeless and what they call a 'high bottom drunk', utterly wasted but able to function...barely.

"I'd split up with my wife. I'd left home. I was working in a warehouse, dumping rubbish just to pay for drink. I thought, 'If I lose this job and can't play anymore, I'll have to go to the Salvation Army hostel. I could go there. I could get a bed.' I had reached the point where I could accept that possibility. I tried to rationalize with myself that I was different from other losers. Of course, I wasn't like anyone else on the skids. I'd wake up in the morning and drink a half a bottle of vodka just to function. People would say, 'You look great,' without realizing that it was taking me half a bottle of vodka to look great.

The Road Ahead

"When the fun went out of it, I could see the road ahead." From that low point Danny began to turn his life around. He stopped drinking and went back to work. He met Sylvie, his second wife and true love (along with Victoria). Sylvie had two young sons that Danny helped raise. Still highly respected and greatly in demand, Danny continued gigging and recording with some of the greatest musical artists of the time. And he started asking questions. "I bought books on Taoism, on Buddhism, on everything except Islam." In 1982 Danny and his family moved into a lovely house in a leafy genteel neighborhood outside of London. Life was good. And then it got better.

The Good Neighbor
In 1985 a new family moved in across the street from the Thompsons. The father was Rehmat Khan, an internationally acclaimed squash player who was also the cousin and coach of world number one squash champion Jahanghir Khan, then in the process of taking ten British Open titles in a winning streak of 555 consecutive matches. As a housewarming gift Danny presented the new neighbors with a sack of potatoes. "Rehmat said, 'We expected maybe getting a box of chocolates or some flowers, but a sack of potatoes?' I said, 'With three kids, the potatoes are worth more than a box of chocolates or flowers." From there a friendship began.

"We'd talk about religion and I'd talk about Catholicism. I always believed in God, even as a kid. I questioned the priests but just because there were bad priests it didn't mean there wasn't a God. He starts giving me books and videos on Islam. And then he gave me a video of Ahmed Deedat. 'Whoah!' I woke up."

The Firebrand
Ahmed Deedat was a South African preacher who, as a boy growing up in Durban witnessed heavily-funded missionaries aggressively trying to convert Muslims to Christianity. Shaykh Ahmed, who was a friend of mine, told me himself that the evangelicals would print millions of flyers with verses of the Qur'an on them and scatter them everywhere. Muslims would find these flyers lying on the ground and on tables and would rush to rescue the verses of the their Holy Book underfoot only to find messages against Islam, defaming the Prophet Muhammad and 'proofs' that Islam was a lie. He was so deeply affected by these devious

scams to undermine his faith that he started studying the Bible to be able to refute evangelical arguments against Islam. He turned his knowledge of the verses of the Holy Bible into an effective arsenal and went on the theological warpath for the rest of his life, challenging Christians to debates throughout Southern Africa and eventually around the world.

Shaykh Ahmed Deedat emerged at a time when the oil boom triggered a resurgence of Islam, after centuries of decline. Muslims were coming out of a low point of self-esteem. He was a blunt instrument and his bold offensive against the white western Christian establishment became hugely popular across the Muslim world.

Given his unhappy experience with Catholicism, it isn't surprising that Shaykh Ahmed's message struck a chord. Danny was bowled over by Deedat's fiery, combative rhetoric. "This bloke is telling the Truth and he's not frightened to tell it like it is. The Pope and a stadium and all these Christian theologians and we'll get it on!'"

No More Mucking About

During this period he was working with Richard Thompson (no relation), the founder of the seminal folk-rock group The Fairport Convention and virtuoso guitarist and songwriter. Richard had quietly become a Muslim and affiliated with a Sufi order during the early 1970s. Over the years Danny played many tours with Richard Thompson's band but never once did they discuss Islam. "Richard was a Muslim but he doesn't wave a flag about it. We never talked about Islam because I'm sensitive to what other people feel and Richard is very private, very humble. I thought, 'Well I don't want to start bending his ear about Islam.'" All this time, for year after year, Danny's preoccupation with Islam gradually became stronger. He kept thinking. He kept reading. He had been alienated from organized religion from his early experiences with Catholicism. It was like the grain of sand in an oyster, creating the pearl of certainty.

"So one day in 1990 we're in a recording studio, doing a film on Richard. And I suddenly said, 'You know, I can't muck about any more. I've got to become a Muslim, because there's no question.' And Richard looked up, stunned. He wept. He came over to me and hugged me. And he said, 'Repeat after me: *Ash-hadu an la ilaha illa 'Llah, wa ash-hadu anna Muhammadan Rasulullah.'* And I did. And he said 'Now you're a Muslim.' There was no big pretentious celebration. I liked that. That was enough. And we went back to work. And since that time we've never spoken about Islam again. We've prayed together. I've been on Ramadan tours with him. For Richard his faith is a very private matter.

"So I told Rehmat that I finally became a Muslim and he said, "We'll have to find you a Muslim name.' We went through so many names until he told me that the Prophet, peace and blessings be upon him, had an uncle who was a womanizing, hard drinking, fighter before Islam and I said, 'That's me! Hamza it is.'

"I was obsessed. When I started out as a Muslim I was doing the obligatory and all the supererogatory prayers even though they told me I didn't have to. Even at a gig, I'd come off stage and go behind the curtain and pray."

Champion

He never forgot his first mentor. "I was working with Cat Stevens (Yusuf Islam) and we were touring South Africa. He said, 'I'm going up to Durban to see some friends and hopefully visit Ahmed Deedat.' This was in the '90s." By this time Shaykh Ahmed had suffered from a devastating stroke that had left him paralyzed and unable to speak. He was incapacitated in this way for the last ten years of his life until his death at the age of eighty-seven in 2005. But in a powerful act of will he continued to communicate through an alphabetic grid that allowed him to spell out words one letter at a time by means of eye movements.

"We went to his house in a suburb of Durban and met his lovely wife who must have been in her eighties. I entered his bedroom. He's lying in his bed. I'm from South London! Battersea! I had grown up with all this emotional baggage. And the man who opened the door for me was in front of me! There's Ahmed Deedat! His son introduced us. I said, 'My Champion! You are my Champion!' He smiled. His wife came and offered us some food. We left his bedroom and food was laid out and I kept saying to myself, 'That's Ahmed Deedat in there! That's Ahmed Deedat.' So I went back in and he was lying there, totally paralyzed, unable to move anything. So I held his big toe and I said, 'Because of you, I'm a Muslim!' He smiled. A tear rolled down his cheek.

"He was my champion."

Certainty

In between gigs Danny/Hamza has performed the Hajj and visited the Mosque of the Prophet. In 2005 he made a pilgrimage to Jerusalem and was the central figure in the acclaimed BBC documentary, 'The Furthest Mosque.' Throughout, this working class musical giant from Battersea has confounded outsiders who have questioned his faith.

"One bloke kept going on about eating bacon. 'Why don't you eat pork?' I said, 'I don't eat bacon.' And he kept on at me, 'Why don't you eat pig?' I said, 'Listen, stop! If you come to my house and I say to you, you can live in my home for as long as you wish, a month, two months, but please don't go into that room. That's the one room I don't want you to enter. You would respect my request, right? If God says to me, 'This is what I give you – family, love, home – but please do Us a favor, don't eat My pigs, that's a good enough reason for me, without going into the theological and medical arguments against eating pork. Allah says, Don't eat My pigs! There's a good boy. That's it. End of story.'

"So he goes on, 'But what if it's all a load of rubbish?' And I said, 'Okay, let's suppose it is a load of rubbish. Right now, I live my life and life is good. I don't steal. I don't commit adultery. I don't hurt people. I try to be good. I make mistakes but generally I try to be a good example. And hopefully when I die I will have left a good example for my family and that's good enough. But if I die and there is Paradise too? BINGO!! So I can't lose. I have a great life. I have my faith. That'll do me. It's common sense and that's what has taken me to Islam.'"

In the late 1990s Hamza's history of hard living and a pre-existing heart condition caught up with him and he suffered a series of catastrophic medical crises that nearly ended his life. He was forced to submit to open-heart surgery.

"I was ready to go. I felt very good within myself. They marked my chest where an incision was going to be made. They were going to saw me in half. They painted me with all this antiseptic. I'm lying there, preparing for this operation that I might not survive. I'm repeating *ash-hadu an la ilaha illa 'Lllah wa ash-hadu anna Muhammadan Rasulullah*. So these hospital attendants come over to me and say, 'Hey brother, why are you speaking in Arabic?' I said, 'I don't want my last words on earth to be *twelve-eleven-ten-nine-eight-seven...*' I said, 'Whatever happens, I'm ready.'"

Almost miraculously Hamza/Danny Thompson recovered and has for decades continued to improvise acutely beautiful, breathtakingly lyrical, richly melodic, sublimely rhythmic bass lines that, instinctively, intrinsically, aim for the glory of God and the recreation of the soul.

When he does finally reach the end of his bass line, *insha'Allah...*
BINGO!

Best Wish

ABU MAHFUZ MA'RUF ibn Firuz al-Karkhi was born of Christian parents in Baghdad during the last part of the 8th century. At the Christian school he attended as a child his teacher instructed him to affirm the Trinity. "Say God is the third of three." Young Ma'ruf refused. "No. He is God, the One." The teacher gave the boy a beating so severe that Ma'ruf ran away from the school and his home. His distraught parents searched for their young son with no success. "If only he would come home we will agree to whatever faith he wants to follow."

Islam was the religion Ma'ruf had chosen and he ran away to an imam to make his declaration of faith. Then he came home to his family. His parents were overjoyed at his return.

"What faith have you adopted?"

"I have accepted the religion of Muhammad, the Messenger of God."

Upon hearing this news his loving parents both accepted Islam.

Ma'ruf studied his religion with the great scholars of Baghdad and disciplined his soul with rigorous practice until he attained a high station and became one of the greatest spiritual guides of his time.

One day he was walking beside the Tigris River with his students when their path was cut by a group of rude, carousing youths on their way to a wine party on the water. Their behavior was outrageous, offensive and profane. Ma'ruf's followers were enraged.

"Master," they implored their guide, "please pray to God Almighty to drown them all, that the world will be rid of their foul presence."

Ma'ruf complied, asking his companions to raise their hands in supplication. They did. Then he prayed, "O God, as You have given them a happy life in this world, even so grant them a happy life in the Next World."

His disciples were stunned. "Master, what is the secret of this prayer?"

"He with Whom I am speaking knows the secret," Ma'ruf replied. "Wait for a moment and, God willing, the secret will be revealed."

Suddenly, the young reprobates noticed the figure of the saint on shore. They were shaken to the core. One by one, every single young man on the barge broke his musical instrument and poured away his wine into the Tigris. They disembarked and rushed to the shaykh. They were trembling and fell down before Ma'ruf al-Karkhi and turned to God, away from their dissolute lives.

His students looked on in amazement. "You see," said Ma'ruf. "Your wish has been realized without drowning or suffering."[41]

41   Retold from the *Tadhkirat al-Awilya* (Memorial of the Saints) of Faridud'din Attar, translated by A.J. Arberry

Leaving Normal

SUSIE GOLDMAN WAS born in Philadelphia into a conventional working class Jewish family. Her father was "a communist-leaning intellectual" who worked for the US Post Office. If pressed he would have said he was an atheist. Her mother "was a little softer", teaching her bedtime prayers without a whole lot of conviction. It was what normal people did in America back in the 1940s and '50s.

The thing is, Susie wasn't really that normal.

Perhaps it was the bump on the head.

"When I was two years old I fell from the second story window. It was summertime and the window was open on the second floor of the house and I crawled out of the window and fell. My father, who loved to read, was supposed to be babysitting me but he was reading and didn't notice. A clothesline below broke my fall but I hit my head and was in a coma for three days. Everyone thought it was a miracle that I survived.

"We lived in a row house in a working class neighborhood in Philadelphia and our next-door neighbors were Italian Catholics. They had eight children – four boys and four girls. My father had a little used-book business on the side. He and my mother would go on book buying trips into the Poconos and upstate New York. They'd be gone for a couple of days and, when I was six, let the Catholic family next door take care of me. So they put me in the room with the girls. They had mattresses all over the floor and it was really fun. They were these lovely girls. They wore pretty nightgowns and things; they were so pretty, like little angels. Every night before they went to sleep they would pray. They would hold their hands in the prayer position. We got all tucked up into the bed and I asked them, 'Why do you pray to Jesus?' They whispered and told me all about Jesus. The day after my parents returned I said, 'Mommy, I have to tell you something.' She could see that it was something very important to me and she said, 'What is it darling?'

"'I love Jesus.'

"'WHAT!'

"My mother called up our neighbor and said, 'Are you trying to convert my daughter to Catholicism?' And the neighbor got hysterical. And I was never allowed to sleep over there again. But years later I realized that it was too late. They had converted me. Because they put this thing in me: 'Why don't we love Jesus? What's not to love?'

"When I was around nine years old I was going to have a birthday party. On my birthday I was allowed to do anything I wanted to do so I decided I wanted my birthday party to be outdoors, in the back yard. I woke up that morning and the plan had been all set for my special outdoor party. *It was raining.* My mom said, 'We're going to have to have the party in the living room.'

"I went up to my room and I knelt down by my bed and held my hands in the prayer position like the little Catholic girls from next door and I prayed with all my heart. My bed was located right next to the window and it was pouring rain outside and I said to God, 'Please stop the rain and *please, please* let me have my birthday party out in the garden!'

"And, hand to God, the rain stopped right then and a shaft of sunlight poured into the room all over me. And that was it. I knew that God had heard my prayer. And I became a true believer.

"I tried to be a good observant Jewish girl. My parents weren't observant Jews. They ate ham and Canadian bacon. My father would say, 'I'd love to be a religious Jew if only I could have a ham sandwich or a BLT every day.' Up until I was 12 years old I was asking my parents about God and all those questions kids have. 'Why are we here?' 'What should we be doing?' And their reaction was 'Oh, not with the questions again!' And they would say, '*Oy vey! She's religious!* Where did we go wrong?'"

In desperation Susie's mother made an appointment with a rabbi at the local synagogue. "I was 12 years old but still very tiny. I hadn't really developed very much. I was still wearing braids, little girl dresses with puffy sleeves and a little sash. We arrived at the rabbi's office at the appointed time. I was sitting down in front of his big desk and out comes the rabbi and he sits down, looks at my mother and says, 'What seems to be the problem?' And she says, 'What are we going to do? She's going through this stage and she's…religious!'

"The rabbi never looked at me or asked me anything. He looked at my mother, put his fingers together and said, 'Mrs. Goldman this is a normal stage of life. She'll get over it. She'll be fine. Don't worry about it. It's not a big deal.' Then I remember him looking at his watch and saying, 'Please excuse me but I do have a lunch appointment.' Then he looked at me and said, 'Susie you're fine. You're going to be okay. Don't worry about this.'

"As we were leaving my mother said, 'You know, honey, we're going to buy you a bra. Because I notice that you could use a bra. And this is to commemorate your realization that this is silly for you to think that way.' So we go and get one of these triple-A little teeny, tiny things. As we left that appointment I was thinking 'Okay, I guess if the rabbi says it isn't true then I shouldn't worry about it. I guess I'll give it up.' And I did. From that point on I became what was considered in the 1950s to be normal. *'Thank God, now she's normal!'*

"I became one of these very straight teenage high school girls, you know, where your boyfriend calls you up on Monday and asks you for a date and he comes to the house on Saturday and the parents talk to the boyfriend and you're upstairs primping and you come down in your crinolines." Susie took normality to its logical conclusion. "I attended the Museum College of Art (now re-named the University of the Arts), graduated with a bachelor's degree in fine arts and married my college boyfriend right after graduation. That was supposed to be my life. He went to Harvard Law School and we were going to have a nice house in the suburbs and two children and I would paint my watercolors and he would take care of the taxes and everything." It was the heart and soul of normal. Except that "it didn't work out that way." The marriage fell apart fast. Susie moved to Washington DC and took a job as the first white teacher in a junior high school with a black student body. She became politically active and then, well, she started leaving normal.

Berkeley
"This was in 1964. The civil rights movement was happening and I was passionately involved. Then I read about what was going on in Berkeley and I was like 'Oh yeah! That's for me!'

What was going on in Berkeley was the Free Speech Movement (FSM), an outgrowth of the civil rights movement, and a generation-defining confrontation between student activists and the administration and Board of Regents at the University of California at Berkeley. That confrontation culminated in the student occupation of Sproul Hall in late 1964 and resulted in a victory for the students. The protest made national headlines and Berkeley became the hub of radical politics and a symbol of social protest.

The non-political side of the social protest movement was finding its form at the same time in the San Francisco Bay Area in what would soon become the hippy movement, which reached its full flowering in 1967 with the Human Be-In in San Francisco's Golden Gate Park. Hippies took the Beat legacy of rejecting the norms of the 1950s and launched a culture counter to mainstream American norms. Free love, Eastern mysticism, mind-expansion, communalism, vegetarianism, and music formed the core of the hippy movement. The Bay Area became the nexus of the Counter Culture and Susie jumped right in. She hopped a flight and enrolled for a master's degree in fine arts at UC Berkeley.

～❀⁀

"To fathom hell or soar angelic
Just take a pinch of psychedelic"
HUMPHREY OSMOND[42]

Angel-Cloud

"I had a couple of really great years studying art, taking LSD and smoking pot." In the mid-1960s political idealism reflected in the Civil Rights and Free Speech Movements in tandem with the social idealism reflected in the Hippy Movement were signs of breaking away from the stifling materialism, conformity and emotional and social repression of 1950s America. In the early days, young people experimented with drugs not so much to get high as to expand the mind, transcend the solid, materialist world of their parents and experience divinity. Early proselytes of psychotropic drugs believed that these substances had a purifying effect that opened the mind and inner vision to transcendent worlds. The celebrated novelist and essayist Aldous Huxley wrote a book

---

42   Dr. Humphrey Osmond (1917-2004) was a British psychiatrist who identified adrenochrome, a hallucinogen produced in the brain, as a cause of schizophrenia, and used vitamins to counter it. This breakthrough established the foundations for the orthomolecular psychiatry now practised around the world. Osmond coined the term psychedelic.

on his experiences with Mescaline (an hallucinogen extracted from the Peyote plant). He titled his book, 'The Doors of Perception' from a poem by William Blake:

> *"If the doors of perception were cleansed*
> *Everything will appear to man as it is, infinite."*

In those days taking LSD, Mescaline, Peyote and other hallucinogens was considered to be a therapeutic, religious experience.

"Taking LSD for me was always this magnificently gorgeous, great thing. One time when I was on a trip I remembered falling out of that second story window when I was two years old and I realized that I wanted to fly. That was my first realization that I wanted to fly and be free. I felt I was an angel. I wanted goodness. So I came back, through drugs to a realization. There's no question in my mind that I came back to a certainty about the existence of God.

"I went into this whole angel thing. My boyfriend at the time made me this extraordinary pair of wings – he was a sculptor – out of turkey feathers and buckram. One of the works of art I did for my master's degree was this amazing robe covered in beaded embroidery with angels on one side and demons on the other." Susie Goldman assumed a new identity. The redhead artist became 'Susie Angel-Cloud'.

The Magic Floating Lotus Opera Company

At about this time she met the poet Daniel Moore who Rolling Stone magazine described as 'the shaping spirit' of the Magic Floating Lotus Opera Company, a counter culture sensation in the Bay Area, producing plays that focused on 'the transformation of evil and dark energies, such as were driving the Vietnam War, into positive and light energies, through a cathartic initiation, which the central hero had to undergo.'[43] As the producer, director and star player in the Floating Lotus Company, Daniel "was a leader in the community. And he was very spiritual. He was always very much into meditation. He was a practicing Buddhist at the time. And he was this person who represented all that was good and sweet, not just to me, to many people."

---

43   Wikipedia entry The Magic Floating Lotus Opera Company

For Susie, "Daniel was a friend. I used to dance with him at parties. He was a fantastic dancer and I always liked him so much. He was so funny and really neat to be around."

Afghanistan

While Daniel Moore was steeped in poetry, theater and Eastern spirituality, Susie had begun to move in darker circles. She lived in an artists' commune with her sculptor boyfriend who was also a womanizer, drug dealer, con man and thief. "We used to travel all over the world to buy *kif* and hashish. On one of these journeys I had a ticket around the world with him. We wound up in Afghanistan. This was in 1969.

"We were having problems and I decided I didn't want to carry on any farther and that I was going to go back to the States. In those days you could buy a ticket around the world like from New York to Australia, and you could stop anywhere you wanted as long as you went in one direction. So I went to the airport with my round-the-world ticket my boyfriend bought me and it turned out that it had been stolen. He had taken all the travelers checks and moved on to Kathmandu and I was stranded penniless and ticketless in Kabul. I prayed, 'God, if You're there, please help me, rescue me!' The next day I heard there was an opening for a job at Kabul University teaching English as a second language and I got the job! I wound up staying in Kabul for a year.

Sunset

"I traveled to Mazar-i-Sharif in northern Afghanistan with a bunch of hippies I'd met at this café in Kabul. We were going to shop in the bazaar for embroidery, jewelry, lapis lazuli, antiques and rugs. On the journey the driver stopped the VW bus on a precipice high in the mountains. Way down below were these rice terraces and one lone Afghan farmer. We watched this spellbinding sunset. Never in my memory have I seen such a gorgeous sunset. It was cobalt blue, purple, fuchsia, gold, orange, pink – a luminous, mesmerizing sunset. There must have been five or six hippies just standing there stunned into silence when suddenly, echoing from this chasm came a call to prayer. It was staggering, beautiful. And we saw the lone farmer, a tiny speck below in the distance, spreading out his prayer mat. We watched him perform the sunset prayer. It was like a lightning bolt had struck me.

"But living in Afghanistan I would never have become a Muslim because I didn't like what I saw and heard about the way women were treated. They were very much oppressed at that time."

Hippy Hell

After one year Susie headed home with the call to prayer resounding in her memory. Back in Berkeley she found the hippy heaven she had left had "turned into a nightmare". By the end of the decade flower power had wilted. The excesses, the rampant promiscuity and the mounting casualties from drug abuse had cast a shadow over the initial idealistic impulses and Utopian naïveté that drew millions of young people to the hippy movement. By 1969 Edward Kern in Life magazine could reduce the counter culture 'sacraments' to 'sex, drugs and rock and roll.' At the same time, the industrial-scale cruelty of the Viet Nam War, which millions of Americans watched on television every night, and the government's increasingly violent repression of dissent polarized the country. The Kent State massacre in 1970 where the National Guard opened fire on anti-war student protestors on campus, leaving four students dead, ended the era. The doors of perception were slammed shut, the promise of illumination and a better world, broken.

"I was deeply unhappy. I was really lost. I just didn't know what to do with myself. I couldn't find a job. I was on welfare. I was having something like a nervous breakdown. I couldn't sleep. I was in agony. I had hit rock bottom. I was in hell. This went on for months until one night, I fell to my knees and prayed. I begged God to take me out of the situation that I was in and put me with the best people. 'Please put me in the company of noble, trustworthy, good people, I want to be like them. I want to be with true friends.' And after I made that prayer, this peace descended on me. I fell into a lovely sleep.

Sufis

"I woke up the next morning and felt this peace was still with me. I took a shower. It was a beautiful day in Berkeley. I walked to a health food store and there was a community bulletin board with a poster that said Sufis were having an open house." She learned that some of her old Berkeley acquaintances, including Daniel Moore and Conrad Archuletta, had joined the Sufis.

Susie told a friend of hers about it. "We had made a huge organic zucchini that we'd cut in half and stuffed with crunchy granola, mushrooms and veggies and topped with melted cheese. It was absolutely yummy. We had eaten one side of it. The other side was untouched. My friend suggested that we give it to the Sufis. So we made a mandala of this beautiful platter, surrounded with veggies. I wrote and decorated a little note saying it was from Angel-Cloud with my address. We dropped it at the door at night and ran away. I later learned that they were afraid that I'd put LSD in the food so they threw it out.

"But two days later there was a knock at the door. The Sufis came to thank me for the food and invited my friend and I to tea the next day. So we went to their *zawiya*. I had tea with them and I was very drawn to that group."

During the tea Susie was asked what her plans were. She told them that she was thinking of driving across country to see her mother in Philadelphia. They asked if she was driving alone. She said she was and their leader asked her if she could take three *fuqara* with her who were traveling to Morocco. She agreed.

The Ride

A week later, Susie and three young men she'd never met before piled into her little Sunbeam and took off for the East Coast. "We had two nights camping out. I was with these angels. These men were so respectful of me, and so kind. They were the answer to my prayer of being with noble people. They were such noble, beautiful men. They were in the car reciting prayers and *dhikr* and stopping along the roadside to perform the obligatory prayer. I was in love with the beauty of it all. They spoke to me about Shaykh Muhammad ibn al-Habib and related wonderful experiences that they had and the saints that they had met in Morocco. And I thought, 'This is it, this is where I'm going.' There was a little thought at the back of my mind that if this doesn't work out I'll just go to New York and find cousins who were Hassidic Jews and join the Hassidim. Because if I'm going to be a Jew I want to find out what a real Jew is. What do real Jews do?

"We were driving along Route 66 through the Navajo Indian Reservation. Route 66 is this long highway that goes as far as the eye can see toward the horizon. And suddenly this pickup truck jumps out and rams right into my cute little Sunbeam, which was probably made out of tin or something. The car was completely totaled. We managed to extricate ourselves from the wreckage. When we got out and looked at this wreck in the middle of the highway, we realized there wasn't a scratch on any of us! We had been doing *dhikr* at the time of the accident. The family that had crashed into us gave us something like twenty-five dollars and disappeared." So the three men huddled and came back to Susie and offered to get money to send her back to Berkeley. "I said, 'I'm not going back to Berkeley. I'm going with you. I'm joining the Sufis.' This is before I became a Muslim."

The Highway Patrol came and took a report. Little did they know that Susie was carrying "this beautiful, Art Nouveau gold compact with twelve or thirteen beautiful, hand-rolled joints, a present from someone who knew I was leaving on this trip." When her traveling companions learned what she was carrying they were horrified. Those were the days when possession of marijuana was a felony. The car was towed away and the four stranded travelers ditched the dope and hitched a ride to the nearest town. Susie called her sister who wired money for them to take a Greyhound Bus to Philadelphia.

Susie left the *fuqara* in Philadelphia. The men carried on to New York to hop a Yugoslav freighter to Casablanca. She stayed with her mother, who was not well. Three weeks later she returned to Berkeley. It was Halloween and her hippy friends met her, all dressed up in Halloween costumes and swept her off to a party. "Everybody was stoned. Everybody was leaping around and dancing. I was done. I was done with all of it, smoking pot, making out, everything. I went home early and went to bed. I woke up in the morning and said to myself, 'Today is the day I'm going to join the Sufis.'"

The Walk

"As I was leaving the house the social worker turned up to make sure I was still eligible for welfare. I said, 'I don't want welfare anymore. I don't need it. I'm okay.'" Susie walked a few blocks to the Sufi *zawiya* and nobody was there. The place was empty and abandoned. Undeterred, she decided to find Daniel and Conrad who both worked at Record City on Telegraph Avenue. "So that began my walk. I walked to Record City and neither of them was there. By this time it was about noon. They told me Daniel had the day off but that Conrad had gone to lunch and would be back. So I sat on the pavement on Telegraph Avenue in front of Record City, smoked a cigarette and pretty soon Conrad came by. I told him of my intention."

Conrad gave her directions to the new *zawiya* they had moved to. It was "way down in another part of Berkeley. I thought I'd take the bus but the bus never came so I ended up walking there. On that walk I kept meeting all these people from my past: artists, strange encounters that I had, my old boyfriend. One of the people I met along the way said, 'Tell me about this' and we sat down on the curb and I smoked a cigarette. He whisked out this mirror with lines of cocaine on it. He said, 'Have some cocaine.' I said, 'No, no, I'm not doing that anymore. I'm with the Sufis. I'm on a path of purification.' And I carried on walking. I lit up another cigarette on the way and I started looking at my hands. I said to myself, 'Okay, I'm not going to smoke any more. This is it. This is the last cigarette I'm going to smoke.' I threw down the cigarette, stomped on it, turned around and there I was, at the *zawiya*. So I go up and knock on the door and I'm full of anticipation. And guess who answered?"

Daniel Moore opened the door.

"I said, 'Daniel, I'm here to become a Muslim. I'm joining the Sufis.' So he welcomed me in."

And Susie Goldman, aka 'Susie Angel-Cloud', recited the declaration of faith, became a Muslim, joined the Sufis and was given the Muslim name of Malika. Her journey from normal to Real was just beginning.

Oh, and after many adventures and much learning in America, England, Morocco and other ports of call, Malika Goldman married Daniel Abdal Hayy Moore. They were soul mates for 36 years until his death in 2016.

The Real Guide

MANY YEARS AGO I was taken to a gathering organized at the Regent's Park Mosque in London. I tend to be gathering-averse and only came along because my friend was the organizer and was working hard to bring Muslims together. So we entered the foyer of the mosque complex and I was standing off to one side when someone came up, shook my hand vigorously and greeted me. "*As-Salaam Alaykum!*"

"*Wa Alaykum Salaam,*" said I.

He stood there grinning. I grinned back.

"You don't remember me, do you?" he stated.

I was taken aback. I studied his face to see if I could place him. I shook my head. "I'm really sorry," I said, "I have a terrible memory."

"You changed my life," he said.

That was a conversation stopper.

He then told me the story of our meeting. And, as he told it, I began to remember.

Years before (sometime in the mid-1970s), I had been invited by one of my best friends at the time, a Malaysian engineering student and Sufi acolyte, to come up to Norwich and stay with a group of young Malaysians studying there. The last time I had visited Norwich was in 1967 with a school madrigal ensemble I was part of. We'd given a concert in the town hall and attended a party in an ancient dungeon where, for the first time, we all heard the Beatles' just-released 'Sergeant Pepper's Lonely Hearts Club' album. Otherwise, I knew nothing of the place until my Malaysian sojourn. When I arrived the students insisted I visit a new British Muslim who had converted to Islam in order to marry a Malaysian woman. They were eager for me to meet the new convert and I was happy to pay him a visit. But as soon as we turned up at his door and were invited in, I wanted to get out of there in the worst way.

I know that my memory is probably playing tricks on me but the image that came back to me that day was of a kind of lugubrious Stanley

Kowalski[44] type, a loutish, humorless working class bloke with empty eyes. The picture would have been complete if he had a beer in front of him (he did not). Our host seemed dull and disinterested with a quizzical look about him, as if he was trying to figure out what we were doing in his house.

But there I was with my Malaysian friends eagerly looking to me to tell the new convert about Islam. So I started talking. I can't remember a word I said because all I could think about was finding a smoothe and gracious exit line. I jabbered on about Islam for about forty-five minutes, telling stories, moving quickly from one subject to another, looking for my cue. His wife came in to serve tea. There was something shrewish about her. He looked dazed and didn't say a word or ask a question. We drank tea. I continued with my monologue until I found the right moment to announce our departure. I shook his hand and thanked him for his hospitality. We said our farewells and made our escape. I remember that once we had descended a flight of steps turning on my Malaysian entourage in the stairwell and scolding them. "Why did you bring me here? What a waste of time! Hopeless!"

"When you came to my flat that day", he said, "I never really knew anything about Islam but I kept thinking about what you said. What you told me that day made me want to learn more about Islam and the more I learned about Islam, the closer I came to the faith. The closer I came to Islam the farther apart my wife and I became. We eventually divorced and now I have remarried a pious Turkish Muslim woman." I think he told me that he owned an Islamic bookstore.

Now it was my turn to be speechless and dazed.

I learned a lesson that day. I learned that all guidance comes from God in whatever form He chooses and that we are nothing more than instruments He uses in His wisdom to guide whom He wills. May God bless this sincere believer and forgive us our arrogance and delusion. There is no power and no strength but from God.

Walk on Water

HABIB AL-'AJAMI WAS a medieval loan shark. He lived in Basra and amassed a fortune from usury in defiance of the Qur'anic prohibition against it:

> O you who believe! Do not devour usury, making it double and redouble and be careful of (your duty to) Allah, that you may be successful. And guard yourself against the Fire that has been prepared for the unbelievers.[45]

In ancient times usury was beyond the pale in Muslim lands. Usurers were considered to be cursed and unclean (*najas*).

> Those who eat Riba (usury) will not stand (on the Day of Resurrection) except like the standing of a person beaten by Satan leading him to insanity. That is because they say: "Trading is only like Riba (usury)," whereas God has permitted trading and forbidden Riba (usury). So whosoever receives an admonition from his Lord and stops eating Riba (usury) shall not be punished for the past; his case is for Allah (to judge); but whoever returns [to Riba (usury)], such are the dwellers of the Fire – they will abide therein.[46]

The Messenger of God (peace be upon him) cursed the one who accepted usury, the one who paid it, the witness to it, and the one who recorded it.[47]

When children playing on the street saw him passing, they would scatter in fear and revulsion. "Habib the usurer is coming! Run away or his dust will settle on us and we'll be as accursed as he is!"

Habib didn't care. His heart was hard and cold. He was a nasty piece

45   Holy Qur'an, *Sura Al-Imran* 3:130-131
46   Ibid, *Sura Al-Baqara* 2:275

47   Narrated by 'Abdullah ibn Mas'ud from the Sunan of Abu-Dawood

of work. He doggedly made his rounds, collecting from his debtors and whoever couldn't pay he would demand compensation for his 'shoe leather.'

One day he made his way to one of his debtors to collect his interest payment. The debtor's wife answered the door. Habib demanded payment.

"My husband isn't here." Habib demanded his 'shoe leather' payment.

"I have nothing to give you," said the debtor's wife.

But the usurer wouldn't leave until he extracted something from the wife.

"We sacrificed a sheep some days ago," she said. "I only have the neck remaining. I can give you this as compensation."

"Good, that's something anyway," replied Habib. "So go put a pot on the fire and cook it for me."

"But I don't have any bread or fuel for the fire."

"I'll go and bring you fuel and bread but I will add this to what you owe me," the usurer said.

So Habib went off to the market and returned with bread and fuel and invited himself into the house and waited for his debtor's wife to cook his meal.

Just before the woman was about to pour the stew from the pot into a bowl for Habib a beggar knocked at the door, asking for alms.

Habib shouted out impatiently, "If we give you what we have, you won't become rich and we will become poor!"

The beggar pleaded with the woman to give him something to eat. In spite of the threatening presence of the usurer, she lifted the lid of the pot to give the mendicant some of the stew and turned pale. The stew had turned into black blood.

She cried out to her uninvited guest, "Look what has happened to us because of your cursed usury and your reviling this poor beggar! What will become of us now, in this world? What will become of us in the Next?"

Habib looked into the contents of the cooking pot and beheld the woman's anguish and the beggar's need and felt a fire rising within him that never left him for the rest of his life.

"Woman," he said. "I have turned away from all that I have ever done."

And he left, chastened and repentant. His heart had turned in *Tawba*.

The next day Habib ibn Muhammad al-'Ajami set out to track down all those he had lent money to and taken usury from with the intention of recompensing them. As he walked through the streets the children scattered and rebuked him and, for the first time, their words cut him to the quick.

On his way to redress the wrongs he had committed, he passed by a gathering. A discourse was in progress. The speaker was al-Hasan al-Basri, the greatest saint of the age, may God be well pleased with him. As Habib passed by, al-Hasan's words struck his heart like a hammer of light and he fainted dead away. When he revived his heart had turned away from the world to God. Al-Hasan was beside him, calming the turbulent penitent. Habib's heart had turned again, in *Inaaba*.

As he left the gathering, he passed one of his debtors who made to run away from him. Habib called after him, "You don't need to run away. Up to now it was for you to run away from me but now I must run away from you."

And as he walked away from the meeting with al-Hasan, the children who had fled from him just a short while before, now cried out, "Here passes Habib the penitent, run away lest our dust settles on him, for we are sinners against God!"

"My Lord and Master!" cried Habib. "Because of this one day that I have made my peace with You, You have beaten the drums of men's hearts for me and broadcast my name abroad for virtue!"

Then he issued a proclamation.

"Whoever wants anything from Habib, come and take it!"

The people gathered together, and he gave away all his possessions until he was penniless. He withdrew to a retreat on the banks of the Euphrates and gave himself up to the worship of God. He studied with al-Hasan al-Basri day and night. Habib spoke only Farsi and despite great effort he could not learn the Holy Qur'an in Arabic and for this he was nicknamed *al-'Ajami* (the Persian).

Habib al-'Ajami became a transcendent saint known for many miracles. In some respects he outstripped his master.

At one point officers of the ruthless Umayyad enforcer al-Hajjaj bin Yusuf were tracking down al-Hasan to imprison him. al-Hasan went into hiding in Habib's cell. They found Habib at the retreat and asked him where al-Hasan was. He said, "He is here."

"Where?" they asked.

"He is in my cell. He is hiding there."

The officers went to Habib's cell but they found no one.

They returned to Habib. "He is not there."

"I swear by God that he is there in my cell."

They returned seven times to the cell and found no one. So they beat Habib and left the retreat. Once they had left, al-Hasan emerged from Habib's cell and upbraided his disciple.

"Habib, you did not observe your duty to your master. You pointed me out. I know that it was from your *Baraka* that they did not discover me but you should have concealed me."

"Master," replied Habib, "it was not because of my *Baraka*. It was because I told the truth that you escaped. If I had lied we would both have been arrested."

"What did you recite that they did not see me?" asked al-Hasan.

"I recited the *Ayat al-Kursi* ten times," Habib answered. "I recited *Amana Rasulu Bima Unzila* ten times and I recited *Qul Huwa Allahu Ahad* ten times and then I prayed, 'Oh God, I have committed al-Hasan to You. Watch over him.'"

On another occasion al-Hasan came to the banks of the River Tigris. Habib approached him. "Master, why are you standing here?" he asked.

"I wish to go to a certain place. The boat is late," Hasan replied.

"Master, what has happened to you?" Habib demanded. "I learned all that I know from you. Expel from your heart all envy of other men. Close your heart against worldly things. Know that suffering is a precious prize, and see that all affairs are from God. Then set foot on the water and walk."

With that Habib stepped on the water and walked across the Tigris. al-Hasan swooned. When he recovered the people asked him,

"Imam of the Muslims what happened to you?"

"My student, Habib, just now reprimanded me," he replied. "Then he stepped on the water and walked across the Tigris, while I remained powerless. If tomorrow a voice cries, 'Pass over the fiery pathway' – if I remain like this, what can I do?"

"Habib," al-Hasan asked later, "how did you discover this power?"

"I make my heart white with contemplation," Habib replied, "while you make paper black with ink."

It would appear that Habib had reached the station of *Awba*, but God knows best.

al-Hasan sighed, "My learning profited another, but it did not profit me."[48]

---

48   Retold from *Tadhkirat al-Awliya* of Attar, translated by A.J. Arberry

Part Three

MIGRATIONS

Mercy

IT IS RELATED in the name of 'Abu Sa'id al-Khudri that the Prophet said: "There was, in the past, a man who had killed ninety-nine persons. He inquired after the wisest man upon the earth, and was directed to a monk. He came to the monk and asked: 'One has killed ninety-nine people, is there [a possibility] of repentance for him? 'No.' The man then killed the monk, completing, thereby, the number of his victims—one hundred. Then he again sought the wisest man in the land and was directed to a learned man, to whom he said: 'If one has killed a hundred men is there repentance for him?' 'Yes,' was the reply, 'Who can prevent him from repenting? Go to such and such a land, where people serve God, worship with them, and do not return to your land, for it is an evil land.'

"He then set out on the road but midway death overtook him.

"Then the angels of mercy argued over him with the angels of chastisement. The Angels of mercy said: 'He came as a penitent, in his heart directed toward God.' 'He has never done any good,' retorted the Angels of chastisement. An Angel in human form approached and they appointed him to judge between them. He said: 'Measure the distance of the two lands; he belongs to the one that is nearer.'

They measured and found him nearer the land [he left, so] God urged this side to move away and the [land he sought] to draw near, then said: 'Measure what is between them.' They found the man closer to the land [he sought] by a span and he was forgiven."[49]

---

49   From *Kitab Al-Tawba* (The Book of Repentance) by al-Ghazali, related in Sahih Muslim and Sahih al-Bukhari, translated by S. M. Stern.

Friends

KENNETH HONERKAMP BUMMED a cigarette off Michael Fitzgerald outside a French class they were both attending at San Fernando Valley State College. This was in 1967 and that was the first time they met. Little did either of them know that this was an auspicious moment—a fork in the road that would take them both to the other side of the world and to another way of life altogether. It was a meeting that marked the beginning of a bond that would surpass a half century.

They were Southern California boys. Michael was born and raised in Santa Monica. Ken was born in Burbank and raised all over the country because his father spent years as an itinerant jobbing aeronautics engineer. After living in thirteen states the Honerkamp family moved back to Granada Hills in the San Fernando Valley. Both ended up attending the same university. Both were already looking beyond America and American values for answers.

Michael: "I had become enthralled with France and French culture. I thought, 'Here were thinkers, history, culture, art, music, cuisine!' I did everything I could to learn French in high school, to save money working part-time jobs, and finally getting my mother's permission to get a passport. I took off from L.A. to Paris in the winter of '64 or '65 very soon after finishing high school. I had some vague idea that I could find in another culture some kind of happiness and coherence that I hadn't found in my own. Generally, it was a great experience to see another place in the world. I spent about forty days living in a cheap hotel in the Montparnasse, seeing history before my eyes and, ironically, also seeing the place where my father had spent weeks hiding from the Nazis with the French underground. That year I was bitten by the travel bug and I never quite recovered.

"By the time I met Ken Honerkamp, I was already pretty convinced that the world was not a particularly happy place. I was the child of divorced parents and had spent my years from the age of eight (when

135

they divorced) to eighteen navigating between a mother and father whom I loved but who had fallen out of love with one another. More than that, both of them had a lot of anger stored up, probably from the war, and I had plenty of chances to witness manifestations of that. It was also probably an indirect effect of WWII that I had grown up with no religious training. Seeing war can do that to people. Also, all through my senior year in high school, the U.S. was ramping up for a new war in Viet Nam, the draft was in place back then, and probably the only reason I went straight into college after high school was to get that precious student deferment.[50] I hated the idea that after growing up watching my parents' personal war, I was going to be sent off to try to kill some peasants on the other side of the world. I was also pretty sure that my homeland was cursed for our having stolen it from its rightful owners, the Native Americans. In short, I was the typical angry young man.

"So I met Ken that day and found out he and I were both against the war, that he too had entertained ideas of escaping the U.S.A., that we both liked country blues and folk music, and that he was also impressed by French thinkers, and was actually reading Sartre's 'Being and Nothingness' (in English) as part of being a philosophy major. That was enough as the basis for a friendship back then."

Kenneth: "My high school Spanish teacher was a Chilean political exile who had been a professor of philosophy. In class he would suddenly stop teaching and say, 'Have you ever thought what the purpose of life is?' The students would roll their eyes and say, 'Oh not again!' but I started thinking 'What *are* we doing here?' We got to know each other and he started giving me philosophy books. My readings of philosophy led me to existentialism and the writings of Jean Paul Sartre and anarchist writings. By the time I got out of high school I decided I had to go to France. That's how I ended up taking French."

Michael: "By the first summer after that meeting, I think we had both switched our majors to anthropology, and had started getting into the books of Carl Jung. His notion of archetypes and the collective unconscious was sort of a revelation and it led us into books on Buddhism and maybe Hinduism. The writings of Herman Hesse, 'Steppenwolf,'

---

50   In the U.S. during this period anyone attending college or university was exempted from mandatory military service for the duration of their studies.

'The Bead Game', and 'Journey to the East', had a profound effect on us as they did on so many young people back then, so I guess, indirectly, we were getting a new perspective on religion, but one that really had little to do with faith and a lot to do with realizing that deep within us we shared what Jung called 'the collective unconscious' with all humanity.

"Anthropology was so interesting. It was about other cultures. Our anthropology professor had these stories of other cultures. They were about other civilizations and other visions of the world. We were both captivated. At that point, in the sixties, we decided that the most important thing was to search for some sort of meaning in life, some meaning in existence. 'Why are we here? What are we doing?'

"The next semester, I took a course called 'Cultures of the Middle East', and Jungian ideas were so much on my mind that I decided to do my term research on the symbol of the labyrinth across cultures.

"This was against the background of the labyrinth that was California in the mid-sixties. There were some really good things that happened during that time - for me, the most lasting and beautiful of which was to meet the woman who would one day be my wife. But there were also a lot of false starts, dead-ends, and encounters with the darkness that had quickly descended on the youth culture as soon as certain people figured out how to make the 'Summer of Love' and the drugs that fueled it a commodity, which was really fast. In those days, both Ken and I also got our share of meeting people who made themselves out to be guides of some sort, but who, in the end, were mainly interested in their own egos, in dominating other people who were sincerely searching, and, since they were inevitably men, in taking advantage of young women. It was the rock-star mentality superimposed onto some deformed version of the spiritual quest."

Both young men decided that they couldn't find the answers to the questions they had in America so they both dropped out of college with the vague notion that they were going to India. The answers would be there. Of the two, Ken appears to have been more desperate to leave— much more desperate.

Instead of India he scraped together enough money to book passage on a freighter to Casablanca. His decision was heavily influenced by the writings of Beat post-modernist writer William Burroughs, author of

'The Naked Lunch.' Burroughs famously lived in Tangiers with other Beat literary figures like Paul Bowles and Alan Ginsberg. Ken had the idea of seeking out this scene but when he arrived he found that "Tangiers wasn't healthy. It was depraved. It was, to be polite, not very full of light." The hippies in Tangiers he met "were tending toward the dark side of life." So Ken turned south toward the desert and landed in Marrakesh. He was driven by an intense desire to abandon his past and find himself. The nineteen year-old took things a tad too far.

Kenneth: "I threw my passport away. It was my identity. I was no longer interested in my identity. (Nowadays I'd do anything to keep my passport.) Things started to go wrong. It came to the point where I disassociated myself from who I was. I was wandering around out of touch, very, very detached. No shoes. I was not in a good state. I had no idea that Moroccans were even Muslims, but from time to time someone would say something about Islam. One thing that we used to do was to sit with the *Gnawa*."

The *Gnawa* are a Saharan *Amazigh* (Berber) tribe that integrated into Moroccan Sufism and are famed for an intensely rhythmic musical tradition that aims to send listeners into a state of *jadhb* (spiritual attraction), which is commonly described as a trance.

"They would always stop when the *Maghrib adhan* came. That was their tradition. In Marrakesh there used to be a big circle in the *Djemaa El Fna* (the main square in the old city) and all the hippies would sit there and listen to the *Gnawa* music. I knew them, they knew me, but I started avoiding them because I thought they were too perceptive and I was afraid they would see the state I was in, which was not good. In those days, the *Gnawa* would take a Moroccan in trouble to the center of their circle and play their drums and make prayers. One day I walked by and one of them ran up to me, grabbed me and pulled me into the center of the circle and sat me down. These were old men with white beards. They started playing those drums in my ears and the disturbances in my heart and mind all drifted away and things were good again. I was all right. A man named Abdul Salaam said to me, 'How are you now? Where were you?' And all I said was '*Allah! Allah!*' That was the beginning of turning away from what many of my contemporaries were following and beginning to think that there was more to life than what we had been doing.

"I ended up in jail for vagrancy. I had no passport, no money. The U.S. embassy sent somebody and got me out. They alerted my parents who generously provided a return ticket. They kept me in a place in Casablanca and put me on a plane back to the United States. There I was, six months later, back home, taking the walk of shame. But after all that, all I wanted to do was to leave again."

So what did Kenneth do? After six months Stateside, he took the same freighter back to Morocco. He traveled around the country, "visited holy men, drank from sacred springs, looked at nature and started thinking about things." He eventually ran out of money again. This time he held on to his passport and managed to avoid jail by presenting himself to the U.S. Embassy and asking them to help him get back home, again.

During all Kenneth's Moroccan adventures Michael - clearly the more conservative of the two - remained in the U.S., living in communes and experimenting with alternative philosophies and lifestyles.

After Kenneth returned to California for the second time he rejoined Michael and they decided that they really had to get their lives together and head for India.

Taking Off
Michael: "We decided that we really needed to get out of that whole environment and head towards India, the place where so many people back then were heading to find spiritual understanding."

The two young seekers needed to save up enough money to make their own 'Journey to the East.'

Kenneth: "I didn't have a job, Michael was not working but he was a very good short order cook so it was very easy for him to get a job almost any time. I had gotten a job working as a draftsman. I said to Michael, 'My mistake was to have gone to Morocco before India. We have to go to India.' Maybe Michael thought he had to go with me to keep me out of trouble. We started saving money to go to India. I'd been studying Eastern religions, Buddhism and Hinduism. The aim was to find a *guru* and go to his *ashram* and meditate. We were going to travel by sea and overland."

Michael: "By the winter of 1969, we were saving up money to book passage on a Yugoslav freighter to 'the East'. That freighter, from a country that no longer exists, was the cheapest way to cross the Atlantic in those days - maybe two hundred dollars for an eight-day crossing, with three meals a day on board plus tea. It carried sixty passengers in pretty nice cabins, along with tons of potatoes and other US exports in its hold. We would be traveling to Rijeka, Yugoslavia, stopping, as I recall, in Lisbon, then Casablanca, and then Milan to unload and load along the way. Then we would take the Orient Express, which was still running, from Zagreb to Istanbul."

Kenneth: "I looked at the map and realized that we would be crossing a huge piece of the Islamic world. I'd tasted something of Islam in Morocco.People talked to me about Islam. I'd heard the call to prayer. So we went down to a bookstore in Hollywood and bought a copy of Marmaduke Pickthall's translation of the Holy Qur'an. Before that time Islam was to me just another religion trying to control the masses with a particular discourse and dialogue. I never gave it any consideration but I said, 'Now I have to.'"

Michael: "My interest in Islam at that point was purely academic. You have to be culturally correct and you have to know what people believe so you have to read their holy book. I had no intention toward Islam whatsoever. I'd read about Hinduism and the Vedas. I started reading Pickthall's translation of the Qur'an. It is not an open book but what *did* get me was that from the very beginning the Qur'an is addressing *you*. I didn't know if it was *you* plural or *you* singular but it was *you*. I came to the conclusion that it was telling *me* something."

The two friends set off to New York and took the freighter to Yugoslavia.

"The crossing took about eight days and, since there was nothing else to do on board, we spent a lot of time reading and sometimes getting mildly drunk on *slivovitz*, the sickly sweet Yugoslav brandy they provided. We had tried to keep our baggage to one backpack each, so there was not much room for books, but Ken had a copy of one of Gurdjieff's books, maybe the *I Ching* as well, and we had a paperback copy of Marmeduke Pickthall's 'The Meaning of the Glorious Quran'. I remember that, for me, this was a very 'anthropological' choice: I didn't want to be the ugly American, ignorant of the people around me. So in those extra days at sea I started reading it.

"The Qur'an in English is not an easy read. You don't get the poetry of the Arabic and the wonderful sounds which can vibrate deep within you even apart from the message of the text. But I started dutifully at the beginning and found myself soon in the story of the *Bani Israel* in *Sura al-Baqara*. Here's where the book started talking to me, because the verses address those people as 'you' and somehow I felt that the 'you' was not just them, thousands of years before, but *me*. So it was a book not just speaking to me, but in some strange way also about me. These were just glimmers at the time and they didn't get any brighter until much later.

"The freighter was full of American hippies and retired people. We had to sit with them and have tea with them in the galley. By the time we were mid-Atlantic, we were thoroughly sick of seeing the other passengers, so we both decided to fast one day. I made my way out to a space where you could actually lie down on some bench or something in the bow of the ship. The sky was clear, the air was fresh, ocean stretching in every direction, and I just lay down there and began repeating slowly the name *Allah*, which I at least knew was the name of the Divinity in Arabic. I just started repeating it. I have no idea why or even if I was saying it correctly, but it seemed right at the time. Much later, when I tried to think if there was anything I did to take a step towards Allah, I thought that maybe that was it."

The Muslim World

Kenneth: "We got to Rijeka (in what is now Croatia) and then we trained through Bulgaria to Turkey. I remember crossing the border into Turkey and seeing the mosques and the domes and feeling this attraction. We didn't know Arabic but seeing the words over the doors and visiting the large mosques, seeing Islamic society, there was something—the mosques, the architecture, the people—it started communicating to me."

Michael: "When we arrived in Istanbul suddenly it dawned on me: 'This is the Islamic world, the world of Allah!' We knew we were somewhere else. It wasn't Kansas City! The mosques were overwhelmingly strange and beautiful, and the people were friendly, even though we didn't speak their language. That was how it started. That was the beginning."

Kenneth: "We traveled from Istanbul, through Iran by train and by bus. This was the time of the Shah. There were statues of the Shah riding horses. There were big buildings in Tehran. Young people would come up to us, asking if we had any Levis. Sometimes we'd see old people on the buses with traditional beards and turbans."

Michael: "Turkey had its modern sides, but as we travelled by train through Iran, it was like going further and further back into time - tiny mud villages surrounded by vast plains and mountains on the horizon. We were traveling through a mediaeval landscape."

Arrival

Kenneth: "We arrived in Afghanistan at night. There was a no-man's land. We got off at the border in Iranian territory and boarded this dilapidated bus that was going to take us to Herat. We were on a very rough road. We saw soldiers wearing these funky uniforms made of thick wool, carrying old weapons, standing there. We finally get to the border crossing and this Afghani man in a suit comes out and says, 'Give me your passports.' This is now late '69. You could tell he didn't like all these foreigners coming into his country, but we had visas. I remember he took us in the office and we waited for a long, long time in the middle of the night. Then he came out and said 'Here' and he threw the passports up in the air. We sorted out everybody's passports, got on a bus and headed for Herat.

"Herat in those days was a small town. There was no electricity. We couldn't see anything. It was pitch black. We got off the bus and here's this guy who was wearing a turban and what looked like pajamas. He said, 'You look for hotel?' We said, 'Yeah! We need to sleep. We're really, really tired.' So he took us to a place that had mats on the floor and we lay down and went to sleep. I woke up and saw the sunlight coming through the shuttered windows and the dust in the sunrays. Everyone was sleeping.

"I opened the window and looked out. There was a caravan of camels swaying with turbaned riders in traditional clothes. There were no cars or trucks. It was dusty. In the distance there was a mosque. I looked at this ancient tableau and said to myself, 'We made it! We made it! We finally got away.' We'd gotten far enough away from America that our programming would no longer be kicking in. I always remember that moment when I realized, 'This is it! We made it!' We're now in the East. *Phew!*"

Michael: "When we crossed the border into Afghanistan, a new element was added: seeing for the first time people in traditional clothes: big turbans, long shirts, pantaloons, women in *burqas*. Everything got that much more intense."

Kenneth: "We got on a bus headed for India. We traveled through Kandahar and spent some time in Kabul. We were walking around the city and we saw a picture of the mosque in Mazar-i-Sharif. We decided to go to Bamiyan and then to Mazar-i-Sharif and continue on to Pakistan and India."

Bamiyan

Michael: "After a few days in Kabul, which was a peaceful place in those days, we heard about the giant carvings of Buddha in the Bamiyan Valley, and since we had read a lot about Buddhism, we decided we needed to visit. There were no trains in Afghanistan (and there still aren't), only two main highways at the time, the east-west one built by the Americans and the north-south one built by the Russians. We travelled by bus as much as we could, but as you get towards the mountains, the transport switches to trucks, standing up in the back if you can.

"It was on that trip that I got to see, for the first time, people offering the Muslim prayer. This was not visible in Turkey or Iran, but the Afghans would stop wherever the prayer time found them. So, every so often the truck would stop near a stream, people would get down, make ablutions, and pray. I don't think I had ever seen any human action as beautiful as the prayer offered by men in their traditional clothes, prostrating on a patch of green near a stream, surrounded by snow-capped peaks and a vast sky.

"After a trip of at least two days, we got to Bamiyan and there they were: these amazing stone statues over-looking the valley, everything feeling so ancient. How many peoples had passed through that valley?

"Bamiyan was absolutely beautiful. There were these huge carvings of the Buddha, which the Taliban later destroyed. I spent a couple of nights on top of the main Buddha's head, looking down at that valley and its peacefulness and also down upon the shrine of the most famous Muslim saint in the area, 'the tomb of the ice-burning saint' who we learned had been given the miracle of being able to use ice as fuel to warm people during a particularly severe winter."

Kenneth had contracted a virulent case of dysentery and stayed behind in the hotel but joined Michael the next day.

The Big Ask

"We checked into the one hotel in the village and found that the only other guests staying there were a few Americans who turned out to be very fervent Christian missionaries. They were definitely involved in proselytizing and it didn't take long for them to ask us, 'Have you taken Jesus Christ as your personal saviour?' I think we both answered no, although I had had a passing phase with Christianity before leaving the U.S. They said all we needed to do was get down on our knees and pray. As I recall, Ken wasn't interested. I will always see him as someone with singleness of purpose who could see a goal ahead before anyone else. (Maybe that's an advantage of being tall!) But I had reached a point in my life where I had inwardly decided that if I did not find some way that was going to show me what I was doing on earth by the time I reached 25, there was no point in continuing to live. So if someone had told me that the way to finding that was to go juggle in the marketplace, I would have given it a try. I got down on my knees in my hotel room and for the first and last time in my life prayed to God in the name of Jesus Christ. I think I said, 'Dear God, dear Jesus, please lead me to a way that is pleasing to You.'"

Three months later Michael received the answer to his prayer, but not exactly the one the missionaries anticipated.

Kenneth: "We made our way to Mazar-i-Sharif and visited the shrine. In Mazar-i-Sharif we met a British guy who told us he had met some Moroccans in Ibiza and entered Islam. I'd never met anyone who'd converted to Islam. I'd never even thought about it. He said, 'Today I went into the shrine of Sayyidina 'Ali and prayed because I had learned to pray in Ibiza. And the people came and gave me money and lots of gifts! They were very kind to me because I had converted to Islam.' And I was thinking, 'You can convert to Islam?'"

144

Pakistan

Michael: "Eventually, we left Afghanistan and made the trip by bus over the Khyber pass into Pakistan. The first real city you come to is Peshawar. It was crowded, hot (I think it was June), noisy and there was a big international hippy scene where hashish and other drugs were readily available."

Kenneth: "There were government opium shops. Because rooms were cheap, several people would be in the same room. Down below in the central courtyard was a mosque, where people would pray. Things were reaching a critical mass where we couldn't stand being around foreigners anymore. We didn't want to be around our own people any more."

Michael: "Many Pakistanis spoke English, the language of the British colonizers, and they were not shy about talking to us. Besides asking the usual questions about where we were going, they would also ask us 'Who is your prophet? Is it 'Isā (Jesus), Mūsā (Moses)? Who?' And it started to dawn on me that it was natural for all human beings to be following a prophet. Neither of us were, but sometimes, thinking back to the time I professed Christianity, I would say, 'Isā.' They would ask, 'Then how do you pray? Can you pray now?', for which we really didn't have an answer. Still we felt that everyone around us knew something that we didn't know. What, really, were we doing even calling ourselves human beings without the least connection to the One who had brought us into existence? This was the question that started nagging at me, and I felt more and more as someone behind a pane of glass, an on-looker to human life. But as for becoming Muslim, I don't think it really occurred to either of us until later.

"Suddenly Peshawar turned incredibly hot. I had never experienced heat like that. There were no air-conditioned places to escape to. They would bring snow down from the nearest glacier peaks and sell it in the bazaar, so you could order a mango drink or a lassi to cool down, but you also exposed yourself to unsanitary water or fruit. We spent a lot of time dealing with dysentery. Finally, we both were so overwhelmed that we needed to find some place else to survive the summer. People told us, 'Go to the Swat Valley. It's very beautiful and cool!'"

Swat

Kenneth: "I had come down with a serious case of pneumonia. I was really sick. We got on the bus. Michael was taking care of me. My health has never been that great but 'This,' I thought, 'this is it. I may just die here.' But then I thought, 'Well, better I die in Swat Valley than San Fernando Valley.'

"We made it to Swat. One man we bought some *dal* from said, 'Are you cooking your own food?' We said, 'Yes, the local food is too hot for us.' He said, 'Come to my house for dinner.' He was a very nice Swati shopkeeper. We came to his house. His father was there, a venerable old man. He said, 'This is my father. He has memorized the Qur'an.' I thought, 'Wow!' He pointed to a high shelf and said, 'Do you know what that is?' There was a very large book wrapped in a cloth. He said, 'That's our Holy Qur'an.' He said, 'Have you read it?' I said, 'I've read a translation.' He said, 'You can enter Islam you know. You can become a Muslim.' I thought, *'Ooooh I don't think I'm ready for that.'*

"In Swat my health improved. The air was good. The people were good. We were walking around in our tattered hippy clothes. We walked by a tailor sitting outside working a pedal sewing machine. He looked at my jeans and shirt and said, *'Oof!* No good!' I said, 'I agree. I don't like my clothes either but I don't know what else to do.' He said, 'Step inside.' He measured both of us and said, 'Come back tomorrow.' We came back the next day and we had Pakistani clothing. The first suit I had was this olive drab green. I said, 'Wow! This is so good.' The tailor gave me a nice embroidered white Swati hat. That hat was so beautiful, so pure that I said, 'I can't wear this. You don't know what's inside me. I'm a terrible person.' In those days it seemed like everybody knew what I was seeking before I knew what I was seeking. I said, 'I'm just a lost person from a ruined society.' I suppose I was feeling sorry for myself. He said, 'Well take it and keep it. One day you might need it.' So I took it and kept it.

"Everywhere we went people were inviting us to Islam. Now that we were wearing Pakistani clothing, when the *adhan* was called people would approach us and say, 'Come brother do you want to pray?' I would say, 'I wish I could pray but I don't know how. My heart isn't pure enough to pray. I can't do it.'

"Then somebody told us about Kalam."

The End of the Road

The village of Kalam is where the confluence of the Gabral and Ushu rivers join to form the Swat River.

Kenneth: "We took the bus from Mingora, the administrative center of Swat, up to Kalam., the end of the road. The Swat Valley is beautiful. The rivers. The forests. The mountains. You pass by people walking to the fields, carrying scythes."

Michael: "It was so incredibly beautiful. The forests seemed to ascend and then disappear into glacial peaks and into infinity."

Kenneth: "On the bus a man sat next to me and said, 'Excuse me sir, what are your qualifications?' I said, 'Well I was a university student but now I'm just traveling.' He says, 'Oh, but what are you going to say to God on the Day of Judgment when He asks you, *What have you done for Me in this world?*' I said, 'I don't know.' I told him that I didn't lie or steal or kill anybody. But I really started thinking about that.

The Voice

"We ended up riding on a bus that was so full we had to get up on top with a lot of other people. We were in the front, holding on. Kalam is down in a valley but to get to it there's a rise and you reach the top of the hill and then you go *doooown* into the valley. I'm on top of this bus. It's very loud. The air is rushing by. I could hardly hear anything. We come to the top of this hill and I look down and central to the whole place in those days was the mosque. The mosque is set upon where the two rivers meet. For the first time in my life I heard a voice. The voice said: *'If you leave here without finding what you're looking for you'll spend the rest of your life traveling and never find anything.'* I looked around, 'What? What?' Then the bus descended into the village.

Michael: "Kalam is one of the highest villages. Beyond that the road starts disappearing into glaciers. It is an amazing part of the world, it really is. People there speak rare Persian dialects. Kalam was stunningly pristine. There was no electricity, no running water. The houses were made of logs and mud. It was just beautiful. The village was on one side of the Swat River and the guesthouse was on the other side. We sat there and looked up at this terraced village. It was cool. We could see the mosque and people heading to the mosque. This extraordinary mosque was made entirely of huge tree trunks, and on the front of it were spiral carvings of what looked like Norse versions of water, maybe also a version of the labyrinth symbol I pondered upon in college. We checked into the government hotel on the opposite side of the river, and once again ran into travelers from the West."

Kenneth: "We were sitting in the center of the guest house surrounded by all these rooms. And the hippies were passing around a water pipe with hashish in it. I was sitting there looking at the mountains and listening to the river. I was looking at the mosque and minaret all made of wood. I saw that the *mu'adhdhin* climbed all the way to the top of the minaret to call the prayer. The water pipe was passed to me at the moment he began calling the prayer. I just passed the water pipe on and listened to the *'adhan*.

"Ten years later the *mu'adhdhin* that day told me he had seen me in the guest house at that very moment. He said, 'I knew you were going to become a Muslim because I saw you pass that water pipe when I called the prayer.'

"We stayed on in Kalam for some time. My health improved. The people were good. I really started thinking. Finally, Michael said to me, 'Your health is better. What are we doing here? Why are we staying? We have to continue to India.' I didn't tell him about the voice I had heard on the top of the bus as we entered Kalam the first time or what I thought about it, but I said, 'I can't tell you why but I just can't go.' He said, 'Well, I have to go.'"

Michael: "After three months our tourist visas had run out. We were supposed to periodically check with the police. There was always a thing about foreign spies."

Kenneth: "I knew my visa had run out. I didn't care."

Separation

Michael: "I decided to go to Peshawar to deal with my visa. The government authorities said, 'You've broken the law of Pakistan. Please report here tomorrow. We may have to put you in jail.' That was very upsetting so I went to the American Consulate. I was in this surreal air-conditioned office with a photo of Richard Nixon on the wall. The consular officer said, 'You really have no choice. You've got to leave the country. Just go out through the Afghan border. They're not going to bother you there. You really have to leave because you are in jeopardy.' I left and went back to Afghanistan."

Kenneth: "An Englishman who was staying in Kalam was leaving on a trek. He had a small simple room. He said, 'If you want to take it, I'm paying about five or six dollars a week for it. Take it and live here away from the hippies.' So I moved in with what little I had. A tailor named Muhammad Gul lived in the cabin next door. I would just sit out on the covered porch of this little cabin and listen to the *'adhan*. I would see the people going down to the mosque very quickly but coming back very slowly. I said, 'Look, they're hurrying to the mosque.' I said to myself, 'Ohhh I wish I could go. I wish I could pray with them. But I don't want people to think that I'm not respecting their religion, that I'm just some foreigner who wants to go into the mosque.' From time to time the tailor would go to the prayer while he was cooking rice and he would ask me to put some wood on the fire and watch the rice. Then I would eat with him.

"I had a small frying pan and one day I put some ghee in and put it on the fire. We were cooking with wood. And I put in a handful of onions. They go *'phhhhhhhhhah'*. They catch fire. I pulled the pan off the fire with all this burning oil and dumped it on my bare foot. I showed Muhammad Gul what happened and he said, 'Not good, not good.' There were no doctors up there and my foot swelled up. I was in terrible condition. In the days after Michael had left I was thinking I should leave too. My will was breaking down. But with this injury I couldn't walk. I couldn't leave. Muhammad Gul looked at my foot—we got some salve for it—he said, 'You know if you don't enter Islam, in the Hereafter all of you will be like that.' I'm like, *'What?!'*

"All these small pointers made me think that this is a serious business. Sometimes at night Muhammad Gul would make his ablutions and pray in his room. I would sit with him and he asked me if I wanted to pray with him. I said, 'No I can't pray. I'm a mess. No, no, no.' He gave me a green plastic rosary (*sibha*). He said, 'When I pray just sit here and say *La ilaha illa 'Llah*.' I knew what it meant so I sat there saying *La lilaha illa 'Llah, La ilaha illa 'Llah, La ilaha illa 'Llah* and thinking. Very soon after that I was sitting on my porch looking at the mountains, looking at the river, looking all around. I thought, 'Well, look at this. Look at nature. Look at the forests, look at the river. Everything is synchronized. Everything is in balance. The people here are in balance with their environment. What am I doing here? I'm out of balance.' I thought that the only thing to do is, metaphorically, to jump into the river to see if I can swim or not.

"I wasn't sure if Islam would change me. I had no idea basically because I didn't think much of myself. I went to Muhammad Gul and said, 'Can you teach me the prayer?' Muhammad Gul taught me how to pray. I wrote it down in transliterated letters. I walked around the forest and memorized it. I would pray with Muhammad Gul. If he went to the mosque I would pray in my little room. I always remember in my first prayer there was this voice yelling at me in my head. *What are you doing? You're prostrating to this black wall!* (The wall was covered in black soot). *What are you doing? Who's there?' Woof!* It was a last real reaction against turning my face towards Allah."

Michael: "On the bus to Kabul I met wonderful people who invited me into their homes. I spent about a month there. Then I headed back to Peshawar.

"In Peshawar I stayed again in a hotel in the Kisahani Bazaar. I went to a bookstore and bought a copy of Maulana Maududi's 'Towards Understanding Islam.' I found a passage in the book where he defines *kufr* (commonly translated as 'disbelief') from the literal meaning of *ka-fa-ra,* 'to cover up."

> The man who denies God is called *Kafir* (concealer) because he conceals by his disbelief what is inherent in his nature and embalmed in his own soul...But the vision of this man has been blurred, his intellect has been befogged, and he is unable to see the manifest. His own nature has become concealed from his eyes and he thinks and acts in utter diregard of it. The reality becomes estranged from him and he gropes in the dark...[51]

"I remember thinking at the time, 'That's me.'

"I was sharing a room in that hotel. There was a big open window that let me look down into the courtyard of a mosque behind the hotel where I could see the people offering the prayer. One of the hippies who

---

51   Towards Understanding Islam by Sayyid Abu'l 'Ala Maududi

were sharing that room had a radio-cassette player that he'd set in the window. They were playing a cassette of the Beatles 'White Album.' The sound went out into the night. I had just heard the call to prayer, so I said to the people in the room, 'We should turn this down. It's the prayer time and it might disturb the people in the mosque.' I can remember very distinctly about six pairs of eyes looking back at me like I was crazy. Then one of them said, *'What's the matter, man? Are you ashamed of our music?'* And I remember thinking at that moment, *'That may be your music but it's not mine.'*

"I asked myself, 'What am I doing? Should I head East to India?' So I decided to see Ken.

Return

"I got on a rickety bus, the kind that some of the passengers would have to get out and push uphill. The bus was going up, up, up. I was looking out at these terraced fields with irrigation canals running everywhere and women in colorful *chadors* tending them, and I just thought of the description of Paradise repeated in the Pickthall translation of the Quran: 'Gardens beneath which rivers flow.' And I really thought I heard a voice ask, in English, *'And where is your Paradise?'*

"The bus kept climbing and at one stop this small man got on. There was no other seat except the one next to me. He was walking with crutches. He was stunted and paralyzed from the waist down.

"He sat next to me and began talking to me. He was a teacher of Islamic studies in high school. He was very lucid and spoke very good English. He started talking about religion. He said, 'You can be a Muslim.' I said, 'I don't think so. I'm an American.' He said, 'No, no, Islam is not for any particular nationality. You can be a Muslim.' Then he looked at me with the most intense gaze I had ever experienced, a look that seemed to go deep into the turmoil of my heart, and said, 'In Islam you will find a complete life and complete happiness.' I couldn't quite believe what I was hearing. Here was a man whose body was half paralyzed and he was talking about complete happiness, while my body was whole, but it seemed like I was inwardly paralyzed. His stop came and he got his crutches under his arms, and looked at me one more time. 'You be Muslim.' He got off the bus at some mountain village, and I never saw him again, but at that moment something had changed. I said, 'I know he's right, but I still really need to talk to my friend and get his counsel.'"

Kenneth: "I'm in my room one day and two venerable gentlemen come up and talk to Muhammad Gul. It was the imam of the mosque and another religious figure. They're speaking in Pushtu and looking at me. They said, 'We hear he's praying.' Muhammad Gul said, 'Yes, he's praying.' They asked, 'Has he entered Islam? Why doesn't he come to the mosque?' Muhammad Gul knew a little bit of English and translated for me. I said, 'I think people might think I'm not respecting their tradition. They might think I'm not serious about this. I don't want to make people think I don't respect their tradition by going to the mosque.' The imam told Muhammad Gul, 'Bring him to the mosque tomorrow.' It would be Friday. In those days my hair was fairly long. The imam made gestures that I understood to mean that I should shave my head and take a bath. I said, 'Alright, if that's what you say, I'll do it.' So in the morning I went to the bathhouse down in the village and took a bath with hot water and had my head shaved. I came back to my room and found that Muhammad Gul had made me a Pakistani suit of white cloth. It was there, waiting for me. I put it on and went to my backpack and found the white hat I'd been given by the tailor in Swat. I put it on and walked down to the mosque with Muhammad Gul. It is an amazing mosque made entirely of wood from the surrounding forests. There were villages all around and this was the central mosque for all the villages. On Friday everybody came. It was packed.

"I approached the entrance with the idea that I would sit at the back, where no one would take notice of me. There were piles of shoes at the entrance to the mosque. I left my shoes and stepped in. The place was full. I was late. Suddenly, all these hands started taking my hand and pulling me and pushing me toward the front. Right behind the imam was a prayer mat. They said, 'You pray here.' I thought, 'Maybe if I keep my head down no one will notice me.' It was a very powerful moment. And then the imam delivered the Friday *khutba* (sermon). I had no idea what he was saying. He then stands directly in front of me. Everyone stands up and cries, '*Allahu Akbar! Allahu Akbar! Allahu Akbar!*' And these rough Pashtun mountain men with beards and blankets all stood side by side in lines. The imam faced the direction of prayer, raised his hands in

Takbir and called, 'ALLAHU AKBAR!' and that was it! My heart broke! I started weeping. It was all I could do to keep going through the prayer. I was totally demolished: that moment, that motion, that place. After the prayer there was the *du'a* (supplication). I was weeping uncontrollably. People were patting my hand, patting me on the back. And they kept putting money under the prayer mat. I kept protesting 'No, no! I'm from the richest country in the world!' People brought eggs and bags of grain, corn and potatoes. When I came out of the mosque people took care of all the stuff that had been given me because I was not organized enough to take care of all my new possessions! Somebody said, 'That room you're staying in is no good. I have a guest house.' Someone else said 'When you want tea come to my *chai khana*.' Another said, 'I will bring dinner from my house.' And another said, 'You come in the morning, I will teach you Qur'an.' Suddenly I had everything. Suddenly everybody took responsibility for me." This is when Kenneth Honerkamp from the San Fernando Valley became 'Abdelhadi' in the Swat Valley.

Michael: "We got to this next stop on the road back to Kalam and the driver announced that the bus could not go further because of an avalanche on the road ahead. I knew that this was a sign from God. No more consultation, no more this, no more that. I have to do what I have to do. I got off the bus at this beautiful village called Bahrayn, which means two rivers or two seas because this was where the Daral and Swat Rivers meet.

"I went to a man selling vegetables by the side of the road and sort of fell down on my knees next to him, 'I want to become a Muslim.' He said, 'What happened? Did your money run out?' In those days there were a lot of Hindus who became Muslims and people would give them alms (*sadaqa*). I said, 'No, no, I have money.' Then he immediately recited the declaration of faith (*shahada*) in Pashto and then Arabic and asked me to repeat it. The instant I did, I felt this huge weight lift off my shoulders and tears flooded my eyes.

"Suddenly there were a lot of people around me. Someone was actually cutting my fingernails which had gotten long and dirty. People were patting me on the shoulder, speaking to me with what I suppose were congratulations and praises to Allah, and then, just at that moment, the call to prayer sounded from the village. A teenage boy who I suppose had been in the group around me, spoke to me in English. 'Okay, now you must pray!' He took me up the path to this beautiful wooden mosque. There was a place where water was flowing in and running through basins carved into the flat side of a huge split tree trunk. He said, 'Wash as I do'. I didn't know what I was doing. 'Now go inside and pray with the men and just do what they're doing'. That was the beginning.

"Right after the prayer, I was asked to wait in a little room between the prayer chamber of the mosque and the door out. There was a poor, thin old man standing there too. Just the two of us. He looked cold. It was cold in those mountains in the evenings, even in the summer. I was wearing a warm vest. I took it off and gave it to him. The imam came to where we were with another man. I sensed they were talking about me. Somehow, the imam made me understand that from there on, I had a new name: 'Abdurrahman'.

"I stayed in Bahrayn until they cleared the road. I was ready to leave. The people said, 'You should stay here for the rest of your life. We have a nice girl you can marry'. That was the way the people were. There was this openness. I finally got back on the road. I didn't know whether I was really Muslim or not. I hadn't made a major ablution (*ghusl*). It was something that came out of a *hal* (state) and not out of a steady intellectual decision, but I do know that when I said the *shahada* on the side of the road with the vegetable seller, something lifted. This heaviness, as if I had been carrying a very heavy burden, it lifted. There was a feeling of great relief."

Abdelhadi: "So I moved to the new house, which was so much nicer that the tailor moved there too. During the following week I was going to the mosque and getting more organized, getting into the routine of the village and the prayers. And then, the next Friday..."

Abdurrahman: "I continued up to Kalam. I got off the bus and saw somebody I thought I knew. I said, 'Where's my friend? The tall guy'. They said, 'Oh him! Maybe he's in the mosque.'"

Abdelhadi: "The next Friday I come out of the mosque and see a group of people approaching and Michael was with them. I'm wearing Pakistani clothing and so was he. I said, 'Michael! How are you?' He said, 'My name's not Michael, it's Abdurrahman. How are you Ken?' I said, 'My name's not Ken, it's Abdelhadi'. We embraced and realized that we had both come to Islam, differently, on different paths, not in the same time or in the same place but very, very close."

Abdurrahman: "We were transformed in some essential way and we were trying to discover what the religion was by practicing it. '*Alhamdulillah*.'"

Abdurrahman stayed on for a time with Abdelhadi but eventually decided to return to America and complete his university education. He returned to California, enrolled in the University of California at Davis, married his wife, Barbara, who became Jameela, and earned his degree. The couple eventually settled down in Morocco and raised their family in Rabat, where Abdurrahman taught English. In 2009 he founded the Center for Language and Culture in Marrakesh, teaching English to Moroccans and Arabic to foreign students. With his collaborator Sidi Fouad Aresmouk, he has translated many classical Sufi texts into English.

Abdelhadi remained in Pakistan for ten years, never returning to America during that time, although he did keep in contact with his friend. He lived an ascetic life of a student (*talib*), learning in the traditional *kuttab* system, becoming fluent in Pashto.

Abdelhadi: "I became very acculturated, very Pathanized. You didn't have real schools but you had a scholar of grammar, the students would come with him and the village would feed the students. I was living on about one hundred dollars a year. They gave us food. The *Khan* (ruler) of the village would give us a new suit of clothes every six months. They would give us a pair of shoes every year. Soap every week. We only needed money for books.

"I wanted to become a scholar like my teacher but it was too late. You must start when you're very young. My teacher had studied for thirty years before he started teaching." Abdelhadi wanted to learn Arabic and realized he would never learn the language in Pakistan. Abdurrahman introduced his friend to a professor with connections in Morocco who promised to arrange a place for him at the Qarawiyyin University in Morocco.

"I asked my teacher for permission to leave. I said, 'Sidi, I'm going to 'Arabiastan' to continue my studies. Do I have your permission?' He gave his consent. I was going to put my thumb out on the road and hitchhike to Morocco but my teacher said, 'Go and say goodbye to the *Khan*' who was a very large landowner in the district where we were living. It was a feudal system. People lived on the land of the *Khan* and they would give back from the land. He also took care of the students and the teacher. I visited him. I said, 'My teacher told me to come and say goodbye. I'm going to Arabiastan to learn Arabic and continue my religious studies.' He sent his retainer out to give me some cash. A few other people gave me enough to get all the way to Morocco overland by bus."

Abdelhadi studied Arabic at the Qarawiyyin University for three years, earning the equivalent of a Bachelor's Degree. He returned to the U.S. from 1983 to 1985 to earn a Masters Degree from the University of Georgia at Athens (UGA) and then returned to Morocco to teach English at a language school in Fez and translate Arabic manuscripts. During his three years in Fez he not only sat with *fuqara* of the Harraqiyya *tariqa* and learned their traditions and knowledge, he also earned his doctorate. "I have French citizenship through my wife, so I went to Aix-en-Provence, the University of Marseille and they accepted me as a doctoral candidate. All the years I was in Fez I worked on my doctorate."

In 1999 Dr. Kenneth Honerkamp joined the faculty of the Department of Religion at the University of Georgia where he is today a full professor. He has distinguished himself as the translator of seminal texts by Sulami, and Ibn Abbad, and, most recently, Imam al-Ghazali's 'Book of Knowledge.' He returns to Morocco frequently.

Abdelhadi and Abdurrahman remain fast friends.

Get Back

"MY EARLIEST MEMORIES begin in Yemen. There were goats and donkeys. I remember an incident when one neighbor stole a goat from another neighbor. A tire was a toy for me. If I found a tire to play with, that was a good day. I remember it used to rain once or twice a year and the streets would fill with water and all the kids would go swimming in this muddy water. It was a Bedouin life. I remember a *shaykha* named Hababa as-Sufiya. She must have been about 120 at the time. It's a place where remembrance of God isn't difficult. It's just what you do. You don't work for it. Life there *is* that. At the time it was just life. It wasn't until leaving that I realized the power of it. It was the best time of my life. It's everything I want to get back. It's a place of secrets. My story is of having something, losing it, then trying to find it again and pick the pieces of the puzzle up and put them back together."

By the time Muhammad Davis was born in 1998 in San Jose, California, his parents were preparing to leave America in search of knowledge. Before he was one-year-old Muhammad was living in Damascus, where his father and mother were studying Arabic. After Damascus, the family moved to Morocco for a time, then to Sudan and then to the ancient city of Tarim in the Hadramaut in South Yemen to study the sacred sciences at Dar al-Mustafa, the new traditional school established by the Ba'Alawi scholar and sage Habib 'Umar bin Hafiz.

Muhammad's first formative years were in this austere, rarified setting, a life that revolved around prayer and remembrance. He lived there until the age of eight.

Then his father landed a job in Abu Dhabi working as media director for the Tabah Foundation, founded by the eminent Hadrami scholar Habib Ali al-Jifri. The family, which now included six-year-old brother Ahmed and four-year-old sister Fatima, moved "from a mud house to a skyscraper."

Transition

For little Muhammad and his siblings, it was a shock to the system. Although the U.A.E. is a Muslim country, "it wants to be western so bad. Most of the youth want to be western. They want to party. They want to have girl friends. In Abu Dhabi you learn that religion isn't cool. Praying isn't cool. I was only eight then but these values informed the way my eight-year-old peers acted, following the examples of older kids. It was the first time in my life when I wanted to hide my prayers. If I was playing with kids in the park and the time for prayer came, I was embarrassed to pray.

"Obviously when you're a child you don't really process these things. You just go. You're in the moment. Gradually I became desensitized to it all and it became normal. In retrospect I see the change. I was leaving what I had in Yemen and who I was and trying to become more western just because of what was around me. Looking back on it now I see Abu Dhabi as a transition period."

It was in Abu Dhabi that young Muhammad discovered *Muay Thai*— literally Thai Boxing and commonly known as kickboxing. "My dad was going to a gym and there was this small class for children on self-defense. It was just a fun activity but it sparked my interest in the martial arts."

It was also in Abu Dhabi that Muhammad started to connect with his American roots. "This was the first period of my life when we began visiting the U.S. regularly. The eight years we were living in Syria, Morocco, Sudan and Yemen we never went back to the U.S."

Reconciling the Past

Muhammad's parents "came from heavy trauma. Both had very rough childhoods and I think they both had a kind of PTSD from the way they were raised." Muhammad's mother, Nejma, is an American of Somali extraction and a direct descendant of the Prophet Muhammad, may God bless him and give him peace. Notwithstanding her noble lineage, her immediate family in America suffered from many of the ills of modern society, including alcoholism and mental illness. Muhammad's father, Mustafa, is the son of a black father and white mother who divorced when he was two. He lived with his mother, who remarried a white man. Mustafa was raised as the only black child among white siblings. His parents were heavy drug users.

"When my dad was growing up, he'd go home and there would be cocaine on the table. His parents were coked-out, out of it." Mustafa suffered from poverty and neglect. "My father had to work full time when he was twelve years-old to buy his own groceries to eat." As a teenager, Mustafa succumbed to drug abuse. At the age of eighteen, on the verge of addiction and homelessness, he tried to commit suicide and failed, and was forced by law to spend three months in a mental institution. From this low point Mustafa fought his way back and at the age of twenty-four discovered Islam and turned his life around. To do that he left America and spent nine months in the Mauritanian desert, studying with the scholar-saint Murabit al-Hajj.

Given their fractured personal histories, "when my parents came together their whole purpose was to create a wholesome, stable family unit. When you see me, and my siblings being as close to whole as you can get, having good childhoods, it's because that was at the forefront of my parents' goal in life.

"One of my earliest memories of my relationship with my father's mother and stepfather was when they visited us in Abu Dhabi. They came and gave me presents. *'You're my grandpa and my grandma. Great!'* Before that we didn't have a relationship with them because my father was still trying to heal wounds from his childhood. In Abu Dhabi was the first time he invited his mother and stepfather to visit. It was very difficult for him."

When Mustafa's mother and stepfather were in Abu Dhabi he introduced them to Habib 'Ali al-Jifri. Habib Ali is a larger-than-life, magnetic figure, radiating love, compassion and forgiveness. In a completely unexpected turn of events, in the healing presence of Habib Ali, their hearts turned. "My grandparents made the declaration of faith (*shahada*)."

After two years in the U.A.E. Mustafa and Nejma decided it was time to return home. "My parents made the decision to go back to the States because of us, out of fear of us not knowing who we are and where we had come from. We had spent ten years abroad. They felt it was time. They wanted us to know our own culture."

Whatever culture shock Muhammad experienced coming to Abu

Dhabi at age eight, was multiplied by a factor of ten when the ten-year-old landed in the U.S. "Had I gone straight to the U.S. from Yemen, I would have been totally lost. I'm able to see the benefit of Abu Dhabi now, as a transition between Yemen and the U.S. You come back to the U.S. and there's this identity crisis that happens. You're living in Yemen and you're a foreigner. You come back to the U.S. and you're a foreigner. You end up doing things to try to fit in.

"When we came back we ended up living with my grandparents for four or five months while my father got all our paperwork sorted out, transferred funds, and tried to find places to live and work. My grandparents lived in Lincoln Village Park in Sacramento," [which the Urban Dictionary describes as 'a small hood on the East Side of Sacramento. Known for drug deals, gang activity, and simply thug shit.']

"During that time, and whenever we visited my grandparents later, we had rules. We couldn't wear red. We couldn't wear blue. They were gang colors. If I wore a red shirt I would have to wear blue shoes at the same time. If I was going to walk in the park I'd have to walk a certain way. My dad came from that environment. If you go to a high school in the hood, even if you're not in a gang, you have to be associated with a gang somehow for protection. My dad went to a Crip[52] high school. He had to affiliate with the Crips to be safe, not to get shot. He'd come back from this Crip school to a Blood[53] neighborhood. They knew he was from a Crip school. When we would go back to Sac he would say, 'Yeah, I got jumped on that block. I got hit there.' We were driving past a bus stop and he said, 'That's where I saw my first murder.' In Abu Dhabi we didn't have to know where to walk. So now I'm back to the U.S. and I have to know these things. It changed me. It made me more defensive."

After a few months in Sacramento the Davis family went south to Los Angeles so that Mustafa could find work in the film industry. After two years they decided that the L.A. lifestyle, with its traffic jams and bleak, impersonal materialism, was not the way they wanted to live.

"We returned to the Bay Area where I'd been born and my dad had

---

52   Crips are one of the largest and most violent associations of street gangs in the U.S. Founded in 1969 the Crips have been involved in drug trafficking, robbery, extortion, murder, racketeering, illegal gambling and theft. Crip gang members wear red.
53   Bloods are an African-American street gang founded in 1972 notorious for its rivalry with the Crips. Blood gang members wear blue.

reconnected with his close friend Usama Canon. They had founded the Ta'leef Collective[54] together years before. In the time my family was away, the organization had grown and my dad returned to supervise media development and run things behind the scenes. That became our life. We settled in Fremont, California.

"I was about fourteen when we came back to Northern California. I was in high school. At that point, I had kind of shifted as a person. I'd lost a lot of the innocence I had as a youth, but the change happened slowly. Coming from a Bedouin lifestyle to American culture, you end up trying to find a new identity. You fight to validate your place in the country you've come to. In Yemen, I was the Western kid. Back in America I was that Yemeni kid. I was overcompensating. It manifested in the way I started to dress. Everything became about Hip Hop. For me I was still trying to hold on to my Islamic identity but in the Muslim community everything seemed to be focused on my physical appearance rather than what was inside me. I'd go to the *masjid* with my baggy pants and my necklace and my cap on backwards and I would get, 'What are you doing here, *ya akhi*, this is *haram* (forbidden).' I felt a lot of judgment and that led me to not want anything to do with those places."

Outside his close-knit family unit, Muhammad did have one constant in his life, his relationship with the Moroccan Sufi sage Moulay Hassan al-Alaoui, the son of one of the great disciples of Sidi Muhammad ibn al-Habib, may God be well pleased with them. Moulay Hassan is a spiritual guide (*murshid*) in his own right and has counseled many young acolytes, including his son-in-law 'Usama Canon and Muhammad's father, Mustafa. "I would visit Moulay Hassan regularly through all my struggles. He knew my flaws and he was always there to aid me in the most compassionate and loving way possible.

"I would say that ninety percent of the people I associated with at that time were not Muslim. In high school the friends I kept around me all had very good hearts but no spiritual grounding. I allowed myself to make compromises to who I am as a person. When you make a compromise to one of your values it becomes easier to compromise

---

54   Ta'leef Collective is an innovative initiative dedicated to serving youth, assisting newcomers to Islam, welcoming guests and building a dynamic community for Muslims in the United States. Ta'leef offers Community Care and educational programs, training courses and lead conversations around community leadership, cultural relevance and overall sustainability.

other values later on. It became a slippery slope for me and the main cause was that I wasn't fighting against what my ego (*nafs*) wanted. In Yemen, even as a child, the concept of the lower self, or *nafs al ammara*, was not difficult to understand. It's ingrained in you. So I grew up knowing that, but coming back to the U.S. I completely shut that side of me off. I didn't want anything to do with it and with spirituality in general. It started in Abu Dhabi with being ashamed to pray. In Abu Dhabi I was still praying. I would pray all five at night. In America I eventually stopped praying altogether.

From the time he arrived in the U.S., kickboxing, or *Muay Thai*, became Muhammad's refuge. He had a natural gift for it. "Coming in to what was for me a new country, I didn't have a routine. Kickboxing became a way of escape. I replaced everything with kickboxing. That became my life. I was good at it and I knew it. I didn't have to work at it to be good at it. At the same time I had this other dual life – the party life.

"I pretended to be a good Muslim kid at home. It didn't trouble me to live this dual existence. Even now I'm only revealing this to my parents little by little. It would be very difficult for them to understand that the whole time in the U.S. what they saw of me wasn't the reality. The reality was that I was having fun, going out with girls. I had a big problem with girls. Oh man, yeah, it was a big, big struggle. Now thinking back on it, I'm able to see the benefit and growth that came with it but there is also great sadness."

At this point in his story, sitting in a sweet shop in Istanbul, Muhammad began to weep with remorse.

The Party

"I was a junior in high school. There was a party. That was the turning point for me. The music was loud. Girls were dancing." Muhammad looked around the room. Eyes were vacant. "Everyone was in a state of heedlessness. They were like animals. These two girls wanted to dance with me. My friend says, 'go, go, go'. For the first time I was struck with terror. I became petrified of God's wrath. In the middle of this party I broke down and cried. I'm sitting on the floor at this party, with a loud musical soundtrack, surrounded by dancing, and I'm making *tawba*. It was as if I had just seen clearly for the first time. I was in tears for what must have been half an hour, weeping, weeping, weeping. I was shaken. My chest felt like it was split open. I left. I made a pact with God: '*Allah, I'm done. I'm not doing this anymore.*' I wanted to run to the *masjid* and make my escape but I felt a lot of judgment in those places. I needed a place to run."

Muhammad ran to the one sure thing in his life at that point. He immersed himself in *Muay Thai*. "I was naturally gifted. I knew my natural ability and because of that I'd been lazy. I didn't put in the work I needed to. I had the skills, I won matches, but I had no drive, nothing to push me. My coach had seen the talent in me at an early age but had a hard time making me work. Now for the first time in my life I felt a hunger and a desire to do well that stemmed from not wanting to go back to that old life style. It all happened within the span of a day. Before that party, I was training maybe two hours a day. After the party I was in the gym for six to eight hours every day.

"My life has been very easy. I've had a lot of things handed to me. My parents always provided me with the best life option. I've come from a life where I've been very comfortable. I've been handed most things. I became spoiled. This was the first time in my life where it was the opposite. I was fighting *for* something. With every win and with any kind of effort that I put in, I saw this in a mental map of putting as much distance as I could between me and that past life I was living. No one saw that.

"My coach is old school. He's hard. He would make us do sprints up a hill and sometimes make us sprint carrying our teammates up the hill with us. We'd run hard for six miles every day. When we'd finish the run my coach would say, 'Muhammad's gonna rest' because he knew I was lazy. But, the day after the party, when we came back from the run, the first thing I said was, 'What's next coach?'

"Muhammad Ali said, 'People don't become champions in the ring. They become champions in the gym.' I felt something take over. Something just switched on. I became a champion on that day."

Winning

The U.S. *Muay Thai* Open (USMTO) is the premiere amateur kickboxing tournament in the Americas, attracting the top amateur players from North and South America. "My coach saw the hunger that I had. It was like a light had been switched on. I was doing everything I possibly could to be the best. I would leave to the gym in the morning and wouldn't come back till the night. So my coach said, 'You know what? Let's do this tournament. It doesn't matter if you win or if you place, let's do it just to give you experience. I think it would be good for you.'

"It was a three-day tournament in Arizona. I went with my team. I was just going for experience. I went in to my first fight. I tap hands with this guy who had more experience than I did and was favored to win the fight. I don't know what happened. I was like a man possessed. I was on fire. I went into the fight and kicked his leg, which is not fundamental. You're supposed to box. I kept kicking. I kicked twelve times in a row. He went down. Everyone was in shock." The next day it took Muhammad one minute to win his fight and on Day Three he went on to become the 2016 United States *Muay Thai* Open Welterweight Champion. He was eighteen years old.

"After I won that title my life started moving fast. I started competing, moving to a higher level. I won every fight. I racked up nineteen wins and zero losses. I won my debut appearance at LionFight *Muay Thai* 36 by unanimous decision. It was broadcast on AXS TV, which was a big promotion. People could watch it online or on television. I achieved a top five ranking in California. It got to the point where I was becoming known in the martial arts world. I was a rising star. I posed for photo shoots. I landed a sponsorship contract. I would go to events and people that owned brands would give me things for free. People wanted to know me for what I'd accomplished. It was a big ego boost. Up until this point, the sport had just been fun."

Things changed.

Change

"When I first started with my coach it was all about gaining experience. My coach put a lot of emphasis on character building. 'This is going to build your character. It's going to make you a good man.' My parents appreciated that. They said, 'Go do your sport. You are with a good man.' But things began moving too fast. My coach is one of the best *Muay*

Thai coaches in North America and is very good at marketing fighters. Things became more about business, about branding and marketing. My relationship with him became less about the experience and more about winning. It even became about the way to win. My coach started saying, 'I need you to be meaner.' He would do things to make me tap into that. I was a martial artist but I didn't want to hurt anybody. I would fight and win, but let's say I hit my opponent and he was dazed. I'd hesitate. I'd let him breathe for a little bit. *I was too nice.* My coach didn't like that so he made me do things to make me be meaner. He needed me to become a killer in the ring, to have that killer instinct, but that doesn't just stay in the ring. It affects your life. *Muay Thai* is a martial art, to be sure, but it's also like a dance. There is beauty in it. But the way I was now fighting wasn't beautiful. It was vicious."

Muhammad's coach tweeted about his fighter: 'If you're an amateur and are fighting between 160-170 pounds… protect ya neck, your liver and your legs… cause he's coming for you!!! Could not be prouder of this young man!!! His future and potential is limitless.'

"I kneed my opponents. I elbowed them. I fought dirty and audiences loved me for it. They went crazy. It was toxic. That year I finished seven fights by knockout."

The World Boxing Council (WBC) is one of the oldest organizations in boxing. To be a WBC champion is huge. Muhammad Ali was a WBC champion. Floyd Mayweather Jr. was a WBC champion. "To win a WBC amateur title is the pinnacle of the sport." The WBC started a branch connected to *Muay Thai* in 2010. In 2017 Muhammad entered the WBC Amateur *Muay Thai* National Tournament, held in Tacoma, Washington. By this time he'd become a 'mean machine'. He went into the tournament as a killer.

"I sign up for my weight class and fight my first opponent. I touched gloves and went crazy. I destroyed him in a gross fashion. At one point I pushed him against the ropes and in kickboxing when you have someone against the ropes you're supposed to break. I didn't. I was elbowing him. I finished him in the first round. I knocked him out with a knee to the liver. He went down." Muhammad's future opponents were watching. The young fighter's brutality scared them off. They conceded. It was supposed to be a two-day tournament but on Day One Muhammad became the WBC *Muay Thai* Amateur Welterweight Champion. "What really was happening was that I was losing to fury."

Egomania

The WBC championship hit social media. Videos of Muhammad's fight went viral. "My fan base went up very fast, from 100 followers to 10,000. When I started out I was fighting on local stages. I wasn't fighting for the crowd. I was fighting for the love of the sport. Within the span of a year, I was fighting in front of huge crowds and it became about pleasing the crowd. It was all going to my head. When I would win a fight my phone would be going off. I'd get five hundred text messages. When I would go to a kickboxing event, I would go expecting people to recognize me. And if they didn't, '*there's something wrong with you. You need to catch up with the times. I'm Muhammad Davis!*' I'm just oozing ego. I went around thinking, '*I'm so bad.*' It messed with my psychology.

"My dad said, 'You know, you're going to have to lose at some point.' I was like, '*Whatever dad. I don't know why you're hatin'. I'm successful. I'm doing well.*'

"I was surrounded by people who were very successful in the sport, but their lifestyle was purely materialistic. At the time one of my closest friends was, without a doubt, one of the best kickboxers in the world. In *Muay Thai* he was my idol. I wanted to be what he was. He took me under his wing. He said, 'We're going to make you a superstar.' He has a good heart but he's very materialistic. When he won one fight he bought two cars to celebrate. *What do you need two cars for?* I can attest to the fact that you become like the people you keep company with. I had essentially made my coach my shaykh and my teammates my companions. I was blind to any of their flaws. I didn't know how to process success. At this point my entire value system and self worth was the sport."

Smack in the middle of his kick boxing triumphs Muhammad paid a visit to his spiritual godfather, Moulay Hassan al-Alaoui, who was staying part of every year in the Bay Area. "He said, 'You should perform a lot of *istighfar* (asking forgiveness of God).' Then he gave me an invocation to recite: *Allahumma, inni a'udhu bika min al-nafs al-ammara.* ('Oh God I seek refuge in you from the commanding [lower] self'). I would say it occasionally when I was in a spiritual mood."

New Migration

Muhammad's parents longed to reconnect with the Muslim world and seized an opportunity for the whole family to live and study in Istanbul. Muhammad rebelled.

"I said, *'No! I'm not coming. My career is here. My life is here. Why am I going to Turkey? In one year I'll be going professional and I'll be able to stay here on my own.'*

"My father was hurt. In a way it was like spitting in his face. *'I don't need you. I don't need what you have to offer. I don't need your advice. I have it all figured out.'* My dad's fathering style is that he lets you learn from your own mistakes. He was never the father to hold your hand and take you. If there's a hole in front of you, he waits until you almost fall in and then he'll catch you and say, 'See the hole?' But in that year my father felt an urgency to let me know what he had seen over the last three years, who I am and what I was becoming as a person. In my own head there was nothing wrong. *'I don't have an ego. I'm successful in the sport. You're being selfish by taking me away.'*

"My father saw what the sport was doing to me. My ego had grown so much that it was disgusting. When I would talk to people ninety percent of the conversation would be me talking about myself. My father said, 'You've lost your compassion. Where did it go?' It wasn't any one thing he said but the accumulation of his counsel began to sink in. I was still fighting, still competing, but little by little I processed what my father said and it began to make sense." Muhammad grudgingly agreed to travel with his family to Turkey. He informed his coach.

"My coach said, 'Okay, you're taking the year off. After this year you're going to go pro.' I have one more fight before I go to Istanbul and this fight brought the top contenders in the U.S. together. There were six guys in my weight class who were the top-ranked *Muay Thai* amateurs in the U.S. All of us were on the same level. The winner of that tournament would get a slot on the U.S. Olympic National Team 2024. My coach's plan was 'You do the tournament, get the slot, go to Turkey. You train in Turkey. After you finish your year you come back.' This shows you the kind of control at this level the coach has over the athlete. He's planning your life. He said, 'If you're going to take a year off, this is the only time you can do it. You can go, but after this you're not going to have time. Being a professional athlete is going to be your priority. So let this be your one-year experience of not having to deal with sport. And then you come back and go pro.'

Olympic Trial

"I go to the Olympic trials. It was a three-day tournament. There was a documentary team and they chose me as a subject for the documentary. 'We want to do a film on rising stars. Can we follow your journey?' My father said, 'Okay, follow him.' By this point I wasn't really invested in the fighting. For me it had become all about the show and the appearance of things. I'm focusing on these interviews. As they were filming my warm-ups I tried to send the message that I'm going to win this anyway so I don't need to warm up.

"The first day I won my fight by unanimous decision. I won my second fight the next day to make it to the finals."

Then Muhammad got what seemed like an extraordinary windfall. The finalist he was supposed to fight dropped out of the tournament and a fighter who wasn't considered to be a contender took his place. No contest. Muhammad was now a shoo-in for the Olympic slot. "Everyone, including the documentary team and the audience was thinking, 'This is like a free win for Muhammad.' I was thinking, 'They're just handing me the spot.' I knew I'd win. I was undefeated." Muhammad's ego was on overdrive. "Before the fight I was more concerned with how I looked to the people. 'Do I look like I'm confident? Do I look like this is going to be easy for me?' I had my gloves on, I warmed up, everything's prepped to make that long walk into those lights when something comes over me. I felt the urge to say the supplication that Moulay Hassan had given me six months before. *Allahumma, inni a'udhu bika min al-nafs al-ammara* ('Oh God I seek refuge in you from the commanding [lower] self'). Before I entered the ring, I recited the supplication the number of times he prescribed. When I stepped into that ring, everything was different.

"In the first round, I knew that this guy wasn't on my level. *'He's not even supposed to be here.'* I'm playing around, showboating, telling him to come to my corner and hit me. I'm dancing around.

"Then he hits me with this vicious right hand. I'd never been hit before in a fight. It was a shock. When I took the hit, I didn't think '*Wow, that hurt*'. I thought '*Hey, you're not supposed to be doing this.*' Then it happened again. My head rocked back. '*What is happening? How are you doing that to me?*' I get angry. Fighting with anger is one of the biggest mistakes you can make in boxing. Anger clouds your judgment. Anger gives you tunnel vision. So I came after him, hitting him, hitting him, hitting him. He took it all. At that point, I'd hit with everything that would normally drop an opponent. He wasn't fazed. He's smiling at me. He hits me with an uppercut and knocks me out cold.

"I opened my eyes. The crowd is in shock. Normally you hear cheering. It was quiet. What just happened?

"I walked out of the ring to silence. I walked into a bathroom and cried. I couldn't stop bawling. I went to the locker room. My teammates weren't there. My coach wasn't there. My father was there, standing back to give me space to breath. My phone was silent: only two missed calls and two texts, all from my mother. That put everything in perspective. That for me was the opening.

Running to Reality

"I came to Turkey, broken and humbled. When I landed, and as we were leaving the airport, we heard the call to prayer. I hadn't heard the *adhan* in twelve years. It was like an earthquake."

In Istanbul Muhammad and his family settled in Uskudar and entered a one-year Arabic program. "For me it was not only a year of learning Arabic but a year of *tazkia*, of purification of the self. It has been a year of having been broken and being forced to look at the parts of myself that I didn't want to see before. I didn't have a choice. My time in the U.S. was a cloud of smoke with a lot of noise. I didn't have to look at myself. I was in a state of distraction. I was in a fog. I came here and it was quiet. The noise is gone. The smoke is gone. *La ilaha illa 'Llah* is everywhere. This city is built on *La ilaha illa Llah*. You are forced to look at yourself. You can't run from it.

"I spent the majority of my adolescence running from the realities of my own heart and my own afflictions. Turkey is the place where I've been forced to see it. Here the flaws are laid out in front of you. Being able to see my flaws is in itself a victory but the real victory will be in rectifying my flaws and changing what is in me. Now I have to do the work.

"After I came to Turkey I found myself again, what I'd buried away for so long came back to the surface. I'm able to look at my life and see the path forward and know that's where I want to go. For me it is something of a miracle."

Part Four

OPENINGS

Discovery

AHMED MOUSTAFA WAS born in 1943 in wartime Alexandria, Egypt and grew up during a period of intense political and social upheaval. After centuries of foreign domination the Egyptian people were "united in their aspiration for a modern nation."[55] But Egypt was in the midst of an identity crisis. On the one hand, as the home of al-Azhar University, Egypt was the bastion of traditional Sunni Islam and steeped in an ancient culture. On the other hand, there was a powerful secular modernist movement led by politicians, reformers, intellectuals, writers, poets and artists who wielded tremendous influence. In the words of art historian Salwa Mikdadi, modern art was seen as "an essential visual expression of [the Egyptian] national identity and freedom from foreign oppression" and "a manifestation of the contemporaneous intellectual discourse... The acceptance of figuration and the introduction of art education in schools were sanctioned by religious scholars. This tolerant attitude toward figurative art was also the outcome of new developments in publishing and photography, as well as the revolutionary establishment of a local cinema industry. Egypt led the Arab world in these fields."[56] In consequence, Egyptian society became polarized between tradition and modernity. Although all Egyptian Muslims identified with their religion and traditional culture to some extent, the modernist educated elite turned away from the old lifestyle and embraced scientific, intellectual and cultural education and achievement, which was, ironically, derived from European models.

Ahmed was raised in the midst of this cultural ferment in post-revolution Egypt. In school he studied art and became a prodigiously gifted young painter in the European tradition, entering the Faculty of Fine Arts and Architecture in Alexandria University's Department of Painting and Stage Design in 1961. He graduated in 1966 with the 'highest

---

55   'Egyptian Modern Art' by Salwa Mikdadi, independent curator, The Met website, www.metmuseum.org
56 Ibid

national distinction in fine arts' receiving an unprecedented 98.5% for his graduation project. He personally received his Bachelor's Degree at the hand of Gamal Abdel Nasser, the President of the Republic. Ahmed settled down to life as a painter and lecturer in Fine Arts at the University of Alexandria until he was sent by the government to England to continue his studies at the Royal College of Art. When he got there he was stunned to be told that his marks were so unusually high that there was nothing they could teach him. "I obviously couldn't return to Egypt with this response. They wouldn't believe me. They would have mocked me." So Ahmed changed course and headed in a technical direction. He decided to pursue a postgraduate degree in printmaking.

Printmaking

"I went to the Central School of Art and Design, which was the best school for the study of printmaking in the U.K. I met the head of the department and told him I wanted to enroll. He said, 'You have to have a portfolio and we need to review your work." Ahmed had never studied printmaking and had no portfolio. "I said, 'Give me twenty-four hours in the studio and at the end of these 24 hours see what I have produced. Give me that chance.' He said to me, 'We've never done something like that before," but he was impressed by Ahmed's confidence and intrigued by his bold proposition. He gave him his 24 hours, lent the brash young Egyptian tools and took him on a quick tour of the engraving department to show him the basic processes.

Everything he saw on the tour was completely new to Ahmed, but as he was observing he had an insight. "The most important thing was to know the exact duration of the plate in the acid, which in itself gives you the result in terms of tonality with the ink." So when Ahmed returned to the engraving workshop for his twenty-four hours, "I took a strip of zinc and totally covered it in masking tape, leaving a portion exposed and started putting it in acid for 5 minutes, 10 minutes and so on, and every time I finished the first 5 minutes I exposed another strip and another strip. Very quickly I taught myself about the tonality of the acid."

When the head of the department came to visit Ahmed and saw what he was doing, "he said to me, 'Who asked you to do this? Where did you learn this technique?' I said, 'Nobody. I thought this was common sense.' He said, 'We spend five years teaching this common sense to students. If you can pay the tuition you are welcome to join us.' I did my postgraduate studies in printmaking at the Central School of Art and Design and earned what was equivalent to a PhD in the field."

Ibn Muqla

During the two years Ahmed was learning and mastering the technical and aesthetic skills of printmaking, he was a voracious reader of journals on art and design. In his readings he stumbled upon an article printed in 1939 that completely changed the direction of his life. The article was a discussion between the eminent 20th century scholar Nabia Abbott and Eric Schroeder, who had done his PhD thesis on the text of *Khat al-Badia* by Ibn Muqla.

Muhammad Ibn 'Ali Ibn Hassan Ibn Muqla (886-940 AD) was a significant figure in mediaeval Islam. Born in the slums of Abbasid Baghdad, he joined the Abbasid civil service as a tax collector, pursuing a career in the powerful Abbasid bureaucracy. Through patronage and forging shrewd political alliances he rose through the ranks to become Chief Minister, a position he held three times over a ten-year period— an unprecedented achievement. But by the tenth century the Abbasid Caliphate was crumbling, marked by loss of central power, instability and political intrigue.

Ibn Muqla was a Machiavellian operator who maneuvered through the shifting power struggles, falling out of favor and being restored to high position then losing favor again. His conspiratorial tendencies proved his undoing. The first time he was arrested, he was imprisoned and his right hand was cut off. The second time he was imprisoned, his enemies cut his left hand off and cut out his tongue. In this pitiful condition he died in prison.

It was not, however, Ibn Muqla's dubious and tragic political resume that gives him a lasting place in Islamic history. It was his unique and transformative contribution to the art of calligraphy. Ibn Muqla was born into a family of calligraphers and became a master calligrapher at an early age. By the Abbasid period, calligraphy had evolved from the crude and angular Kufi script to more variegated and aesthetically pleasing forms of penmanship. Calligraphy, as the expression of the Divine Word of the Holy Qur'an, had begun to form the foundation for all the arts and architecture of Islam. What Ibn Muqla discovered and introduced was a theory of proportion, which Nabia Abbott defined as 'a mathematical control of the basic forms of letters of the Arabic alphabet'.[57] This profound insight 'provided a scientific basis for the art of writing and penmanship and, in doing so, laid the foundation of the geometric principles which the art of Islam as a whole were to be guided by in their diverse manifestations.'[58]

The article he had discovered had an overwhelming impact on Ahmed. "They [Abbott and Schroeder] were talking about a subject essential to the art of Islam. Here I was, a Muslim who knew everything about occidental art, its practitioners, its main figures, its historians, and I felt ashamed that I knew nothing of what they were discussing: the method of investing Arabic letters with proportionality; the method that was responsible for the transition from the Kufic state of writing to the cursive writing, which is still with us today.

"In the absence of knowing the true nature of that particular theory, we can know nothing about the true nature of Islamic art. Most books published on Islamic art do not address its source, which is the power and proportionality invested in the 28 letter shapes of Arabic. Most of the literature speaks about domes, colors, tiles, patterns, and even definitions such as Arabesque. Geometry for the Muslim creative mind was a palette based on a Divine order. Man simply utilizes it for creative purposes, creating a piece of work that places him in proximity to his Creator."

The Voyage
Ahmed became obsessed with this new discovery, and, like a 19th century explorer, he set out on a scientific voyage that would dominate the rest of his creative life. "After I'd come across the article I went back to the Central School library and asked the librarian if he had further reading on the subject." The librarian told Ahmed that he had never heard of the subject but that, as luck would have it, Nicolete Gray, a distinguished

57   The Contribution of Ibn Muklah to the North Arabic Script, Nabia Abbott
58   The Geometrical Cosmos of Arabic Numerals, Dr. Ahmed Moustafa

scholar of calligraphy who taught at the Central School, was in the library at that moment. Ahmed was introduced to professor Gray. A specialist in Roman letters, she professed to be unfamiliar with Arabic calligraphy but she promised to ask her husband, the art historian Basil Gray who was a scholar of the history of Islamic miniatures and the head of the Oriental Department at the British Museum.

"The following week she came to me and said, 'Ahmed, Basil recommends that you should register for an MA to research the subject and explain to us what this theory is about because all academic attempts over the last one hundred fifty years have failed to uncover the true nature of this theory.' Basil Gray felt that the fact that Ahmed was a practitioner and technician and not a scholar was what was needed to solve this mystery. "'We don't have an enquiry from a practical perspective,' he said."

Ahmed accepted the challenge and launched his investigation. He visited the Zaytuna Library in Tunis, Dar al-Kutub in Cairo and the Topkapi Museum in Istanbul and collected every shred of scholarship he could find on the theory of proportional script. What he found was baffling and incomprehensible. "When you read it, it is almost like reading gibberish." Ahmed realized that the meanings were encrypted in a code language nearly impossible to decipher. Cryptology was used in mediaeval Islam to conceal political, scientific and artistic secrets and as a political operative Ibn Muqla would have been well versed in the use of code. Moreover, apart from Ibn Muqla's short treatise on proportional script, which is only a summary, nothing survives of the two more detailed books he wrote on the subject. Therefore, "the only way to gain a coherent understanding of the full range of [Ibn Muqla's] thinking is to piece it together in detective fashion from a labyrinth of citations, references and partial explanations which appear in the works of later authorities... "[59]

Ahmed spent two years sifting through fragments of scholarship scattered across a millennium. "I spent one year investigating every one of the nineteen shapes from which twenty-eight letter shapes of Arabic are based. I investigated them as individual shapes, so each one has its own drawing, it's own criteria."

59   The Cosmic Script by Ahmed Moustafa and Stefan Sperl Vol. 1, pp 23-24

He submitted his thesis ten days before he was scheduled to meet his assessors and defend it. Nicolete Gray was his tutor.

The Message

Then, five days before the defense of his thesis he had a vivid, fleeting dream that changed everything.

In the dream an anonymous figure in silhouette against a harsh backlight stood before Ahmed and said, 'Ahmed, all letters emanate from one geometrical grid'.

"I pulled my blanket over my head and tried to sleep again, but the dream kept returning. It returned three times until I left my bed. 'All letters emanate from one single grid.' I went back to my drawings and suddenly *I saw the grid!*"

In the middle of the night Ahmed drew a grid and inserted each letter of the Arabic alphabet into it. Suddenly it all became crystal clear. He had unlocked the secret that Ibn Muqla had encrypted one thousand years before. As this revelation took hold of him, he realized with a mixture of elation and dismay that the thesis he had just submitted, which was based on careful research and erudite speculation, was "total rubbish. I realized that this new discovery should have been the outcome of my investigation."

What Ahmed had discovered through this dream was "that the geometric instructions in the sources, when taken together, implied the existence…of a geometric grid based on a circle inscribed within a square, which governs the construction and visual harmony of all the letter shapes and hence functions as the unifying element in Ibn Muqla's theory."[60]

The young scholar worked feverishly over the next three days to explain and prove his new breakthrough. "In the course of those three days, I made more drawings than I had made in the previous twelve months." A secular man, a western trained artist, had the overpowering sense that he was being divinely guided.

"This was the first time in my life that I felt there was a Supreme Knower.

"I felt that the figure I had seen in the dream was a messenger who

---

60   Ibid

cared what was in my heart. He wasn't reprimanding me for not praying, for not making supplication. He was addressing my investigation."

When Ahmed reached this part of his narration to me, his voice broke and he wept at the memory.

The Challenge

"It was a humbling experience. I took all my drawings with me to the oral examination. I remember having my portfolio with me on a double-decker bus. I felt as if a devil was with me, whispering, *'Why are you taking these drawings with you? You should keep quiet about this in order to get your M.A. If you start stirring the waters as this drawing might do you're not going to obtain anything.'* I answered the devil back, saying, *'Who are you to tell me this? Why don't you ask yourself who actually commissioned that figure to appear in my dream and even to inspire that dream in the first place? This is something out of my domain and out of my control. So you shut up. I'm not after an MA or a degree or anything. I'm now after the truth about this theory.'*"

So Ahmed scrapped his thesis and presented his new revelation. After his presentation "one of the assessors opened the discussion by saying, 'Ahmad, you are not going to pass.' Nicolete Gray was looking at the floor. It was very clear that they had already made up their minds and they were not going to pass me. So I said to them, 'I'm not here to discuss whether I'm going to pass or not going to pass. I am here to tell you that you are not qualified to assess this work. I demand an arbitrator to judge the decision.' Nicolete almost jumped for joy. She said, 'Ahmad, this is your right. We are going to put your request to the Council for National Academic Awards and see who they recommend as an arbitrator.'"

Dr. Michael Rogers, who had been professor of Islamic Art in the American University in Cairo for fifteen years, was chosen to arbitrate. "He spoke to me in Arabic. He said, 'I'm not interested in the subject of this thesis but I am interested in the drawings Nicolete told me about.' I showed him the drawings. He looked at them carefully. After fifteen minutes he said, 'Ahmad, this is not an M.A. level investigation, this is a Ph.D. investigation. This is amazing because now I understand what Abu Hayyan Al Tawhidi has said about Ibn Muqla:

He [Ibn Muqla] is a prophet in the field of handwriting. It was poured upon his hand, even as it was revealed to the bees to make their honey-cell hexagonal.

"I said, 'What do you mean a PhD? I haven't yet obtained my M.A.' He said, 'You will get it with distinction but you must carry on to explain to us with some certainty where the dot comes from.'" Ahmed was awarded his M.A. His thesis was considered a serious breakthrough in the study of calligraphy.

But he was only beginning. In 1978 Ahmed embarked on a new journey of exploration—a doctoral study—to unlock all the secrets of Proportioned Script. It would take him eleven years.

In the course of his research Ahmed discovered that the traditional calligraphers he interviewed "knew nothing about the theory of proportions. They were emulators of exercising sheets but they didn't even know the foundation of these exercising sheets. It was their livelihood and that's all that they knew and they didn't want to know anything more."

The study led to "a second breakthrough no less important than the concept of the grid, namely the realization that the term *misaha* or 'surface area', which appears repeatedly in [Ibn Muqla's] instructions, must be taken literally in the sense that it refers to the actual surface area occupied by the stroke which draws the letter form concerned. It thus became clear that previous reconstructions of Ibn Muqla's theory... all had one major flaw: they were, in effect, one-dimensional and only reflected measurements relating to length but not to breadth. Once the thickness of the stroke was accounted for by correct understanding of the term *masaha*, the instructions suddenly appeared more meaningful and precise, and it became clear that Ibn Muqla's theory is far more sophisticated than had so far been presumed. Covering both the length and breadth of the stroke of the pen, it operates not in one dimension only, but in two. In doing so, it takes account of the fact that the stroke produced by the reed pen is analogous to a two dimensional ribbon which moves and twists in space as though hinting at a third dimension. This peculiar way of moving gives the stroke the tangibility in space on which its calligraphic quality depends. It is a defining feature of this art form which no theory of Arabic calligraphy can afford to ignore."[61]

What this meant was that Ahmed had to completely recreate his geometric grid from a square to a hexagon. He then "proceeded to design all letter shapes on that basis,"[62] painstakingly "reconstructing some of the more complex letter shapes."[63]

Coming to the Point

"The objective of my PhD was to know with certainty where the dot as a measuring unit comes from. It required that I should have some higher knowledge of mathematics and geometry." As it turned out, it also demanded a deep exploration of the metaphysics of Islam. Reflecting on the dot (*nuqta*) took the artist into spiritual worlds he never anticipated.

"Seen from a symbolic perspective, the emanation of the letter shapes out of a single, unified source recalls the multiplicity of creation brought forth by the oneness of the Creator. Both the seminal dot and the *alif* figure are symbols of the One in theosophical[64] writings. The Islamic theosophical tradition provides numerous...reflections on the nature of the dot and its relationship with the *alif* and the letter shapes." Ahmed realized that the "dot as the smallest building block...appears like the manifestation of a universal abstract symbol—the point... The point is a one-dimensional, disembodied entity, while the seminal dot traced by the pen is its concrete, two-dimensional embodiment. Both represent sources of emanation: the scribal dot for the letter shapes, and the abstract point for the entirety of space."[65] His quest to understand the *nuqta* in its most profound meaning exposed Ahmed to the writings of the great scholar and spiritual master Muhyid'din Ibn 'Arabi.

"He [Ibn 'Arabi] describes the dot (*nuqta*) as the *ruhaniyyat al-alif taqdiran*, which may be translated as 'the spiritual essence of the *alif* through ordained measurement'. The term *taqdiran* here evokes Qur'an 25:2, which describes God as *'measuring out all things to perfection'*. Applied

---

61   The Cosmic Script Vol. 1 pp. 27-28

62   Ibid

63   Ibid pp.29

64   In this context the speaker refers to 'theosophical' as what the Oxford Dictionary defines as a philosophy 'maintaining that a knowledge of God may be achieved through spiritual ecstasy, direct intuition, or special individual relations,' not the 19th century spiritualist movement associated with Madame Blavatsky.

65   The Cosmic Script Volume Two by Ahmed Moustafa and Stefan Sperling, pp. 585

to the human sphere, it recalls God's command to David that he should *make coats of mail and measure out the chain-links well (qaddir fi s-sard, 34:11)*. The context of the phrase suggests that David is in effect being urged to observe the well-measured apportionment which mankind should aim for in all pursuits, not only in physical manufacture but also in ethical dealings. By truly observing the right measure, humans engage in an act of spiritual devotion, for in doing so they emulate the Creator, who is the source of all measure. As the fundamental unit of measure of the Proportioned Script, the dot is a symbol of such divinely sanctioned apportionment. It measures out the correct dimensions of *alif*, and can therefore constitute its 'spiritual essence'.

"As for the *alif* itself, Ibn 'Arabi sees its relationship to the other letter shapes as equivalent to that between the *qutb*, the Perfect Man and mystical paragon of the age, and the rest of mankind. The *alif* and the *qutb* share a quality he describes as *qayyumiyya*, which in the literal sense denotes the ability to stand up straight without support. Thus it points to a physical similarity between the two: the *alif* is formed of an upright stroke, while the term *qutb* literally means 'pole' or 'axis'. The metaphorical meaning Ibn 'Arabi intended is best understood by reference to the divine attribute *Qayyum* to which it clearly alludes. The latter denotes God's self-sustaining constancy which depends on nothing else, while all else depends on it. Both the *qutb* and the *alif* mirror this quality in their respective domains: the *qutb* through being the spiritual exemplar which all others need, while he is not in need of them; and the *alif* because—in a phrasing which clearly recalls Ibn Muqla—all other letters are composed of it and derived from it, while it does not derive from them. Through its 'self-sustaining force' (*qayyumiyya*), and through the 'spiritual essence' (*ruhaniyya*) it is granted by the dot, the *alif* becomes at the level of the letter shapes, the equivalent of the Perfect Man and a pointer to the divine presence."[66]

This abstruse and complicated quest for the truth of Qur'anic lettering utterly transformed Ahmed Moustafa's life. "I took an oath between me and my Creator, to try to be a better man, to have good conduct in everything." He gave up drinking completely. He began to pray sporadically. With single-minded intensity he abandoned everything

---

66 Ibid p. 584

that did not lead to his path of discovery. It was for him a spiritual journey.

The Artist

At the same time, and throughout this intense period of research and academic preparation Ahmed supported his family through what became a spectacularly successful design practice. By 1983 he had completely abandoned representational (occidental) art forms and devoted himself exclusively to the creation of complex, layered works of calligraphic art using silkscreen and other printmaking techniques. His works were virtuoso *tours de force* that attracted international acclaim and clientele that included royalty, philanthropists, industrialists, art collectors and cultural institutions. He had by this time become recognized as a leading expert in the art of lettering although he considers himself an artist, not a calligrapher.

Then one night he had a curious dream that left him giddy.

Elephants Can Fly

"I found myself riding an elephant. The elephant is flying, taking me to greater and greater heights. My hair was flowing behind me. I remarked on the irony. 'To fly on an elephant! How was this heavy, flying elephant going to land?' Suddenly the elephant landed in a very peaceful manner but upon a very weird landscape: there were incredible well-paved highways with towering lampposts stretching out to infinity. There were no [distinguishing features] other than a mountain. The elephant left me there.

"I woke up."

Ahmed had no idea what the dream meant. That morning, while he and his wife had breakfast, the phone rang. The call was from 'Abdul Wahab 'Abdul Wasi, Saudi Arabia's Minister of Hajj and Awqaf. "Dr. Moustafa, we would like you to participate in the washing of the Ka'ba."

He had reconnected with his inherited faith, but in truth, he didn't know much about it. He was praying "on and off, really. I wasn't strict. At that time I didn't even know what 'washing the Ka'ba' meant.

"I said to him, 'washing what?'" The Minister didn't quite believe his ears. "He said, 'It sounds as if you just got up. I will ring you in an hour. Perhaps you will be more awake.' During that hour I contacted a friend of mine who was very pious. I asked him, 'Is there such a thing as *ghaseel al-Ka'ba?*' He said (with great emotion), 'Only the most fortunate people have the opportunity to participate in this symbolic act.'" It began to dawn on Ahmed that he was being offered a sacred opportunity.

"When the Minister's office called back, I asked, 'Why do I deserve such an honor?' They said, 'We have a problem inside the Ka'ba. We have a shaft with a spiral staircase leading to the roof and we wanted suggestions on how to make this shaft, which is constructed in T section steel and marble to appear truly worthy of such a place.'" Ahmed immediately agreed. He was then told that they had scheduled a flight for him for seven o'clock that evening. "I said, 'Are you serious? I have no visa.' They said, 'Everything is prepared. Just send your passport by courier and you will receive your visa and ticket.'"

By seven o'clock that evening Ahmed found himself on a Hajj plane surrounded by pilgrims. All the passengers were in *ihram*. "I didn't even know what an *ihram* was. I was the only one in a business suit." When Ahmed arrived in Jeddah everybody left the Hajj terminal except for him.

He waited all alone in the vast terminal. He didn't know who was meant to receive him or if anyone was actually waiting for him. Finally someone approached him diffidently. "Are you by any chance Dr. Ahmad Moustafa?" Ahmed confirmed that he was. "In a gentle, reproachful way, he said, 'Doctor, where is your *ihram*?' I said to him, 'What do you mean, *ihram*? I was invited for consultation on a particular issue and here I am.' He said, 'But Sidi, this issue is inside the Ka'ba.' Ahmed's guide, 'Abdullah, couldn't believe that his charge had not even this basic understanding of Islam.

"I said, 'Please, brother Abdullah, I want you to consider me a total outsider who knows nothing. Please consider me an idiot and please help me get through this experience intact and to do it well.' Then 'Abdullah smiled and said, '*Abshir, abshir.* (I give you good news.) Come with me.' It was something like four o'clock in the morning. He bought me an *ihram* and flip-flops (*shabaship*) and took me to the hotel and told me exactly what to do and how to do *ghusul bi niyyat al ihram* (full ritual ablution with the intention of entering *ihram*)."

Inside

When Ahmed entered the shower to purify himself in preparation for donning the *ihram*, his heart burst. The floodgates opened. He began to weep. "I had never cried in my life the way I cried in the shower. As if I was newly born. My eyes were inflamed with anguish. I performed two prayer cycles with the intention of entering into *ihram*."

'Abdullah drove Ahmed to Makkah Al Mukarrama. He advised him to stay awake and continue reciting 'Labbayk Allahumma Labbayk...' By the time he arrived in Makkah he was overwhelmed with emotion. "Tears were flowing from my eyes without control." In this fragile state, Ahmed was introduced to one of the Banu Shaybah, the family that had held the keys to the Ka'ba since the time of the Prophet Muhammad, peace be upon him. "He embraced me with a big hug and said, 'Please stay as close to me as my shadow. Forgive me if I am not paying attention to you.' They awaited the arrival of the designated member of the royal family, the al-Saud, to give permission to begin the Hajj season. A large circle of high-ranking army personnel was assembled around the Ka'ba. Outside the circle, people continued to make their circumambulations. I was standing there next to a high-ranking officer until the royal figure arrived. They put up an ordinary ladder and I was the third person on the ladder after the key holder and incense burner carrier. The key holder opened the door and the incense burner carrier stepped in. I stepped inside the Ka'ba, trying to hold myself together. Burning incense blew into my face and that was the final blow. I entered a state I had never experienced before; I began to lose consciousness."

Ahmed fainted within the four walls of the Ka'ba in the crush of dignitaries and the attendants who were washing the interior walls of the ancient House of God. He was revived by water that splashed on his face from the ritual washing. He came to completely disoriented; he didn't know where he was. "I opened my eyes and asked the first person I saw, 'Where is the *qibla*?' He said to me, 'My son, you are inside the *qibla*. This is the only place on earth you can pray in any direction you like.'" And this is what Ahmed did. He prayed two cycles of prayer (*rakas*) in each outward direction.

"They handed me a tape measure. The minute I looked at it I knew exactly what to do. I didn't need to take measurements or anything. I had the answer."

When Ahmed descended from the interior of the Ka'ba he set out to make his first circuit of God's House, clockwise, in the wrong direction! A member of the entourage gently corrected him and they proceeded to make the *tawaf* with the other pilgrims. He joined the entourage in kissing the Black Stone. He knew nothing about it and assumed it was just one of the building blocks of the House. "So I kissed the Black Stone and somehow I felt sorry that here I was granted the honor of being in this place but was not prepared for it.

"When I met the Minister, I told him that I had to go back to London. He was surprised. He said, 'Aren't you going to perform Hajj?' I said to him, 'Hajj has to be performed if I invite myself to perform it, not by an invitation from a third party.' He said, 'You are absolutely right.'"

The Elephant's Landing Pad

Ahmed returned to London, set down the solution he had realized inside the Ka'ba and sent it to the Minister of Hajj and Awqaf. Then he tried to absorb what had happened to him on his lightning journey to the epicenter of Islam. "I spent one whole year contemplating my experience. The next year I performed the Hajj with my mother. After the third day of stoning (*jamrah*), walking back to our tent, I suddenly found myself standing before the very place that the elephant landed! I stood there, speechless, this time of course, it was full of people, but it was in Mina. I said to my mother, 'I saw this place in a dream one year ago but this is the first time I see it in reality.' She looked at me. She didn't ask me what I meant. She just said, 'My heart and my Lord are happy with you.'"

And again, for the second time in his narration to me Dr. Ahmed Moustafa, the distinguished artist, intellectual and scholar, now in his eighth decade, broke down and wept at the memory.

Sacred Meaning

His exploration into the secrets of Arabic lettering and Proportioned Script led this gifted secular artist into the depths of faith. His voyage of discovery didn't end when he received his PhD in 1989. He continued his explorations and applied his learning to his works of art. In 2005

Dr. Ahmed Moustafa set to work with his collaborator Dr. Stefan Sperl on what became a monumental, groundbreaking two volume, study, exquisitely illustrated, of the sacred art and science of Proportioned Script based upon Dr. Moustafa's definitive investigation.

He attributes his discovery to his "glimpse between the unknown and the sensual world. I find it amazing, this meeting point between the sensual world and the unknown. If man can experience a glimpse—just a glimpse—of that meeting point, that's enough for him to understand what righteousness is about. It is an Opening (*Mufatah*).

"[For me] it manifested in Hajj but originated in a dream."

Recognition

IN LONDON I gave a book reading. Throughout, and during the question and answer session that followed, I kept returning to the face of a woman in the audience. It was like a haunting. Her face was luminous, like a moon. I had met her before, of that I was absolutely certain, but I couldn't for the life of me remember how, when or where. It was all I could do to concentrate on the gathering. When the evening ended audience members surrounded me to continue the discussion, but my mind was on the mysterious face in the crowd. I managed to pull away and scanned the room in hopes of catching her before she left. I found her outside.

"I know you. Where have we met?"

She looked surprised. "We've never met."

"But I recognize you."

And that was how we met… in this world.

Yasmin Khatoon was born in the seaport city of Southampton into a first generation immigrant family that retained strong ties to their homeland in East Pakistan, what became Bangladesh after the War of Independence in 1971. Immediately after the war, when she was still a baby, her mother took her and her older sister back to live in Bangladesh and she grew up as a Bengali child until the age of nine, when the family rejoined her father, who was working as a chef in London. It was a rough transition for the young Bengali girl.

"As a child you don't prepare yourself that you're leaving everything and everyone you know behind. We were told that we were going to a land of opportunity and as a child you kind of go along, not realizing the emotional impact of the loss. I didn't understand it at the time. I just knew there was something missing, the sense of belonging. She suffered from what she calls 'migration trauma.' "I remember crying myself to sleep at times, the loss of it, the transition. You've got to find yourself a place of belonging again.

"I grew up with elemental weather in Bangladesh - the Monsoon weather. Bangladesh is a country that overflows with rain. Sometimes we were trapped in the house for days because the water was flooding to knee height around the house. Nature and the environment had a huge impact on who I am. I was a bit of a tomboy, climbing trees, running with kites. I lost part of myself when I came to Britain, with four bedroom walls and the concrete streets of London."

To begin with, even though she was a British citizen, Yasmin spoke only Bengali when she returned to England so she had to start learning English. "I picked it up fast because of my love of reading." But almost immediately she had to face a more intractable reality: racism.

"When I was about eleven I was walking home from the playground when two white girls charged at me and pushed me to the ground and started beating me and calling me names. I didn't know what to do. I was in shock. I couldn't understand why I was rejected because I was Asian. I remember walking home crying and telling my dad.

"He reassured me. He said, 'Don't worry, it'll be fine.' I think about my dad, when he came here in the fifties with limited qualification and little knowledge of English, I feel sad for him because he must have been treated very badly. He left everything behind to make a better life for us. He was alone for so many years."

In Yasmin's household Islam was "something intuitively there as part of life. It wasn't something where at home our parents said, 'We're Muslim, we're going to talk about what that means, you can do this, you can't do that.' It was just part of the environment. It gave our lives a spiritual quality. We fasted and prayed but it wasn't something we talked about. It was just there in the background, fasting, praying, going for Eid, learning 'Arabic in the morning, Qur'an classes. It was something that was encouraged, but, looking back, I think it was more cultural than religious.

"Being a migrant, it forces you to stay close to your ethnic community. We didn't really go out like traditional English girls. We stayed home. We played together. We watched the telly. Our social activities revolved around our extended family. We would visit our aunts, uncles and cousins, cooking together, talking. I had lots of girls around me from my extended family and we've stayed connected with one another. That was our social life. There wasn't anything out there. We would watch other people going out through our windows. It was another life to us, another culture. It wasn't our identity and that was fine. I was protected. I had food on the table. My parents always made sure to show affection. Not so tactile as in Western culture. English families did that. I saw them kissing their kids at the school gate. I used to think about that, how our expressions of affection were different."

But Yasmin was different from many other Bengali girls. "I always aspired to do something different with my life rather than to end up a traditional housewife in an arranged marriage. A lot of my friends had arranged marriages and didn't have any aspirations beyond that. I was always curious. I wanted to make something more out of my life."

She attributes her independence to her father. "He always encouraged us. 'Ah, if I knew the English language the way you speak, I would be able to do so much more.' He encouraged us to get a higher education."

Yasmin attended the School of Oriental and African Studies (SOAS), University of London with a major in history. "The fact that I had another cultural identity, I was finding myself through the study of history. It wasn't really a career I wanted out of it. It was very personal."

At university she met the man she would marry. "He was Bangladeshi; the same culture. We were introduced through mutual friends. We liked each other. He proposed to my father and my parents agreed and we got married after I graduated." It didn't last.

"I was brought up to believe that you go to university, you meet someone, or it's arranged, you get married and settle down. And I suppose part of me wanted that." Yasmin became pregnant almost immediately after the wedding but within one year the marriage was on the rocks.

"We were young. We were naïve. We were incompatible. I knew what I wanted in life. I was confident. I had traveled around as an undergrad, doing things that many Bangladeshi girls didn't do back then. My husband liked that I was independent but ultimately wanted a submissive Bengali girl that fit into his family. He tried to force that on me. I was living with his extended family. They didn't like that I was so independent and the marriage quickly started falling apart. We were together less than a year."

In the end her husband walked out on his wife and baby daughter after a quarrel and disappeared for months. Yasmin's world was abruptly shattered. "My daughter was only a few months old. I was still post-natal. Suddenly I was divorced with a child. *That's not who I am. What am I going to do with myself? How do I manage this?'* I was abandoned at twenty-four. I was a single mother.

"For a long time I was angry with men being able to do this. They could decide on my daughter's life. My in-laws could decide to influence their son. It seemed to me that it was easy for men to walk away from their responsibilities. I had so many plans for my life and all of a sudden they were taken away. My role became to survive the day, raising a child on my own. I was angry. I was frightened. 'How can I do this on my own? What do I know about being a parent?' I was petrified. 'Will I survive this? *O Allah what do I need to do to bring some peace and happiness into my life?'*

"For my family it was very difficult. In Asian cultures people talk a lot. There's a lot of peer pressure. I fell into this cultural trap, feeling that I had brought shame on my family with my divorce.

"I felt that I'd let my father down. I felt that I'd lost his respect. I was his bright child. I was given so much. He was so proud of me. Suddenly, I come back with a baby in my arms, saying, 'Dad, I don't know what to do.' I felt I'd let my parents down.

"My father tried not to make me feel that I was a disappointment, bless him. But in the early stage people would ask him, 'Why is your daughter back at home? Why is she divorced with a child?' And he didn't know how to respond to that. In my community at that time divorce was seen as a disgrace."

Yasmin's personal misfortune propelled her in a new direction. She pulled herself together and set up a community project to help single mothers raise their children. In the process she found her calling. "I witnessed so much pain and sadness." Hearing the stories of these women awakened a desire to alleviate the traumas of women in distress. Through this work Yasmin discovered systemic family psychotherapy and fell in love with it. She went back to study and train for six years.

"Without my parents I wouldn't be where I am today. I wouldn't have been able to train and qualify as a psychotherapist with a young baby to bring up while working full time. Most of the time my dad would pick my daughter up from school while I was working and studying. I didn't have to cook in the evening. I would come to my parents' house every day and have supper. We would go back to our flat, sleep there and start the whole process all over again."

Yasmin discovered an empathy for the unfortunate "through the personal challenges I faced in my own life: as a child, struggling with the emotions of loss and migration and the impact it had on me; as an adult, trying to fit in to the UK, not knowing how; through my university experience; and through the breakdown of my marriage. I had to confront the feeling of alienation; that I don't fit in, I don't belong."

When she qualified as a psychotherapist she not only entered a new profession but set out on a journey of self-discovery. "In my training I took my first step into the process. What was missing from that was faith. My training was very western. Very much centered and couched around the ideas of science since the Enlightenment, which is what Freud and others followed: the duality, that mind and body are separate. Faith and spirituality were more or less absent from the process."

Spirituality and faith crashed into Yasmin's life with brute force. Her father was diagnosed with terminal cancer. "It was my first real, meaningful encounter with death. I had to face it. My father was dying." This man who had been her pillar of strength, her protector, her guiding light, was "fading away, skin and bones, in front of us." In the trauma of loss Yasmin reevaluated her life, asking, "What does death mean? What does it mean that I am going to lose my father? I remember thinking, 'I have to live every second of this year, every breath that I take is his breath. I must live because he is going to die, I must live for him to make it count.' So I used to think that every breath I'm taking, I am racing against time. Somehow this had to mean something."

In retrospect this was the beginning of Yasmin's spiritual journey. The aspiration of the people of the Path is to become slaves of the moment (*abeed al-waqt*) and this race against time, this acute awareness of each passing second, of each breath, established an interior dynamic that launched her search for something that transcends death.

When Yasmin's father passed away "we turned my father onto his side, facing the *Ka'ba*. We closed his eyes. I'd been repeating *La ilaha illa 'Llah* for three or four days and it pierced my heart. I thought, 'How can I stay connected to my dad between this world and the Next? How can I understand his existence and his loss?'" Up until the death of her father Islam had been for Yasmin an identity and a fallback in times of crisis. "I would pray when I felt the need and then stop. I didn't cover my hair. After my dad died I began to read the Qur'an. I began to pray again. I began to attend the mosque and listen to discourses. I began to learn Arabic. When I returned to work I covered my hair as according to the *Sunna*."

Yasmin began reading spiritual literature: Rumi, 'Abdul Qadir al-Jilani and others. She read 'The Secret of Secrets' by Shaykh 'Abdul Qadir al-Jilani over and over again.

In 'The Secret of Secrets', al-Jilani refers to the Hadith *Qudsi*, where God speaks through His Messenger, peace be upon him:

> Man is My secret and I am his secret. The inner knowledge of the spiritual essence ('ilm al-batin) is a secret of My secrets. Only I put this into the heart of My good servant, and none may know his state other than Me.

"There was another passage in The Secret of Secrets, relating the saying of the Prophet, peace be upon him, that really made me stop and think:"

> One moment of contemplation is better than seventy years of worship.

She began to listen to the devotional songs, the *qawwal*, of Nusrat Fateh Ali Khan. She attended discourses all over London.

I met Yasmin about this time. On the surface she seemed to be dabbling in spirituality, randomly attending lectures and reading. But I sensed that there was a deep, almost frantic, longing just beneath the surface that impelled her toward some kind of path. I gave her a course of *dhikr* to perform and recommended books to read and spoke with her every so often.

Suddenly, out of the blue, Yasmin decided to visit Morocco on her own. This was so extraordinary for a prim, conservative Muslim woman who had never visited an Arab country that I volunteered to meet her in Morocco and take her to visit spiritual masters in the Sufi tradition, to make sure that her journey was safe and easy.

192

The sages advise:

> Sit with the masters, drink in their *baraka*, for their mere presence radiates such light that whoever is with them is penetrated by it through and through.[67]

I wanted Yasmin to be penetrated by the *baraka* of these masters.

Then she got cold feet and cancelled. And that, I thought, would be that. After she backed out I assumed that my intuitions about her might have been wrong; that she really was simply dabbling in spirituality as many do.

But this wasn't the case.

"I felt that I was on the verge of great change. I'd been going through these leaps and leaps over the year. I was thinking something's got to happen. The tension was building. I just thought, 'I can't to this now. I'm not ready.'"

But then Yasmin changed her mind and hopped a flight to Fez. "I knew I had to go. I didn't know why but I had to go. And I was really quite scared because I was going alone and I'd never been to Morocco. I didn't know anyone. I traveled at night so I call it my *'isra'*, my Night Journey. I landed late. I was really scared but I prayed to Allah, *'I trust in You to look after me and protect me. I'm here for whatever the purpose You've planned for me.'*

Yasmin had let me know she was traveling at the last minute and I arranged for a close friend and experienced faqir to meet her, translate for her and accompany her to visit the men of God.

Yasmin took a taxi to the hotel she had booked. She had the number of a young man who belonged to the Naqshbandi *tariqa* living in Fes, given to her by his sister. Yasmin texted him and he invited her to stay with his family. While in Fez she visited a spiritual teacher.

"We went to his house and as soon as I walked in I felt something. He reminded me of my father, my uncles and my grandfather. 'Oh my God, he could be someone from my family.' He was majestic. I sat down. The introduction was done. I greeted him and when I looked at him, I began to cry. I just sat there crying. He asked me who I was, who was my father. I told him my father had passed away. He asked me why I had

---

67 From 'Sufi Sage of Arabia Imam 'Abdallah ibn 'Alawi al-Haddad' by Mostafa al-Badawi

come. I said, 'I don't know, I'm here to find something.' He spoke to me. His words were wise. He passed me incense burning in a *mabkhara*. A young man was trying to pass a gift to me and the Shaykh said, 'No, no, I want to give it to her directly.' So I went forward to receive it from him. I felt a connection. Something touched me deeply and I wept again. I felt that I had come home. Something happened and I couldn't put it into words. I felt I was at home."

Yasmin took her leave in a cathartic state. A few hours later she met my friend who had come from Casablanca to take her to a great teaching shaykh in Meknes. When she met the shaykh she was, again, overcome with weeping. "He was so gentle but his presence was like a whoosh, a force."

Yasmin stayed at the shaykh's home for three days.

"The whole time I felt very looked after spiritually and I was rich with this. The first night I had a dream but I didn't tell the shaykh. On the last day before we were to leave he asked, 'Did you have any dream while you were here?' I said, 'Yes.' He said, 'Tell us your dream.'

"*In the dream an old man came to me. He was wearing white cloth across his shoulders and wrapped around his waist and he had a staff. He wore nothing else. He took me by the hand and we walked up some steps. We climbed over this stage-like platform and we looked out at this beautiful ocean. He said, 'And so what do you see?' And he pointed with his finger and said, 'That's your star' I looked across the ocean full of little star-like flowers and lights floating on the water. Wonderful white doves were circling. And everything was beautiful. The stars were just wonderful. 'They're all beautiful but which one is my star, which one?' I asked. I couldn't understand because the stars and the doves were here close around me. He says 'Yours is the brightest one'. I said, 'Which one is the brightest one?'*

"'And I woke up.'

"The shaykh and your friend entered into an ecstasy. They said, 'You have had a great dream.' Your friend said, 'This is the kind of dream that kings and queens wish for. You are so blessed.'

"Then the shaykh asked if I had performed *Hajj*. I said, never. He encouraged me to perform the *wird* of Sidi Muhammad ibn al-Habib and gave me the prayer on the Prophet, peace be upon him, to perform. He said, 'You will see him in your dreams.' He said, 'Whatever you've seen you've been blessed. It is a great gift.' Your friend confirmed the shaykh's counsel to keep to the *Salat an-Nabi*. 'He has seen him many times. I have made this *du'a* and I have seen him too, and if you recite this prayer you will see him as well. May Allah bless him and give him peace.' They spoke in Arabic with excitement. I didn't understand. Your friend briefly translated that they were both very pleased. I felt very nourished.

In Fez Yasmin had another dream. "I saw myself in a shower. Water poured over me, washing and purifying me and I was told 'All your sins have been washed away by that water. You've been cleansed. Your sins have been washed away and you're blessed.'

"I feel that Allah has been knocking on my door for some time now, perhaps all my life. *'But you just haven't recognized Me,'* He says, *'You haven't recognized Me. You keep waiting but I have been there all along.'"*

Fifteen Degrees to the Left of Kensington Park Road

DR. ANN COXON is a kind, soft-spoken neurologist and general practitioner in her late seventies. A gifted and compassionate Harley Street physician, her practice has attracted a vast and stellar list of patients that includes movie stars, divas, tycoons, royalty, politicians and of course many ordinary people who trust both her professional integrity and her medical acuity. Privately she leads a life suffused with a deep, abiding spirituality. Raised a Catholic, Dr. Coxon is a devout, practicing Muslim. Her journey is worth a story.

For starters, she had intoxicating origins.

Ann was born in 1940 in Saigon in French Indochina. "Dad ran a cigarette factory there. The Japanese were invading. My mum was heavily pregnant with me and went to the ship to leave and was told, 'We're not taking anyone who's going to have a baby. We don't have the facilities,' so my dad and my brother took the ship while my mum took a friend and a bottle of gin and drove over some very rough ground to escape overland. She went into labor, having drunk the bottle of gin. They went to a local obstetrics unit along the way and were lucky enough to find a midwife in the process of stealing all the abandoned equipment. Mum bribed the midwife to stay and deliver me. I was officially born drunk.

"We left on the last ship out of Saigon that was not torpedoed by the Japanese and many of my parent's friends who dragged their feet because they had a good life there had a terrible fate. I was always aware of what might have happened had my parents stayed."

Cigarettes and Matches

Ann's father hailed from British aristocracy. "Mine is a large and well-known aristocratic family. My cousin is Lord Cadogan. My dad was the first member of his family to go to work. He was what they called 'a gentleman.' His father was an artist and failed to contribute to the exchequer of the family but there were sufficient trust funds to pay for my father's education. Dad found himself leaving public school as an

English gentleman but unable to work in England because he was too much of an English gentleman to go into trade. So he went to Belgium and got work on the shop floor in the cigarette industry. He ended up as chairman of British-American Tobacco."

Ann's mother was a third generation American from German immigrants. Her grandfather, Henry C. Traute, made his fortune as a salesman for the Diamond Matchbook Company. According to the arcana of matchbook lore, in 1902 young Traute came up with the idea of printing advertisements on matchbook covers. He had a lithographer reprint a magazine ad for Pabst Beer, took it to the Brewery's headquarters in Milwaukee and landed an order for ten million matchbooks. Traute managed to convince bar owners to give matchbooks away with the aim of doubling tobacco sales. Bull Durham, a tobacco company, gave Traute an order for thirty million matchbooks. In those days matchbooks had the striking surfaces inside the flap. What this meant was that you could set the whole matchbook on fire by striking a single match. Ann's grandfather further secured his place in matchbook history by coming up with the idea of putting the striking surface on the outside of the matchbook.

"He made his fortune and ended up with a house on Park Avenue in New York. That was the world my mother was born into, a sophisticated *nouveau riche* life. Dad made cigarettes, Mum's father sold matches. Mr. Cigarettes married Miss Matches."

After their escape from Saigon, Ann's family settled in Los Angeles for the duration of the War. Her father enlisted in the British Army. "They asked him what he did for a living and he said, 'I make cigarettes' and they said, 'Okay, we don't want you to shoot anyone. We want you to make cigarettes for the British troops.' They'd found a disused Italian cigarette factory in Eritrea and Dad spent the rest of the war there making cigarettes for the army."

Egypt

Ann's family left L.A. soon after the war in 1945. Her father had relocated to Cairo to run British American Tobacco operations in Egypt. "So I was brought up in Cairo. We started off in the district of Maadi, which was lovely." She remembers the beauty of the *adhan*, the Muslim call to prayer. "I loved the *adhan!*" And she remembers the family's Sudanese cook with fondness. "I completely trusted him. He wouldn't harm a fly." Otherwise, Ann's childhood memories of Egypt were marked by peril. "You had to shake your slippers in the morning to make sure there were no scorpions in them. And sometimes you'd go into the shower room and there would be a cobra coiled up on the floor." More dangerous than the occasional cobra was the anti-British insurgency. Nationalism and anti-colonialism boiled over in postwar Egypt. For safety reasons Ann's family moved from the leafy suburb of Maadi to Gezira Island "where things were safer because they could raise the bridges to the mainland. On one occasion my brother and I were put into a taxi to go to church or something like that. The taxi was going in the wrong direction and my brother said to me, 'You've got to jump out.' So there were kidnappings. On this occasion nothing happened."

On another occasion something did. "I was downtown at a hairdressing salon with my mother. I told my mother that I could hear bumble bees and my mother said, 'Nonsense, there are no bumblebees anywhere.' But then the lady hairdresser suddenly told everybody to be quiet. And there were bumblebees! It was the sound of rioters approaching. The hairdresser panicked and ordered everybody to go home. But she couldn't do anything with my mother and me because we had to cross the town to get to the island so she put each of us into a basket and threw dirty laundry on top of us. I remember I could see through the basket. I heard the noise of all the windows being smashed and the mirrors being smashed and a lot of voluble Arabic and people walking past the baskets but nobody opened them. Even though I was only six years old I knew not to make a sound. This was serious." The incident convinced Ann's parents to send her to boarding school back in England.

The Candle and the Priest
"I was sent to a Catholic boarding school. For me it was a deep shock because I'd been in affluent surroundings and suddenly I was in postwar Britain. The school was a Victorian priory with extensive grounds. It didn't have heating because in the postwar years there was no money for fuel. You had to chip the ice off the windows to put water in your jug in the morning. It was horrible. I was unhappy. I was regarded as a

spoilt American brat and bullied mercilessly. But there was one place where I felt utterly at home and I went there as often as I could. That was one of the side chapels in the church where there was always a candle. When I looked into that candle I didn't know what it was that I saw, but whatever it was, I felt completely at peace and completely safe. I didn't have a sense of a personal God as such at that time but we had a priest, who's name was Father Damien. His skin and hair were so white. His neck was scraggy and his white collar much too big. He seemed to be already dead and coming down from heaven to teach us. At the beginning of every lesson Father Damien would make us put our heads on our hands on the desk and in a very sweet voice he said, 'Now remember, God is in heaven and He is all around you and He is within you and He loves you, and always will.' That was the beginning of every lesson. And that, plus the candle, never left me.

"My great aunt was a nun and she echoed that level of spirituality. But because of the rules of the convent (she was in an enclosed order) I was only allowed to see her once a week for only one hour, which started at three o'clock on a Sunday afternoon. So even at that point I realized that religion had rules, which didn't seem to make too much sense to me. I didn't see why the only member of my family that I had was someone I couldn't see except for one hour a week. I think I started to question the difference between my natural mystical understanding of the presence God and what I saw as the rules governing religious expression in society and ritual tradition. I don't think that questioning has ever stopped."

Hidden Treasure

Ann was transferred to another school. She was a bright student who ended up as head girl but, away from her parents and without any emotional anchor, she began to misbehave. One of her classmates later described her as 'feisty and daring'. Although her new school "had the ritual of religion, it didn't have the soul of religion that I'd had back in my other school with Father Damien." So Ann behaved badly. "In the refectory, the eating area, they served chocolate sauce ahead of the pudding, we had meat with gravy. So I put chocolate sauce on my beef, pretending that I didn't see that it was chocolate and not the gravy. The person who was invigilating the table knew perfectly well that I knew what I had done and I was sent to do the washing up, which is where I met the nun in charge of the kitchen."

In the kitchen Ann had her first encounter with a true woman of God. "She was radiant. I was once washing up and she came silently in behind me. I sensed her presence. I felt warmth all around me. There was light, warmth and love that came from her eyes. After that I constantly misbehaved in the refectory in order to be sent to that nun. I thought I'd discovered someone unique and special. I thought I was the only person who knew the treasure of what a real being in touch with God was all about, until one time I pranced out of the refectory into the kitchen with a great smile on my face, happy again to do the washing up, only to find the Bishop there asking for her guidance and blessing. And I realized she was recognized. She was one of the hidden ones. This upended the structure of things. I saw very clearly at a young age that the person wearing the feathers is not necessarily the person who's important."

Marooned

Ann matriculated through school, graduated and left for university and went through "a very horrible time. It was good in terms of study and the external things of life but I completely lost track of spirituality. I tried very hard, but within the Catholic tradition I just found it formulaic: lots of rules, no essence. I tried really hard. I prayed more. I went to mass every day for periods of time. There was a nun who'd left her order and was running a silent weekend retreat. In Catholicism there's always an image of the door that is closed with Jesus standing and saying, 'Knock and it will be opened unto you.' And so I kept reminding God that I'd been given a great gift at my Christening, the gift of stubbornness, and that I was knocking and I hadn't had an answer but I'd wait because I knew He would answer when the time was right. I said, 'I'll wait for as long as it takes, but I'm waiting.'"

During this prolonged period Ann had two dreams. In the first dream: *"I was lost in an anonymous landscape. I saw a light. It was a soft, glowing light. I stumbled and struggled to reach the light. The light kept receding and because of this I was in distress."*

The second dream was more disturbing.

"I was in a ruined cathedral. Through an opening I saw the same soft glowing

light I had seen in my previous dream. A priest came between the light and me. He pointed a finger knowingly at me and said, 'You are not worthy'. And I became an ugly homunculus, a grotesque, a gargoyle."

As the years passed the light continued to recede and the world mushroomed. In the course of her education, Ann discovered medicine, studied at Guys Hospital Medical School and St. Barts and qualified as a neurologist in 1963. She established a Forensic Psychotherapy Association, did research work, got married and divorced (twice). She raised two stepchildren after their father abandoned her and them for another woman. "But in essence, I was spiritually marooned."

The Queen Mother

Dr. Coxon eventually set up a private practice in neurology and general medicine in 1982 and things began to change. By now in her early forties she had been spiritually adrift for twenty years. In the late 1970s and early '80s Gulf Arabs with petrodollars flocked to London for medical care and Ann began to treat a growing number of Arab patients. Although she had a few fond memories of Cairo from her childhood, "my image of Islam had been formed by nearly being kidnapped and witnessing political upheaval."

It was when she began treating Sultana Mazoon al-Mashani that she came into a full confrontation with this alien faith. Sultana Mezoon was the mother of Sultan Qaboos, the ruler of Oman. Ann treated the Queen Mother for diabetes and other ailments that come with age. She would make monthly visits to Oman to check up on her royal patient. Ann still considered herself a Catholic and had no special interest in Islam. On one visit she discovered that there was a small Catholic church in Muscat, so early one morning she hired a taxi to take her to attend mass. When she returned she was braced by a royal protocol official who wanted to know to where she had disappeared. She explained that she had been to church. The official left to report to the Queen Mother and returned with the message that Her Majesty was pleased that she was going to church and that a limousine would be placed at her disposal to take her to and from the Church whenever she wanted to attend services. This kind and tolerant gesture touched Ann. She also discovered that the church had been paid for and built by Sultan Qaboos. Ann became increasingly fascinated by her royal patient.

"I was looking after her in Salalah in the South and one morning she went into heart failure. I was completely alone with a Filipina nurse. We worked intensively to save her and within about an hour she was okay. But having that level of heart failure is the equivalent of running a marathon. It is utterly debilitating. So I said to her, 'You can't carry on with your appointments today.' She said, '*La*! (No), I will!' She was a very strong woman. That day Her Majesty insisted that I remain in the corner of the room while she met with family after family. There was no hint that she had practically died in the morning. She saw seven families that day, each one a large group, and she would even ask about uncles and aunts who weren't there. At the end of each meeting she set an exact appointment for the next year's audience: 'Next year come on June 23rd at 4 o'clock,' 'Next year come on August 4th at 10 o'clock,' and so on. I never saw anyone take notes or come in with any pieces of paper or reminders.

"After witnessing this, I said to her, 'Where's your PA (personal assistant)?' And she said, 'What's a PA?' I said, 'The person that writes down the appointments.' She said, 'Why should I have anyone write down the appointments?' I said, 'How do you know who comes and when?' She said, 'I remember.' And then she said, 'You have weak minds because you can write things down. I can't write so I remember.'

At that moment this simple, illiterate woman from a mountain tribe—a 'Jebali'—challenged Ann's European prejudices and sense of cultural superiority. "I suddenly understood that just because someone's illiterate doesn't mean they're not intelligent. And I realized I was in the presence of somebody with a brain I couldn't comprehend.

"I assumed that the Filipina nurse had told someone about her medical crisis that day. I saw how exhausted she was and I was annoyed that nobody—and I mean nobody—had rung to see how she was even though she nearly died in the morning. We had a straightforward relationship and I was very honest with her. I said, 'It's all very well for you to take care of everybody else, but who looks after you?' And this exhausted woman whose skin was gray, who had just gone through a devastating medical crisis, raised herself off her pillows with a look of contempt—it was more than anger, it was complete contempt—as if to say, 'you stupid white woman. I befriended you and you know nothing.' Her finger went up pointing to the heavens and she said, '*Allah looks after me, and I need nothing more!*'

"I thought, 'I don't know what that is but I want it. I want that in my life.'"

Although this exchange had a powerful impact on Ann, she had trouble grasping how to reach 'that' in her life. "I thought all I needed to do was to sort of look at some nice Islamic principles. I wasn't quite sure but I thought they had to do with hospitality and being kind to people and rather anodyne things like that. But I thought, 'I know, I'll fast during the month of Ramadan.' Catholics had bowdlerized Lent. All you have to do is give up chocolate. I thought, 'Ramadan is better. I'll do Ramadan.'"

The Ramadan 'Fudge'

For two years Ann fasted during Ramadan in England. "It was tough because it was the summer. And I knew if I went home I would drink something so I would take myself to Hyde Park and sit under a tree because I wouldn't be tempted to go home where I knew I would have a glass of water." Ann knew all along that she was 'fudging,' that is, she was practicing part of the religion without really making a full commitment to Islam. As the time approached for her third Ramadan, she began to feel uneasy.

Fifteen Degrees to the Left of Kensington Park Road

Ann went on holiday with her family in the South of France. "We have a small mediaeval stone house in Gassin village near St. Tropez." One day while she was sunbathing there Ann fell asleep and had a dream.

"*In the dream I was driving and I looked up to my flat, which is at the top of a big Edwardian building in Notting Hill. The flat was on fire. I tried to call out but I couldn't and people were walking up and down, paying no attention at all. I looked back up and there was this neat little square, where the flat had been but nothing else was affected. Rocks were coming down on to the car and all around the car, bang, bang, bang! And people were still walking around as if nothing was happening. So I thought, 'I guess I better get out of here, there's nothing else for me here.' In the dream the car turned itself around* and, fifteen degrees to the left of Kensington Park Road, a new road opened and there were no cars on it. I always liked taking a new journey. I thought, 'Oh, I'll take that road.' I found myself completely alone on that road and it went absolutely straight. It had its own bridge across the Thames. It went into a Surrey-like area with trees. It went up on to a hill and down again. And it went into some rocks. After the rocks was a twin track across the desert, going into infinity toward mountains in the distance. And the Light! It was clear and penetrating and crystalline. I could see a pattern forming in the Light. And the pattern was the Name of God in Arabic, 'Allah'.

"I woke up shaking. I thought I might have had an epileptic seizure. Then in the depths of my heart I realized I really was a Muslim." She had struck up a personal friendship with one of her patients, a lighthearted, sweet-natured Kuwaiti. She would come to his house and play backgammon with him. About one week before Ramadan, in the middle of a backgammon session, suddenly and without warning, in her heart, Ann became certain that she had to formally become a Muslim, and she confessed this to her jovial host. "He went white, burst into tears and rushed off to his wife who was in the other room. I saw them hugging one another and jumping up and down. A couple of sons joined them.

"He came back to me and said, 'I'll take you to the mosque tomorrow.'" He gave Ann her Muslim name Amina, which was the same as his wife. They went to the Regent's Park Mosque. Ann explained to the Imam that she knew very little about Islam, "but I knew it was the only way I might stand a chance of saving my soul from the drudge and triviality of the world", which she had been trapped in for decades. The imam asked her about Jesus and she shot back defensively, 'If you expect me to repudiate Jesus I'm out of here because he's been on my shoulder all my life. He is absolutely with me and will always be with me!' "And he said, 'I wanted you to know that Jesus is our Prophet of Islam, the *Ruh Allah* (the Spirit of Allah).'" This put Amina's heart at ease and she made her declaration of faith before the imam of the Regent's Park Mosque, just a walk away from her Harley Street surgery.

After this, though, Ann/Amina returned pretty much to the *status quo ante* of her life. She didn't learn to pray or anything about Islam. She had no one to teach her. She was left to her own devices. But she made her third Ramadan fast, this year as a Muslim. "I didn't go to the mosque or anything but as far as I was concerned I began to feel different fasting as a Muslim.

"After Ramadan I decided to find out the direction of prayer and how to pray and the knowledge I needed as a new Muslim. I managed to get hold of an imam who visited my flat to help me learn to pray and determine the direction of prayer (*qibla*). When he did his calculations for *qibla* it turned out that *the direction of prayer was 15 degrees to the left of Kensington Park Road!*"

The Real Deal

Amina started praying. She found a group she liked and began to attend dawn (*fajr*) prayers at the mosque in their center even though it was a long way from where she lived. It was a congregation "who clearly liked praying. It wasn't a duty for them. It was something they wanted to do. I started praying regularly. I realized that this was the real deal and I had to take it seriously. I got into the pattern of praying."

At first Amina kept her new faith a secret from her family but she did confide in the brother of her brother's wife "who dabbled in many religions. We would talk about religion a lot and I told him I had converted to Islam. He was dying. The day before he died he said, 'I want you to be with me when I'm buried. I don't want my sister there. I only want you and no one else. The rest are to be up at Gassin having a party in my name. And you must be dressed as a Muslim. You are the custodian of my soul.'"

Amina took his dying wish to heart. "I had to announce to everybody the day before the funeral mass that I would look a bit different because this is what Michelangelo wanted. His sister knew this was his wish but didn't know why." It was in this way Amina's brother learned of her conversion. He was naturally upset. He said, 'So what's this that you're Muslim?' "I said, 'We're all looking at the same horizon. I just moved to another window.' 'Oh that's all right, then,' he said, and we've never fought about religion. What I've been pleased about is that because of our long conversations about Islam and religion, he's taking his own religion much more seriously."

Over the years Amina has built up a wide circle of friends "for whom their faith and the deepening of their faith is central to their lives." The most meaningful relationship she had was with an aged Bangladeshi gentleman, to the extent that she took her elderly friend to perform the annual Pilgrimage (*Hajj*) with her five times. "He was what I would call one of the Hidden Ones. His patience with me was extraordinary. He was connected with Allah. That was the only important thing for him, nanosecond to nanosecond. There was nothing else that mattered. And all the spiritual courtesy (*adab*) of the conventional Muslim – don't waste time, don't talk about trivia, all of these things – it came from the fact that he was connected. He didn't have to make the effort. He wouldn't involve himself in trivia.

"On one occasion I was being attacked. I was hurt and offended. It was all to do with my ego. I was crying, driving the car on the way to take my teacher home. He was sitting silently beside me as I wept and wailed nonstop all the way. He didn't say a word. We parked beside the old people's home where he lived and I finally stopped. Very quietly and for the first and only time in my long association with him, he put his hand on my arm, and said, 'What they did, that was wrong.' That's all he said. He was saying that what they did was wrong but you don't have to go on about it. People fail. You get hurt. It's not important. There are so many little ways he taught me. This is real teaching."

Insight

One of the by-products of her faith and practice of Islam has been the opening of a profound, almost uncanny insight into infirmity, the ability to make an informed but intuitive diagnosis, a snap judgment that allows her to send her patients to exactly the right specialist. I have no doubt that it is a gift, a form of spiritual insight that comes from a deep compassion and acute awareness of the presence of God.

"I know that I am not in charge anymore. I've watched as thoughts come into my head, which logically would have been inappropriate in a diagnostic or therapeutic situation. I've learnt to follow these instincts and they prove true. It invariably turns out that the patient does have the condition I've just thought of. I once told a specialist, 'You've got to examine this person's thyroid.' 'Why?' 'I don't know, it's in my head.' And there it was! A malignant nodule I wouldn't have found otherwise. So things happen that have nothing to do with me.

"Every day as I leave the house I have this default setting. I dedicate my day to reliance on God. I am the slave of God. Obviously I'm thinking and engaged but if I suddenly have five minutes or even one minute between patients I immediately remember God, I do *dhikr*. If I'm walking down stairs I'm in *dhikr*. I don't try to be. It's there. It bubbles up. When I'm driving my car I'm in *dhikr*. When I'm walking down the street it's there. I am not alone. I'm never alone. I feel I'm lighter. I see terrible things happening all the time. Sad people. Terrible struggles. Terrible burdens. And I spend more time than I used to with patients, yet I don't get tired as much. And although I take on more burdens, I'm not as burdened."

Mortality

In the 1990s Amina was diagnosed with cancer. "When I became sick with cancer I became fascinated. Allah had given me this gift. What did He want me to learn from it? Did He want to take my life and take me to Him? Or did He want me to remain, in which case, what was I to learn from it? At no point did I think, 'Oh, this is a punishment.' I just thought it was a gift. I know God would never give me anything that wasn't for my benefit." As it turned out Allah wanted Amina to live. She responded to treatment and her health was restored. Now twenty years on, she is busier than ever.

"The older I get the fitter I feel. I don't understand why. And I don't know what I'm meant to be doing differently. Allah will tell me what I'm meant to do differently and when. And how. I'm seriously old. I'm trying to listen. In the past when I sat stubbornly in the Catholic Church, what the Catholics call the Dark Night of the Soul, I got my answer. I have every trust that I'll get my answer. But I don't know what it'll be.

"I'm at a stage where I already know after decades of being a Muslim that certainly I want no other path. But I already know how far I've come and how it's affected me. Certainly, I don't sweat the small stuff."

Learning

Hajja Amina Coxon has set herself on a life-long trajectory of learning more and more about her faith. Well educated and highly cultured, she finds her learning curve to be steep and challenging and more to do with practice and good company. "Like most Muslims today I have to get most of my education from books. I have about 2,000 books on Islam. I've probably read half." Yet, there is a thirst for transmission and realization and a concern that the knowledge she finds in print may not be enough.

"One of my friends described a dream he had, that I can certainly relate to. In the dream:

"He was suspended in infinity climbing a rope ladder higher and higher toward Heaven. The higher he climbed the harder the ascent. It was if he was carrying a heavy weight. The climb became so slow and difficult that he stopped. A voice from Heaven called down.

'DROP THE BOOKS!'"

On a Crumbling Bank...

VIRGINIA GRAY HENRY was born and raised in Louisville, Kentucky. Blonde, blue-eyed, she was from a patrician family that could trace their local lineage back eight generations. For his service to the nation, Gray's ancestor George Gray was given a four thousand-acre land grant by George Washington, which became the original downtown Louisville. She grew up in a beautiful house in Mockingbird Valley designed by her father, surrounded by woodlands and set along the elite Louisville Country Club golf course. Her father was a distinguished architect who designed churches, but wasn't himself religious. Her mother was a Unitarian but never attended church. Virginia did. "I went to a church my father had designed. I always loved religion. I would paint icons. I wanted to be a saint."

The southern gentility of Gray's life and her adolescent piety was shaken by a string of deaths. "I experienced the death of many friends I had grown up with, in car accidents, through sudden illnesses." This challenged her beliefs. "We go to church. We say we believe in the community of saints, the forgiveness of sins, the resurrection of the body and the life everlasting. Amen. But I became aware that there was not very much belief in the resurrection of the body or the life everlasting because people are too scientific minded. It's not rational. So people go to church and they enjoy the rites that they're used to and all the rest of it, but there's the underlying disbelief that there is anything but this life. And I found that hard to handle in the light of so many friends' deaths. They were just kids. We're sitting here and you go into the other room and drop dead, are you really gone? There's nothing?"

Her parents didn't pay much attention to Gray's religious demonstrations. She once wore a Sari to a debutante ball. In conservative Kentucky society Gray's heterodox eccentricity was overlooked.

Metaphysics

She left Louisville to attend Sarah Lawrence, a prestigious liberal arts college for women where she majored in art history and world religions with a focus on Hinduism. Her don was Joseph Campbell, a towering figure in the study of mythology and comparative religion. At Sarah Lawrence Gray learned about all religions—except for Islam. The study of Islam was excluded from the curriculum in the 1960s. "In fact, the only image anyone had of the Islamic world (this was before the Oil Boom of the 1970s) was of camels and harems and Baghdad and the Thousand and One Nights." Gray studied "the Vedanta and Shankara and the whole idea of the Small Self and the Real Self. I was saved by Hindu metaphysics because I realized that there is an underlying structure and everything is just coming off of that. It's the same thing that the Eastern Orthodox call 'The Essence and The Energies,' in Islam, 'The Ninety-Nine Names' and in the Tao, 'The Ten Thousand Things'—the Divine qualities.

"So I didn't know anything about Islam, but after Sarah Lawrence of course I really wanted to realize the spiritual states I was reading about in all the texts. You know, we're all being handed our particular lives, skills, connections and tendencies but what they're really for is just to find a way to humbly serve, to point the way back to God."

One way available to point the way back was the experimental use of psychedelic drugs. While studying at Sarah Lawrence, Gray, who was living in Manhattan, took classes at the New School with Jean Houston who, with her husband Robert Masters, had been conducting, with U.S. government support, pioneering research on the effects of LSD on the human psyche, which resulted in a landmark study, 'The Varieties of Psychedelic Experience.' Dr. Houston was teaching a course on the varieties of religious experience.

Gray described herself at the time as "very straight", and perhaps precisely because of this Jean Houston approached the bright young undergraduate with a proposition: "I'm writing a book on LSD. Would you be interested after you graduate in coming to New York and taking LSD and writing an article on your experience?" Gray accepted the proposal and wrote about it. "I did it because I had a godmother who had actually taken LSD with Jean Houston." The experience "was very 'art history' for me. There were incredible colors and patterns." It began what she calls "an interesting phase" because "the few times I bothered to take a drug it was an experience I could not categorize. It went beyond duality and was ineffable. I don't think that it was a hallucination. I think it reflected something very profound." Gray embraced the new liberated spirit. "Initially I thought that Flower Power was wonderful. It really was about love."

New York

She wanted to stay on in New York after graduation. "I wanted to live there because at the time Louisville seemed to me to be just a bunch of people playing golf and bridge." Her father wouldn't continue to support her in New York, so she reached out to a man she had had a blind date with. She sent Feodor Gouverneur, a Venezuelan filmmaker studying for his master's degree at Columbia University, the article she had written on LSD and asked him if he could help her find a job in the city. And he did.

"He got me a job at Third World Film Studios in Lower Manhattan, a studio Feodor had co-founded with Bob Lowe, his professor at Columbia." Bob Lowe introduced Feodor and Gray to Eastern mysticism. "Bob had studied Sanskrit and had lived in Korea. We were like twenty-two and he was forty-something and we considered him to be a wise man. We had three lofts on the Bowery and East 2nd. We had a beautiful brick meditation room with polished wooden floors devoted to Sri Ramana Maharshi. We took some lessons with a disciple of Maharshi on the Lower East Side." The room was also used to throw the *I Ching* and read from the *Baghavad Gita*, Maharshi and the writings of the Romanian philosopher Mircea Eliade. "I took what I learned there and created a film-making department for Dalton, a private college preparatory school, and taught filmmaking to 12-14-year-olds, and then taught film to nuns and priests at Fordham University."

During that period Gray met Dr. Ralph Metzner, the German-born American psychologist and writer involved in the study of consciousness, who had participated in Harvard University's controversial research program into psychedelic drugs with Dr. Timothy Leary[68]. Through

---

68   Timothy Leary was a clinical psychologist who led Harvard University's scandalous

Metzner the studio produced a series of audio-visual shows on various religions—'The Christian Show', 'The Buddhist Show'—all presented at the Second Avenue Theater in the East Village (which later became the legendary Fillmore East), followed by a film production shot in Dayglow fluorescent colors. "I was doing the makeup and coloring horses and Indians."

This free-wheeling experimental period came to a sudden, sobering end for both Feodor and Gray when Feodor was plunged into a profound and prolonged spiritual crisis, which in the end propelled him to the discovery of Islam.

Certainty

Through Feodor, Gray, the graduate of comparative religions, was exposed for the very first time to Islam. Feodor was spending his days in the New York Public Library reading about Islamic history and spirituality. Gray joined him one day and found a copy of 'The Faith and Practice of Al Ghazali', Scottish orientalist W. Montgomery Watt's translation of al-Ghazali's 'Deliverance from Error' (*Munqidh min al-Dalal*). "When I read al-Ghazali, I thought, 'Oh my God, this is true'. al-Ghazali wrote: 'I am on a crumbling bank. My soul is crying 'Up, up and away. If not now, when?'"

> So I became certain that I was on the brink of a crumbling bank and already on the verge of falling into the Fire, unless I set about mending my ways... Mundane desires began tugging me with their chains to remain as I was, while the herald of faith was crying out: 'Away! Up and away! Only a little is left of your life, and a long journey lies before you! All the theory and practice in which you are engrossed is eyeservice and fakery! If you do not prepare now for the Afterlife, when will you do so? And if you do not sever these attachments now, then when will you sever them?'[69]

Psilocybin Project before being fired and becoming a controversial advocate of psychedlic drugs, who U.S. President Richard Nixon called 'The most dangerous man in America.'

69   Deliverance from Error (*Munqidh min al-Dalal*), translated by R.J. McCarthy

"I was about twenty-three years old and I thought, 'My God, I am on a crumbling bank! If I don't do it—'up, up and away'—I've blown it! I knew that if I didn't do it now, I would have blown it." Gray had been looking for a spiritual path all along and was drawn to Sufism. She embraced the religion of Islam and took the name Aisha.

Emigrants

After they had both entered Islam the young couple got married and, yearning for deeper knowledge of their new, unfamiliar faith, they left New York behind and set out on a migration East into the unknown, crossing the Atlantic and then overland in a tiny Citroen *Deux Chevaux* car across North Africa. Their destination was Cairo, the home of al-Azhar University. Feodor, now Faarid Rahmatullah, had written a letter to the venerable institution and received a written invitation to study there. The journey took the better part of one year and along the way they experienced the overwhelming, deep-rooted generosity intrinsic to traditional Muslim cultures. They reached Libya in 1968. At the time, Aisha was in the final stage of her first pregnancy and Cairo was being bombarded by the Israeli air force. In the noble tradition of Muslim hospitality, the young couple were welcomed by the government of King Idris Senussi and provided housing in the Islamic University in al-Beida and a stipend to live on. There they met and befriended Muslim students from around the world, including future Filipino leaders Nur Misuari and Sharif Zain Jali and a young Yugoslav Muslim studying in Libya, Haris Silajdzic, who many years later would play an important role in his country's and Aisha's life.

Aisha gave birth to a daughter. They were emigrating to a new life in Islam. They were *muhajireen* and they named their daughter Haajar (Emigrant). Haris was the first visitor to see Haajar. The Gouverneurs left Libya for Egypt in 1969. Within months of their departure from Libya, their generous host King Idris was overthrown in a military *coup d'etat* led by Muammar Qaddafi.

Aisha, Faarid and Haajar settled into life in Egypt. Aisha gave birth to her son Mustafa there and for the next decade the family lived in a beautiful villa in the leafy suburb of Maadi. Faarid taught filmmaking at Cairo University. Aisha worked as a teacher at the Azhar School for

213

Girls. The eminent scholar and Sufi saint Dr. Abdel Halim Mahmoud, who later became Shaykh al-Azhar, supervised their studies. Faarid eventually took a job in Saudi Arabia heading the film unit at the newly established Hajj Research Center. Aisha taught at Cairo American College.

The Islamic Texts Society
As part of his work for the Hajj Research Center, Faarid was sent round the world to make a film on the Hajj, and Aisha and the children departed Egypt to accompany him. They traveled East, meeting Muslims from Taiwan, Japan and Indonesia. At the end of her husband's Saudi contract in 1979 the family moved to Cambridge, England. They brought with them a decade of study and experience from within the heart of the Islamic world', which culminated in 'An Introduction to Islam: A Pictorial Essay in Four Parts', the first audio-visual presentation on the religion of Islam in English. This beautiful, groundbreaking initiative served as Aisha's master's thesis.

For his part Faarid established The Islamic Texts Society (ITS), dedicated to bringing the traditional knowledge of Islam to the English-speaking world, through the translation of its great sacred texts. Aisha joined him. One of the earliest projects they initiated was the first translation of al-Ghazali's *Kitab dhikr al-mawt wa-ma ba'dahu* ('The Remembrance of Death and the Afterlife'). To translate this classical text, they identified a brilliant Cambridge undergraduate. His name was Timothy J. Winter. His Muslim name was 'Abdal Hakim Murad.

Aisha was, before all, a teacher. Her focus has always been on children and youth. During the first years of the Islamic Texts Society she collaborated with Leila Azzam on a biography of the Prophet Muhammad for children, 'The Life of the Prophet Muhammad', which has become a classic of Islamic children's literature.

During the following decade Aisha was a cyclone of activity, traveling across the Muslim world to raise funds for ITS's landmark publishing projects, planning, writing, studying, lecturing, publishing, socializing, keeping house, cooking, raising her children and visiting her aging parents in Kentucky. During that period we all remember her as an inspiring 'force of nature', with seemingly inexhaustible energy. "I could always, somehow, get to my feet to do one more thing." But she received three successive shattering reminders that she was, as are we all, still poised precariously on a crumbling bank.

Even at Night the Sun is There

In 1987 Aisha and her family were living in Meldreth, a village about ten miles southwest of Cambridge. Her husband was away on a business trip and the children were away at school. "I was lying in bed at night. As I reached out my hand to turn off the bedside lamp, I couldn't lift my arm. When I tried to take a deep breath, it seemed as though my lungs were incapable of expansion. At the approach of a cough or a sneeze I held my arms tightly around my chest for fear the sudden and painful enlargement of my breast would rip me apart. I was virtually paralyzed. I wanted to pull the blankets up over me but I couldn't. In the morning the only way I could get out of bed was to hang my knees over the edge and slide off on to the floor since my upper torso had become powerless. I couldn't even raise my arms to brush my hair. Turning on the bathroom faucet was an excruciating affair. By holding the bottom of the steering wheel in my fingertips I was able to drive to the village clinic. The doctor concluded that I had some kind of virus for which there was no treatment other than time."

Reassured that it was "just a virus that would pass", Aisha went ahead with plans to fly to Boston to attend the Middle East Studies Association (MESA) Congress. "I started noticing that it was hard to walk up and down stairs, but we were leaving the next morning. We flew across the Atlantic to Boston and by the time we got to the hotel I couldn't go to the bathroom on my own anymore. More and more of my system seemed to be shutting down. I could no longer write or hold a teacup, dress myself or even get out of a chair unassisted. Everything ached. I couldn't do anything. I lay on my back but I couldn't shift position or roll over." Indomitable, Aisha dragged herself out of the hotel to attend an event at the Boston Museum. "I couldn't move my head in the direction of the persons to whom I was speaking—I looked straight ahead, perhaps seeing them from the corner of my eye. Everyone kept saying, 'Don't you think you ought to go to Mass General [Hospital]?' I kept shrugging it off, saying, 'It's just a virus.'

"The worst part was lying in bed at night. It was impossible to roll onto either side. My whole body felt on fire with pain. It was terrible to lie flat, unable to make any shift of position whatsoever all night long. I thought to myself, 'If only I could scratch my cheek when it itched. If only my eyes were not dry but cool. If only I could swallow without it feeling like a Ping-Pong sized ball of pain. If only I could reach for a glass of water when I was thirsty during the long night.'"

After the Congress, Aisha and her husband took a plane to New York. "I was sitting on the aisle. The stewardess brought some tea and I said, 'Could you tear the sugar and stir it in there for me?' And then I thought, *'What am I saying? I can't tear a piece of paper!'* I called her back and asked her to arrange for a connecting flight to Louisville, Kentucky, a wheelchair when I get there and asked her to arrange to call my father to pick me up in Kentucky.

"A kind soldier returning to Fort Knox helped me during the flight to Louisville. I felt like a wounded fox that wanted nothing more than to curl up alone in the nest of its childhood. My father met me, and the next day took me for every test imaginable." The results from the battery of tests Aisha underwent were inconclusive. "These doctors were really fooling around in the dark with the symptoms. They were saying things like, 'Maybe this is Lou Gehrig's. Maybe it's Lupus.'"

Aisha was brought back to her parents' home and to her childhood bed by the window. She refused painkillers. "Since I found I could tolerate great pain, I wanted to observe my situation and know where I stood. I started to view my body as an object separate from myself, witnessing its ever-declining condition. When my knees became swollen to the size of grapefruits and my feet became incapable of holding me up, I mused with a kind of detached interest, 'Oh, there go the legs!' The body seemed to be mine, but it was not me.

"It was November, and moonlight was shining through the branches and making patterns all over the blanket. I thought, 'Look at that, even at night the sun is there,' (even in death life is there). Later that night, as I lay gazing out my bedroom door, I noticed the yellow carpet in the hallway. I thought, 'Thank God I'm not in a hospital with a linoleum hallway and the chatter of nurses.'

"Moments later I became aware that I was solidifying. My body had stiffened and I became like a solid log, totally paralyzed. Then I seemed to separate from my body and rise above it. I glanced down and saw my head on the pillow below and thought, 'This is remarkable—I've read about this kind of thing. I'm thinking (up here) and my brain is down there, in my head! I must be dead!' Then I remembered to think '*La ilaha illa Llah*' and when I did, I fell back into my body. I'm lying there clumped in, totally paralyzed.

"During that night, before Mother and Daddy found me, I began to imagine my future. I have friends who are in wheelchairs who have always been placed along the sidelines. Had I now joined them? Was I now out of the normal life of others? I began to see myself like a hunchback or a dwarf. My active life was now over. I would no longer be able to do anything. I realized that what was exemplary in the people I admired was not what they did but what they were. It was their state of being that inspired others. And so I set upon a plan of inward action: the best thing I could do for others would be to sanctify my soul, to let my state of being become radiant.

"In the morning my parents found me, fixed in place. I was brought downstairs and given eggnog to drink through a straw. Chewing was over. My husband came in from New York and I recall marveling when I observed him. He could, without considering the matter in depth, shift his position in a chair; scratch his forehead or lean over to pick up a dropped pencil—all painlessly! Imagine—reflex action! Occasionally if I really wanted to move my fingers, for example, I would think to myself, 'Alright, now I am going to try to move my fingers,' and I would concentrate all my attention on the task. With incredible pain and focus I would, at most, shift a few millimeters. It struck me profoundly that when someone is able to move in this world without pain—that is, in health—that they are experiencing a foretaste of Paradise on earth without ever being aware of it. Everything after that is extra."

It was decided that the best thing for Aisha would be to return to her home in England and seek diagnosis and long-term treatment for her mysterious condition. She was given a week's course of cortisone to allow her to move. "The cortisone was miraculous...and frightening. I could actually walk and pick things up, yet I knew that I couldn't." Back in England she went to the Evelyn Nursing Home in Cambridge for treatment but was told she had to be taken off cortisone immediately so

217

they could begin testing. "I then discovered what withdrawal symptoms are—a level of pain that seems to consume one alive with fire. But the pain was nothing to the frightening mental confusion I experienced. I could not grasp proper thinking, or even normal reality. What I needed was not only a doctor, but also a kind of scholar-saint who could describe to me the hierarchy of meaning so that I would not be so painfully lost. I held my prayer beads like a lifeline. I made it to dawn on the invocation of God's Name, my sanity somehow still intact."

The British specialist also could not make a conclusive diagnosis. "I had come to the point that the very ill come to, where inside something had dimmed and I no longer cared or wished to make an effort. I had reached a great calm within. Each day I was brought downstairs where I directed the preparation of meals. I was resigned to never moving again. I had never experienced such peace. I felt like an upright pole in the middle of a stream. I had come to feel that it would be wrong to pray for my affliction to be lifted, as its good had come to outweigh its bad, in terms of my heart and soul. I could now see what was of real importance.

"In the spring my husband had work in Saudi Arabia and suggested that, as he would be traveling by private plane, they could manage to get me on board. I could as easily sit in a warm climate as I could in cold, damp Cambridge." Aisha was accustomed to giving a talk every year to students at the women's university in Jeddah. This year she declined, explaining that she was unable to research and prepare a topic properly. Her friends in Jeddah offered to step in and provide her with all the assistance she needed to make the talk if she could come up with the topic. "I answered, 'Alright, [my topic is] Why does this Job-like affliction happen to someone, in the view of Islam?'

"In Islam illness is understood to be a great blessing because it is an opportunity, if borne with patience, free of complaint, to purify oneself of past sins—to burn away wrong thoughts and deeds. As I delivered my talk, it began to dawn on me why Muslims always reply with *Alhamdulillah* whenever anyone inquires about their health. I had always wondered why one could ask someone who suffered from an obviously terrible physical or emotional pain or loss, 'How are you?,' and the only reply one would receive is *Alhamdulillah*. I wanted them to talk about their pain with me, to share their suffering, and I wondered why they would not. Suddenly I realized that they were praising God for their state of being. The suffering they endured, no matter how great or small, was an opportunity to be purified, which is the very aim of human existence. In an instant, as I was speaking before an audience of five thousand students, I saw my own illness in this new light. I no longer patiently tolerated my affliction. *I loved it.* I flowed with it. I saw how blessed I was to have been tried with something that was not small but something as total as paralysis. God had considered me up to this affliction.

"As I loved my illness, or shall we say, loved God's will for me, my fingers began to regain movement. Bit by bit, the movement in my hands returned. And I flowed in the river because I loved my paralysis."

When Aisha reached this part of her narration, a look of wonder overtook her, and she wept at the memory.

By the spring of the following year Aisha had recovered and her illness had been diagnosed. It was an extremely rare autoimmune disorder called Guillain-Barré syndrome. "What had been the most painful and difficult time in my life turned out to be the best thing that ever happened to me. I had gained a deepened perspective, a sense of proportion and freedom. God had blessed me with near total dependence on others, a symbol reminding me of my utter dependency on Him. And even when I had not been able to move one inch, I was able to be in touch with His Divine Presence.

> *God created suffering and heartache*
> *so that joyful-heartedness might appear through its opposite.*[70]
> JALALUD'DIN RUMI

Loss

In 1991 Aisha gave up publishing and returned to Kentucky on her own to care for her aging and ailing parents. Faarid returned to Venezuela to care for his mother. This parting of ways signaled the end of their marriage. They were amicably divorced. Aisha stayed with her parents until they both passed away. "My father had a long death because his legs had been amputated from gangrene. And mother couldn't walk." Aisha set up two hospital beds in a large enclosed porch off the kitchen. Her

70   *Mathnawi* VI 104

mother passed away first. When her father died in 1992 someone asked her if she was experiencing grief. "I replied, 'Actually no. Daddy was old, and he died.'

"My cousin encouraged me to visit her spiritual counselor to discuss my grief—the grief I didn't have. In order to please her I drove over one rainy Sunday afternoon to meet this man at his home. He said, 'Tell me about your grief.' I said, 'I'm not experiencing grief. He was really sick and wanted to die.' He continued, 'Then what are you experiencing?' I explained that I felt the loss of protection, which Daddy was giving me up until the time of his death, and I was in my early fifties. I was also experiencing the loss of unconditional love.

"The man I had come to see did not say anything. He allowed me to take that bit of time with him out of my busy life to reflect backwards deep into my heart to see what I really knew. So I continued, 'I suppose that God is the Protector, and He is also the Source of Unconditional Love...and I suppose, in His Wisdom He gives us parents whom we can see and touch in our time of small faith in the Unseen, and they are manifestations of His Protection and Unconditional Love and stand in for Him, as it were, on Earth. And then I suppose when He draws them back into His Divine Presence, we have nowhere left to turn save unto Him for protection and unconditional love.' Realizing this from deep within my own heart I was able to be at peace at last."

Heartache

In 1993, after the deaths of her parents, Aisha wanted to give something back for all the blessings she had received in her life. "I was free then. I could do something." The Bosnian War was raging and her old friend from Libya, Haris Silajdzic, had become Prime Minister of Bosnia and Herzegovina. She offered to help his cause. For the first time in her life she faced the inhumanities of war. "It was like hell on earth." She joined aid workers trying to evacuate children, the infirm and the elderly from Mostar. We had a plane to take them out of harm's way, but they were blocked by the Serbs." Aisha couldn't fathom the wanton hatred and cruelty. "I didn't get it. There is a point at which you can't get it."

She returned to her home in Louisville "feeling very down. Bosnia broke my heart. It was a period of my life when nothing was going on. I wasn't working. I didn't have publishing. My parents were dead. I had no projects to keep me occupied. I was running on empty. You know, we're very rarely on empty on every single level at which we can be functioning. No family. Nothing. So I am at home, sitting at the dining room table with a friend of mine. I told her, 'You know I feel a real tightness here. My heart hurts.' I thought my heart had broken over Bosnia.

"I was living alone in my father's home and, after my friend left, that night, the deep pain in my heart became more and more unbearable. It was so bad and the skipping of the heartbeats had become so alarming that I concluded, as I cried out, that I was about to die." It occurred to Aisha that she had never written a will and she thought the state of Kentucky might take everything from someone who dies intestate. "I reached over and took a yellow legal pad on which I wrote a few simple instructions. It was very comforting to think that everything had been put in order. I put the will on the stairs so if I died upstairs anyone would step on it walking upstairs. And I crawled back up and went to bed

"In the morning, finding myself still alive, I called a cousin of mine who worked at the Louisville Heart Institute. She sent a car for me. A kind Lebanese doctor informed me that every time my heart beat, blood was escaping out into the surrounding cavity. He would need to operate the following morning, and I was not to eat anything from that evening onward. I explained, however, that I was not free on the following morning. I had tickets to Santa Fe. 'One of my childhood friends whose husband died is getting married again and I'm attending the wedding.' He said, 'Well, you can't actually go in a plane to Santa Fe because you won't be able to deal with that kind of altitude in your condition.'

"I didn't know how to tell him this, but when I made that little will of ten lines it was like a love affair that is over and you tie it all up in ribbons. My life was packaged and I was free. Because I wasn't involved in anything and I chose not to be lying on a cold metal operating table when I could be in the autumnal paradise of New Mexico. He said, 'I want to tell you I think you may be one of the most irresponsible people I've ever met.' And I said, 'If I'm alive in a week, I'll come in.'

"A friend came and helped prepare my tiny bag and took me to the airport. I was having a great deal of trouble walking and speaking. On the plane I found myself to be too frail to even turn the pages of a book. I was simply holding on. But I did scribble on a tiny yellow Post-It the words: 'What is actually happening to me is not physical. It's spiritual. My true being is trying to separate from its shadow.' What I meant was that my spirit was trying to free itself from the hypocritical quagmire I had been calling my 'spiritual life', the crumbling bank!

Surrender
"When I arrived in New Mexico my friends, having heard of my condition, insisted that I stay in their home although it had been arranged for me, as a wedding guest, to stay in a hut in the desert, not far from the Indian Museum. I thanked them for their kindness and said, 'I'll take the hut.' The next morning I awoke and decided to slowly make my way out into the desert to enjoy the Dante-esque mountains and the golden trees. As I slowly walked out, my inner emptiness, my concluded life, my lack of concern for any future or past, were mirrored by the void of the desert around me. I seemed to be on a vertical alignment with nothingness and completion.

"In all faith traditions we are asked to surrender, but I think that must be impossible to do because we always have an agenda at some level. But as I began to sit down, I got surrendered—was surrendered. Time simply stopped." Aisha experienced "an infinite, luminous being, in pure consciousness and absolute bliss". She realized that "what we are living in is Divine Beauty." She realized in the depths of her being that "It is actually true! God is Love.

"In an utter reverence and a joy that I had never known, my hardened heart began to melt from relief—I could finally *see*. Tears of relief completely soaked my blue sweatshirt as the waves of myself subsided into a Sea of my Self. Although I had a body, it seemed cool and I couldn't really feel it. Somehow, through my eyes, I could see an unearthly glory surrounding me—nature's unveiled Paradisal archetypes were shining through. But, what was really going on was that part within my heart that participates in God was recognizing Itself. Somehow, Itself was recognizing Itself. There was/is no time. There was/is no duality—no past or future, no male or female, no birth or even death. There was/is nothing but Divine Reality—there is nothing but God. *La ilaha illa 'Llah*. That's all

222

there is. And that's all I want. It is everything and yet no thing. The Eternal Now: I belong here forever. I am from here—it is the true me—even if I forget.

> *Only Thou, oh Best of Helpers, canst transform the eye*
> *That sees non-existent things into one that sees the Existent![71]*
> JALALUD'DIN RUMI

"What is the vehicle that can transport us to this Glorious Other Shore? Perhaps something like this state of being that I was blessedly shown. It exists in the place of 'no thinking'—where opposites meet, between good and bad.' This state of utter happiness and inherent transcendence of our temporal 'selves' is always there and we just have to remember to be in touch with It, to recall that who we really are is absolute reverence, serenity, beauty, humility and awe. It would seem that access is through stillness, slowness and reverence.

"As the afternoon faded, the tear-soaked shirt chilled my body. I slowly rose to return to the hut. I walked almost in slow motion. I wondered whether if I lived, I would abuse and lose this greatest of graces, this taste of Divine Unity. That night in the hut I dreamt of His Holiness the Dalai Lama who, for me, embodies qualities of Mercy and Compassion:

"*I opened the door of my home in Kentucky, and my heart, and there he was on the front steps. Behind him were eight earth-colored, log-like bundles and I thought to myself, 'He must be bringing me the Eightfold Path.' He came in through the door and, standing a couple of feet away, facing me, appeared to condense into a Cheops-shaped pyramid, which penetrated my heart. At the same moment I felt an energy descending through my fontanel and coming up through my feet.*

"When I awoke in the morning my heart no longer hurt but I could no longer speak or even move except extremely slowly. I concluded that a real person moves slowly and in silence—my exact opposite."

> *Silence! Silence! For the allusions of love are reversed.*
> *The meanings become hidden from much speaking.[72]*
> JALALUD'DIN RUMI

---

71   *Mathnawi* VI 825

72   The *Diwan* 12073

Fons Vitae

Aisha returned to her home, kept her promise to her doctor and underwent treatment on her physical heart. She recovered, and in 1997 she re-entered publishing with the establishment of Fons Vitae, resuming the work she had started with ITS. She has commissioned and publishes a wide range of works on spirituality, with a focus on translations of key works by Ibn Ata'illah al-Iskandari, Ahmad ibn 'Ajiba, Jalalud'din Rumi and Imam al-Ghazali, including a new translation of the book that brought her to Islam in the first place, 'Deliverance from Error' (*Munqidh min al-Dalal*). She also remarried, to Kentuckian Neville Blakemore. Aisha has become a pillar of the Louisville community and a driving force behind interfaith initiatives across the U.S. and around the world.

The Rush

Toward the end of October 1999 she experienced a third decisive event on the crumbling bank of her life.

"I went out to the Louisville airport to catch a flight to Cincinnati, which would connect me to JFK in New York to take an Egypt Air flight to Cairo. When I arrived the agent at the counter informed me that the flight to Cincinnati had been cancelled. I replied, 'Then put me on any flight to New York.' She looked and said there were none, but that she could book me for the next day. Two business people from New York were standing behind me and pushed their way forward. They were very frustrated by the inconvenience and asked the agent if there would be enough time to rent a car and drive to Cincinnati to make the New York flight. She replied that indeed there was enough time to do this. So the couple turned to me and said, 'We're New Yorkers and we don't drive but if we rented a car would you drive us and then, hopefully, all three of us would be able to make our flights?'

"I called my husband and said that it was doubtful that I would be able to fly to Egypt that evening but would probably stay in Cincinnati or New York and take the flight the next day, October 31st. When we got out on the highway I noticed a sign indicating that Cincinnati was ninety miles away. We only had two hours before the flight would leave for JFK so I decided that as long as we had made this effort I might as well drive ninety miles per hour. I'm not used to driving fast but a strange calm came over me and I concluded that, if the police stopped us, we would have at least given it our best shot.

"As we pulled into the airport the New York couple jumped out and ran for the flight. I gave the check-in porter twenty dollars to return the rented car and proceeded inside with my baggage. The agent explained that, unfortunately, it was too late for me to make it. Tears welled up in my eyes and I said, *'But I have to make this flight!'* As I turned to leave, she called me back and said that the New York flight had just, at that moment, been delayed and she could, in fact, put me on and have my bags transferred in New York directly to the Egypt Air flight.

"When I boarded the plane the New York couple were pleased and said that they had a car waiting for them at JFK and that they could take me directly to my terminal on arrival. When I reached the terminal at JFK the Egypt Air check-in desk had already closed. I knew where the gate for the flight was so I ran as though my life depended on it. My lungs burned from the exertion. As I reached the gate the door of the plane was being shut and I was told it was too late for me to board. Again, I begged, *'I have to make this flight!'* I reminded them my luggage was already in the hold. So they decided it would be easier to board me than offload my bags.

"Late the next day I was sitting with my daughter in our family house in Maadi when the phone rang. My husband had assumed that I hadn't made the connection and was on that day's flight, Egypt Air 990. A friend had just informed him that Egypt Air 990 leaving from JFK to Cairo on October 31st had plunged into the ocean. He called in panic, thinking I had been on the flight. My daughter burst into tears." But Aisha was calm. "I knew it wasn't my time. I knew that I was compelled to drive ninety miles an hour, to plead, to run and do all of that without knowing that I was running not to die at that moment. Now isn't that something?"

> Solomon said, 'Whatever you want, just ask!'
> He pleaded, 'Please assign the wind this task'
> To transfer me to India with its breath.
> So, over there, I might escape my death.'
> (Solomon questioned Azrael right at the chime:

'Angel of Death, did you drive that good man
From home and family—was that your plan?'
He answered, 'Now you know I wouldn't lie,
I just looked on amazed as he strolled by,
For God had said today he would be dead
Not over here, but India's tip instead.'[73]
JALALUD'DIN RUMI

God has seen fit to keep Aisha into her eighth decade and give her strength to continue her inestimably valuable work to bring the sacred texts of Islamic spirituality to the English-speaking world and to find common ground between all the world's spiritual traditions. Her distinguished imprimatur has published more than one hundred and fifty titles.

Aisha has embarked upon what she considers her reason for being born: the creation of a comprehensive educational package for children, families and schools based upon the wisdom and knowledge contained in Imam al-Ghazali's 40-volume seminal masterwork *Ihya 'Ulum Ad-Din* ('Revival of the Religious Sciences') translated into language and concepts that children can grasp, to give them an ethical foundation and understanding of faith and practice in Islam.

More than this, Sayyida Aisha Virginia Gray Henry Blakemore brings the wisdom and love that she has realized on her long, precarious and resolute stand on the edge of the crumbling bank of a life well-lived to all around her, eliciting a reciprocal love, reverence and longing for knowledge that calls 'Up, up and away!'

Return to yourself, oh heart.
For from the heart a hidden road can be found to the Beloved.
If the world of the six directions has no door, then come into the heart,
the place of contemplating God, though it is not so now, it can be so.[74]
JALALUD'DIN RUMI

---

73   *Mathnawi* 1:957-63
74   The *Diwan* 6885-87

Heartbreak

IN CAPE TOWN beneath a huge tent set up adjacent to a neighborhood mosque in a mixed gathering of several hundred souls, I was asked to accept two African women into Islam. I had never seen them before. The faces of these women were, to put it gently, careworn, marked by poverty, hardship and suffering. I sat down at a long makeshift table across from the two apprehensive middle-aged ladies. I pulled my rosary from around my neck and offered one end to one of the two. The new convert (my South African hosts prefer the word 'revert') took the *tasbih* and waited. By my side someone translated my English into Afrikaans. I briefly explained the meaning of the *Shahada* (*ash-hadu an la ilaha illa 'Llah wa ash-hadu anna Muhammadan Rasulullah*—'I witness that there is no god but God and I witness that Muhammad is the Messenger of God') and asked her if she understood and accepted this statement. She said that she did. I then asked her to repeat after me. And she did, and when she did she received an ovation from the assembly. I then turned to the lady sitting beside her. She seemed almost forlorn. I offered one end of my rosary to her. She held the *tasbih* for dear life until I thought she was going to pull it out of my hands or snap the string. She didn't speak English or Afrikaans, so we found someone from the gathering who spoke Zulu. I continued my explanation, which was haltingly translated into Zulu. Then I carefully asked her to repeat the declaration of faith. She could not articulate the Arabic so she repeated the declaration in her mother tongue. When she finished her *shahada* and we told her that she was now a Muslim, she suddenly lit up, leapt out of her chair and, with unbridled joy, danced back and forth across the room. It was one of the most beautiful spontaneous acts of faith I have ever witnessed.

Over a period of just four years one small group of dervishes from Cape Town has received over eighty-six thousand (and counting) Africans into the fold of Islam. I have been engaged, off and on, and in one form or another, in calling people to Islam for over forty years.

In all that time I have never heard of or experienced anything close to those numbers of mass conversion (reversion?). When I first heard these awesome statistics, my skeptic meter jumped to red. How is that possible? Are they cooking the books? Are these people really Muslims? Why are they doing it? How are they following up?

Since the end of apartheid many South Africans have prospered—the whites, the Cape Malays, the Indian communities—but the indigenous African communities have been largely left behind. This can be seen in the vast, sprawling informal townships of ramshackle hovels, reeking with poverty, crime, addiction and hopelessness. One can see Africans walking along the roads, heads wrapped in black garbage bags, soiled and tattered clothes, broken shoes. There is a heartbreaking sadness that overshadows these settlements and the people who live in them, the cruel legacy of vicious institutionalized racism.

By contrast the traditional Muslim communities have thrived—the Cape Malays and Indo-Pak South Africans. For Muslims Cape Town is a city founded and surrounded by saints. Sufism runs deep through Cape society.

When the late Turkish Cypriot Naqshbandi murshid Mawlana Shaykh Nazim Al-Haqqani, may God have mercy on him, visited his disciples in South Africa, his first observation was that there were no Africans among them. He ordered his *khalifa*, the venerable teacher Shaykh Yusuf Da Costa, to reach out to the African communities and call them to Islam.

The Townships

The prospect of venturing into impoverished, crime-ridden townships to invite a downtrodden disenfranchised and possibly dangerous population to an unfamiliar religion was intimidating. The members of this community were mostly middle-class Cape Malays and Asians who had little or no connection with the people of the townships. After a few tentative and less than successful attempts to attract people to Islam through the local Muslim imams and lectures in the mosques, the community reassessed their efforts.

Shaykh Yusuf began to completely reexamine the project and realized that to reach out to these communities they had to start from a *tabula rasa*, and go back to the origins of Islam, when the declaration of faith was all there was. Talking and lecturing wouldn't work. They had to aim directly for the heart. Many of the Africans were illiterate or, at best, under-educated. They lived on the periphery of civilization in grim poverty. Alcoholism, drug addiction, gangsterism and rape were endemic and yet there were many decent, God-fearing people in these communities. The issue was not religion, as such. It was about a kind of spiritual conversion that transcended religion. It was about compassion, mercy and love. Shaykh Yusuf "realized that there was only one route and that was the spiritual route. This work absolutely could not be done without spiritual guidance, spiritual support, spiritual help and individual sacrifice. The whole process has to be spiritualized." So how to take this spiritual route?

The Spiritual Route

The first thing Shaykh Yusuf did was to impose a rigorous discipline on his dervishes. He divided them into small groups and appointed an *emir* or leader for each group. This new approach meant that the community had to internalize their mission. They had to give up any illusions that they had any power to bring anyone to Islam. They had to surrender everything to the Will of God. They had to depend on God and place all their trust in God. They had to purify their actions and intentions. Their outward mission thus became an inward journey.

Every weekend delegations of Naqshbandi dervishes (sometimes more than twenty groups) would visit Shaykh Yusuf at his home and he would lead them in supplication, acknowledging their powerlessness and asking for the protection and mercy of God. They would then set out for the unknown, with no stratagem, no forward planning, to visit townships they had never been to and people they'd never met carrying nothing more than some food, benches, good intentions and the remembrance of God.

The first time they ventured out in this way, Shaykh Yusuf sent them to Malmesbury, a small town about sixty-five kilometers north of Cape Town. They didn't even know for sure if there was an African settlement in the vicinity. When they arrived in Malmesbury, they went to the local mosque and asked if someone could take them to a black township. They were told, 'You can't go there! You'll be murdered!' They thanked them for their advice and then went straight to the township with warnings of impending homicide ringing in their ears.

They entered the settlement with no more plan than to start knocking on doors. Their aim was to find a place to pray and make invocation (*dhikru'llah*). They had no idea what would happen. The very first person whose door they knocked on was a Christian lady. She invited them into her shack and allowed them to pray and hold their meeting there. Members of the group were shy at first, not sure whether they should invite the township people to Islam outright or simply pray and remember God and let things take their natural course.

The township people who attended this tentative, informal gathering started asking questions about Islam. After answering questions for about forty-five minutes one of the dervishes asked if anyone was interested in accepting Islam. "The first person to come forward to accept Islam," said one member, "was the Christian lady who hosted us. And after that there was a continuous flow of people from the township who came and accepted Islam. We were thunderstruck. It just happened, without any effort."

The Breakthrough

The Naqshbandi community had tapped in to something mysterious, almost primordial. Once the group left their egos behind and turned to God for success, a new dynamic took over.

In a settlement near a small town called Ceres about one hundred thirty kilometers from Cape Town, one group led by Fadeel Sambo, an IT service manager, entered and began knocking on doors. "We were inviting people to join us for a large gathering. We knocked on one door and a lady answered and was adamant that our group should come into her home. We said, 'No, thank you, we're holding a program down the road. We'd just like to invite you to join us.' She said, 'I will join you but I would like you to come into my home.' So we entered her home and the lady said, 'I've already taken a bath and I am coming to your program because last night I had a dream of my mother who passed away a few years ago. She told me that people will come knocking at my door and she said that the men would be wearing turbans and pointy hats and she

230

described what the women would be wearing as well. My mother told me to take the religion they bring to me because it will take me to the Light.'"

One of the Naqshbandi groups was scouting a new, unfamiliar township for a place to set up. They made supplication, asking God to guide them to the site He had chosen for them. They were driving around slowly and came upon a couple. The couple approached the van and the lady poked her head inside and said, "I know you." They said, "How do you know us? This is the first time we've been here." She said, "I saw you in a dream." She looked inside toward the back of the van and said, "Yes, I saw all of you. I saw you all right here, on the soccer field. You came to pray with us." So the soccer field was the site they were scouting. They assembled there and performed remembrance of God and over two hundred souls entered Islam on that day including the lady with the dream who poked her head in the van.

Water is scarce in the townships and that same day one of the dervishes was looking for a place to make ritual ablution (*wudhu*). "I went to the house of a lady who hadn't participated in our program that morning but she gave me permission to make my *wudhu* at her home nonetheless. I asked her why she didn't attend. She said, 'My cousin is a Muslim but I'm not very interested. I have other things to do.' She walked with me toward the soccer field and we met my wife who was walking toward us with this little girl. It turned out that the little girl was the lady's daughter and her daughter had just entered Islam. After she had entered Islam she prayed that her mother would accept Islam. And her mother entered Islam on the spot. Then we met her Muslim cousin who told us, 'I've been trying for ten years to convince her to become a Muslim!'"

The Unseen
In a settlement on the outskirts of Darling, a town on the Western Cape about seventy-five kilometers from Cape Town, Ahmet Kriel, a chiropractor by profession, and his group knocked on doors and were greeted by a lady who gave up her house for them to perform *dhikru'llah*. She had embraced Islam and took the name Hajira. She married a Muslim man. She died of cancer sometime after that. Ahmet said, "Not

long after her *janaza* (funeral prayer) my wife had a dream. She was in a gathering of *dhikr* and saw Hajira. My wife stood up and greeted her and said, 'But Hajira you're dead. What are you doing here?' Hajira replied, 'No, [I'm not dead], I still attend the *dhikru'llah* whenever it is held.' The rest of Hajira's family was non-Muslim. They live in Mossel Bay on the Southern Cape, about four hundred kilometers from Cape Town. After she died Hajira appeared to her family in a dream and told them, 'It is time now for you to become Muslim because this is the right way.' Hajira's husband received a phone call from her sister to tell him that she and her husband had accepted Islam."

One dervish group entered a township in the vast desert region of Karoo in the Northern Cape. One group member remembered, "It is very difficult to explain but it felt as if the environment was set up for us, as if we were just instruments of Allah and that the way was already prepared for us in the Unseen to do our work. We witnessed the power of supplication, which was a struggle for our egos because we all tend to think that we are doing everything. In this situation we had not brought shading or seating and we worried that people wouldn't come out in the heat. So we were inspired to make supplication to Allah and ask for clouds. And clouds formed! And people came. The next day we failed to make supplication and the sky was cloudless. So we asked Allah for shade and we found the shade of a tree and, beneath the shade of that tree a massive gathering formed and many people accepted Islam."

It is as if extreme deprivation opened up the Unseen and an overflow of dreams. At one township outside Cape Town I met a woman who had very recently embraced Islam. On the surface she was sad and broken but, in a state of awe, she related a dream she had: "I was in Makkah. Three men came to me. They were wearing white robes and one asked me, 'When will you make Hajj? When will you make Hajj? When will you make Hajj?' over and over and over again." This was a woman with almost no knowledge of Islam and, almost no material hope of being able to actually perform the Pilgrimage and yet inwardly there was a spiritual imperative, a command from the Unseen. May God transport her to His House! And God is Powerful over all things. At another township an old woman who had converted shared with me a beautiful dream she had of the Night of Power (*Laylat al-Qadir*). These are women who appear to have been beaten down and brutalized by life. I can't imagine the indignities and suffering they have endured. And yet they have been transfigured by belief. They are some of the most heartbreakingly beautiful women I have ever seen.

Change of Faith

In an immense commercial farm near Kimberly in the Northern Cape the Naqshbandis entered a squatters' settlement. One of the group remembered, "We were knocking on doors to invite people to a Muslim gathering. We passed a church where a worship service was in progress and someone said, half-jokingly, 'I wish we could invite these people to the gathering.' We moved to the area we had chosen for the gathering and we started our invocation. It was about half past eleven in the morning. Suddenly crowds of people entered the gathering. We sent someone to see what was happening. It turned out that the church service had finished and the entire congregation had walked from the church to the Muslim assembly. All these churchgoers were standing there holding Bibles. And here we were telling people that Jesus was our Prophet but not the Son of God. We were worried that we would offend these pious Christians. But the entire congregation—every single person, from eight years old to eighty years old—accepted Islam. We were stunned. We asked an elderly gentleman in Afrikaans, 'Have you really accepted that Jesus is not the Son of God?' He looked at us almost annoyed and said, 'I understand very well what you said.'"

In Clanwilliam in the Western Cape, about two hundred kilometers from Cape Town the Naqshbandis were holding a gathering. One of the dervishes told me, "A priest from the area approached. He began to ask questions about Islam. 'How can you say that Jesus is not the Son of God?' We explained how God put the spirit into Mary and that Jesus was considered by Muslims to be the Spirit of God (*Ruh Allah*), not the Son of God. And he began to cry. He fell down and cried. He said, 'I'm a priest. You've brought me this message now? How am I going to tell my congregation? I've been preaching for twenty-eight years. What do I tell them now?' They said, 'This is God's message of Truth. You must be someone who wants to know the Truth.' And he accepted Islam."

Through their work in the black townships it became clear that the good people in these settlements had a tenuous connection to Christianity. Shaykh Yusuf said, "They tell us, 'We can't attend church because we don't have money.' The churches charge parishioners ten per cent of their wages. We come into these areas and we don't ask them for money. We bring love to them and the truth that there is only one God. In fact, as poor as they are and no matter how they look and how they smell, they understand. You would look at them and imagine them ignorant and illiterate, but they are not. They invariably say, 'We've always believed that God cannot have a son. How can we worship Jesus?' When we ask if they would like to accept Islam, many at the moment they recite the declaration of faith, cry, and say, 'Why, why are you only coming now?' And we see how the remembrance of Allah has touched their hearts. We stand there in awe."

Nadeem Williams, a debt counselor by profession and a Naqshbandi group leader, explained, "The people we reach out to are the most deprived of the poorest of the poor. The Church rejects these people so they don't have a religious home. We come and offer them a home. They are the people no one else is interested in. We don't discriminate against any of them. They come drunk, dirty, smelly, it doesn't matter. We accept everyone. And we give love and affection to them. We show them that we are genuinely interested in them."

Alcoholism is common in these townships. One of the women in the community told me that a drunk came staggering into one of their gatherings. "The locals were mocking him, but this gentleman was so sincere. He was the only person who took off his shoes. Nobody told him to take off his shoes, but he did and he was crying so much and he came to pray with us even though he was drunk. We try to show the people love. We don't make distinctions. We don't chase anyone away. This man was so humble. He was so sincere, even though he was drunk."

Understandably young Africans from the townships are seeking ways of escape from the misery they face. Alcohol and drugs have been the traditional escape mechanisms but they have destroyed already devastated communities. Spirituality offers a glimmer of transcendent hope.

Tradition

Many of the poorest Africans are the Xhosa people and by reaching out to these people the community discovered many similarities between Xhosa culture and Islam. One community member told me, "The way they bury their dead is similar to Islam. They bury their dead wrapped in cloth before sunset. They practice circumcision in a way similar to Islam. Ladies who are married cover their heads. Traditionally, Xhosa men weren't allowed to wear tight clothing. In earlier times they were bearded." Other tribes like the Zulu share the same similarities. The Xhosa have historical ties to Islam. Their ancestors traded with Persians and Arabs and there is some evidence to suggest that the ancestors of many of these tribal people were Muslim. Many Xhosa and Zulu people still have Muslim names.

When the Naqshbandi community members were relating their experiences to me, their sense of wonder was palpable. They were witnessing a phenomenon that they realized they had no power over.

"Allah is at work. Allah is at work," Shaykh Yusuf said. "He determines and He implements. Our job is to be sincere. It is *Allah Subhanahu wa ta' ala* Who decrees whether or not these people will become Muslim. If one person comes to Islam, *Alhamdulillah* and if many come, *Alhamdulillah.*"

In the event thousands upon thousands of Africans have embraced Islam through the simple, self-effacing effort of a few dozen sincere believers. The program developed by Shaykh Yusuf and his community proved so effective that delegations were sent out to neighboring countries, including Namibia and Malawi as well as Surinam in South America. Thousands more embraced Islam.

I couldn't help wondering what kind of follow up there was after so many had come into Islam. Obviously, one small community couldn't solve all their problems and rescue all these disenfranchised people from desperate poverty. What I learned was that each and every person that entered Islam through the ministrations of the Naqshbandi groups was registered with names and contact details recorded. Each time a *da'wa* group would enter a new township, they would identify a contact person who could keep them informed of developments and needs. They then established places of prayer (*Salah Khanas*) and community centers where people could learn more about Islam. Each *Salah Khana* included a soup kitchen. The Naqshbandi community formed alliances with other organizations like the South African Zakah Fund (SANZAF), which equips and supplies the soup kitchens. Food is provided to anyone who comes, Muslim or non-Muslim. And, most importantly, they brought the remembrance of Allah in to every township.

The Power of Remembrance

At Drift Sands, a black township just outside Cape Town hundreds converged on the *Salah Khana* the day I visited. Many children were there and I figured they were coming for the free lunch, which was probably more or less true. But when we sat down and started to perform invocation (*dhikru'llah*) everybody—and I mean everybody—joined in with gusto, even the naughty boys in the crowd. When the *dhikr* stopped and someone started talking, the naughty boys zoned out and started fidgeting. When the *dhikr* resumed, so did they. I discovered that many of the young children had embraced Islam even though their parents had not and that many non-Muslim parents encouraged their children to enter Islam, to attend the *Salah Khana* and to keep learning. They recognized that this place was a safe haven that could keep their kids away from crime and drugs.

The day I came I was told that there was a young man who had been hanging around the *Salah Khana* and who had decided to enter Islam. Evidently I was the reason. When the imam told him that a white person was coming to visit who was a Muslim, he said in amazement, "You mean Muslims can be WHITE?" The imam said yes, so the young man said right then and there, "Cool. Then I'm going to be a Muslim too!" And they asked me to witness his *shahada* and he decided to take my Muslim name, Haroon, for his own. Go figure.

"Never have people of a different color come into those areas and given love," one of the dervishes told me. "There are people in these settlements who can't wash themselves because there's no water. Nobody has ever hugged them. Nobody has ever brought love and compassion to them. We come in and we let them know who God is, in their language. It is the remembrance of God that touches them."

When one of the women from Drift Sands first heard the Name of Allah recited, she fell to the floor in prostration. They asked her why she had fallen to the floor and she replied, "When I heard this word, '*Allah*,' it struck my heart *here*." She pointed to her heart. "And it pushed me down to the ground!" Witnessing these beautiful people respond so deeply to the act of *dhikru'llah* it dawned on me that this kind of primal reaction, based on nothing more than the invocation of the Name, was exactly the same powerful impulse that drew me to Islam in the first place. Affluence, education, privilege had nothing to do with it. When I heard the Name, '*Allah*,' it struck my heart, *right here*.

Tin Can Town

I was taken to Blikkiesdorp (Afrikaans for 'Tin Can Town'), an appallingly desolate relocation camp thirty kilometers outside Cape Town consisting of flimsy two-room shacks made from thin tin and zinc sheets. Blikkiesdorp was built in 2007 as 'temporary' housing for poor families evicted from other parts of the city in the lead up to the 2010 FIFA World Cup. Many of these dispossessed people had lived for two years on the pavement in ramshackle hovels along Symphony Way. The Symphony Way settlement was desperately poor but safe, with a sense of community and self-determination. The residents built makeshift houses big enough to accommodate their families. They grew vegetables. They created a football field for their boys. And then the government evicted these evictees again, forcing them into Blikkiesdorp, which has been compared to a concentration camp and called 'a place worse than hell.' Whole families are crammed into tiny one-room shacks that are unbearably hot in summer and unbearably cold in winter. Four shacks share a water tap and toilet. And there is nothing temporary about it. Families have been trapped in this hellhole for a decade with no hope of relocation. Crime and violence are rife and drains overflow with sewage. Despair is widespread.

In the middle of all this misery is Auntie Rashieda's soup kitchen, supported by the Naqshbandi community. She serves lunch every day with a radiant smile to anyone who comes and, in her tiny tin shack she teaches the basics of Islam and leads circles of invocation. Auntie Rashieda Levember and her husband were among those living on the pavement along Symphony Way. In the face of truly terrible poverty she never stopped teaching Islam to her community. When she was forced to move into Blikkiesdorp she continued serving the Muslims and others in the settlement, cheerfully and with great patience and compassion. Auntie Rashieda's is a haven in a hellish hopeless dumping ground. Most of those who gathered in the soup kitchen were women and schoolgirls. They were sweet and luminous, overflowing with faith. They eagerly related extraordinary spiritual dreams they had. They remembered God. They are the best of people. They break my heart.

When God's Help and Victory come
And you see mankind entering God's religion in throngs
Hymn the praise of thy Lord, and seek forgiveness from Him.
Truly He is Ever-Relenting (Tawwab).[75]

---

75   Holy Qur'an, *Sura al-Nasr* (Help): 110

Dream Progression

I RETURNED FROM my first visit to Cape Town filled with wonder at the vast numbers of men, women and children who had entered Islam in South Africa through the sincere and self-sacrificing efforts of a small group of Sufis. I had a sense that this was an indigenous phenomenon, something deep in the African spirit and this intuition was confirmed a few months later during a visit to the Gambian Qadiri master Shaykh Muhammad Hydara al-Jilani, God bless and protect him. He had just returned to Dubai from an annual conference he holds in Banjul, The Gambia, celebrating the teachings and traditions of his ancestor Shaykh Abdul Qadir al-Jilani, may God be well pleased with him. He also appeared to be filled with wonder for reasons similar to my own.

A Muslim convert had come from neighboring Guinea Bissau to attend the conference, take on the teaching of Shaykh Muhammad and follow the Qadiri Way. What made this visitor unusual was that he was from the Balanta people who had for centuries fiercely rejected both Islam and Christianity. The very name of the tribe tells this story. 'Balanta' is a Mandinka word meaning 'Those Who Refuse'. So it was remarkable in and of itself that one of the Balanta had, on his own volition, embraced Islam. This was not the whole story. What made this Balanta visitor unique was that he had single-handedly brought a big group of his tribesmen (and women) to Islam. A really big group.

Given that the Balanta had a reputation for being belligerent and warlike, Shaykh Muhammad had urgent concerns that they should be rightly guided in Islam. As a young man he had spent much time traveling through the deserts of West Africa and had seen the dark, destructive radicalization of Muslim youth across the region. He told me once that after spending time in Timbuktu with young people there he went to the elders and said to them, "You've got a serious problem with your youth and you need to deal with it now." The elders dismissed the young Gambian scholar's warning out of hand. "They're just hotheaded.

Nothing will happen." Of course, something did happen. These same young people joined the *Ansar Eddine* extremist group that took over the fabled city in 2012, terrorized its population and destroyed priceless and irreplaceable features of its ancient heritage.

Shaykh Muhammad wanted to bring these new Balanta Muslims into the Qadiri Way before they could be seduced into Boko Haram, ISIS or any of the other violent jihadist groups proliferating across the continent. He told me, "If this happens it is very dangerous." I was keen to meet the man who was bringing his traditionally obstreperous people—'Those Who Refuse'—to the way of Islam. Shaykh Muhammad told me that there were many who were waiting for him to receive them into Islam so I started making plans to accompany him to Guinea Bissau. In the event, that particular journey didn't happen but the Shaykh encouraged me to come to The Gambia the following January.

'Through Me You Will Find the Path'

It was there, in Banjul, that I met Antonio Montero Fernandes, now known as Mawlana Abdullah. He appeared to be a simple, soft-spoken workingman with strong face, a beard flecked with gray and the rough hands of a builder, which was how he earned his living. Beneath this working-class exterior was a deep well of spirituality. Born in Guinea Bissau on September 5, 1958 Antonio showed signs of intense piety from childhood. "I didn't know through which religion, but I knew with certainty that I would call people to God." There was a game the children played in which they would give themselves nicknames. At the age of only ten years Antonio gave himself the name *Winda Bogobate Sina*, which in his language means 'Through Me You Will Find the Path'. When he was a small child, and through primary school, he wanted to be a doctor. As he moved into adolescence he aspired to the priesthood. He studied the Bible with great passion but at the age of seventeen, disenchanted by organized religion, he left the Christian Church while continuing his Bible studies.

Dreams

Then he fell ill. For three months he was at death's door. "I thought 'If I die I won't be able to fulfill what I came to fulfill." He began having

240

dreams. Night after night he would dream of the Prophet Jesus, peace be upon him.

"*In the dream Jesus, peace be upon him, would take me by the hand and lead me to a river that was not a river in my land. He would tell me of virtues and show me beautiful things. The dreams were long.* When I returned to myself I realized that if I had seen an Angel I would die but as I have seen a Messenger I will continue to live." Antonio continued to have vivid dreams. In a single night he would have as many as seven dreams. "I never told anyone about these dreams with the exception of a sage who simply said, 'You are on the right path.'"

After he regained his health Antonio continued his search and discovered the Baha'i Faith. It struck him as similar to Protestantism, "but they said, 'This is something new. This is a new faith.' So I thought I would try it out. I attended a gathering and decided to accept it."

The Baha'i Faith is a heterodox cult that emerged in Persia in the mid-19th century and was immediately reviled as heresy in Iran and throughout the Muslim world. In other parts of the world the Baha'i attracted a growing number of adherents through its soothing and seemingly open-minded messages of universal brotherhood, the unity of religion, the promotion of world peace and its easy and unchallenging religious obligations. The fact that this new 'religion' didn't appear to be dogmatic in the way established religions seemed to be would have been compelling. Antonio learned the fundamentals of the faith and began to teach and call others to Baha'ism. It was, in a way, a vehicle for his charisma: through his preaching he brought over twelve thousand people in West Africa to the Baha'i Faith. Eventually, though, he became disillusioned with the flaws and egoism he found in the Baha'i organization and stopped proselytizing. He continued for the time being to identify as a Baha'i.

Throughout this period he was inwardly driven by a series of celestial dreams. In 1993:

"*I ascended to Heaven and was presented to three Prophets of God: Jesus, Moses and Abraham, peace be upon them. I shook each Prophet's hand. I then saw a figure sitting upon a higher level. I ascended stairs to reach the figure and found myself in the presence of the Prophet Muhammad, may God bless him and give him peace. We did not speak but communicated telepathically.*

I saw a door behind the Messenger and wanted to pass through that door but after a silence the Prophet Muhammad spoke. 'Go back [to the world] so that you can educate your children and grandchildren.' At that moment I began descending to the Earth but never arrived."

"My daughter was only five years old at the time and when I awakened from the dream I thought, 'It will be a very long time before I'll have grandchildren.'"

Time passed. More dreams. In another dream:

"I ascended to the heavens. Arabic script was written on the sky. A rope dangled before me. I took the rope in my hands and the rope swung me to a place I had never seen before but I knew that it was Rio de Janeiro. I tried to descend to the city but could not. The rope then swung me to South Africa, then to Morocco. I descended to Morocco.

In real life Antonio would retrace part of his dream trajectory, visiting Brazil, Portugal and eventually Morocco.

In 2006, thirteen years after his first dream of the Prophets of God, Antonio had another powerful and decisive dream.

"In the dream I found myself on top of the moon. I felt something hold me with great force and hurl me down to earth. I was falling with such force that I thought 'If I hit the earth I'll break into a thousand pieces' and then I decelerated and found myself descending onto the shoulders of a powerful man who picked me up and placed me down on the earth."

Antonio had reached an impasse and crisis point. He journeyed to Morocco in 2008 at the beginning of Ramadan, seeking answers. He stayed with a Muslim friend there who he had met earlier in Guinea Bissau. He joined in the fast. He spent most of his time alone and slept. He looked in vain for a Qur'an translated into Portuguese. He settled for a Spanish translation. He had picked up a Qur'an before in Guinea Bissau and had seen something beautiful in it but someone tapped him on the shoulder and took it from him. He wanted to see it again.

He was deeply affected by a verse from *Sura al-Furqan* (The Criterion):

Have you not seen how your Lord stretches out the shadow?
If He had willed, He could have made it still. Then We made the
sun a guide to it. We withdraw it unto Ourselves, gradually.[76]

76   Holy Qur'an, *Sura al-Furqan* XXV:45-46, from The Majestic Qur'an, Nawawi Foundation

Seeking a Sign

He read the translation of the Qur'an. It gave him strength and propelled him to retreat to a Moroccan forest to meditate. "I meditated for a very long time. Tears flowed from my eyes continuously." Antonio was in a state of perplexity. "As the sun was setting I raised my hands in supplication and said, 'Oh God, if Islam is good for me guide me to Islam and if the Baha'i faith is good for me then keep me in this faith. I asked God to give me a sign that night and if God did not give me a sign, to accept my decision. When I returned from the forest, I broke my fast and went to sleep and in a dream:

"A man came and killed another young man who was my companion. The man that killed the companion said, 'My master is going to come to kill you as well'. So this master came and they were fighting and I looked up and saw the moon was very near to me. The longer I gazed at the moon I felt my body growing larger and larger and when my adversary saw this he fled."

Antonio awoke from the dream with conviction and clarity. "I said to myself, 'There is nothing in this world to prevent me from entering Islam.'" The next day Antonio Montero Fernandes became a Muslim. He went to his friend and declared his acceptance of Islam.

Astonished, Antonio's Muslim friend confessed that before he had met him he had seen him in a dream dressed in the white robes of a Muslim and praying as a Muslim. "When I arrived in Guinea Bissau and came to meet you, I found that you were not Muslim. Now, today, you tell me that you wish to enter Islam!" So his friend formally received Antonio Montero Fernandes—*Winda Bogobate Sina*—into Islam through the declaration of faith. Antonio took the Muslim name of Abdullah.

For three years he studied the Holy Qur'an and meditated on its meanings. He left everything and spent time in Morocco, Mauritania and Senegal. "I left my wife and children with God." Throughout this time, he performed remembrance of God "a lot, a lot, a lot". While in Senegal he had a dream.

"I saw feet. Many feet. Then I saw legs. Then I saw bodies. I saw the Balanta people. In the dream, as I watched the Balanta people I heard the call to prayer and I realized that my tribe would become Muslim. The Balanta people were calling the prayer."

Through this dream Abdullah became convinced that the Balanta were already spiritually Muslim. It was then that he decided to call his people to Islam. The very next day he returned to Guinea Bissau and began.

"I went from village to village. I would spend three months in one village teaching my people about Islam. I gave them the freedom to study and find the secret themselves." The door was already open for him because he had called so many thousands to the Baha'i Faith. So he returned to these congregations and told them, "'I have reached the final message. It has been a progression.' And the people trusted me."

On the very first day he invited people to Islam "I met the powerful man in my dream whose shoulders I descended on. He was the chief of the village (*tabanka*) where I began calling people to Islam." That very first day the chief and one thousand five hundred men, women and children of his people became Muslim. Within three days six thousand souls had come to Islam. Since that time seventeen thousand Balanta people have entered Islam through the ministrations of this simple builder and inspired teacher who had tapped into the spiritual yearnings of ordinary people from his tribe. "When one village would enter Islam, the neighboring village would follow suit and embrace the faith." Twenty mosques were established.

On the day I sat with Mawlana Abdullah he told me that two tribal chiefs representing nine thousand souls had just asked him to call them to Islam. "There are four hundred thousand Balanta people in Guinea Bissau and I believe that every one of our people can enter Islam. But we are taking our time."

I went away after Mawlana Abdullah related his story and realized that I had forgotten to ask him how it was that he came to the Qadiri Way and the guidance of Shaykh Muhammad Hydara al-Jilani. Months later I put the question to Shaykh Muhammad himself. I should have guessed the answer.

He had a dream.

Part Five
A FEW BAD HABITS

It is necessary for those who repent to hold themselves to account at every single moment, to leave aside every lust and abandon vain acts. These (consist of) six items: abandoning idle talk, abandoning idle looking, abandoning idle walking, and abandoning idle eating, drinking and clothing. [77]

ABU TALIB AL-MAKKI

77   *Qut Al Qulub*, translated by W. Moh Azzam b. Mohd Amin

Logorrhea

I SET OUT on the Path in silence, not from fear of God or some lofty ascetic sacrifice but out of a neurotic inferiority complex. I became tongue-tied and introverted, wallowing in insecurity, self-pity and self-doubt. While I was in this lugubrious state, someone counseled me that silence from self-obsession was ungenerous and that the cure for this form of parsimony was to come out of oneself and talk. With great effort I opened up and rejoined the social conversation. But then, once I loosened up it was hard to shut me up. I went through periods when I went on endlessly about things I knew and things I didn't know. I liked to hear the sound of my own voice. Since I was usually talking to people who knew even less than I did I began to exchange my inferiority complex for a superiority complex. I later on became a professional communicator and felt that this justified my verbosity. And then I came across the following passage from the Letters of Shaykh Moulay al-'Arabi al-Darqawi:

> Let me tell you about how I was once with my brother in God, the devout and noble Hasani Abu'l-'Abbas Ahmad at-Tahir (may God's mercy be upon him) in al-Qarawiyyin Mosque. We were both of us deeply wrapped in contemplation when all of a sudden my companion allowed himself to be distracted – or, let us say, weakened – to the point of falling into chatter like ordinary people. Abruptly and in anger, I said to him: 'If you wish to win, strike, and throw (it) out!' ... You also, my brothers, cast out idle talk completely and without fail, for it is one of the worst temptations and does not become your spiritual station and state. And say only good of people, for the Prophet (on whom be blessing and peace) says: 'He who is not grateful toward men is not grateful toward God.'[78]

---

78   The Letters of Moulay al-'Arabi al-Darqawi, translated by Titus Burkhardt

This made a deep impression on me and set me on a different course. The problem with prattle, I realized, is that it can easily lead to heedlessness, gossip, backbiting and slander, which are great sins.

When she was a young girl, my eldest daughter was sitting in the company of a group of Saudi women in Makkah. They were chattering away about one of the women's new son-in-law, commenting on a mistake he made in serving her tea. This comment initiated an escalating slanging match against the hapless (and absent) son-in-law that ended in all the women agreeing that the woman's daughter absolutely had to get a divorce, all over a *faux pas* in tea service.

Jabbering on reinforces the ego, dissipates light and hardens the heart. Most damagingly, excessive talking takes one away from the remembrance of God, which is the supreme medicine of the heart and the source of happiness and peace. It took a long time but eventually I turned away from idle talk. And then I became excruciatingly aware of how much time we spend blathering on. What a waste of breath! *Yakity yakity yakity yak.* I've reached the point where idle talk repulses me and my heart sickens whenever I find myself engaged in inconsequential conversation. I try to follow the practice of my beloved teacher, *al-marhum*, Sayyid 'Umar Abdallah, *Mwinyi Baraka*, who, before rising from any conversation would recite the Prophetic supplication, *Subhanaka 'Llahumma wa bi hamdika, ash-hadu an la ilaha illa anta, astaghfiruka wa atubu ilayk* (Glory be to You, O Allah, and with Your Praise. I witness that there is no god but You. I ask forgiveness of You and turn to You).

At the same time, I had to learn to make a distinction between idle talk and spiritual conversation that is helpful and heals the heart. I was able to do this by sitting amongst men of God and gnostic saints and observing their exchanges. I noticed that while their talk was never frivolous, there was never anything somber, self-serious or sanctimonious in these conversations. I discovered that the best conversation is when one has to speak by force, out of courtesy to others, to give sincere counsel from the heart, to help relieve a listener's anxieties, or to draw someone to the good, while being fully aware that all good comes from our Creator and that we have no knowledge, no power and no strength except from God. In this context, then, spiritual conversation is a source of healing and excellence and can elevate the spirit.

I remember driving one day with Sayyid 'Umar 'Abdallah and my friend the journalist 'Abdallah Schleifer. We were deep in discussion about a range of subjects that included, among other things, politics and homosexuality. When we parked, Sayyid 'Umar exclaimed with great enthusiasm, "Now *this* is the kind of discussion we should be having!" He said this because we were all learning as we talked, and we were all remembering God at the same time. In fact, while avoiding idle talk is a necessity on the spiritual path, spiritual conversation is indispensable. Moulay al-'Arabi al-Darqawi wrote in his Letters:

> Spiritual dialogue (*al-mudhākara*) is one of the most important practices of the Way and no one would dispense with it unless they did not know its worth. The master of our master, Sīdī al-'Arabī ibn 'Abdallāh, used to say, "Their wine is in the sacred dance (*al-haḍra*) and our wine is in talking together (*al-haḍra*)". He also used to say, "Two who converse about the Way is better than carrying two loads". [79]

> *When 'Uthman became Caliph he mounted the pulpit. The people waited to see what he would say, but he remained silent and said nothing. As he looked at the people, they were overcome by such a state of ecstasy that neither could they leave nor did they know where they were. Not a hundred homilies or sermons could have put them into such a state. They learned more valuable lessons, and more mysteries were revealed to them than could ever have been acquired through any amount of deeds or preaching. Until the end of the session 'Uthman kept looking at them in silence. As he was about to come down, he said, 'It is better for you to have an active leader than a talkative one.' And he spoke truly, for if the end of rhetoric is to impart something of benefit and to transform character, it can be imparted much better without speech than with.*
> MEVLANA JALALUD'DIN RUMI[80]

79   Letter 92, Letters of Mulay al-'Arabi al-Darqawi, translated by Michael Fitzgerald and Fouad Aresmouk.

80   Discourses of Rumi (*Fihi ma Fihi*), translated by W.M. Thackstone, Jr.

Standing on the corner watching all the girls go by.
Standing on the corner giving all the girls the eye.[81]

The First Glance

I WAS DRIVING along Speedway Avenue in Tucson, Arizona with a young man who had recently entered Islam. It was a brilliantly sunny day and at a stoplight a convertible with the top down rolled up beside us, driven by a gorgeous blonde. My young companion turned his head and—let me see if I can find the right word—he *ogled* the blonde. He stared out the window slack-jawed until the light turned green. While he was staring I said, "Abdul Jalil, the Prophet Muhammad, peace be upon him, said, "There is no fault in the first glance, but you have no right to a second glance." Without missing a beat or taking his eyes away from the blonde he said, "That's alright, I'm still on my first glance."

Funny.

In actuality, we men (sorry, but I can't speak for women here) find every loophole we can to try and get away with (here's the 1950s word again) ogling women, openly or surreptitiously. In the non-Muslim world it's a kind of national pastime. Then you enter Islam and suddenly you're not supposed to do that anymore. So how can we turn away from our red-blooded heterosexual proclivity for giving all the girls the eye?

Anatomy of a Leer

My beloved mentor Sayyid 'Umar 'Abdullah was in London with a British Muslim friend of ours, waiting to meet someone in a hotel lobby. He noticed his young companion looking with more than passing interest at a well-endowed woman crossing the lobby. Sayyid 'Umar then set about deconstructing the follow-up from his young companion's first glance. The next step would be to act on the ogle. Get up and approach the well-endowed woman. Then flirt with her. Then...do what? Ask her out on a date? (The young man was married). If he took her out on an illicit date, what then? Would he try to seduce her? How would that work out?

81   From the musical 'Most Happy Fella' by Frank Loesser

Would he go on and meet her family? Would he not feel guilty? How would this affect his marriage? By the time Sayyid 'Umar had finished his quiet narration, the thrill was gone.

～〇

Look-See

My younger brother is a talented craftsman in Southern California and for many years would sell his wares at beach shows up and down the coast. He was married and a Muslim and he came back from one of these weekends really frustrated. He said, "All weekend beautiful women are coming up to my stand in their bikinis, leaning over my table. It's driving me crazy. They're virtually naked. I don't know what to do." I said to him, "Don't look at them. *See* who they are." What I meant by this is that all these nubile and seductive young women are people, with insecurities, anxieties, bad habits, flaws, personality defects and all kinds of emotional baggage. They are other men's daughters and sisters. If you see them in all their humanity and human frailty they will cease becoming sex objects. It is a very big anaphrodisiac. My brother is an intelligent man and he understood exactly what I meant. The next weekend he went out to his next beach show. When he came back, he said, with a sense of amazement, "It worked!"

～〇

> A single glance may have a huge effect on a person's heart. A person's hearing and vision are like two doors which open on to the heart. Everything that a person sees and hears reaches the heart and has either a positive or a negative effect upon it. Therefore the believers must be careful what they allow their gaze to fall upon.[82]
>
> HABIB 'UMAR BIN HAFIZ

Consequentiality

Let's face it, we don't take these things seriously, but we should. An illicit glance can lead to lust. It may begin as something incipient and

---

82   'The Clarification of Noble Character', translated by Ibrahim Osi-Efa, Yahya Rhodus, Faiz Qureshy and Amin Buxton

innocent enough, at least in our heavily sexualized world, but, if one seeks illumination and salvation, letting lust get the best of us has consequences. Take the case of Abū 'Amr ibn 'Ulwan, a 9th century disciple of Imam Abu'l Qasim al-Junayd, God be well pleased with him:

> One day, I was standing to pray when my heart was overcome by a passion about which I thought for a long time until lust was generated from it. I fell to the ground and my whole body was blackened. Then I concealed myself in my house for three days and never came out, and I was trying to wash it away in the bathroom with soap and various cleansing substances, but it only grew blacker. It was removed from me after three days and the whiteness (of my skin) came back. Then I met Abu 'l-Qāsim al-Junayd, may Allah have mercy upon him, who had sent for me and brought me from al-Raqqa. When I came up to him, he said to me, "Are you not ashamed before Allah ta'ala? You were standing before Him, and you conversed with your lower soul in lust until it overcame you at al-Raqqa and it drove you away from the presence of Allah ta'ala. If I had not prayed to Allah and repented to Him on your behalf, you would have met Allah ta'ala with that color." I was very astonished as to how he knew that when he was in Baghdād and I was in al-Raqqa. Nobody was aware of this but Allah, may He be praised and glorified.

One of the sages commented on this narration, saying, "This was from the kindness and generosity of Allah ta'ala to him, since his heart was not blackened and the blackness appeared on his body. If it had been concealed in his heart, he would have been destroyed.

"There is no sin committed by the servant who persists in it but that his heart is blackened because of it, just like the blackness of body, which he mentioned, and it cannot be cleaned away except by repentance."[83]

---

83   From *Qut al-Qulub* (Nourishment of the Hearts) by Abu Talib al-Makki translated by W. Mohd Azam b. Mohd Amin.

A Close Call

A young man from New York had just embraced Islam. He hadn't shaken off his bad habits and was still vulnerable to the temptations in his old neighborhood. The biggest temptation of all was a beautiful young woman. She never gave him the time of day. Then, after he had entered Islam, he met her on the street and she was all over him. He couldn't help himself. He ended up in her apartment, in her bedroom, in her bed.

Suddenly, buck naked, under the sheets, seduced by the hottest girl he'd ever seen, he came to his senses. A wave of terror passed through him. He leapt out of bed. "I can't do this! I can't do this! *Astaghfirullah!* I'm a Muslim! I can't do this!" he cried out as he jumped into his clothes and fled the girl's bedroom and apartment, full of remorse and fear of God.

One year later he was walking in the neighborhood. From a distance he spied a young Muslima he had never seen before, all in white, head covered in *hijab*. As he passed her, he greeted her, "*As-Salaam Alaykum*". She replied, "*Wa alaykum Salaam.*"

And then he did a double take.

She was the girl he had run away from. He stopped. "You've become a Muslim!" he exclaimed. "How did you find Islam?"

She told him, "No man had ever run out on me the way you did and when you cried out, 'I can't do this! I'm a Muslim!' I had to find out what it was in your religion that was more powerful than sex. And when I did, I discovered Islam and became a Muslim."

Sensory Deprivation

I once had dinner with Muhammad Ali, the legendary boxer, may God have mercy upon his soul. He was a genuinely lovely person, a true gentleman with great humility, sweetness and a warm sense of humor. We were in Saudi Arabia and, as we ate, I asked him what he thought about being in the Kingdom. He thought for a minute and said, "Well I miss McDonalds." (That shows you how long ago it was). He was quiet for another minute. He said, "You know, when I was younger I had a lot of women. I don't do that anymore but, you know… *I like to look.*"

"You and me both," I thought to myself, but for me the fact that women were veiled was one of the things I liked best about living in the Kingdom of Saudi Arabia. What a relief! No distraction. I could see that from a woman's point of view gazing through a film of black gauze could be suffocating and oppressive, but it was very helpful for hapless heterosexual men like me who wanted to avoid second glances, if you know what I mean.

"Say to the believing men that they must lower their gaze."[84]

The Male Veil

In traditional societies the veil of the man is the lowered gaze. Back in the 1970s I was once in a group with Moulay Hassan bin Muhammad al-Alaoui from Fez. He was and is an extraordinarily beautiful man, physically and spiritually. He was quite young then. We were negotiating a Fez passageway when some women passed by and Moulay Hassan turned toward a wall and lowered his eyes in what was a completely natural and inherently graceful move that knocked me sideways. I've tried to copy him for forty years and have never been able to match the sheer elegance of his modesty (*hishma*). This courtesy was ingrained in Muslim men in traditional societies.

I remember my first wife, God bless her and protect her, who was from Makkah Al-Mukarrama, telling me that when she was a teenager she was out walking in the *Ajyad* district, where her family lived. Her face was veiled and she encountered her father walking in the opposite direction in an alleyway too narrow to allow two people to pass. Her father, who was a *mutawif* (pilgrim guide), immediately lowered his eyes and turned to face the wall to let the young woman pass. My wife was very funny and always up to practical jokes. She stopped in her tracks and stayed in place, blocking the alleyway. Her father kept quietly facing the wall. She stood there for a very long time and finally had mercy on the poor man and continued on her way. When he got home he was fuming about a crazy woman who kept him stuck facing a wall in an alleyway. I'm not sure whether my wife ever fessed up that she was the one who pranked him, but how beautiful was her father's traditional

84   Holy Qur'an *Sura al-Nur* 24:30

courtesy.

Of course, I liked the idea of veiling because I was escaping from a highly permissive society that revels in female pulchritude, on the streets, on TV and movies, in advertising and now online. On the other hand, I noticed that the enforced veiling of women had an altogether different effect on more than a few young men in Saudi society...

Skin

A European woman who reportedly in her past life had been an exotic dancer or something like that, had embraced Islam, quite sincerely I believe, and had become extremely pious, 'extreme' being the operative word here. She settled in Makkah and would come to the Holy Mosque every evening to perform the circumambulation (*tawaf*) of the Ka'ba, but instead of keeping the general pace of the other worshippers she would make her circuits slowly–*veeeery* slowly–with head turned up dreamily gazing at the heavens. Of course, she was completely veiled except for her pale white hand holding her *abaya*, but that was enough to drive the pious young Saudi male population crazy. Young men would approach my wife in the *Haram* with notes of affection and their telephone numbers and ask her to deliver these romantic missives to the pious white woman. They had no idea what she looked like (she was by then apparently middle aged and no pin-up) but the white hand was enough. It got so bad that I was told there was actually a municipal law enacted prohibiting male Saudi nationals from having anything to do with the excessively pious European woman.

This phenomenon was so widespread that Saudi satirists Abdullah Sadhan and Nasr al-Qasabi devoted an episode of their popular television series *Tash ma Tash* to it. They put a completely veiled little old lady in a limousine, rolled down the window part way enough to expose her bare hands and had her driven around the city. At the end of her tour the car door opened and an avalanche of paper scraps that hot-blooded young Saudis had tossed through the window poured out.

That kind of absurdity is offset by what can be the most romantic innocence...

Love at First Glance

During the Oil-Boom period in Saudi Arabia in the late 1970s a close friend of mine, an American procurements expert, served as senior consultant for major government construction projects, including the National Guard Headquarters. He was assigned two young men as his assistants: Muhammad, a Saudi of Moroccan extraction and 'Abdullah, a pure Bedouin. They were best friends, inseparable. Muhammad had two sisters and although Muhammad and 'Abdullah were close, in accordance with Saudi customs 'Abdullah never met the female members of Muhammad's family.

As 'Abdullah's father was an officer seconded to the Jordanian army and away most of the time, my friend became a kind of surrogate father to the young man. At one point 'Abdullah accompanied my friend and his wife to al-Madinah al-Munawwara. They were walking in the street near the Prophet's Mosque and ran into Muhammad and his family. It was the first time 'Abdullah had laid eyes on Muhammad's sisters who had their heads covered but were without face veils. One of the young women smiled at 'Abdullah. It must have been some smile because he instantly fell in love. He dragged my friend's wife aside, pointed out the sister and asked what her name was. "I think her name is Zuleikha." He then asked my friend if he could act as his guardian and approach Muhammad's father to ask for Zuleikha's hand in marriage. A meeting was set and my friend accompanied 'Abdullah to Muhammad's house and asked his father for the hand of Zuleikha.

"'Abdullah, you are like my own son and we would be pleased to have you as a member of our family," said the father of Muhammad, "but my eldest daughter Fatima is not yet married. It is not right that Zuleikha precedes her. I must make sure Fatima is married first. Would you consider taking Fatima as your wife? "No," said 'Abdullah. "It must be Zuleikha. I love her!"

Zuleikha's father said, "I'm so sorry 'Abdullah but I really must make sure that Fatima is married first. Please be patient. When Fatima is married please come back."

'Abdullah was devastated. He pleaded with Muhammad to intercede with his father. Muhammad explained that if Zuleikha married, families of eligible young men would think that there was something wrong with Fatima not to have attracted a suitor first. His father had the best interests of both his daughters at heart. He couldn't sway him.

'Abdullah was inconsolable. He moped around the office. He couldn't focus. After a couple of weeks like this he went back to my friend and begged him to set up another meeting with Zuleikha's father. He felt sorry for the young man and made the arrangements. This time 'Abdullah was genuinely desperate. He pleaded with her father to reconsider and allow him to marry Zuleikha. The father was unmoved. "I'm sorry 'Abdullah but I must marry Fatima first. Would you reconsider and take Fatima as your wife?"

"*Never*. It must be Zuleikha!"

"Then I'm really sorry but you will have to be patient until my first daughter is married."

After this second meeting 'Abdullah really and truly fell apart. He stopped eating. He stopped grooming himself; his hair was wild, his beard untrimmed. He never changed his thobe. He lost interest in everything. He would stand outside Muhammad's family home like a lunatic and gaze up at the second story windows in hopes of getting a glimpse of his beloved Zuleikha. He was like Majnun yearning for Layla. This went on for days and weeks. My friend became concerned for the young man's sanity. Finally, after a long vigil, a second story window opened and his beloved peeked out.

Abdullah was ecstatic. "*I love you Zuleikha! I love you!*" he cried out.

She beckoned him to come closer to the house. He gazed up at her.

"*I'm Fatima,*" she said and then ducked back into the house.

A few days later my friend and 'Abdullah returned to Muhammad's family. The young man was cleaned up and groomed and beaming with delight. He sat down in the salon and this time asked for Fatima's hand in marriage. She came out, served 'Abdullah tea and cakes, a sign that she accepted his proposal.

Abdullah and Fatima were married and raised a family. I don't know if they lived happily ever after. It was a long time ago, but how about that for a first glance?

The seeker of God, as he walks, should know at each step he makes whether that step is against God or of God: if it is against God, he must ask for pardon, and if it is of God, he must persevere in it, that it may be increased.[85]

'ALI 'UTHMAN AL-HUJWIRI

Step by Step

SO MUCH OF our lives is spent walking from one place to another: around the house, to work, school and market. Our expressions of faith and practice are rooted in ambulatory lexis. We follow the *Sharia*, the Road. We are on a spiritual Path, *Tariqa*. Those who follow a Path are called *Salikeen*, or Travelers. The apotheosis of our worship is the *Hajj* and *Umrah*, which involves circling the Ka'ba in the *Tawaf* and walking and running between Safa and Marwa in the *Sa'i*. Many pilgrims walk from Arafat to Muzdalifa and Mina. We walk to the mosque and step up to pray in hope that we will gain forgiveness, blessings and salvation.

> Abu Huraira reported that the Prophet Muhammad said, may God grant him peace: "Whoever purifies himself for ablution in his house and walks to a house among the houses of Allah in order to fulfill an obligation among the obligations of Allah, then one step of his will expiate his sins and another step will elevate his status."[86]

So, we are either walking of God, or against God, in the right direction or the wrong direction.

⁓

The Wrong Direction

Many years ago I had to fly from London to Amsterdam for one day for a brief appointment. Afterwards I had the rest of the day free and nothing to do but ride the canals and wander around the city before my flight back to London. Someone had told me that a walk through Amsterdam's *De Wallen*, or Red Light District, in the middle of the

85   *Kashf al-Mahjub*, translated by Reynold A. Nicholson
86   al-Nawawi from Sahih Muslim

mediaeval city center, was something I had to do. I'd never heard of a red-light district being a tourist attraction before, but I looked it up and, sure enough, there it was in all the guidebooks and they made it sound fairly innocuous. I'm not exactly an innocent but I'd never knowingly been to a red-light district before and had no idea what to expect. I set out along the canals, my lurid curiosity aroused, walking toward what had been touted as a colorful and atmospheric neighborhood. I don't know what I was thinking. I rationalized my visit as a harmless touristic walkabout I suppose.

I turned a corner, entered *De Wallen* and scanned the ancient walkways and quaint buildings along the canal. It *was* colorful and atmospheric, that's for sure, just not quite in the way I anticipated. Scantily clad women danced lifelessly in neon-lit windows, dead faces and empty eyes beckoning passersby to come inside. It conjured a vision straight out of Hieronymus Bosch, a squalid version of the Garden of Earthly Delights and the Last Judgment. It was dark, bizarre and hellish, and my heart seized up. I dropped my eyes in shame and rushed along the street repeating *astaghfirullah* (I ask forgiveness of God) over and over again, regretting every step I'd taken in the direction of that sordid, depraved tourist trap. God forgive me that, and all the many other steps I've taken in the wrong direction.

The walk of the seeker of God should always be of such a description that if anyone should ask him whither he is going he should be able to answer decisively: '*Verily, I am going to my Lord; He will direct me.*'[87] Otherwise his walking is a curse to him, because right steps (*khatawat*) proceed from right thoughts (*khatarat*): accordingly, if a man's thoughts are concentrated on God, his feet will follow his thoughts.[88]

ALI BIN 'UTHMAN AL-HUJWIRI

87   Holy Qur'an, *Sura al-Saffat* xxxvii: 99
88   *Kashf al-Mahjub*, translated by Reynold A. Nicholson

Right Steps

I was living in Dubai not far from the largest shopping center on earth. Apart from groceries, printer ink and an occasional hot dog, I used to marvel that there was virtually nothing in Dubai Mall that I wanted or needed. But then I came upon this *hadith*:

> The Messenger of Allah (may the peace and blessings of Allah be upon him) said: "Whoever enters the market and says *la ilaha illa 'Llah wahdahu la sharika 'Llah, lahu l'mulku wa lahu'l-hamd, yuhyi wa yumit, wa Huwa Hayyu la yamut, bi yadihi l'khayr, wa Huwa 'ala kulli shay'in Qadir.* (There is no god but Allah, alone, without partner, to Him belongs all sovereignty and praise. He gives life and causes death, and He is living and does not die. In His hand is all good and He is powerful over all things.) God will erase one million sins from his record, and record one million good deeds, and elevate him one million degrees, and build him a house in Paradise."[89]

After reading this glorious narration, I made it a practice to drive over to Dubai Mall and walk round and round that vast shrine to conspicuous consumption for no other reason than to repeat the Prophetic invocation in hopes that my innumerable sins would be erased and replaced with one million good actions, that my station would be raised and that I would be making an investment in Paradisiacal real estate. Next time you hit your local mall, try it out. I highly recommend it.

❧

✺ Vicarious Walking

A shaykh was walking with a young disciple. They came to a river. There was no bridge. No crossing. A beautiful young woman on the opposite shore was trying to ford the river. She was floundering. Her clothes were wet and clinging to her body. She implored the two wayfarers to help her cross the river. The shaykh waded into the river. When he reached her, she wrapped her arms and legs around his body. He held her close to

---

89   Reported by al-Tirmidhi and Ibn Majah, from Prayers of Muhammad, translated by A.H. Farid

him. She placed her face against his neck. He turned around and carried her across to the other side. He set her down and she went on her way. The young disciple watched, wide-eyed. The two men continued their journey crossing to the other side of the river and continued walking. The young man was lost in thought. As the two men walked, the disciple turned to his master and asked, "What was it like to carry the young woman across the river?" The shaykh smiled. "You tell me," he replied. "I set her down on the other side of the river. You're still carrying her with you."[90]

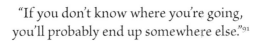

Pace

Nasrud'din Khoja was tilling his field. A traveler walking on the road stopped and addressed the lone farmer. "Excuse me. Could you tell me how long it will take to walk to the next village? Nasrud'din Khoja did not look up from his tilling and kept quiet. The traveler said, again, louder, "Excuse me. I asked you if you could tell me how long it will take for me to walk to the next village." Again, Nasrud'din Khoja continued his tilling and did not respond. This made the traveler angry. "What is *wrong* with you? I asked you a simple question and you have ignored me! How rude!" Nasrud'din Khoja kept tilling and made no reply. At this the traveler continued down the road, fuming and cursing the rude farmer, when he heard a voice behind him. *"Twenty minutes."* The traveler turned. "What?", he said. Nasrud'din Khoja said, "It will take you twenty minutes to walk to the village." The traveler shouted back, "Why didn't you say that in the first place? I asked you three times and you refused to answer. Now you're telling me?" Nasrud'din Khoja replied, "I didn't know how fast you were walking."

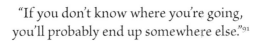

"If you don't know where you're going,
you'll probably end up somewhere else."[91]

Spiritual Compass

This amusing insight could as easily be applied to the spiritual path as to

---

90   From a *Sohbet* of Muzaffer Ozak
91   Peter's Quotations: Ideas for Our Time by Laurence J. Peter

corporate planning. Indeed, God challenges us to define our objectives.

Where then are you going?[92]

Every step we take, every decision we make means something and takes us in one direction or another. The Prophet Muhammad said, "Actions are according to intentions, and everyone will get what was intended."[93]

Of the true people of the Path I have had the blessing to walk with, sit with and observe, whether they showed signs of majesty or beauty, every single one of them was possessed of heart-rending humility and this is reflected in the way they walk. They walk full of certainty and purpose, without pride or pretention, but with an absolutely natural self-assurance and nonchalance. They always know exactly where they are going because they are walking 'of God.'

Walking with the people of the Path in this world gives one a tangible sense of a walking step by step toward the Next.

The servants of the Merciful are those
who walk humbly on the earth.[94]

---

92   Holy Qur'an, *Sura Takwir* lxxxi:26
93   Sahih Bukhari and Sahih Muslim
94   Holy Qur'an, *Sura al-Furqan* xxv:63

Eating is part of religion.[95]
ONE OF THE PIOUS PREDECESSORS[96]

Breaking Bread

WHEN I WAS a teenager I decided to become a vegetarian. I'd seen some film showing how animals were slaughtered and it put me off meat right up to the time I entered Islam. I think that changing what I ate was a necessary preparation for turning my life around and taking a spiritual path and I've observed the same pattern in other seekers as part of an instinctual process of purification. In the beginning you don't know how to change yourself spiritually so you start by making physical or behavioral changes.

When I started practicing Islam I abandoned my vegetarianism in favor of the *halal* because meat was so central to the Muslim diet. I was a reluctant carnivore, but the concept of the *halal* made sense. Eating meat that had been killed by hand humanely in the name of God and refraining from ingesting anything impure or toxic was easy enough to understand. Not eating pork was no problem for me because I hadn't been eating any kind of meat, including poultry.

I didn't need any justifications or rationale for keeping to the *halal*. I took everything on faith and didn't spend too much time thinking about it. Over time, through my readings, I started to realize that food could have a very serious and immediate impact on one's spiritual health.

🐟 The Young Ecstatic

The 8th century gnostic Ibrahim ibn Adham learned of a young man who manifested signs of sainthood. The youth was, by all accounts, in perpetual ecstasy, leading a life of extreme asceticism and relentless worship. Ibrahim expressed an interest in meeting the young ecstatic, and his companions arranged an introduction. When they met, the

95   From *Kitab adab al-akl* from the *Ihya 'ulum al-din* by Imam al Ghazali, translated by Dennis Johnson-Davies,
96   'Pious Predecessors' refer to the first two generations of Muslims after the time of the Prophet Muhammad, peace be upon him.

young man invited Ibrahim to stay with him for three days. During that time, Ibrahim was able to observe his host at close range. What he witnessed was more impressive than the reports he had heard. The young man was overcome by a powerful state. He wept continuously. He never slept or rested for an instant throughout the day or night. Ibrahim felt as if his own devotions paled beside the exertions of the young ecstatic. Yet, something wasn't right. Ibrahim had an intuition.

He thanked his host and reciprocated with his own invitation.

"I have been your guest for three days. Now come and be my guest for forty days." The ecstatic youth accepted.

Born a prince and raised in the lap of luxury, Ibrahim gave up his Kingdom for a life of poverty and devotion on the Path to God. He was famously scrupulous about the source of his income. He refused to beg and would support himself with honest labor like grinding corn or tending orchards. Whatever he ate came from the labor of his own hands. He firmly believed that "the root of the matter is what a man eats."

When the young ecstatic came to Ibrahim's home, the first thing the Shaykh did was to serve him a meal, in accordance with the courtesies of the Path. When the young man partook of the meal his ecstasy instantly vanished. He lost all the intensity that made him sleepless. His tears dried up. He shrieked. "WHAT HAVE YOU DONE TO ME? *I have lost everything!*"

Ibrahim answered the distraught young man. "The food you've been eating was *haram* (forbidden), from unclean sources. Because of this, satanic impulses invaded your state and overwhelmed you. As soon as you swallowed *halal* (lawful) food from pure sources, the satanic impulses deluding you were revealed for what they are." The young man had to start all over again, from square one.[97]

> Watch carefully what you eat, and then there will be no harm
> for you in not staying awake during the night or fasting during
> the day![98]

IBRAHIM BIN ADHAM

---

97   Retold from *Tadhkirat al-Awliya* (Memorial of the Saints) by Attar, translated by A.J. Arberry

98   *al-Risala al-qushayriyya fi 'ilm al-tasawwuf* (Al-Qushayri's Epistle on Sufism), translated by Alexander D. Knysh.

I learned that, from a spiritual perspective, what is *halal* or *haram* is not only determined by whether an animal is sacrificed properly but whether the food one eats comes from a permissible source. This can be a grey area, defined by one's own spiritual condition and the limits one sets on oneself, in accordance with one's own sense of purity. When I was starting out in Islam I came across a passage from *Ruh al-Quds* by Muhyid'din ibn al-'Arabi, which described the discretionary nature of whether provision is *halal* or *haram*:

> It happened one day at Ceuta…that the Sultan Abu al-'Ali, may God grant him success, sent two lots of food for us…the brethren who had come to that place…ate it, while my special companions [99]did not partake of it. On the second night the Sultan did the same, but I myself neither accepted nor refused it. When they heard that the Sultan had sent down food, the brethren came to us to eat of it.
>
> I, for my part, performed the night prayer. One of those who had come and who claimed to be a shaykh, said to me, "One may not pray on a full stomach." I remained silent and did not answer him, which made him angry; so I said to him, "I did not accept the food, nor did I see fit to eat it because it is, in my opinion, unlawful food; nor could I order you to eat it since I wish for you what I wish for myself." Then, having explained to him the reason for my opinion regarding the food, I said, "The food is available, so let him who considers it lawful eat it, otherwise not."[100]

Ibn al-Arabi and other adepts of his time considered food from rulers to be forbidden for them to eat, but they did not forbid 'the brethren' (*fuqara*) and other Muslims from partaking.

Some contemporary scholars have given Muslims living in Judeo-Christian dominated countries (Europe, North and South America, Australia and New Zealand) where *halal* meat is often difficult to

---

99   He refers to two living saints of the time, Abu Muhammad 'Abdallah al-Fakhkhar and Ibrahim Tarif

100   *Ruh al-Quds*, from Sufis of Andalusia, translated by R.W.J. Austin

come by, dispensation to eat non-*halal* meat because they consider the population of these countries to be 'People of the Book.' Other scholars have gone a step further, saying that it is enough to invoke Allah's name over chicken or meat to make it *halal*. I'm in no position to pass judgment on these judgments and I have many devout Muslim friends who have no problem eating meat that has not been sacrificed according to *sharia*. I would never think of making this an issue for them but, personally, I don't consider meat that is not properly sacrificed permissible for me. Fish and vegetables will do me just fine, thank you very much.

Before entering Islam eating was all about what you ate. After entering Islam I discovered that eating was all about *how* you ate. Keeping company with people of the Path introduced me to eating as a kind of sacrament. Sitting at a table amongst *awliya* and *saliheen*, literally breaking bread with them, had a profound impact on me. The act of eating seemed to be given equal importance to the act of worship. Every gathering was for the purpose of remembering God, but would always be sealed by a meal. Vibrating with the resonance of *dhikru'llah*, there was a sense that we were being nourished and sustained by the *baraka* (blessing) of the remembrance and that this blessing was delivered through the meat, vegetables and grains we were eating. I noticed that the men of attainment at my table would take food with great relish but would, in fact, eat very little. The whole transaction was a life lesson, as *fuqara* carried out the *adab* (spiritual courtesies) detailed by Imam al-Ghazali in his *Kitab adab al-akl* (Book on Manners Relating to Eating). Observing the way the brethren ate completely transformed the way I looked upon eating. When I began living in the Muslim world I discovered that this spiritual dimension of eating informed even the most worldly and secularized Muslims. Food is central to hospitality and hospitality is inherent in Muslim culture and Muslim culture emanates completely from Prophetic tradition.

> Abdullah bin 'Amr bin al-'As (May God be pleased with him) reported: A man asked the Messenger of Allah, (may God grant him peace): "Which act in Islam is the best?" He replied,

"To give food, and to greet everyone, whether you know them or not."[101]

Hajj Jalali was a wealthy and deeply devout disciple of the celebrated Moroccan Shaykh Sidi Muhammad ibn al-Habib, may God be well pleased with them both. Despite his wealth Hajj Jalali was an austere, taciturn gentleman with the most serene face I have ever laid eyes on. To purify his wealth the Shaykh ordered him to feed forty people every day for the rest of his life. And so he did. We were regular beneficiaries of his largesse. We would pile in to cars and vans and head out to his home in Meknes, then file into and sit around a large *majlis* room on raised couches. Hajj Jalali would enter the *majlis*, greet his guests, then sit off to the side, directing his staff to bring in huge trays with mountains of delicious meat and couscous. He sat quietly as we ate, cane leaning on his knee, watching us, making sure that we were well served and well fed. I had never seen anything like that in my life. It was so graceful, so utterly beautiful. He did it every single day.

Hajj Jalali continued to feed people until the end of his life. He knew when the end was near and, with the same quiet serenity he had while serving a feast, he sat, cane on knee, to oversee the digging of his own grave. He was buried in the *Zawiya* of Sidi Muhammad ibn al-Habib beside the resting place of his beloved master, may God be well pleased with them both.

---

101   Sahih al-Bukhari and Sahih Muslim

Disintoxication

I WAS WITH a Greek friend in Thessaloniki. He introduced me to his father-in-law, who was genial and welcoming. He said to his son-in-law, "Let's take Haroon out and drink *ouzo*."[102] My friend explained, "Haroon doesn't drink." His father-in-law repeated, "We really should take him out for *ouzo*." My friend said, "No, really, Haroon doesn't drink." I nodded. My friend's father-in-law said impatiently, "Yes, I know. You said that already, *but he should try!*" On another visit to Greece, in Athens, I ran into a Greek who'd been working in Saudi Arabia. We talked for a bit and he also invited me out for *ouzo*. When I told him I don't drink he pulled back in shock and exclaimed, "*Are you not a man?*"

The Greeks may be more forthright and melodramatic in their passion for drink but in the West, and indeed through most of the world, every occasion is celebrated with some kind of alcoholic beverage. Every holiday, every social function, every business event, every milestone is alcoholized in one form or another. Unless you're a recovering alcoholic it is nigh on unthinkable to refuse a drink. In social gatherings teetotalers can make drinkers uncomfortable and, in some societies, where drinking is a big feature of the culture non-drinkers can be ostracized.

I attended a conference of journalists in Europe and passed by a group of newsmen drinking in the hotel bar. The life of the party was a rather loud, almost stereotypical Aussie, the international editor of a major newspaper. I didn't think much of it. Journalists do have a reputation. A day or two later, the Aussie approached me. He said, with some sense of urgency, "Can I talk to you in private?" It was a strange request given that we had never spoken before. We retired to one of our rooms in the hotel. When we sat down he said, furtively, "*I'm a Muslim!*" as if he was letting me in on a deep, dark secret. I registered surprise. "I would never have guessed. I've seen you drinking, rather heavily, at the conference." He said, "You see, I have to drink or I might even lose my job. In

---

102   A strong anise flavored *apertif*, called *arak* in the Levant and *raki* in Turkey

Australia, if you don't drink you're an outcast." He went on to explain the prejudice against non-drinkers in Australia and how he coped by going to the bar with his colleagues after work and then going home to his Muslim wife and doing his prayers. I found that kind of duplicitous existence difficult to fathom but he insisted that it was necessary for his professional survival.

Although intoxicants are forbidden in Islam, there has always been a fair bit of intoxication going on throughout the Muslim world, even where alcohol is illegal and supposedly unavailable. My next door neighbor in Makkah was a roaring drunk Saudi who beat his wife when he was on a bender. His wife and children would take refuge with us until he sobered up. Because the government considered alcoholism a crime, not an illness, he ended up in and out of jail. Back in the 1980s it was rumored there was a fully functioning bar in Jeddah patronized by the chief of police. A lot of 'liberal' Muslims drink. I've noticed that, unlike non-Muslim social drinkers, when Muslims drink socially they tend to get absolutely plastered. I think the reason for this may be that they know what they're doing is forbidden so they figure they might as well go for broke.

In fact dipsomania has been a feature of Muslim history from the very beginnings of Islam. Lest we be too smug or morally superior, there have been Muslim drunks in every age. And there have been many who have made *tawba* and teetotaled.

✺ Tell Me About My Lord

Bishr ibn al-Harith was a full-blown alcoholic. Born near the city of Merv in 767 AD (150 AH), he moved to Baghdad where he lived an utterly dissolute life, moving from one drunken orgy to the next.

One day, wine-soaked and reeling down a road, looking down to find his uncertain footing, he came upon a piece of paper on the ground. He picked it up and read it. On the trampled scrap was written the *Basmalah*, 'In the Name of God, the Merciful, the Compassionate.' An irrational flood of devotion overcame him and he lurched to the bazaar, purchased some rose essence and lovingly perfumed the paper. He took the inscription to his dwelling and set it reverently in a place of honor. He then proceeded to his next wine party.

That night one of God's Friends had a dream. In the dream he was instructed to find Bishr al-Harith, and to relate the dream to him. In the dream a voice addressed Bishr:

"You have perfumed My Name, so I have perfumed you. You have exalted My Name, so I have exalted you. You have purified My Name, so I have purified you. By My Majesty, I will surely perfume your name in this world and the Next."

When he awoke from the dream, the saint was perplexed. He knew about Bishr. He shook his head. "He's a degenerate. This can't be a true dream." The saint performed the ritual ablution, prayed and returned to sleep. And he saw the same vivid dream. Once again, he refused to believe the dream could be true. He returned to sleep and then, for the third time, he saw the dream.

So, in the morning the saint went out in search of Bishr. He was told that Bishr was at a wine party. He found the party and approached the group of drunkards. He asked where he could find Bishr.

"He was here but he staggered away in a drunken stupor."

"I have a message for him," said the saint. Bishr's drinking buddies formed a search party and they tracked him down, barefoot and blind drunk. The saint told him that he had a message.

"A message from who?" demanded Bishr.

"A message from God," replied the saint.

Bishr shrieked and burst into tears. *"Is it a message of reproach or punishment?"* he cried out in fear. The saint related the dream. Bishr's heart turned. Suddenly sober, he faced his drinking companions in contrition. "I have had a call! I am leaving. I say goodbye to you. You will never see me in this condition again!"

And from that day until the day he died, Bishr lived a life of extreme austerity, remembrance and devotion. He never wore shoes for the rest of his life. He remained barefoot, he said, because "I was barefoot when I made my peace with God and since that moment I have been ashamed to wear shoes. And God has said, 'I have made the earth a carpet for you,' so it is wrong for me to walk with shoes on the carpet of the King." For this he became known as *al-Hafi* – 'the Barefoot'.

Overwhelmed with the vision of God, Bishr al-Hafi became one of the greatest saints of his time.

Imam Ahmad ibn Hanbal would visit Bishr often. The master's students protested, saying, "In our time you are the world's pre-eminent scholar of traditions, law, theology, jurisprudence and every science, yet every spare moment you seek out the company of this degenerate? How can that be right?"

The famed scholar replied, "It is true that of all the sciences you have mentioned I have more knowledge than Bishr, but he knows God more than I do." Imam Ahmad ibn Hanbal would come to Bishr al-Hafi, and the great imam, heart full of yearning, would say to the broken, barefoot ascetic, the knower of God, "Tell me, Bishr, please tell me about my Lord."

Proximity

For many years Sidi Muhammad ibn al-Habib, may God be well pleased with him, had the same driver whose name was Hajj Muhammad. Hajj Muhammad was a pious *faqir* who would transport the Shaykh from his *zawiya* in Meknes around the town and to other cities, towns and villages across Morocco to see to the spiritual needs of his many followers. However, Hajj Muhammad was in love with Makkah and kept leaving Meknes to make the *Hajj* and *Umrah* until he finally settled in Makkah permanently, working for a Saudi landowner to help him rent his property during the pilgrimage season. When I lived in Makkah I became friends with Hajj Muhammad. He was married and living in the *Shamiyyah* District, which has since been razed to make way for the expansion of the Holy Mosque complex. Hajj Muhammad left all his salary in trust with his sponsor. In the end the sponsor cheated him. He left Saudi Arabia for Tunis where he lived the rest of his life. May God have mercy upon him.

With the departure of Hajj Muhammad, the Shaykh asked his *fuqara* to help him find another good driver. After looking all over Meknes they returned empty-handed. They couldn't find a decent driver who was available. "There is one driver who's very good," he was told, "but you wouldn't want him."

"Why not?" asked the Shaykh. "He's dissolute," they told him. The driver in question was also named Muhammad. He was, according to the *fuqara*, a drunkard who lived in a brothel, but they admitted he had a reputation for being a very good driver. The Shaykh said, "Find him and bring him to me."

The *fuqara* brought the driver to Sidi Muhammad ibn al-Habib. He appeared before the great saint, sheepish and guilt-ridden. The Shaykh said, "I want you to be my driver. Your pay will be such and such. You will drive me wherever I need to go. There's only one thing I ask of you. I want you to refrain from drinking when you are with me because, you see, I don't like the smell of alcohol. Will you do that for me? Would you accept this job?" He took the job.

So he began to work for the Shaykh, driving him to circles of *dhikr*, to mosques, to the homes of his *fuqara*, to *mawlids*, to the tombs of the saints. Day in and day out he was with one of the greatest living saints of the age surrounded by his followers, stone cold sober. Gradually he began to join in the ritual prayers and then the circles of *dhikr*. Finally, one day he turned up at the *zawiya* door asking if he could stay there. It turned out that he had started to perform his daily prayers in the brothel and the ladies threw him out.

When Sidi Muhammad ibn al-Habib died in 1972, Muhammad was devastated, inconsolable, shipwrecked. Proximity to the Shaykh had transformed this good-for-nothing-but-driving lowlife into a noble man of the Way.

> Shaykh Muhammad al-Bajli is said to have seen the Prophet, may God's blessings and peace be upon him, in a dream-vision and asked him which was the best of all deeds? His answer was, *to sit with a saint of God for as long as it takes to milk a goat or cook an egg.*[103]

~~~~~

🌺 My Saint

Imam Abu l'Hassan al-Shadhili, may God be well pleased with him, had a son named 'Ali. Shaykh Abu l'Aza'im Madi, one of al-Shadhili's

---

103   From 'Sufi Sage of Arabia: Imam 'Abdallah ibn 'Alawi al-Haddad' by Dr. Mostafa alBadawi

greatest disciples and a saint in his own right, ran into 'Ali on the street in Alexandria. The young man was drunk. Madi was horrified, as drinking wine is a major sin in Islam. He forcibly dragged 'Ali back to his home and beat him in front of the boy's mother with such severity that the young man grabbed hold of his mother. Madi said, "I dragged him away with such force that he pulled with his hands the cords of her hair. She cried aloud and wept." Madi continued to beat 'Ali for some time and then left him. Imam al-Shadhili came upon his wife in tears and asked why she wept. She told him that Madi had dragged their son into the house and was beating him, but she didn't tell her husband that 'Ali was drunk.

Imam al-Shadhili was deeply disturbed by this news. He went in to his *zawiya*, found Madi and confronted him. "Why have you done this? Why have you beaten my son even as he clung to his mother?" Madi replied, "I found him *drunk*. By God, even if he had clung to you I would have flogged him according to the punishment prescribed for drunkenness!" When he heard this, the Shaykh's face fell in distress. "*So it is*," he whispered and withdrew into solitude. After an hour the Shaykh emerged from his retreat and called for Madi. He was exultant. "O Madi," he said, "I withdrew into solitude to revile and repudiate my son! But I was told [by God], 'O 'Ali (Imam al-Shadhili's first name) what has come between you and My Friend? Leave him until that which I have decreed for him shall come to pass." And a short time later his son's heart turned away from the world. He became an ascetic and wanderer. He ended up in the Maghrib, bearing the marks of sainthood and lived out his days as one of God's beloved Friends.[104]

We drank from the lights in the tavern of the Presence
a wine that removed confusion without a doubt.[105]
SIDI MUHAMMAD IBN AL-HABIB

104   Retold from *Durrat al-Asrar wa Tuhfat al-Abrar* (The Mystical Teachings of al-Shadhili), translated by Elmer H. Douglas
105   The Diwan, 'We Drank from the Lights', translated by Abdurrahman Fitzgerald, Fouad Aresmouk and Moulay Abdelkebir al-Belghiti

The Tavern

The imagery of intoxication pervades the mystical poetry of Islam, from Attar to Hafiz to Rumi to Ibn al-'Arabi and Ibn al-Farid, to Sidi Ahmed al-'Alawi and Ibn al-Habib. 'The Tavern', 'Wine', 'the Cup', 'Drunkenness' are powerful mystical symbols that indicate the deep rapture and illumination experienced by the lovers of God. Those who deny the intoxication that comes from worship and remembrance are those who have never experienced it, but I can give you one example of collective intoxication that anyone who has been there should be able to relate to.

Throughout the month of Ramadan Muslims perform the *Tarawih* prayers in congregation. In Makkah al-Mukarrama, hundreds of thousands of believers congregate around the Holy Ka'ba to break the fast and pray at sunset and for the Night prayer (*salat al-'Isha*), followed by the *Tarawih* prayer. In many places, eight cycles of prayer are performed, in accordance with the *Sunna*, and signalling an end to congregational worship. In Makkah the imam leads the assembly in twenty cycles with extended recitation. During the last ten days of the month, the additional twelve cycles of the *Tahajjud* prayer are performed in congregation, finishing just before the dawn prayer is called. Many Muslims who may only perform the obligatory prayers throughout the rest of the year find themselves praying all night long through the month, listening to the entire Qur'an recited in the most sacred place on earth. It is an incredibly intense experience. By the end of Ramadan, thousands of worshippers become collectively overwhelmed, hearts overflowing with remembrance of God, filled with Light. Through worship and self-abnegation, they share a taste of the intoxication experienced by those who have entered the Tavern of the Presence and drunk the wine of Light.

To deny the possibility of spiritual intoxication is to remove a powerful incentive for purification and worship: an intoxication that removes confusion, a drunkenness with no hangover. What a difference between effulgent rapture and the darkness of an alcoholic stupor!

Uniformity

"CLOTHES ARE LIKE a uniform." This is what my mentor Sayyid 'Umar 'Abdullah used to say. We dress to identify ourselves in some way as part of something: a nationality, an ethnicity, a profession, a social class and of course, a religion. Suits and ties, blue jeans, *haute couture*, *prêt-à-porter*, *djellabas*, *abayas* (plain or designer), *chadors*, *jilbabs*, sarongs, bikinis, burkinis, cotton, linen, leather, polyester, silk - take your pick. We dress to stand out or blend in, to conform or rebel. One way or another, we're all in uniform. Clothes make a statement, mark status or can become a kind of camouflage. In other words, what we wear sends a message, either subliminal or overt. Sometimes, we send the wrong sartorial message altogether and sometimes we can't see the person for the clothes.

The Honored Guest

As the local religious authority Nasrud'din Khoja had been invited to a feast in his honor, hosted by the district governor. During the day of the feast Khoja worked in his fields. As the daylight waned he left the fields and proceeded directly to the grand mansion of the district governor to attend the feast. He wanted to arrive early. Nasrud'din knocked on the door, which was opened by a servant. "Here I am for the feast!" said Nasrud'din cheerfully. The servant beheld a dusty farmhand and slammed the door in Khoja's face. Nasrud'din went away for a while, then returned and knocked again. Again, the door was slammed in his face. He returned once more and, for a third time, he was refused entrance.

He went home, bathed and changed into fine robes and a luxurious fur coat he had been given by a wealthy student. This time, when he knocked on the door, he was welcomed with great deference and seated at the place of honor beside the district governor. Dinner was served. The guests commenced eating the delicacies before them. Nasrud'din Khoja picked up his plate and, with delectation bordering on gluttony, dumped the contents into the pocket of his luxurious fur coat. He then began stuffing the pockets of his elegant robes with bread and side dishes. The guests were appalled. "What are you doing, master Nasrud'din? What is the meaning of this behavior?"

The Khoja replied cheerfully, "I am feeding the honored guest!" To everyone's horror, he continued stuffing delicacies into every pocket, dribbling sauce over the fur coat and pouring yogurt into the sleeves.

"What are you talking about," cried the guests.

"There is no doubt that the honored guests are the robe and fur coat so I am making sure that they are well fed."

Going Native

There's a tendency for Muslims entering Islam for the first time to 'go native' and start dressing up in 'Muslim' clothes, whatever those are, which can mean anything from a Pakistani *shalwar* to an Omani *dishdasha* to a Mauritanian *boubou* to a multi-ethic mix of vestments. What I found living in the Gulf countries is that Gulf Arabs don't appreciate non-Arabs donning their national garb. I realized that wearing a Saudi *thobe* (robe) and *ghutra* (white head scarf) made Saudis uncomfortable. So, when I went into business in Saudi and elsewhere in the Gulf, I changed uniforms and started wearing suits and ties when dealing with the locals.

At the same time, in non-Muslim countries 'going native' doesn't necessarily identify you as a Muslim. You might, instead, be sending a confounding set of mixed messages.

A Scottish Muslim convert I know of had to sort out some tax problem with the Inland Revenue in the U.K. He swaggered into the government office with his documents to meet with the tax man, wearing a Moroccan *djellaba* and turban. He was a bona fide Scotsman with a white face, an undeniably Scottish name and a thick Scots burr. Yet, when his business was done, the tax man asked, "So which part of Pakistan are you from?"

Spiritual Garments

Fundamentally, as Muslims, we clothe ourselves out of modesty and to comply with the prerequisites of purification and prayer. Aesthetics have always been secondary. It has been pointed out that Muslims have maintained the Biblical profile: flowing robes, turbans, veils. Traditional Muslim dress is beautiful, but what is more beautiful is the purity of the believer's excellent character, beautiful manners and the spiritual garments we must don to travel on the Way.

Imam Abu'l Hasan al-Shadhili, God be well pleased with him saw the Prophet Muhammad in a dream[106] who said:

> "Cleanse your raiment of defilement and you will obtain the help of God with every breath." I asked, "What is my raiment, O Messenger of God?" He replied, "God has clothed you with the vestment of mystical knowledge, then with the vestment of love, then with the vestment of belief in the Divine Unity (*Tawhid*), then with the vestment of Faith (*Iman*), and then with the vestment of Submission (*Islam*). If anyone knows God, everything becomes of little importance for him. If anyone loves God, everything becomes contemptible for him. If anyone asserts the Unity of God, he associates nothing with Him. If anyone has faith in God, he is safe from everything. If anyone is resigned to God, rarely does he disobey Him. If he does disobey Him, he begs of Him to be excused. If he begs of Him to be excused, his excuse will be accepted." With these words I understood the meaning of His Words:

> *And thy garments keep from stain.*[107]

---

106   From *Durrat al-Asrar wa Tuhfat al-Abrar*, The Mystical Teachings of al-Shadhili, translated by Elmer H. Douglas
107   Holy Qur'an, *Sura al-Muddaththir* 74:4

In Paradise you can get anything to smoke that you desire. The only problem is that you have to go to the Fire to get a light.

HAJJ BIKHAYR[108]

Up in Smoke

AT BEST, SMOKING is a bad habit, but most scholars have declared that it is forbidden according to Islamic law. The saint Sidi Abdul 'Aziz al-Dabbagh, who died in 1719 wrote:

> "Tobacco is forbidden (*haram*) because it harms the body, because those who smoke it have an addiction to it that keeps them from worship of Allah and cuts them off from it...and because the angels are hurt by its smell." His student asked, "But garlic and onions and the like have a bad odor and eating them is not forbidden." He replied, "If the right of the human and the right of the angel come into conflict, then the right of the human is given precedence because everything was created for the sake of humans, and therefore that which benefits humans is not forbidden even if it harms angels. And in garlic and onions are clear benefits, in contrast to smoking, for it has no benefit..."[109]

And yet, for all this, in Muslim lands smoking is widespread, and not only among the impious. In some countries—Turkey for example—it would not be unusual to see a religious scholar or Sufi shaykh smoking unapologetically and with pleasure. One eminent shaykh used an amusing rationalization for his habit: "Everything in creation confirms the Name of God except the Tobacco plant...so I burn it." All kidding aside, one only needs to see the tragic results of a lifelong smoking habit in the form of emphysema, lung cancer, heart disease and strokes, to realize the truth of Sidi 'Abdul 'Aziz al-Dabbagh's words.

One of my Muslim friends had been a chain smoker since he was

---

108 A learned Algerian disciple of Sidi Muhammad ibn al-Habib
109 *al-Dhahab al-Ibriz*, Pure Gold From the Words of Sayyidi Abd al-'Aziz al-Dabbagh; al-Lamati, translated by O'Kane and Radtke

a teenager. He was a tough businessman, full of energy and otherwise fit. When he was about sixty years old I introduced him to his future wife and helped them get married. I did so on condition that he stop smoking. He promised. A year late he kept his promise after a doctor told him he would contract emphysema if he continued. He stopped cold turkey and said, "There! I stopped. No problem." Within months he had a series of strokes and remained an invalid for the last two decades of his life. God is Merciful: his bride was a pious, compassionate and infinitely patient nurse who cared for him until the end.

In 1975 'Abdallah Schleifer relocated from Beirut to set up NBC's Middle East News Bureau in Cairo, Egypt. During that period he was in and out of Beirut as Middle East Bureau Chief covering the Lebanese Civil War. I was living in Cairo at the time and Abdallah was a friend. He was a hardened war correspondent who thrived on the dangers of combat reporting. Not surprisingly he was a high-strung, self-confessed adrenaline junky. The celebrated French photojournalist Catherine Leroy was doing a story on snipers in Beirut. She needed an authentic shot of journalists drawing sniper fire. She knew that the only journalist brave enough and crazy enough to intentionally draw sniper fire was 'Abdallah. She went straight to the tall (6'5") journalist and without a moment's hesitation he agreed. "I wasn't fearless. I was terrified, but back then I believed that I should do whatever frightened me." 'Abdallah and his crew ran back and forth across an open street gratuitously dodging bullets while Catherine captured a memorable set of images for her story. With those kinds of self-inflicted stress levels it isn't surprising that 'Abdallah was a heavy smoker.

He would come over to my flat in the suburb of Ma'adi, usually once a week when he wasn't traveling, for a meal or a coffee. 'Abdallah was a hardcore chain smoker, lighting one cigarette off another while he kept up an always-captivating commentary on his two passions: Islam and the convoluted politics and history of the Middle East. One evening 'Abdallah turned up and held forth. He was in great form, but he wasn't smoking. At the end of the evening I remarked on this. He told the following story.

Shaykh Sobhi was an Azhari scholar who had dedicated his life to getting Muslims to give up smoking. 'Abdallah knew about him and avoided him like the plague. He'd been a heavy smoker most of his adult life and had no intention of giving it up. "If I saw Shaykh Sobhi walking down the street, I would cross to the other side of the street to avoid him."

One day, however, 'Abdallah was caught by surprise. He was visiting a friend in Ma'adi with a German Muslim, a young Palestinian scholar and an Egyptian from the Oasis (*Wahat*). Except for their host and the Palestinian scholar, everyone was smoking like chimneys. There was a knock on the door.

"Shaykh Sobhi! *Marhaban!* (Welcome!)"

As soon as he heard Shaykh Sobhi's name 'Abdallah stubbed out his cigarette, stashed his pack, folded his hands and feigned innocence. The other two smokers knew nothing about the shaykh and in blissful ignorance continued inhaling and exhaling clouds of cigarette smoke into the room. The shaykh entered, greeted everyone and sat down, ignoring the elephant (the two smokers) in the room.

The young Palestinian was fully aware of Shaykh Sobhi's reputation and opened the subject. "Mawlana, we have smokers in our midst. Aren't you going to admonish them?" Shaykh Sobhi, who was also the proprietor of a perfume shop, demurred that he was a guest and it would be impolite to do so. The subject would almost certainly have rested there except that the young Egyptian from the Oasis spoke up. "Mawlana, everybody knows that smoking is *makruh* (reprehensible), not *haram* (forbidden)," giving Shaykh Sobhi his opening. He quietly began to speak to the young smoker in Arabic. At first the Egyptian was agitated and defensive but gradually as the shaykh talked to him he began to calm down. Then he began to lean in and listen intently. Then he pulled out his pack of cigarettes and, like a sacred pledge, handed it over to Shaykh Sobhi who opened up the pack, pulled out the cigarettes and broke each one before returning them to the pack. The others looked on in amazed silence.

The German spoke up first. "I've been trying to give up smoking for years. Could you ask the shaykh to repeat what he just said to our friend but this time translated to English?" So Shaykh Sobhi rewound and started over, this time with a translation. The shaykh went through most of the conventional religious and health-related arguments against smoking. But then he said something that struck 'Abdallah to the core. He said, "In earlier times, when people became upset they would pull out their prayer beads and say 'Allah, Allah' and peace would come to their hearts, as promised in the Holy Qur'an:

Surely with the remembrance of Allah the hearts become serene.[110]

"They would exhale the Name of God and their stress would vanish. Today, what do people do? They reach for a cigarette and light up. The man of remembrance has the Name of God on his lips but what does the man of cigarettes have on his lips? Fire and Smoke."

When he heard this, 'Abdallah pulled out his hidden pack of cigarettes and handed it to the shaykh. His German friend did the same. Over forty years have passed and all three men have never smoked again.

The day after hearing 'Abdallah's story I mentioned it to the host. I asked him, how, after a quarter of a century of smoking, he was holding up. He said, "He's fine... except that today I walked in on him in his office and found him lifting the *safroggi* (tea man) off the floor and strangling him over five *piasters* (equivalent to about one penny). Otherwise he's just fine."

And the greatest waste of money is in tobacco. For I heard that in a previous year in which it was scarce, people used to buy it for 11 riyals a pound. What mind does such a person have? Is there a mind behind this? No, it is far behind! Did he clothe he who has no clothes, or feed the hungry? And it doesn't nourish or satiate.... And it causes illness: do you not see the chimneys of kitchens, how their shafts become blackened from the smoke that passes through them? So how do you think is the chest and throat of the smoker? Rust has piled up in them, so what benefit is sought from a person whose state is thus? For we have known many who quit it and became much happier, had

---

110   Holy Qur'an, *Sura al-Ra'd*, 13:28

lesser expenses, and their disposition came back to balance as they have told us; and they were able to sleep better, sleep being the source of man's rest and mental stability. So what waste of money is worse than this waste?

And I was told by him in whose truthfulness I have no doubt, and in whose story I trust, that he saw the Prophet, peace be upon him, in his sleep and said to him: 'Oh Messenger of God, is tobacco *halal* or *haram*?' So he turned to Aisha who was next to him and said: 'If she smoked it I would not come near her.' So he said, 'Is it *halal* or *haram*'? He said, 'If she smoked it I would not come near her' three times. The man of the vision said, "I thought about saying to him: Did you forbid it in the *Sharia* and if so, in which part of hadith? But I forgot because of the state I was in.

SIDI AHMED IBN IDRIS[111]

---

111   *al-Iqd al-Nafees*, Sidi Ahmed ibn Idris (1760-1837), was a great scholar from Fez in the spiritual lineage of Sidi Abdul Aziz Al-Dabbagh, and who founded the Idrisiyya Sufi Order.

*You accustomed us to Your Excellence before we (could even) ask,
when we were still in our mothers' wombs, and You nurtured us
with the gentleness of Your Nurturing in a way that (even the most)
illuminated minds cannot fully grasp.*[112]

SIDI MUHAMMAD IBN AL-HABIB

---

112   From the Noble Litany (*Wird*), translated by Michael Abdurrahman Fitzgerald, Mohamed Fouad Aresmouk and Moulay Abdelkebir al-Belghiti

Part Six
A SERIES OF
FORTUNATE EVENTS

In my experience an insane person (and I have met a few) is someone who believes that the entire universe and everything in it is conspiring against him. The sane person, on the other hand, is the one who believes that the entire universe and everything in it is conspiring *for* him. I, fortunately, am a denizen of the latter category.

THE AUTHOR

Disappearing Acts

WHEN I WAS a boy, sitting up high in an oak tree, hidden by the long, rough, grey twisted limbs and pointed oak leaves clustered at their ends, staring out across open fields of dry yellow grass, I reveled in my imagined invisibility. Or when the sun seemed to melt me, obliterating me in heat and light, I luxuriated in my imagined evaporation. Plunging through a cold Pacific wave into oblivion was like a medicine for the illness of existing. Sneezing, for one sudden, explosive moment, was a relief from the intractable problem of being. I longed to vaporize, to melt away... to disappear. Yet here I am, seven decades past, still here, still hanging on, years closer to my inevitable Last Exit. My first blissful childhood longings for obliteration have long since been displaced by the stubborn polarities of clinging to the trajectory of life – a curious arc leading to a mystery – and the longing for effacement. The longing is not masochistic, morbid or mad. It is not in any way suicidal. It is the longing for loss of self and release into light.

The irony is that the more I am here, present in this world, the more I am alone, the more I feel distant, alienated even, isolated. And the greater my longing for release.

The act of disappearing has marked my life. When I was a boy, I spent my days with Franciscan monks at the Mission in Santa Barbara, not for any spiritual reasons – I didn't have any idea what they believed in or what they actually did – but because I was drawn to their brown robes and rosaries, and that they disappeared behind the alter and into the seminary where they lived. I would ride my bicycle from the top of the Riviera down along Alameda Padre Serra coasting swiftly to the Mission every day and take the tours led by the Franciscan brothers and revel in their disappearing acts.

I was drawn to the theater for the same reasons – the drama and mystery of disappearing behind a curtain. My parents took me to a puppet show at a theater by the railroad tracks that featured three-quarter life-sized marionettes that were taller than I. The darkness, the curtain, the stage lights and the ritual of performance was riveting for a six-year-old and haunted me until I took up the theater in earnest a few years later.

The theater was a chance to disappear – into a character, behind a curtain. To emerge in darkness as someone else – a fictional creation that did not exist. To transform and then to disappear again behind the curtain, was intoxicating. Walking from darkness into a light and then disappearing.

When, finally, I embraced Islam, I disappeared again, from a life that I had led, to a new life, dedicated, curiously, to disappearing altogether.

Fallen Idol

MORE THAN ANYTHING in my memory, I am haunted by a meadow in the moonlight, glowing silver and sweeping up to a dark forest. I could see the meadow from my window at night and could hear train horns in the distance. As a small child I imagined that the trains ran just beyond that dark forest upon the opposite slope. Just beyond. Even after I came to learn that the tracks ran far from where we lived, down the mountain, along the Pacific, I couldn't shake the image of the trains behind the forest. To this day that meadow is the single most beautiful image of my childhood. I fell in love with its glow and sweep and the dark ring of oaks that enclosed it.

We called it the horse pasture because it was where our neighbor, who lived in a large ranch house on the hill above us, pastured his horses. There was a tack room filled with polished silver and carved leather saddles that festooned his horses when they were trotted out on display during Fiesta season. There was a riding trail through the thick oak forest surrounding the pasture fitted out with salt licks all along the way. At first there was no separation between our property and the pasture. Then Teo, the wrangler who worked for our neighbor, put up a crude post fence from eucalyptus logs that I could easily get through. Eventually my father rolled out a rickety green-stained picket fence tied together with wire to keep me inside our property and out from under the horses' hooves, but it didn't really work. I'd walk round to the street side of the property and get in through the gate.

I idolized Teo. He was my first hero. He would gallop up to the fence and we'd talk. He was a Mexican Indian dwarf who wore a beat-up denim jacket and a crumpled, sweat-stained cowboy hat. He was the first adult that talked to me like a friend and almost an equal. I'd climb up and sit on the top post of the fence and he'd pull me up onto the saddle and we'd canter across the meadow and back. I was only 4 or 5 at the time. I'd known Teo as long as I could remember. He was my friend.

When I got older and went to elementary school I saw less and less of Teo but he remained a romantic figure for me, a tiny, leathery Indian cowboy galloping across my childhood.

The closest shopping area to where we lived was down at the base of the Riviera, along Milpas Street, which was, for Santa Barbara at the time, a low-rent area. One afternoon my mother left me alone in the car while she went in to one of the shops to pick something up. I was gazing across the street at a seedy bar called Mecca Cocktails. Teo stumbled out, red-eyed and blind drunk. For the first time I saw a sad, pathetic ugly drunken dwarf. For the first time I sensed his pain and loneliness. It was the last time I ever saw him – staggering out of Mecca.

Twenty-five years later I staggered in to Mecca – Makkah al-Mukarrama – wrapped in two large white terrycloth towels called *ihram*. Getting there had been a complicated process full of impossibly convoluted and fortuitous twists and turns.

Who Am I?

WHEN I WAS sixteen I had an unexpected awakening. At that point in my life I was interested in three things: theater, music and girls (not necessarily in that order). I was not reflective or particularly well read. I was almost totally untroubled; there were no tragedies or disruptions in my rather idyllic adolescence. I reveled in my youth and my talents. One summer night, after a day's rehearsal and an evening out on the town (I was now driving my first car, a red Renault Dauphin), I climbed into bed and closed my eyes.

In the nether world between wakefulness and sleep I was suddenly, without warning, plunged into an involuntary contemplative state. One by one, I was stripped of my senses – sight, hearing, smell, touch and then breath itself. I was paralyzed, driven deeper into an abyss of sensory deprivation and identity loss. Finally, over the precipice, I careened toward nothingness, and in this petrifying state of loss I was overcome by a shattering, unfathomable fear. In this unanticipated darkness, my soul cried out in the deafening silence, *"If I am not my senses, if I am not my breath, then who am I? What is this that still exists?"*

Suspended in this terrifying, infinite chasm for what seemed like an eternity but was probably only a few seconds, my life changed. I knew, without a shadow of a doubt, that I was going to die.

Years later I came across the teachings of Ramana Maharshi, the Hindu sage, who, in 1895 when *he* was sixteen, had a similar unexpected awakening:

> It was about six weeks before I left Madura for good that the great change in my life took place. It was quite sudden. I was sitting alone in a room on the first floor of my uncle's house. I seldom had any sickness, and on that day there was nothing wrong with my health, but a sudden violent fear of death overtook me. There was nothing in my state of health to account for it, and I did not try to account for it or to find out

whether there was any reason for the fear. I just felt 'I am going to die'...[113]

When I regained a semblance of normal consciousness I leapt out of bed and crossed my room to a mirror to confirm that I still existed, that I still looked the same. My reflection was the same as before, but I was profoundly disoriented. Relieved to have survived this trauma, I managed to lie back down and drift off to sleep. The next morning, when I awoke, the estrangement remained. I was dislocated, haunted by my momentary metaphorical death. I felt utterly alienated. The world had an unreal, dreamlike quality I couldn't shake.

I broached the subject to my parents. They were, after all, adults. Surely, this was a normal part of growing up, like going through puberty and getting facial hair. Trying to sound as casual and offhanded as I could, I asked them whether they had ever experienced the recognition of death. I expected a reassuring confirmation that this was all normal and not to worry. Instead, I drew a blank. They looked at me uncomprehendingly. Did I detect a tiny glimmer of fear?

I had a girlfriend and, at a debutante's ball, gazing out upon the moonlit Pacific, I asked her the same question. Nothing. I drifted for a while, isolated for weeks, until I came to the conclusion that I couldn't resolve this enigma on my own. I relaxed, but the experience hovered in the background of my life, like a haunting.

Maharshi found his answers then and there.

> The shock of the fear of death drove my mind inwards and I said to myself mentally, without actually framing the words: 'Now death has come; what does it mean? What is it that is dying? This body dies.' And I at once dramatized the occurrence of death. I lay with my limbs stretched out stiff as though rigor mortis had set in and imitated a corpse so as to give greater reality to the enquiry. I held my breath and kept my lips tightly closed so that no sound could escape, so that neither the word 'I' nor any other word could be uttered. 'Well then,' I said to myself, 'this body is dead... But with the death of this body am I dead? Is the body 'I'? It is silent and inert but I feel the full force

---

113   From 'Gems from Bhagavan', compiled by A. Devaraja Mudalia

of my personality and even the voice of the 'I' within me, apart from it. So I am Spirit transcending the body. The body dies but the Spirit that transcends it cannot be touched by death. That means I am the deathless Spirit.' All this was not dull thought; it flashed through me vividly as living truth, which I perceived directly, almost without thought-process. 'I' was something very real, the only real thing about my present state, and all the conscious activity connected with my body was centered on that 'I'. From that moment onwards the 'I' or Self focused attention on itself by a powerful fascination.[114]

This overpowering contemplation produced in Maharshi a deep enlightenment that persisted until his death in 1950. Maharshi's teaching revolved around this one central question: Who Am I? (*Nan Yar?*).

The gross body, which is composed of the seven humors, I am not; the five cognitive sense organs, viz. the senses of hearing, touch, sight, taste, and smell, which apprehend their respective objects, viz. sound, touch, colour, taste, and odour, I am not; the five cognitive sense-organs, viz. the organs of speech, locomotion, grasping, excretion, and procreation, which have as their respective functions speaking, moving, grasping, excreting, and enjoying, I am not; the five vital airs, etc., which perform respectively the five functions of in-breathing, etc., I am not; even the mind which thinks, I am not; the nescience too, which is endowed only with the residual impressions of objects, and in which there are no objects and no functionings, I am not.

If I am none of these, then who am I? After negating all of the above-mentioned as 'not this', 'not this', that Awareness which alone remains - that I am.[115]

It took me years to find an answer to this mystery. In fact, it has taken my life. The secret lies in the statement of the Prophet Muhammad, may God bless him and grant him peace: "He who knows his self knows his Lord."

114   Ibid
115   Ibid

Who Am I?

Say unto brethren when they see me dead,
And weep for me, lamenting me in sadness:
'Think ye I am this corpse ye are to bury?
I swear by God, this dead one is not I.
I in the Spirit am, and this my body
My dwelling was, my garment for a time.
I am a treasure: hidden I was beneath
This talisman of dust, wherein I suffered.
I am a pearl; a shell imprisoned me,
But leaving it, all trials I have left.
I am a bird, and this was once my cage;
But I have flown leaving it as a token.
I praise God who hath set me free, and made
For me a dwelling in the heavenly heights.
Ere now I was a dead man in your midst,
But I have come to life, and doffed my shroud.[116]

IMAM AL-GHAZALI

---

116   An ode translated by Martin Lings

God Exists!

AT THE END of my first year at university I took another entirely unconscious and involuntary step toward the Path. I was a cocky (and probably obnoxious) young actor/singer, voted the most promising freshman in the Theater Department. In the summer I left the dormitories and had my first taste of independence, sharing a flat with a very talented and much older character actor in the school's graduate program. My girlfriend from high school was a dancer studying in Hollywood, who lived in housing for single women performers with a curfew. She and her friend had come over to our flat in Westwood. After a few hours they had to rush back for the curfew and my flat-mate Tom and I decided to head toward Norms for a midnight ninety-nine cent breakfast, something we did in those days. We were down in the parking lot when I suddenly remembered I had to call my friend, a fellow actor, about a backpacking hike into the Sierras we were planning. We lived in a walk-up apartment over a laundry, accessed by exterior wooden steps with a landing outside the door. I bounded up the steps and entered the kitchen where we had a wall phone. I didn't bother to turn on the light. I dialed my friend. Tom waited outside sitting perched on the landing rail.

My friend had been busted for possession of marijuana, which at that time was a felony in California and he had spent a day or so in jail before lawyering up and getting released. In the course of our conversation on the backpacking trip I said, "I know you've been in jail. I'm an actor and I need life experience to nourish my craft. I want to spend a night or two in jail. I have a couple of traffic tickets. The fines are $50. I don't have the money to pay them now so I was thinking of going to the judge in traffic court and asking if I could spend time in jail in lieu of paying the tickets. What do you think?" My friend said, "Michael, I don't think that's a very good idea." But I went on, "I seriously want to experience what it's like in jail, behind bars. I really want to have that experience."

As we were having this wacky conversation about going to jail, I noticed two guys in windbreakers outside talking to Tom. I wasn't paying much attention and continued talking as Tom led the two through the kitchen swing door into the living room. I kept on at my friend trying to convince him that it would be a good idea for me to go to jail. And my friend kept on discouraging me. "Michael, that's just crazy." Suddenly there was a sharp noise and shouting in the next room, so I said, "Something's going on here. I'll have to call you back."

I hung up the phone at exactly the same moment that one windbreaker burst through the swing door pointing a revolver at my head screaming, "PUT YOUR HANDS UP! YOU'RE UNDER ARREST!" I said, "For what?" He screamed, "SHUT UP AND PUT YOUR HANDS UP!" I said, "Not until you tell me what I'm being arrested for." And with that he whacked me on the side of the head with his revolver, slammed me against a wall, handcuffed me and pushed me roughly through the swing door into a chair on the other side of the room.

Wow! This was intense. Tom was already in handcuffs sitting forlornly on the couch I used for a bed. The two Metro Squad cops were ransacking the place. I was completely jacked up – a combination of adrenaline, fear and elation. I had been talking about going to jail and now, here I was, on my way!

What had happened, I later learned, was that the two plainclothes Metro Squad detectives who arrested us were patrolling Westwood with an eye out for burglars. They noticed Tom sitting in the dark on the landing with the door open and he looked suspiciously like a lookout in a break-in. They climbed the steps and confronted him while I was on the phone telling my friend I wanted to go to jail. They asked him what he was doing. He told them that this was his flat. They asked him to prove it and he said he had rent receipts in his desk. So he walked in to the flat past me and through the swing door between the kitchen and the living room to get the rent receipts. The windbreakers followed, uninvited. Tom went over to the desk and pulled open the drawer to fish out a rent receipt when he saw a small bowl of marijuana seeds. Instead of calmly pulling out the rent receipts Tom panicked and slammed the drawer shut, triggering the arrests.

I couldn't stop talking. As the detectives turned the flat upside down looking for drugs (there weren't any) I launched into a barrage of questions. "Is that legal? I don't think you're supposed to do that. Do you have a warrant? What is it you're looking for?" One of the detectives kept answering my questions until his partner swung around on him and barked, "You don't have to answer him!" He said, "Yeah, you're right, I don't have to answer him." Comic relief aside I started to get a little more scared when I realized these two armed and violent cops were not the sharpest tools in the shed. But I kept up the patter. "You know, you hit me. I think that may constitute excessive force. I wonder if I should bring a lawsuit."

All through this poor Tom, who was a wonderful heavy set and balding character actor about thirteen years older than I, kept pleading, "Michael, please shut up." I couldn't. I was in a state of euphoric terror. When one of the detectives found a prosthetic nose I had used to play Cyrano De Bergerac he asked, "What is this?" I told him what it was. "I want to be an actor when I grow up. What do you want to be when you grow up?" Tom was beside himself. "*Michael, please, please shut up!*"

The Metro Squad cops called for backup and two uniformed patrolmen came up to the flat. I saw them through the living room window calming the two hotheaded detectives down. They put us in the squad car and drove us to the Santa Monica police station. They were clearly more experienced and saw that we were harmless. One of the cops talked to me. "You've never been arrested before?" "No sir," I said sheepishly. "This was the first time you used marijuana, right?" "Yes sir," I said, lying through my teeth. "You're never going to do it again are you?" "No, NEVER," another bald-faced lie, although I was so scared by that time I think I believed myself. We were booked at the Santa Monica police station and put in the drunk tank where we met some former major league baseball player Tom recognized, who had played in a World Series but was now on the skids. I called my girlfriend, whose father was a nice man but a John Birch Society Republican. She was horrified. No help there. (The incident ended our relationship altogether – I never saw her again). I then girded myself and called my father.

They transferred Tom and me into adjacent cells. We cooled our heels all night and in the morning were served tasteless rubbery omelets in aluminum containers on steel trays. We waited. My euphoria of the previous night had turned to dread in the cold light of day. We waited.

Lunch came. It was grim and unpalatable. Then they came for me. I was out on bail.

I'm not sure if I had ever been as frightened as I was then. I imagined seething fury from my father. I walked out of the cells in relief and trepidation. I saw my father standing in the hallway. But instead of moral outrage and shame, he was smiling and shaking his head. He said, "Well, Michael, now you've done something I've never done," almost with a trace of amused admiration. Nevertheless, I was thoroughly chastened by the experience. Back then you could do hard time for possession of marijuana. What had I got myself into?

One of our family friends was a lawyer, who came to the rescue. He reviewed the case and determined that there wasn't enough evidence or significant substance to make a case. Still I spent a few weeks in limbo. When we went to the preliminary hearing the judge threw the case out and expunged our records.

I had my night in jail.

Why am I telling this mortifying story from my misguided youth? I am telling it because this was the first time I experienced the convergence of what is in the heart and what is in creation. This was the first time I believed in the immediate existence and presence of God.

Not in the Cards

I WAS JUST beginning a professional career and had high hopes for success as an actor. I was playing Mercutio in a production of Romeo and Juliet. One of the costume girls was an intelligent young woman who did Tarot card readings on the side. I didn't know anything at all about Tarot cards and still don't, but when she offered to do a reading I agreed just for the fun of it. Backstage in the dressing room she laid out these cards with strange images on them. Then she started to interpret the cards. What she said was unsettling. She looked at the cards and told me that something unexpected was going to happen to me that would stop everything I was doing and change my life forever. (It was like one of those old Wolf Man movies when the gypsy looks into a crystal ball and screams.) That was not something I wanted to hear given that I was pretty happy with the way my life was going. I didn't really take the reading any more seriously than I would have breaking open a fortune cookie and reading the strip of paper inside, but what she said sounded ominous and I couldn't help thinking about it.

The industry newspaper Variety gave my Mercutio a rave review. I had also just won a prestigious musical award. A friend of mine, who was already gaining success in films and television, introduced me to his agent. (Without an agent an actor was pretty much locked out of television and movies.) So I had a rave review, a prestigious music award and an agent. To top it off the Variety critic who had written the review asked me to come to his office and gave me a tip about a 'cattle call' audition for a big movie. In Hollywood you can only audition or interview for parts in movies or television if you have an agent. (I had just acquired one but I think he only took me on as a favor to my friend and wasn't sending me out on interviews.) So sometimes movie studios hold 'cattle calls', which are open auditions for anyone, with or without an agent. With the information I received from the Variety reviewer I joined the cattle—lines of aspiring (out of work) actors—at the office of the casting director. When my turn came, I did a reading for the casting director, who was a legendary figure in Hollywood at the time. The reading was good enough for him to give me a scene script to prepare and come back to read a few days later. It was a comic part so I called a friend of mine who was a very funny and successful comic screenwriter, and later film director. I went over the script with him and he gave me a couple of great tips on timing, which helped me nail the scene.

A few days later I turned up at the casting director's office as he had requested and read the scene. He became pensive. Then he got up and went into his inner office. I could see through the glass partition that he was on the phone. He came back and told me to come with him. We drove over to the Goldwyn Studios and walked through the lot to a rather nice bungalow. This was the office of the Oscar-winning director of the film I was reading for. I waited in the outer office while the casting director went in to see the director. They asked me to come in. I met the director. He was pleasant and friendly, so I relaxed. He had an intense-looking assistant director (AD) with him. They asked me to read the scene. I did. They laughed. That was a good sign. Then they asked me to wait outside.

A few minutes later the AD came out. He took me for a walk around the lot. He was incredibly serious, not at all like the director. He said, almost violently, "That was the most brilliant reading I've ever seen! *Absolutely brilliant!* We are giving you a screen test in three days. But it's for the romantic role." I was both elated and deflated because I knew I had the comic character down pat, but the romantic character was not really in my wheelhouse, if the truth be known. Nevertheless I was chuffed. My very first audition for a movie, and from a cattle call no less, and I had come away with a screen test. I was on a roll. All I had to do was work on the new script. I was pretty sure I could ace it.

Then I got sick. Really sick.

I came down with a terrible throat infection that totally wiped me out. I had no energy to work on the second role. I was completely drained. I came to the studio on the day of the screen test with my lines memorized but bringing nothing to the character. The screen test was bittersweet. The director couldn't have been gentler. The assistant director was as intense and supportive as ever, but the scene didn't work. The spark and timing weren't there. When the shooting wrapped I looked over at the AD. He shook his head. I shrugged and nodded that I knew it wasn't good.

So that was the way that went.

But then the director came up to me and said with great kindness, "You like the other part better don't you?" I nodded. He said, "Okay, let's roll film." I did the comic scene to camera. When it was over and the director called "Cut!", the entire sound stage full of cynical studio people and technicians burst into applause. It was deeply gratifying. But that part had already been cast and I lost the romantic role. I didn't know it then but that ovation would be my very last moment of glory in show business.

I went home, went to bed and stayed there for six months with a prolonged infection that stopped everything and, in the end, changed my life.

For week after week and month after month, I was down with a mysterious, undiagnosed condition, unable to work, unable to practice, unable to do anything but read, sleep and think. I was, for the first time in my life, stuck with myself. I couldn't stop my mind from churning on endlessly. I realized that, apart from these ephemeral talents I seemed to have and that I thought were so important, I was basically an idiot. I had no knowledge, no wisdom and no control over my hyperactive mind. I started to read books on mind control and meditation. Then I found a book that really appealed to me. It was called, 'Zen Showed Me the Way' by the Japanese actor Sessue Hayakawa, who won an Oscar as the brutal camp commandant in 'The Bridge on the River Kwai'. It turned out that Hayakawa was also a Zen Roshi and attributed all his success in show business to practicing Zen. Up to that point I had always considered spirituality to be something followed by monks, nuns, fakirs and other unworldly misfits. This was the very first time that I took the hint that a spiritual path might actually help me to live in the world.

After six months in bed, culminating in a throat surgery, all my career momentum had come to a grinding halt. I was back to square one. By this time I had begun to reconsider a career in Hollywood. I had done some television and didn't like it. I found it almost unbearable sitting around in sound stages for hours waiting for a shot that took ten minutes to do. But I was put up for the starring role in a movie written by my friend who had coached me on the scene for the screen test. I was one of a number of actors up for the part, but the director seemed to have taken a shine to me and favored unknowns, so I was hopeful. During this period I was having dinner at a vegetarian restaurant in Westwood with an actor friend. A woman was moving from table to table. She was offering to do... *Tarot Card Readings!*

I should have dived for cover, but I didn't. My curiosity got the better of me. The last reading was so disturbingly prescient that I couldn't resist. I had her read my cards. This time, the reading was even more disconcerting and more explicit. The lady looked at the cards and said, "A group of men are going to offer you a large sum of money to do something, but you must not do it because your life is going to change forever."

"What? *Not again!* Give me a break!" I thought to myself. It was hard to believe that anybody would offer me anything at that point in time but the reading had a creepy specificity about it. So I decided to wait and see.

Now a word about Tarot cards and other soothsaying practices. They are, as we know, totally forbidden in Islam. The Prophet Muhammad, may God bless him and grant him peace, said, "Whoever goes to a fortuneteller or soothsayer and believes in him, then he has disbelieved in what was revealed to Muhammad." But as my friend Abdallah Schleifer has said, "God finds you where you are." There I was. It wasn't that I believed in the Tarot. I didn't. But since my jailhouse experience I had begun to sense that the course of my life was not in my hands, that I was being guided through the world by something immediate and unseen, through indications and signs.

About ten days passed. Then I get a call from my agent. He says, "The lawyers [a group of men] are drawing up a contract for the film role. They will be paying such and such amount of money", which was a very large sum for me at the time. "Just my luck! It *had* to be the movie."

I found myself in an emotional dilemma. On the one hand, I wanted success in show business. I'd been working for over a decade toward this goal. On the other hand, I kept getting these weird messages that coincided with my own growing misgivings about the course my life was taking. I wasn't so sure that I really wanted the life I had chosen. I wanted something more, but I wasn't sure what it was.

I had this overwhelming sense that there would be unfortunate consequences if I took the money and did the movie. It really wasn't superstition. It was accepting signals I was reading both in my heart and in the world. I wrote the director a note, saying that I had decided not to do the movie. It was a crazy thing to do. It was an intuitive step into the unknown.

Disillusion

I WAS A CHILD of the theater. I began in children's theater when I was eight years old and continued until I started practicing Islam. I never imagined doing anything else. It was a religion for me. The creative act was a form of worship. But when I entered the profession just out of my teens I had a nasty shock. I discovered to my dismay that while I loved the artistry and creative process of the theater, I absolutely loathed the business, 'Show Business'—the agents, the interviews, the bad movies and worse television, the dearth of theater and the perpetual desperate search for employment until you 'made it', which was an elusive accomplishment at best. I thought that, perhaps, there could be answers in the *Avant Garde*, the theater of Antonin Artaud, Samuel Beckett, Ionesco, Sartre, Genet and others. So I auditioned for the inaugural year of the California Institute of the Arts and was awarded a full scholarship in theater and music.

The California Institute of the Arts was a new school that had grown out of the Schounard Institute in Los Angeles. The late Walt Disney funded it, now represented by his brother Roy. Strangely, given its far right-wing backers, the school was being developed as a cutting edge, *avant-garde* academy, which boasted artists and educators with distinctly liberal-left credentials. Herbert Blau, co-founder of the San Francisco Actors Workshop and, later, the Lincoln Center Repertory Theater, was both the school's Provost and my mentor.

The tension between Disney funding and leftist administration became evident almost from the start when they tried to recruit the illustrious/notorious Marxist sage Herbert Marcuse, an appointment that was soundly quashed by the Disney-controlled board. But the board couldn't really control the student body, most of whom were heavily influenced by '60s radical politics and life-style. The inevitable clash came very soon after classes began, and it was triggered by a swimming pool. While the new purpose-built campus was under construction in

Valencia, California, a semi-rural community at the very edge of the L.A. exurbs, the first-year classes were held on an old abandoned high school campus in Burbank. The temporary campus had a swimming pool. The students, who were a strange assortment of freaks and geeks, took to swimming nude in the pool, which was raised up and visible from just about anywhere on the property. On Roy Disney's first tour of the facility after classes started, he caught sight of students cavorting co-ed in the buff and blew his stack. Disney demanded that administrators force students to wear proper swimming attire. Word circulated that Disney ordered that the school enforce a swimming attire code.

The art students immediately responded by silk-screening Mickey Mouse mainlining heroin and female pudenda all over the campus walls. The administration displayed open contempt for the Disney culture and did nothing. So when Roy Disney made a second tour and found the students still frolicking nude poolside, he threatened to have the pool drained if a dress code wasn't enforced. This precipitated a formal showdown between Disney and the administration and staff. According to reports I heard, during the meeting a teaching assistant quietly disrobed at the back of the room until he was suddenly noticed listening attentively, stark naked. Naturally things couldn't continue this way and just as naturally the bankrollers won out. Herbert Blau and Chancellor Robert Corrigan were fired and by the time Cal-Arts moved into its bright white pristine new campus, the educators had moved closer to the center. By that time, I'd had enough.

The problem with Blau was that he never brought anything to fruition. Everything was some kind of fluid work-in-progress. He had grand intellectual ideas but not a single one was ever realized. This had a demoralizing effect on the actors, directors and writers working in the program. The creative artist lives for the culmination of the creative act.

We were cloistered off into an almost monastic grouping and thrown into a kind of hothouse laboratory where we did intensive physical exercises supplemented by a fairly heavy course of reading from a list of Blau's favorites, including Frantz Fanon, Antonin Artaud, Jean Paul Sartre, Jean Genet, Albert Camus and Herbert Marcuse. Blau had this theory that the greatest actors were mad, or at least that the best acting came out of insanity. He repeatedly used the example of a favorite actor of his named Michael O'Sullivan who was, evidently, barking mad and who ultimately committed suicide. O'Sullivan was Blau's ideal. He used to cite an incident in rehearsals where O'Sullivan playing King Lear literally tried to throw himself IN to the floor, in an act he described approvingly as totally self-destructive. So at Cal-Arts Blau set about applying this bizarre theory. His favorite actor in our company was a young African-American named Dennis. Dennis had no technique at all but he did have an arresting stage presence. Dennis and I became good friends during this period. He was a very introverted, very troubled kid, but highly sensitive. Blau decided to put on a production of 'The Screens', Jean Genet's epic nine-hour surrealistic play on the Algerian War, and he cast Dennis as Sa'id, the central character. Instead of ordinary rehearsals, Blau decided we all had to work on what he called ideographs: symbolic physical contortions culled from Jerzy Grotowski's celebrated Polish Laboratory Theater, which was highly influential in the *avant-garde* at that time.

Apart from the physicality and Blau's intimidating intellectualization, rehearsals were a mess. He tried whipping the cast into a near-psychotic frenzy to capture whatever he thought the essence of Genet's disturbing play was. He referred to Beckett's line – "I want to be the wind. I can't be the wind. I'll be the wind anyway". He talked about sets made of Mylar. He conceptualized but he never brought the play to any kind of finished form. And then Dennis did what I suppose Blau was looking for all along. He went mad. He had a psychotic episode that sent him to Camarillo State Mental Hospital. I wasn't there when it happened, but when he came back he was very fragile.

I seemed to be his only friend. I wanted to cheer him up, so I took him to a showing of the MGM musical 'Singing in the Rain' at an art theater in Silverlake. Big mistake. When Donald O'Conner was doing his 'Make 'em Laugh' number, which ends by the dancer throwing himself through a wall I thought Dennis was going to have another psychotic break right then and there in the cinema. He didn't, but he never really recovered.

He had another episode, again out of my sight, and became a catatonic ghost, wandering around the school, unable to talk. I could see that he experienced pure neurosis all around him. I was seeing the same thing, but for him the perception was paralyzing. The only time he and I reconnected was when we were sitting silently together, and I recited Blake's poem:

> I wander thro' each charter'd street,
> Near where the charter'd Thames does flow.
> And mark on every face I meet,
> Marks of weakness, marks of woe.[117]

He almost leapt out of his skin in recognition.

By that time I was becoming increasingly troubled and withdrawn. There was something wrong with this whole enterprise. Then Blau unwittingly sent me a gift that changed my life. Throughout rehearsals of 'The Screens' he would have excerpts from writings he considered to be relevant to the play circulated to the cast. One day he distributed some mimeographed sheets with passages from the Holy Qur'an translated by A.J. Arberry. We were filing out of the gymnasium that served as our rehearsal hall and theater and one of his assistants passed them out. I started to read the passages while walking out of the gym and stopped in my tracks. There were two passages, one was the Light Verse (*Ayat al-Nur*) and the other was from the chapter of Pilgrimage (*al-Hajj*). I didn't understand any of what I was reading but I was thunderstruck by the fragmentary rhetorical flow, the sudden shifts of the verse. "Oh my God, this is the way we think, in waves and fragments," I remember thinking to myself.

At the same time my cousin, rest his soul, who was a bibliophile and omnivorous reader, had discovered Sufi writing and enthusiastically put me on to it. Some of it, like Idries Shah's books, was dodgy, but some, like the translation of Farid'udin Attar's classic 'Conference of the Birds', was authentic. I didn't know the difference.

Most of the cast finished the first term deeply disturbed. Dennis's breakdown cast a pall over the company and Blau abandoned his ambitious production. Also, I think the directors in the program protested at being sidelined and Blau gave each a play for the second term.

During the Christmas break I had reached a low point. I was

---

117   'London' from 'Songs of Experience'

disillusioned with the whole program and I didn't want to go back to show business. All this intellectualization had driven me inward. I had acquired a few crude contemplative tools, like the practice of *Tai Chi Chuan*, and I began to use them with a vengeance. I got in my car and drove south to Calexico, crossed the border at Mexicali and drove into the desert to a place I had discovered while on location for a film shoot. It was at the far end of the *Laguna Salada*, a salt flat used by movie companies for its arresting parched desert flatlands. The *Cañón de Guadalupe* was one of the most haunting places I'd ever been to. I drove into the middle of the canyon and tried to meditate. I stood for hours at the canyon ridge in what our *Tai Chi* instructor called the 'Cosmic Stance'. Energy flowed through my arms and out from my fingertips, like an electrical charge. A catharsis. I returned from the break with a renewed sense of self-discovery. And I had become obsessed with Sufism.

~⁊

Repetition

Actors rarely talk about this, but it's one of the secrets that keeps them addicted to an incredibly neurotic, insecure and frustrating business. It is the moment when, after days, weeks or months of reflection, inner struggle and rehearsal, flailing about, wrestling with the role they're playing, that, suddenly, mysteriously, they 'become' the character. Sometimes it happens in one intoxicating rush, sometimes in stages. Sometimes it never happens and then, as professionals, they just soldier on, doing the best they can, saying their lines, faking it. But when it does happen it is indescribably satisfying.

This moment happens when the character 'sinks in' and becomes internalized. And this takes place in the context of rehearsal. In the theater rehearsals are daily, organized collective events proceeding for weeks. In film, rehearsal periods are rare and mostly technical. And in television they are almost non-existent, so the actor rehearses privately, with or without fellow actors. In French rehearsal is called *répétition*. Through repeating the same action and saying the same words over and over and over again, an actor gradually internalizes and 'becomes' the character. This is not just an inward experience. It is noticeable. Spectators recognize it. Actors use all kinds of techniques to achieve this moment: physical mannerisms, accents, attire, sense-memory, research, and even meditation. The Russian director Konstantin Stanislavski would have his actors undertake yoga-like meditations on their characters before they slept so that the character would enter their unconscious imagination and become part of their on-stage personalities.

But I began to have a problem with this. In the theater most great characters are deeply flawed. Actors have to invoke rage, jealousy, greed, lust, hatred, grief and other intense and highly destructive emotions. They rationalize this by asserting that acting is cathartic and a way of experiencing the scope of human experience without suffering the consequences of action. It's true enough that if you play the character of a murderer you will not suffer the actual consequences of committing murder. On the other hand, there are inner consequences to any kind of behavior. So while I had always wanted to play characters like Iago in Shakespeare's Othello or Macbeth, I began to have reservations about contemplating evil actions and invoking the emotions that drive these characters to destructive behavior. I silently and quite naively began asking myself why we couldn't create theater that was benign, with positive emotions. Of course, then there would be no drama, no catharsis. And audiences would be bored out of their skulls. I had entered the *avant-garde* looking for answers. What I found instead were many more questions.

When I began reading about Sufism I discovered something I understood immediately and experientially. The concept of remembrance or the repetition of Names and Phrases that link one to the Transcendent – the act of *dhikru'llah* – made total sense to me. It was my 'Aha!' moment.

The next term I was cast in Shakespeare's 'Twelfth Night' in two roles – as Sebastian, the twin brother of Viola and as the fool Feste. We had a limited number of players, so being cast in two roles made some kind of sense. However, the British director came to me with an utterly bizarre proposal—that both characters were actually one and the same person. There is nothing in Shakespeare's text that justifies this interpretation but, hey, this was the *avant-garde*. Anything was possible. So I set about trying to find some way of playing the two characters as one single persona.

In researching the role I came upon 'The Fool: His Social and Literary History', a study by the Oxford literary scholar Enid Welsford, first published in 1935, about court jesters and fools in literature and history. In it the author traced the roots of the fool in European literature to the great Middle Eastern Sufi literary fool Joha, otherwise known as Nasrud'din Khoja or Mulla Nasrud'din, who was thought to have originally been the court jester of Tamburlaine the Great, or Timur. The stories of Mulla Nasrud'din have endured since the 13th century and have profound meanings subsumed in satiric humor. Moreover, the stories of Mulla Nasrud'din were universally considered to be Sufi teaching stories.

In the same volume Professor Welsford addresses the concept of the holy madman, mentioning that in the court of the Abbasid Caliph Haroun Al-Rashid there was a court fool known as 'Buhlul the Madman', who the author characterized as a 'fool-saint'. In ancient Muslim courts the ruler would include what we would call a *majdhoub* as part of his entourage. The *majdhoub* is a God-intoxicated saint who appears to be mad and who may say or do outrageous things, but who is in fact wise. The Sultan would keep a *majdhoub* close to him to tell him the truth while at the same time appearing to be crazy so that the ruler would not be humiliated in front of his courtiers. The author characterized such a fool as an "inspired 'poet-wizard' of Islam", and referred to a commentary on Ibn Khaldun's discussion as to "whether 'buhluls' can exhibit sainthood." In the commentary "Ibn Khaldun opines...that there occur in them wonderful things by way of stories of the Unseen, for they are not limited by anything, and they give their speech full course therein."

I latched on to this idea and tried to create a poet wizard "not limited by anything" with supernatural powers who could manifest himself as Sebastian. It was a preposterous approach because there was no way on earth to justify it from the text and I think the performance was pretty much a failure. But by this time I had become more interested in Sufism than I was in Shakespearian histrionics. I had crossed over to the Light

Side.

The year ended and I set off to find a Sufi. I didn't have a clue what to look for or how to look so I started with the Yellow Pages - that's how clueless I was. But, guess what? I found a listing for Sufis! Imagine that.

The Key

I DON'T KNOW what I expected to find when I looked up Sufi in the Yellow Pages but it certainly wasn't a sweet old lady with a French accent who turned out to be a devout Christian Scientist. Suzanne was something like the secretary for the Sufi Order of the West. She was very pleasant on the phone and invited me to visit her. I had nothing else to go on, so I drove over to her house in the San Fernando Valley. It turned out she followed the teachings of someone called Hazrat Inayat Khan.

Inayat Khan, I came to learn, had been an accomplished musician from India, whose Sufi master had sent him to the West in 1910 to spread the message of Islam through his music. The young Indian musician landed in Los Angeles and found work as an accompanist for the celebrated modern dance artist Ruth St. Denis and her husband Ted Shawn. At that time there was virtually no interest in Islam in the West but there was a growing fascination with oriental mysticism popularized by Theosophists Madame Blavatsky and Annie Besant, which culminated in the discovery of the child avatar Jiddu Krishnamurti, who later rebelled and spent the rest of his life debunking the idea of avatars and gurus. Inayat Khan became a spiritual figure in this scene, teaching Sufism without much reference to Islam.

In fact, most of Inayat Khan's disciples were not Muslim but professed to be Sufis (a contradiction in terms). During the year I was affiliated with this curious crowd I met an elderly lady who had been a direct disciple of Inayat Khan and on the surface appeared to be just an ordinary senior citizen but who, in fact, was a 'secret' Muslim. Apparently, Inayat Khan would 'initiate' certain disciples in to the obligatory practices of Islam like 'Wazoo' (ritual purification) and the five daily prayers ('Namaz') as if they were esoteric mystical practices. I can understand that back in the first decades of the 20th century in America and Europe the open practice of traditional Islam might have alienated many but after Inayat Khan died in 1926 any references to orthodox Islam seems to have been lost.

Inayat Khan had married Ora Ray Baker who was a second cousin of Mary Baker Eddy, the founder of Christian Science. The couple moved to Britain and then to France where he invented the Universal Worship Service. This took the inherent spiritual tolerance of Sufism and the recognition of all Prophets and Messengers way beyond orthodoxy. The Universal Worship Service was a kind of watered-down Christian service with a sermon, a congregation sitting in pews and a ritual where worshippers lit candles for all the religions. Even I, ignoramus that I was, found this ritual cloyingly sentimental and spiritually inane. When Hazrat Inayat Khan died he left behind four young children, among them Noor-An-Nisa, who became the legendary allied spy in occupied France during World War II, code-named 'Madeline,' who was captured, tortured and executed by the Nazis.

By the time I turned up, Inayat Khan's son Vilayat, who was 8 years old when his father died, was leading what was called the 'Sufi Order of the West.' When he passed through Los Angeles Suzanne invited me to attend a meditation he was conducting, which I did. The meditation session was held somewhere in downtown Los Angeles at a kind of East-West center. Vilayat was urbane, handsome and soft-spoken and he talked his way mellifluously through meditations for an audience of little old ladies. This was not at all what I expected Sufism to be, but then, what did I know?

So Vilayat had this coterie of mostly sweet little old ladies, who were all mostly Christians, meditating to his silky, fluent and erudite narrations. I would most likely have drifted away from this bland, geriatric cabal had it not been for my introduction to another, almost schizoid side to this group in the high desert of Arizona.

Suzanne gave me a mimeographed announcement about a Sufi Camp that was being held during the summer in Arizona. I was at loose ends and keen to find out anything I could about this new spiritual path I'd discovered, notwithstanding my first impressions. I signed up, hit the road and found myself smack dab in the middle of what I can only describe as a hyper-intense New Age spiritual orgy, a kind of acid trip without the acid. It could have been a scene out of the musical Hair (including the nudity) absent the anti-war slogans.

Everybody was pretty much my age, and everyone was doing one kind of spiritual practice or another from just about every religion under the sun. There were plenty of Buddhists, Hindus, Christians and Jews but, curiously, only one Muslim, a convert from New Jersey, who seemed altogether out of place. He was performing his five prayers solo, which fascinated me, but then jumped right in to all the mayhem as soon as he rolled up his prayer mat.

At the center of it all was Pir Vilayat Khan, the elegant gentleman who had been conducting soft-spoken meditations for the elderly a week before. Here he was serenely presiding over this hippy free-for-all. I have to admit that I was carried away. This was altogether more like it: longhair freaks, nubile young women, mantras, music, yoga, religion everywhere, brown rice and veg and brotherly love – OMG!

Vilayat was the main event and would give discourses on various subjects and lead meditations. I was trying very hard to get my head around his tranquil commentaries without much success... until he introduced a phrase that changed my life: *La ilaha illa 'Lllah* – No god but God – the first part of the Muslim declaration of faith. This statement hit me like a railroad train. It seemed to me to encompass the entire spectrum of belief, from atheism to absolute faith. To my complete astonishment and without any warning I broke down and wept uncontrollably for an hour after hearing the phrase. This was why I had come.

I became obsessed with *La ilaha illa 'Llah*. I learned nothing about Islam at that camp (significantly, Vilayat refrained from explaining the second half of the *shahada, Muhammadun Rasulullah* – Muhammad is the Messenger of God) or, in fact, anything else about Sufism, but I came away from this queer Aquarian Age camping trip with a key.

One Year

THE DISCOVERY OF the *Tahlil* (*La ilaha illa 'Llah*), propelled me on a year-long Cook's Tour of Aquarian Age spirituality. My one constant was the invocation of *La ilaha illa 'Llah*. But, beyond this, there was nothing in the Sufi Order of the West that suggested any special link to Islam. Instead, Sufism was presented as a kind of spiritual buffet: Buddhism, Hinduism, Christianity and Zoroastrianism and, yes, Islam, all loosely tied together with the benign spiritual homilies of Inayat Khan. Islam remained an abstraction, mainly because no one actually practiced it or, in fact, knew anything about it. I took up yoga. I read everything I could get my hands on and head around. I tried meditating. I stared at statues and images and tried to find meaning in this cocktail of sacred iconography. I visited every group and every guru I could find. I attended retreats and prayer sessions. I watched a swami walk over hot coals. I watched an assembly of devotees prostrating *en masse* to a teenage guru who looked to me like nothing so much as a tubby busboy.

Curiously, in all this mélange of New Age faiths, and supposedly following a Sufi path, Islam was nowhere to be found. Yet I continued to invoke *La ilaha illa 'Llah*. It was the only thing in everything I'd been exposed to that made any sense to me.

I couldn't put my finger on it because I thought I was doing something real, part of an ancient tradition, but there was a huge, gaping hole in the smorgasbord approach to self-realization. There was no coherent practice. I wanted to know what to do. I wanted to know how to talk to God directly. I wanted to know how to pray, what to ask for and when to pray. I yearned for structure. I wanted knowledge and wisdom. I longed for peace of mind. I wasn't finding any of it. I probably could have found at least some of these things had I joined a Vedanta Temple or a Zen Buddhist fraternity but my initial readings about Sufism convinced me that this was the path for me. I kept at it, but this mad metaphysical farrago I had joined up with was doing my head in. I was in a desperate state of mind.

Almost exactly one year after my first encounter with 'Sufism' I traveled to Northern California to a second 'Sufi' camp, this time around with a queasy feeling that something wasn't right. For one thing, all the New Age spirituality and bliss the devotees were acting out seemed increasingly unreal, masking deep, unresolved neuroses. The ecstatic, beaming faces that on first encounter seemed so spiritual, began to seem, frankly, weird. And, what was more disquieting was that I was becoming one of them. I knew very well that inside I was the same neurotic narcissist that I had always been. I was beginning to feel like a big fat phony.

I noticed a woman from the camp the year before who taught yoga. She was memorable because she did everything in her birthday suit. This year she wasn't stark naked, she was stark-raving mad, as if she had been possessed, wandering around vacantly and then shouting out in a strange voice. Years later, when I understood a little about *jinn* and the Unseen, I became aware that covering oneself was more than a matter of modesty. Those who understand the sciences of the *jinn* warn against sleeping uncovered under the sky beside a river or body of water because you make yourself vulnerable to possession. I didn't know that then but I found this woman's condition deeply unnerving. Moreover, among all these 'enlightened' beings, no one seemed to be helping her. She was a strange benighted fixture, a lost soul loose in this bucolic setting.

I immediately wanted to escape from the very thing that I thought was so cool the year before. But when Vilayat announced a spiritual retreat, I volunteered. I thought that perhaps this was the serious business I had been reading about and working up to. I had read Martin Lings' classic, 'A Muslim Saint of the 20th Century' about Shaykh Ahmad Mustafa al-'Alawi, which was the only book I had come across that directly linked Sufism to Islam, and remembered the Shaykh put his disciples into spiritual retreat. So, here it was. A small group of volunteers was sent up on to a forested hillside to meditate and invoke God. Once assembled, Vilayat told us that what was going on down in the valley was silly and of no consequence; that what we were embarking on was what the path was all about. We were, he said, the elite. I should have, I don't know, been flattered by what he said, but, instead, it struck me as hypocritical given that he was presiding over all the inane revelries below. The only instruction he gave us was that we were not to speak to anyone. Otherwise there were no guidelines. Nothing. We were left to our own devices.

I was way out of my depth. I began to invoke *La ilaha illa 'Llah* hundreds and thousands of times, as well as *Ya 'Aziz* and other Names of God I had learned. After several days of this, I really thought I might lose my mind. I became very frightened and begged God to help me and protect me. When finally I finished I was in an extremely fragile state of mind. I could see auras and emanations from people, but I felt deeply disoriented – lost in a storm at sea.

I returned to Los Angeles in this condition. Although I felt completely unhinged, I also had a heightened sense of the Unseen and a delusional feeling of power and destiny. Everything seemed portentous. I was walking in Westwood, aimlessly and without any specific intention. As if I were on tracks, I walked into a bookstore straight to a display of books with Kufic calligraphy on the cover. I bought the book. It was, along with the book on Shaykh al-'Alawi, the only book I read up to that point that linked Sufism directly with Islam. I read it and then gave the book to a girl I knew who was also interested in spirituality. And forgot about it.

A couple weeks later, I ran into her. She pulled the book out of her purse, put her finger on the photo of the author on the flyleaf and said, "Guess what? I just met this guy!"

Clarity

"GUESS WHAT? I just met this guy!"

When my friend told me she'd met the author of a book about meeting real Sufis who were Muslims, I took this as a sign from God and immediately made plans to travel north to Berkeley to find "the guy". My friend and I stood on Highway 101 in Santa Barbara, put our thumbs out and hitched a ride up to the Bay Area. (Those were the days when you could do that without taking your life in your hands.)

We arrived in the evening and made our way straight to a public hall where a ceremony had already started. An austere looking group of Muslims were sitting in two circles – women, hair covered, in one circle, bearded, robed and turbaned men in another – reciting a litany in Arabic. I didn't understand a word of it but the sound was breathtaking. After this recitation, the group stood up and formed lines facing a direction. And they prayed. I had seen the lone Muslim at the Sufi camp perform his prayers the year before, but I had never seen an assembly of Muslims pray together. They stood behind an imam who recited the prayer. They bowed and they prostrated. There was a sacred gravitas that I had never seen anywhere else. I was blown away. This is what I had been looking for all along.

After the prayer the assembly chanted a series of songs in Arabic, which I also didn't understand. The singing gave way to a kind of dance, in which the two circles stood up and started to sway back and forth. The dance was simple, sober and focused. The audience was allowed to join and I jumped right in, swaying back and forth with the rest and, I was later told, whirling around (I have no memory of this). It was very intense. I didn't have a clue what I was doing but this seemed infinitely more real than anything I'd ever encountered.

When the dance was over, the Muslims split up and mixed with members of the audience. I sat down with two members of the Sufi Order. I was still incredibly spaced out from all the invocations that I had done during the recent retreat and almost certainly looked jumped up and crazy. They were polite and friendly but reserved. I was still under the illusion that what I'd been doing was part of Sufism and I thought that I would find kindred spirits to welcome me into their circle. Instead, I was suddenly and roughly disabused of my illusions when the leader of the group, the author of the book, swooped down on me and in the harshest and most unpleasant way possible, ordered me to stop what I was doing immediately. He said that what I was doing was very dangerous and it had nothing to do with Sufism and that I would go insane if I continued. He was downright nasty. He then jumped up and left me in a state of shock, sitting in front of the two Muslims. Unlike their leader, they were very kind and considerate and invited me to stay the night with them.

I was in a daze. My head was swimming. I knew there was something wrong with what I'd been doing but wasn't prepared for the grim and hostile reception I'd just had. I was having trouble taking everything in. I stayed the night with a pleasant couple. We had breakfast and repaired to a white clapboard house that served as a kind of center. I spent time with a group composed of a mix of Americans and Brits with an Iranian thrown in for good measure. What struck me about this group was that everyone was so grounded and normal. No beatific smiles, no straining to project an aura of holiness. They were just ordinary men and women on a spiritual path. This was inexpressibly refreshing. What is more, I liked them all. Except for the leader.

I noticed that he kept himself separate from the rest of the group and cosseted in a private room. He would call individuals to his inner sanctum. People were coming and going. I had calmed down from the night before and was able to carry out a conversation. They asked me where I was from and what I did for a living. I told them I was an actor.

After a time, I was called to the inner sanctum. I told the leader that I liked his book. He said that the first part, which was set in some anodyne future and which I found derivative and not very interesting, was important, while the second part, about encountering Sufis in the desert, was not. This struck me as odd because the only part of the book I actually liked was the second part. He then asked me innocently, "Are you an actor?" I said that I was, knowing full well that one of his group had briefed him about me before I came in. "*Really?*" he exclaimed, as if he was surprised by his own clairvoyance. This put me off. Did he take me for an idiot? (He probably did.) Otherwise, he told me a few things about Islam and let me go.

I spent the rest of the day with these people, who called themselves *fuqara* (literally, 'the poor'). In spite of my first impressions of the leader, I found them far and away the most sane, sensible and sincere group of seekers I had met in my year-long search. More than this, I felt as if a crushing weight had been lifted from my heart. I walked away from this group with an overwhelming sense of clarity. Suddenly the world seemed lucid and vibrant. Suddenly, I had certainty.

My friend and I crossed the Oakland Bay Bridge to San Francisco. As we walked through the North Beach district past the City Lights Bookstore, the strip clubs and gay bars, I said to her, "I don't trust their leader but I'm going to become a Muslim."

One Week

I HAD FINALLY found the path that I was looking for. I was going to become a Muslim. I returned to Los Angeles in a state of exhilaration. Then something else happened that underscored this new awakening. My career had languished for a year after I turned down a leading role in a big movie. Hollywood is a small town and casting directors keep their ears to the ground. A young unknown who turns down the chance to be in a big movie is just plain crazy. I couldn't get an interview, much less a job. But when I got back to LA suddenly all these prospects began turning up in the space of one week. I was asked to read for another, even bigger part in a bigger movie. It seemed like a good omen.

The character I was reading for spends much of the movie drunk. I had stopped drinking before I was 21 and had forgotten what being drunk was like so I took to drinking one or two six packs of beer every day while going over the script just to get a sense of the rhythm, delivery and speech cadences of the inebriated character. Other than preparing for the reading my mind was on returning to Berkeley the next weekend and formally becoming a Muslim.

On Friday night I took the Red Eye from LAX to San Francisco. I arrived just after midnight. I had to make my way from San Francisco to Berkeley. I took a shuttle bus to Oakland and got out. It was about half past two in the morning. The streets were empty. I walked from Oakland to Berkeley and turned up at the white house before dawn. I didn't want to wake anybody up (they didn't know I was coming), so I sat on the porch for a couple of hours until I heard someone stirring for the dawn prayer. I then tapped on the door. One of the Muslims came to the door. I told him that I had come to enter Islam. He welcomed me. Someone showed me how to make ritual ablution and told me just to follow along in the prayer. I was in alien territory but armed with certainty.

After the prayer and the litany, the congregation dispersed and I stretched out in the living room and slept for a while.

After breakfast the leader called me in to his inner sanctum and explained the basics of Islam to me. He told me that as a Muslim I must affirm that there is no god but God and that Muhammad is the Messenger of God; pray five times a day; fast from dawn to sunset during the month of Ramadan; pay the *Zakah*, or poor tax; perform the Pilgrimage to Makkah once in life if I had the means. He then enumerated the basic prohibitions: things I couldn't do as a Muslim. "You can't worship idols." (What a relief!) "You can't commit adultery or fornication outside marriage." (I figured as much.) "You can't commit murder." (Duh!) "You can't drink alcohol." (Huh?)

"Wait, as a Muslim I can't drink alcohol?"

"No, it's forbidden."

"What about...*just a little?*"

"No, not even a little."

"Hmm. Okay."

One more spanner in my career works.

I was directed to take a shower. Dried off and redressed, I joined the noon prayer. When it was done, the leader took my hand in front of the entire group and had me repeat the *shahadah*: *ash-hadu an la ilaha 'illa 'Llah wa ash-hadu anna Muhammadan Rasulullah* three times. Then he looked at me and said, '*Haroon*'. And everybody started saying '*Haroon*'. I thought this was some kind of ritual invocation, so I started saying '*Haroon*' to fit in. And everyone was greeting me and congratulating me and saying '*Haroon*.' And I was greeting them back and saying '*Haroon*'. When the whole ceremony was over I went up to one of the group and quietly asked, "What does this word '*Haroon*' mean?" He replied, "That's your Muslim name. Haroon is Arabic for Aaron, the brother of Moses." So I entered Islam, clueless, but with a new name and a new future.

I left Berkeley the same day and returned to Los Angeles. On the following Monday I visited my agent. Suddenly, I was flooded with interviews and offers. There was a moment straight out of a 1930s showbiz movie when my excited agent grabs me by the shoulders and exclaims, "You're gonna be BIG!" I remember thinking to myself, "Hmm.

It's tempting, really tempting... but I think not." I sensed that this was a test from God – *Allah.* "Do you want the world? You can have it. Or do you want knowledge and wisdom? Make a choice."

I packed my few possessions, wrote a note to the director of the big movie, telling him I was leaving show business, called my agent, informed my parents and set off back to Berkeley. I had turned over a new leaf. I had turned to a new life in search of knowledge and peace of heart.

Of course, I had no idea what I was getting myself into.

Part Seven

BEGINNING OF THE END

I seek forgiveness from God, the Almighty, beside Whom there is no god, the Living and Eternal, Forgiver of sins, Majestic and Noble, and I turn to Him in repentance from all disobedience, the greater sins and lesser, from every sin I have committed intentionally and mistakenly, outwardly and inwardly, (in) word and deed, in all my movements and rests, my thoughts and my breaths, all of them, always, forever, eternally...from the sin I know and the sin I do not know.[118]

SIDI AHMED IBN IDRIS

118   From *Istighfar al-Kabir,* translated by Abdurrahman Fitzgerald, Fouad Aresmouk and Moulay 'Abdulkebir al-Belghiti

"We have met the enemy and he is us."[119]
POGO

From Hero to Zero

I ENTERED ISLAM on sheer instinct. I didn't read my way into it, that's for sure. I didn't figure something out ahead of time. I was in completely alien territory. I wasn't looking for enlightenment at that stage. That seemed to me a presumptuous ambition, a bridge too far. I just wanted to find some peace of mind. I knew with some certainty from looking around me that all the blandishments and aspirations of modern life were not going to do it for me. I reasoned that Islam seemed to be a viable and seemingly safe way to arrive at some sense of ease and equilibrium. Islam did, after all, mean 'Peace'. I figured that at the very least I would be doing something that was decent, moral, sensible and sane.

I could never have imagined that this truly beautiful, grounded way of life I'd taken on would become synonymous with fanaticism, hatred and atrocities. But I learned early on from reading the saying of the Messenger of God, peace be upon him: 'Show endurance, for you will not come to a time that is not worse than the time before it until you meet your Lord' [120] to anticipate the entropy and keep going. Still, whenever there is a new ghastly outrage that hits the headlines I can't help thinking, 'It can't get any worse than this'. And then it does. And the hits just keep on coming.

Going in I really had no preconceptions, just a hope of escaping what seemed to me to be a bleak, self-involved and infinitely meaningless future that produces agitation, loneliness, disappointment, sadness, false hopes and disillusion; a world of shattered dreams. I suppose I thought that I might be able to become a wise, spiritual being but I didn't have the faintest idea what that would look like and how it would happen. The five prayers—the *Salat*—were enough for me, and the gnostic litanies that I loved to recite but didn't understand for longer than I'd like to admit.

---

119   The title figure in a long-running syndicated cartoon strip by Walt Kelly. The quotation appeared in 1970 on an Earth Day poster.
120   Reported by Az-Zubair ibn Adi in Sahih al-Bukhari

322

Somehow I thought that I was going to turn myself into a better version of me. What I didn't realize at first was that me, my 'self', was the thing that had to go. It dawned on me gradually and when it did, it scared the daylights out of me. I had spent my whole life up to that time building up my ego, doing everything in my power to be great, to be amazing, to stand in the limelight, because I had been raised to think you had to go out and make your mark in the world. I had seen enough of the world, though, to realize that making a mark in the world was a mixed blessing at best. The mark one makes could easily end up turning into a pretty ugly stain. I had a very close friend, a really beautiful soul, who became a movie star overnight at the age of eighteen and I watched it ruin his life. I remember driving up the coast with him immediately after he was 'discovered', going on about how great it was that he had shot to stardom and that now he could concentrate on what was really important. How wrong I was.

Still, here I was, stuck with my oversized ego and with absolutely no way to use it and not an inkling of the way out of it. And, to top it off, I was discovering that instead of becoming the hero in my own epic saga, I was, in fact, supposed to become a zero.

'Prostrate and Draw Near.'[121]

In prostration (*sujud*) you become zero. This is when you are before God, when there is only God before you. When you have made yourself zero you are able to be in the Divine Presence. Otherwise, the ego is there.[122]

SHAYKH MUHAMMAD HYDARA AL-JILANI

It was only by associating with men of true knowledge and illumination that I began to understand. Moulay Hachem al-Belghiti, my shaykh, may God protect him, told me a story that illustrates the ideals of the people of the Way. His father, Moulay Kebir, was sitting with his uncle. Both men were *'arifin* (those possessed of knowledge of God). His uncle smiled and addressed his brother as they gazed at an

121   Holy Qur'an, *Sura al-'Alaq* 96:19
122   From a conversation with the Shaykh

unseen world. "Do you see our destination?" he asked. "Yes," said Moulay Kabir. The destination they both witnessed must have been sublime for Moulay Kabir's brother said, "Let us go there together." Moulay Kebir replied, "I cannot now." His brother said, "Then goodbye," and died.

Moulay Kebir was so moved by his saintly brother's sudden and willing abandonment of life that he built a shrine over his grave to honor him. The masons completed work on the dome under Moulay Kebir's supervision. They all stood back to view the beautiful structure. Before their eyes the entire shrine collapsed into a pile of dust and rubble. Moulay Kebir immediately went to his brother's widow to tell her what had happened. She replied, "Last night my husband came to me in a dream and he showed me the shrine you built. In the dream he said, 'This is what will happen to the shrine they built for me' and before my eyes the shrine collapsed as you described." He didn't want to leave a mark and today no one knows exactly where he's buried. His grave lies somewhere beneath a taxi stand. May God be well pleased with both these men of God.

This is the ideal we strive for. It is expressed in a hadith of the Messenger, may God bless him and grant him Peace:

> God the Almighty and Majestic has said: 'Verily, for Me, the happiest of My saints is the believer who lives modestly, who finds satisfaction in prayer, worships his Lord in the best manner, and is not pointed out. He is content with a meager living and bears this with patience.' Then [the Prophet] snapped his fingers and continued: 'His death is hastened, few people weep for him, and he leaves very few possessions as inheritance.'[123]

That was not quite what I was ready to come to terms with.

I wasn't alone. I was in the company of members of a once successful rock band, a rock and roll photographer, and a well-known poet, among others, who had also dropped out of ordinary life. But, that didn't make me feel any better.

I had no idea how to deal with my new enemy: myself. I thought about myself all the time. I tried to grasp these new concepts I was

---

123   Narrated by Abu Umamah and quoted by Tirmidhi, in 'Spiritual Teachings of the Prophet,' translated by Edin Q. Lohjia

learning about: *Nafs al-ammara bi su'* (the Self that commands to evil), al-*Nafs al-lawwama* (The Self that struggles), and al-*Nafs al-mut'ma'inna* (The Self at peace). I learned the saying attributed to the Prophet, peace be upon him, '*Man Arafa Nafsahu fa qad Arafa Rabbahu'* (He who knows his self, knows his Lord).

And then, the saying of the saint Dhu'l Nun al-Misri: "He who knows his self (*nafs*) best, is the one who has the lowest opinion of it."[124]

I had a terrible time getting my head around it all. "So, let me get this straight: the self is the enemy, there is nothing good in the self. The goal is *fana fi'llah* (effacement in God) but there are three selves and if you know the self you know the Lord? And if you really know the self you have the lowest opinion of it." It seemed to me that there was an awful lot of talk about the self.

> A man full of self came and said, 'Tell me the secrets.'
> I said, 'I can't tell you the secrets. I tell the secrets to the one in whom I don't see him—I see myself. I tell the secrets of self to myself. I don't see myself in you, I see someone else.[125]
>
> SHEMS-I-TABRIZ

So the question was, "How can I get rid of a self that I absolutely need in order to know my Lord?"

I first began to comprehend these principles through the admonitions of Moulay al-'Arabi al-Darqawi who wrote:

> There is no approach to God save through the door of the death of the self (*nafs*). Now we see—but God is wiser—that the *faqir* will not kill his self until he has been able to see its form, and he will see its form only after separating himself from the world, from his companions, his friends and his habits... The *nafs* is an immense thing; it is the whole cosmos, since it is the copy of it. Everything that is in the cosmos is to be found in the *nafs*; equally everything in the *nafs* is in the cosmos. Because of this fact, he who masters his *nafs* most certainly masters the cosmos, just as he who is dominated by his *nafs* is certainly dominated

---

124   From 'Sufi Rules of Conduct' by Sulami, translated by Elena Biagi
125   From the *Maqalat*, translated by William Chittick as 'Rumi and Me'

by the whole cosmos.[126]

One of the things we bring with us from modern western life is the idea of instant gratification. It is the source of a great deal of unhappiness because people are conditioned to think that things are supposed to happen fast and that they are supposed to be gratifying. So we come into Islam, thinking we're following the Sufi Path (oh ho!) and how cool and mystical we are. We expect to have some incredible flash of light and float away on a cloud or magic carpet. In my generation this expectation was intensified because of psychedelics, which could give you a sense of something spiritual just by putting a chemical tab under your tongue. What most of us had no concept of was not only the hard graft of spiritual practice, but the length of time it can take to transcend or efface the self. If you go back and read some of the ancient texts you will find many references to a dervish praying and fasting for forty years. That was a norm, not an exception. And that was when it was presumably easier because the world was a much less distracting and profane place than it is now. It is a lifelong process. Along the way you have what God gives to you in His Mercy, Generosity and Kindness.

Imam Al-Ghazali wrote:

> What you must realize is that this path of ours, in both its length and its shortness, is not like the physical distances traveled by the lower selves. They traverse them on foot, so their traversing them depends on the physical strength and weakness of the lower selves. This is a spiritual path, traveled by the hearts, so you traverse it with thoughts in accordance with beliefs and perceptions. Its origin is a heavenly light and a Divine glance, which penetrates the servant's heart, so by it he sees the state of the two abodes in reality.
>
> The servant may sometimes seek this light for a hundred years, without finding it or any trace of it. That is due to his error in the search, his shortcomings in dedicated effort, and his ignorance of the method thereof. Another may find it in fifty years, another may find it in ten, another in a day, and another in an hour or an instant, through the providential care of the Lord of Might and Glory. He is the Custodian of guidance, but

---

126   'Letters of a Sufi Master Mulay al-'Arabi al-Darqawi,' translated by Titus Burkhardt

the servant is commanded to strive with dedicated effort, so it is incumbent upon him to do as he has been commanded, and the commandment is predestined, foreordained. The Lord is a Just Judge, who does whatever He wills and decrees whatever He wishes.[127]

My ego is a vast landfill of experiences, memories, emotions and all the detritus of an appallingly misspent life. I have chosen solitude so as not to waste my remaining years. I am trying to call my own bluff, to increase my dedicated effort and correct my errors. I have more than enough of the world to give me more enjoyment than I deserve. I only want the companionship of people of the Path, people that I love for the sake of God, Who has been overwhelmingly generous to me. I have received more of the world than I have ever asked for or intended. And in those things I've received I've been tested and continue to be tested. My priority is the remembrance of God and correcting my woefully unreformed self. In all of that, my days are overflowing with moments of relief and I am trying to perceive those moments as they unfold because these are — everything is — from our Creator — and God is Powerful over all things.

For it is the heart that is accepted by God when it is free from all save other than Him, but veiled from God when it becomes wholly occupied by other than Him. It is the heart upon which claims are made, with which conversations are carried on, and with which remonstrance is made, and which is punished. It rejoices in nearness to God and prospers if kept true, and is undone and miserable if debased and corrupted.

The heart is that which, if a man knows it, he knows himself, and if he knows himself he knows his Lord. It is that which, if a man knows it not, he knows not himself, and if he knows not himself, he knows not his Lord.[128]

IMAM ABU HAMID AL GHAZALI

127   'The Path of the Worshipful Servants to the Garden of the Lord of all the Worlds' (*Minhaj al-'Abidin ila Jannati Rabbi l'Alamin*), translated by Muhtar Holland
128   *Kitab sharh 'aja'ib al-qalb* ("The Marvels of the Heart"), translated by Walter James Skellie

O You Who sees and hears what is in the mind,
You are the One we will resort to in whatever might befall.

O You in Whom we place our hope in all hardships,
You to Whom we complain and is our sanctuary.

O You Whose storehouses of provision is in the word "Be!",
Bestow upon us generously, for Your goodness is comprehensive.
I have naught as means to You but my own poverty,
So by virtue of this need for You I seek to allay my poverty.

My only stratagem is to knock upon Your door,
But if I be turned away, on what other door may I knock?

To Whom else can I pray, and call out by His name,
If Your bounty were denied to one destitute (faqir) before You?

Far be it that Your generosity leave a sinner despairing,
For Your bounty is greater than that, and Your gifts more ample.

In lowliness I have come to Your door, in the full knowledge
That it is submissiveness before Your door that serves best.

I have made my dependence upon You entrusting You,
And spread out my palms in supplication and humility.

So by the right due the one You have loved and sent [to mankind],
And have answered the prayer of whoever used him as intercessor,

Grant us a way out of every constricted situation,
And be kind to us, O He Who is our retreat.

Then prayer be upon the Prophet, the Chosen,
The best of humanity, he whose intercession is sought.

IMAM SUHAYLI[129]

---

129   A *Qasida*. Sidi Abu al-Qasim Abd al-Rahman b. Abd Allah al-Suhayli was an Andalusian
saint born in Fuengirola, which was formerly called *Wadi Suhayl*, in 1114 AD and died in Marrakesh
in 1185AD. He is one of the Seven Saints of Marrakesh.

Oh God, send down to us at this time Your goodness and blessings as you send (them) down to Your saints, and choose for Your beloved friends, and give us a taste of the coolness of Your Pardon, and the sweetness of Your Forgiveness, and spread over us Your Mercy which envelops all things, and grant us Your Love and acceptance, sincere repentance, an answer (to our prayers), and forgiveness and pardon embracing all those who are present, absent, living or dead... by Your Mercy, O Most Merciful of those who are merciful!
SIDI MUHAMMAD IBN AL-HABIB[130]

---

130   A supplication by Sidi Muhammad ibn al-Habib contained in the Noble Litany (*Wird*)

When the believer reaches fifty years of age, God lightens his account; when he reaches sixty, God grants him penitence (inaba); when he reaches seventy, he is loved by the inhabitants of the heavens; when he reaches eighty, righteous deeds are recorded for him and God pardons his misdeeds; when he reaches ninety, his sins are forgiven, he is allowed to intercede for his household, and he is God's prisoner on earth; and when he reaches one hundred and is unable to perform (righteous) works, he will have written for him all of the righteous works he used to perform during his period of health and youth.[131]

THE PROPHET MUHAMMAD

---

131   reported by Anas bin Malik

The Later, the Better

IN RECENT TIMES a sincere young novice implored his spiritual master to take him to the station of *ma'rifa* or direct knowledge of God. His shaykh said, "Don't ask for this." But the young disciple was insistent. "I beg you to take me to the goal." The Shaykh repeated, "Don't ask for this." But the disciple persisted, demanding that his master take him on the path toward *fana fi'llah* (effacement in God) right then and there. So the shaykh replied, "Alright, if this is what you really want, go now to your wife and divorce her, settle your affairs, say goodbye to your children and then come to me." The young disciple was stunned. "I...I can't do that," he said. His master said, "Then don't ask for this."

We have become impatient. We want quick results: Instant Coffee, Fast Food, Speed Dating, Speed Reading, Overnight Success, Accelerated Learning, Enlightenment Weekends, Instant Nirvana. We celebrate youth and mourn old age. To be sure old age is to be mourned if we have wasted our time in this world and have nothing to show for the Next. That 'youth is wasted on the young' is, alas, mostly the case, but not always, as evidenced by the sincere young novice. Nevertheless, the search for knowledge is a continuum, a long haul. We have no other way of knowing God except through ourselves. This requires continuous repentance and constant purification of the heart. This takes time. This takes a lifetime. There are exceptions, of course, but the idea that we should expect to be catapulted to great spiritual heights in record time is delusional.

When I was young and impatient my shaykh Sayyid 'Umar 'Abdullah *Mwinyi Baraka* used to quote his shaykh Habib 'Umar bin Sumayt, may God be well pleased with them both, who said, "The Later, the Better." What they meant by this was that it is better to receive spiritual knowledge later in life, when one has reached maturity and attained a measure of wisdom and balance, rather than to receive spiritual gifts prematurely before one is prepared to handle them. The wisdom of our great sages in this time dictates a slow and gradual path.

I once asked Sayyid 'Umar why it was important to know about exalted spiritual stations such as *fana fi'llah* (effacement in God) and *baqa bi'llah* (subsistence in God) when we were so far from them, and he replied that God is so generous that He gives His servants everything they desire before they die, even if it be minutes before death.

Persistence and patience is a common admonition from spiritual adepts to novices. A friend of mine once asked the Moroccan saint Sidi Muhammad Sahrawi what to do if one performs invocation (*dhikru'llah*) and it never reaches the heart. Sidi Muhammad replied that he should persist in invocation. "Sometimes," he said, "the invocation doesn't reach the heart until moments before you die."

An old man came to Abu 'Ali Shaqiq b. Ibrahim al-Azdi and said to him: "O Shaykh I have sinned much and now wish to repent." Shaqiq said: "You have come late." The old man answered: "No I have come soon. Whoever comes before he is dead comes soon, though he may have been long in coming."[132]

The Mediaeval Egyptian saint Dhu'l-Nun al-Misr (796-861 AD) had an incredibly devout disciple. This man had entered into a forty-day spiritual retreat (*khalwa*) forty times. He had made the pilgrimage forty times. And for forty years he had stood the entire night in prayer and observed the supererogatory fasts. For forty long years he watched over the chamber of his heart. And yet, after all that, he came to Dhu'l-Nun in desperation.

After recounting his sincere exertions he said, "I have done all this and for all my effort, self-denial and sacrifice, the Friend has not spoken one word to me, nor has He favored me with a single glance. He takes no account of me and reveals nothing to me from the Unseen World. I am not saying this to praise myself nor to complain against God. I am simply stating the facts. I have done everything in my power to devote my heart and soul to His service. I am not saying this because my heart has grown weary of obedience. I am only relating my sad misfortune. For my entire

132   From *Kashf Al Mahjub*, translated by Reynold A. Nicholson

life I have knocked on the door in hope, but after all this time there has been no answer, and the silence has become unbearable. My fear is that if further life remains ahead of me, everything will remain the same. You are the physician of the afflicted and the sovereign prescriber of the sages. Please give me a cure for my sorrow."

Dhu'l-Nun replied, "Perhaps if the Friend will not show Himself to you with kindness and gentleness, He will reveal Himself with reproach. So, tonight eat a big meal and go to sleep without performing any supererogatory prayers. Don't rise in the night but stay asleep until morning. If He will not look upon you with compassion, then perhaps he will look upon you with severity."

The disciple left the company of his Shaykh and returned to his home. He reluctantly ate his fill but couldn't bring himself to omit his prayers. He lay down, closed his eyes and fell into a deep sleep.

In his sleep the Prophet Muhammad, peace and blessings be upon him, appeared to the troubled worshipper: "Your Friend greets you. He says, 'An effeminate (*mukhannath*), unmanly (*nā-mard*) wretch is he who comes to My Court and is quickly satisfied. The root of the matter is a lifetime of righteousness without complaint. God the Exalted says to you, 'I have given your heart its desire for forty years and I fulfill your desire and I grant you the attainment of all you hope for. But convey my greetings to that bandit and pretender Dhu'l-Nun! Say to him, 'Pretender and Liar! If I do not expose your shame before all in the city, then I am not your Lord. See that you never again seduce the lovers away from My Court.'

The disciple awoke, overcome with weeping. He rushed to Dhu'l-Nun and related his dream. When Dhu'l-Nun heard the words God spoke through His Messenger, denouncing him, he wept for joy, fell down and rolled on the ground in ecstasy.[133]

No sincere effort for the sake of God is ever wasted. The reward can be hidden for a lifetime but have no doubt, it will come to you.

Mawlana Jalalud'din Rumi said that the Way of Jesus was the way of purifying the soul by withdrawing from the world into solitude, while

---

133   Retold from *Tadhkirat al-Awliya* (Memorial of the Saints), translated by A.J. Arberry

the Way of Muhammad was the way of purifying the soul *with* the world. There is no monasticism in Islam. By engaging with the world according to the revealed law (*Sharia*), the heart can be purified over time.

One of the 19th century masters from the Moroccan desert placed his disciples under fierce discipline. They lived lives of intense austerity and asceticism, enduring sleeplessness, hunger, continuous worship and perpetual remembrance of God. There were those from the nearby village who esteemed the People of the Way, sometimes joined their circles of *dhikru'llah* and gave gifts of food and money to support these men of God. These pious citizens were known as *muhibbin*, those who had not taken an initiation of commitment to the spiritual Path but who loved and respected those who did. One from among them was a local shopkeeper, who only had a casual association with the Shaykh and his disciples. When he became old he retired, gave up his shop, approached the Shaykh and asked to be initiated. The Shaykh received the shopkeeper into the order and immediately put him into a *khalwa* (spiritual retreat). After one day, the shopkeeper experienced *fana fi'llah* (effacement in God) and reached the goal of *ma'rifa*.

In astonishment and frustration the Shaykh's disciples protested. "We have been on this path for twenty years, enduring great privation and hardship for the sake of God and yet none of us has experienced *fana fi'llah*. How is it that this ordinary shopkeeper who has done nothing all these years other than to observe his obligatory religious and worldly duties has reached this exalted station so quickly while we are deprived of *ma'rifa*?

The Shaykh replied, "He was dry wood. All I had to do was strike a spark and he was consumed. You all are still green and wet. You have yet to dry out."

> *If you do not believe that God can take you at this moment and make you one of His Friends (Awliya) then you are ignorant of His power.*[134]

IBN ATA'ILLAH AL-ISKANDARI

---

134   Related in 'Purification of the Heart' by Hamza Yusuf

My mother was born in 1920 in Grand Junction, Colorado. She was a small-town girl, a country girl really. She grew up in a more innocent time, during the Great Depression. She went off to university in California and graduated with a teaching credential. She married at the beginning of the Second World War and adopted me in 1949 when I was three months old. She wasn't my biological mother but in every other sense she was my real mother. She instilled in me an interest in reading and learning. She was curious and open-minded but was perplexed when I entered Islam. For her it was a jarring turn of events, me dropping out of what might have been a successful career and joining this utterly strange religion. Was I becoming a religious fanatic? Was it a cult? It certainly wasn't something she could relate with parental pride to her friends and family. She didn't like it at all. It wasn't normal. We became estranged for a few years. It was only after I got married that our relationship improved. My mother fell in love with my wife, and then head over heels in love with our daughter when she was born in her home.

I never spoke to my mother about Islam. She never really asked me questions. She may have spoken to my wife. I don't know. When we moved to Saudi Arabia we kept in touch by phone. One day, out of the blue, my mother said, "I think I should become a Muslim. I believe in it." That was all. She mentioned that she had read 'Islam and the Destiny of Man' by my friend Gai Eaton and this convinced her. I can't remember whether I recommended the book to her or whether she discovered it on her own. I was stunned and delighted. We made arrangements for her to come to Saudi Arabia and stay with us in Makkah. Apart from some European tourism after she was widowed my mother had never ventured into such alien territory. Here she was at the very heart of Islam.

I introduced her to my shaykh Habib Ahmad Mashhur al-Haddad, may God be well pleased with him. I simply wanted her to sit in his presence for a few minutes. Habib instructed me to personally push my mother in a wheelchair in the *sa'i* between Safa and Marwa during the *'umra*. When she left the room, he shook his head and said to me, "*Miskeena* (poor woman), she has *waswas* (whisperings)." This was true. In old age inner chatter increasingly overwhelmed her.

We made the *'umra* and I had the blessing of pushing her wheelchair in the *sa'i*. We made *ziyara* to al-Madinah. My mother marveled at the Ottoman vestiges in the Prophet's Mosque. She stayed with us for one month. We wanted her to stay longer but she felt homesick and returned to California. I advised her to keep her Islam a private matter so as not to alienate her from her close friends, who she was greatly attached to and were her support system.

Many of her relatives lived to very advanced ages and I used to tease my mother, saying I thought she was going to be this increasingly ancient lady. She demurred. "I don't want to live much longer," she said. She flew to Hawaii to visit one of her oldest friends, a college classmate. She had a wonderful time. On the flight back she began to feel weak. She had a checkup and discovered that she suffered from a terminal blood disease, similar to leukemia. Her body could no longer produce white blood cells. She would be required to have blood transfusions in order to survive. She related this news calmly, with only a hint of surprise. With the first transfusion she was able to carry on for about two months. My wife came from Saudi Arabia and raised her spirits, God bless her, keeping my mother continuously in stitches. She stayed for some time and then returned to Makkah to resume work. The second transfusion worked for about six weeks. The third transfusion lasted less than a month. Her time in this life was quickly diminishing. The next transfusion lasted two weeks.

I flew to California in time for what was to be her final transfusion. I arrived and went directly to the hospital, arriving immediately after the transfusion. The doctor told me that this last transfusion was given so that my mother could see me. She was transferred home by ambulance and placed under hospice care. I have never seen anyone so calm in the face of death. My two younger brothers, my eldest son and I stayed by her side night and day. Her best friend, who was twelve years her senior, came by, distraught. "Michael, this is not supposed to happen. I should be first. I can't bear it." (She outlived my mother by many years, passing away at the age of 102). I read Qur'an for her and recited *adhkar* and *qasa'id*. My younger brother played the guitar and sang folk songs for her. She never complained. She was not afraid. She was ready.

My mother was a good woman. She was loving and kind. She never hurt anyone. She always had a favorable opinion of God. At the back of my mind, though, I was unsure. While my mother believed in the principles of Islam, she rarely carried out any of its practices. Would that be enough?

During our vigil I was reading from 'The Remembrance of Death and the Afterlife" (*Kitab dhikr al-mawt wa-ma ba'dahu*) from Imam al-Ghazali's "The Revival of the Religious Sciences" (*Ihya 'ulum al-din*). I came across this passage:

> It is related that the Prophet (may God bless him and grant him peace) once said, 'Watch for three signs in the dying man. If his forehead sweats, his eyes shed tears and his lips become dry, then the mercy of God (Exalted is He!) has alighted upon him.'[135]

I found this last statement wondrous and strange for its extraordinary specificity.

Time passed until we began to think that my mother might recover. She seemed to be gaining strength. I had to fly to New York. I wasn't sure what to do. I asked my brothers. They advised me to go on and return when I had finished my business. The day I left, my mother seemed to further revive. She ate a relatively large meal. Things seemed to be looking up. I drove down to Santa Monica to stay with friends so I could catch a flight to New York the next morning. Within minutes of my arrival the phone rang. It was my son with the news that his grandmother had just passed. He was beside her when she took her last breath. He recited the *shahada* in her ear and the *adhan*. I turned around and drove back to Santa Barbara. By the time I reached home, my mother's body had been removed. I sat down with my youngest brother and asked him to tell me what happened. He knew absolutely nothing about Islam, nor had he any interest in learning. When he replied, this is what he said:

"When she died her forehead was wet with perspiration, there was a tear drop from the outside corner of each of her eyes and her lips were parched and white."

A wave of relief swept over me. God is the Most Merciful of the

---

135   The Remembrance of Death and the Afterlife" (*Kitab dhikr al-mawt wa-ma ba'dahu*), translated by T.J. Winter.

Merciful! We buried her as a Muslim. May God cover her in His Infinite Mercy, illuminate her grave and raise her close to Him on the Day of Rising.

And may God give us the opening, union and the salvation we seek before we die.

ACKNOWLEDGEMENTS

THIS BOOK WOULD have been an impossibility without the courage, candor and eloquence of the men and women who took the time to share their stories. They are its heroes and I am beholden to each and every one of them.

I am indebted to all my dear friends around the world who have advised me along the way and reviewed the text as it was being composed and given me much needed feedback. My thanks to Karim Lahham, Abdullateef and Tahira Whiteman, Shems Friedlander, Abu'l Qasim and Aziza Spiker, Peter Gould, Emin Elzueta, Ahmad James (Baraka Blue), Muhammad Abdul Bari McCabe, Sohail Nakhooda, Amir al-Islam, Peter and Hafsa Sanders, Muhammad Isa Waley, Ovidio Salazar and Radia Massoud.

In addition, my friend Abdullateef Whiteman generously shared some of his long experience and expertise as our finest book designer in providing me with invaluable advice and a beautiful design template to build the book upon.

I could not have done my interview with Mawlana Abdullah in the Gambia, which forms the basis of the chapter 'Dream Progression,' without Rebecca Slenes sitting beside me and translating from Portuguese into English. My thanks to her.

My thanks also to the faqir and my friend 'Azzad'dine Bettach for tirelessly serving seekers in Morocco and for being my constant companion there.

I am deeply indebted to Shaykh Yusuf Da Costa, Shaykh Shamiel Da Costa and members of the Naqshbandi Community in Cape Town for their incredible generosity in hosting me in South Africa, twice, and for introducing me to their work and the beautiful people of the townships. Sadly, Shaykh Yusuf passed away before the publication of this book. He was one of the inspired giants of spirituality in Southern Africa, a great educator and guide to generations of Muslims. It was a blessing for me to have known this wonderful soul. I have dedicated this book to his memory. May God have Mercy upon him.

My dear, scholarly friend Shakir Massoud is one of our hidden treasures. I first met him about forty-six years ago when he was eighteen years old, bound and determined to become a Muslim. Since that time he has been devoted to learning and research and brings a reservoir of knowledge and rich experience to whatever he's engaged in. He is as self-effacing as they come but many of us rely on his learning, judgement, editorial integrity and attention to detail. He is an impeccable editor and meticulously worked through the text of this book and gave me valuable counsel throughout its composition. More than this, I am honored to call him my friend.

I received much needed encouragement from two towering figures in the Muslim world. Shaykh Abdal Hakim Murad (Dr. Timothy Winter), Cambridge professor and the Founder and Dean of Cambridge Muslim College, has been a good friend for over thirty years. He is one of our finest scholars and a man of beautiful character and deep humility.

I have known Shaykh Muhammad Hydara al-Jilani for only a few years but when we met it was a case of love at first sight. Wherever he goes he galvanizes seekers and gives them a way forward in a difficult and troubling world. He has invariably supported the work we are trying to do and he introduced me to the extraordinary story of Mawlana Abdullah from Guinea Bissau. I am grateful to know these great men of God.

GLOSSARY

A Note on Terms

Although I have tried to make the language and references as accessible and easy to understand as possible, there are necessarily some technical terms that may require explanation.

Adhan: The Muslim call to prayer.

Allah: God. I have used the Name Allah and God interchangeably in the text. For the purposes of this exposition, there is no difference whatsoever.

'Arifbi'llah or **'Arif**: Knower of God or Knower; most commonly translated as Gnostic. The *Arifbi'llah* is the possessor of direct knowledge of God.

Baqabi'llah or **Baqa**: Literally, 'to remain with or subsist in God'. This is the supreme state of spiritual enlightenment where the slave has full awareness of duality, but sees phenomena as not other than God. The concept was first articulated by the 9th century Sufi master Abu Sa'id al-Kharraz in 'Book of the Secret'.

Bay'a: A pledge of allegiance. In *Tasawwuf, Bay'a* refers to a spiritual initiation and connection with a Teaching Shaykh (*Shaykh Murabbi*) with spiritual authorization. The *Bay'a* connects the *murid* with the *murshid* in the Unseen.

Burnoose: A cloak.

Cantor: A person who leads prayer and singing in Jewish worship services.

Dervish: The Persian term for a follower of the Sufi Path. The Arabic name is most commonly *Faqir*, or poor man.

Dhikru'llah: Remembrance of God - the linchpin of all Sufi practice, indeed of all Muslim practice, is the act of remembrance or invocation of God (*dhikru'llah*). I would argue that the practice of invocation or remembrance is essential to all religious practice from Muslim,

Christian, Jewish, Hindu and Buddhist traditions and the traditions of all true faiths. The recitation of the Qur'an, Bible, Torah, Vedas, Sutras, Upanishads and other sacred books is a form of remembrance. The Sufis consider recitation of the Qur'an the highest form of remembrance of God. In the Holy Qur'an there are many references to remembrance of God.

Diwan: a collection of odes, usually in rhymed couplets. Each ode is called a *qasida* (plural: *qasa'id*). In the Sufi tradition the diwan is composed by a teaching shaykh or spiritual master.

Djellaba: a traditional Moroccan/Algerian robe. The Northwest African *djellaba* has a hood. The Egyptian robe, without a hood, is called a *gellabiyya*. In the Gulf countries the robe is called a *thobe* or *dishdasha*.

Du'a: Supplication.

Eid: The feast or celebration marking the end of Ramadan, the month of fasting (*Eid Al-Fitr*), and the culmination of the annual Pilgrimmage (*Eid Al-Adha*).

Fanafi'llah (*Fana*): Literally effacement in God. This is the goal of the seeker, when the self is obliterated in Divine light. Again, this doctrine was first articulated by Abu Sa'id Al-Kharraz (see *Baqabi'llah*).

Faqir (plural *Fuqara*): Literally a poor man (female, *faqira*) or, in plural, the poor. In Sufism faqir refers to a man on the Sufi Way in reference to the disciples having "renounced all things external and internal, and have turned entirely to [God]". One of the Sufis explained that "the *faqir* is not he whose hand is empty of provisions, but he whose nature is empty of desires." In Eastern Sufism the word used is *Dervish*, or *Darwish*.

Ghusl: Full ritual ablution, performed after the act of sex or in preparation for a sacred act, such as the performance of *Hajj* or *Umrah*.

Hadith: A reports tracing back to the beginnings of Islam on the actions and declarations of the Prophet Muhammad, peace be upon him.

Hadra: Literally "Presence", this is an auditory practice that in Western Sufism takes the form of a dance where devotees invoke the Names of God, usually standing in a circle, hands joined, often swaying or moving to the rhythms of the invocation and the collective breath.

Hajj: the Greater Pilgrimage to Makkah Al-Mukarramah, one of the Five Pillars of Islam.

I Ching: An ancient Chinese manual of divination, one of the five classics of Confucianism.

Ihram: The two pieces of seamless white cloth prescribed for male pilgrims to wrap around their waists and cover their upper torso during the greater and lesser pilgrimages (*Hajj* and *'Umrah*).

Ihsan: Literally 'Excellence'. The Messenger of Allah described Ihsan as 'to worship God as if you see Him, for while you do not see Him, surely He sees you'. Ihsan is the spiritual dimension of Islam and is integral and necessary to its faith and practice.

Jadhb: Literally 'attraction', an ecstatic state where the worshipper is overwhelmed with the presence of God.

Jahiliyya: The word is derived from the root JA-HA-LA, which means 'ignorance' and refers to the way the Arabs were living in the period before the advent of the revelation to the Prophet Muhammad and the establishment of Islam.

Janazah: Muslim funeral. *Salat Al-Janazah* is the Muslim funeral prayer, also called *Salat Al-Mawt* (prayer for the dead).

Ka'ba: The House of God, built by the Prophet Abraham and the epicenter of Islam. All Muslims pray toward the Ka'ba.

Kashf: Unveiling, literally raising of a curtain or veil. The term refers to an opening of spiritual intuition or insight.

Khalifa: Literally "one who stands in place of". In Sufism a *khalifa* is a designated representative of the shaykh.

Khalwa: Spiritual retreat.

Kol Nidrei: the first communal prayer service of Yom Kippur.

Laylat Al-Fuqara: Literally "Night of the Poor"; a gathering of Sufis for the remembrance of God.

Ma'rifa: Direct spiritual knowledge of God; gnosis.

Mabkhara (plural *Mabakhir*): Incense burner.

Maghrib: The obligatory prayer after the setting of the sun.

Majdhoub: One who is ecstatic, God-intoxicated, overwhelmed by *jadhb* (rapture) to the point of madness; sometimes described as a Holy Madman. When the great ancient Sufi Shibli was accused of being mad, he answered: "In your eyes I am mad and you are sane. May God increase me in my madness and increase you in your sanity!"

Majlis: Literally "Place of Sitting"; a gathering for remembrance or learning.

Mas'a: The track between the mounts of Safa and Marwa where Sayyida Hajar ran in search of water for her infant, the Prophet Isma'il, peace be upon them.

Mataf: The circular area around the Kaaba where pilgrims and worshippers perform the *Tawwaf* or circumambulation of God's House.

Mawlid: Celebration of the birth of the Prophet Mohamed, peace be upon him.

Minyan: a quorum of 10 men over the age of 13 required for traditional Jewish public worship.

Mu'adhdhin: One who calls worshippers to prayer (makes the *adhan*).

Muhajireen: Emigrants, referencing those who migrated with the Prophet Muhammad from Makkah to al-Madinah. Plural of *muhajir*.

Muqaddam: An appointed deputy of a spiritual master. The *muqaddam* of a Sufi order is generally a more experienced disciple who has been assigned by the Shaykh to help guide disciples and administrate the practice. The title does not indicate spiritual knowledge.

Murid: The root meaning of this word relates to willpower and in Sufism refers to a disciple or follower of a Shaykh. In one sense the murid surrenders his will to the Shaykh. In another sense the murid exercises his will by taking the path to God.

Murshid: Literally, "one who guides", which in Sufism refers to a true spiritual master.

Mutawwif: Literally one who makes *Tawaf* or circumambulation of the Kaaba but in common usage the word refers to one who guides pilgrims during the Hajj. This entails the organization of accommodation, food and transport during the pilgrimage. Originally the *mutawifeen* (plural of *mutawif*) were learned men who guided pilgrims from their home countries to Makkah and helped them perform the Hajj rituals. In Saudi Arabia the position became hereditary and commercial until the government restructured the *Mutawwifun* into organizations, serving specific countries and regions.

Nafs: The self, or ego. It is also sometimes referred to as 'soul'. The word is related to *nafas*, meaning breath.

Passover: A Jewish Holy Day celebrating the biblical narrative of Exodus which describes God's liberation of the Children of Israel from slavery.

Qasida (plural *Qasa'id*): An ode, usually in rhymed couplets. Qasa'id have been written by great Sufi saints for the purpose of imparting wisdom teaching and spiritual knowledge and as a form of *dhikru'llah*. One of the earliest composers of *qasa'id* in the Islamic tradition was the Companion Hassan bin Thabit.

Qibla: Direction Muslims face in prayer toward the Holy Kaaba in Makkah Al Mukarramah.

Qutb: Literally the 'Pole' or 'Axis' and refers to a living saint who is the highest spiritual authority of his age and the axis of the unseen hierarchy of living saints. At times the *Qutb* is well known, as was the case with Shaykh Abu Madyan Al-Ghawth and Imam Abu'l-Hasan al-Shadhili. At other times the *Qutb* is hidden. The hidden *Qutb* of this time was revealed to the Shaykh Moulay Hachem Belghiti in an encounter at Moulay Idris Zerhoun.

Rabbi: a Jewish religious leader.

Ru'ya: A true visionary dream.

Sadaqa: Alms.

Sa'y: The seven circuits between the mounts of Safa and Marwa Muslims must walk as part of the 'Umrah to commemorate Hajar's search for water. Literally Sa'y means "effort".

Salafis: Those who believe that Muslims should return to the essential practice of the first Community at the time of the Prophet Mohamed, peace be upon him, and reject all other subsequent historical iterations of Islam. Many follow the teachings of Ibn Taymiyya and Mohamed ibn Abdul Wahhab. *Salafis* completely reject Shi'aa Islam and Sufism as innovation (*bida'a*). In the media *Salafis* are often described as fundamentalists or Islamists. Sunni extremists who advocate violence claim to be *Salafis*. However, not all *Salafis* are extremists.

Salat Al-Mawt: Literally, prayer for the dead.

Shahada: the Muslim declaration of faith - *ashadu an Lailaha illa 'Llah wa ashadu Muhammadun Rasulullah* (I witness that there is no god but God and I witness that Muhammad is the Messenger of God).

Sharia: Literally "The Road"; Islamic canonic law, based upon the Qur'an and Prophetic traditions.

Suhba: Spiritual companionship.

Sunna: The practice of the Prophet Muhammad, peace be upon him, based upon hadith literature.

Tabernacle: An altar in a Jewish synagogue.

Tahajjud: A voluntary prayer that can be performed any time between the obligatory night (*isha*) and dawn (*fajr*) prayers.

Tasbih: A Muslim rosary, or prayer beads. Also called *Sibha*.

Tarawih: Literally, "to rest", which refers to resting between every four cycles of prayer. *Salat al-Tarawih* are prescribed supererogatory prayers recited during Ramadan, after the night prayers.

Tariqa: Literally, "Path" or "Way". In Sufi terminology, a *tariqa* is a Sufi brotherhood or order, composed of disciples (*murideen*) who follow the teachings of a spiritual master (*murshid*), or *shaykh*. A Sufi *tariqa* can be large, with thousands or even millions of followers, as in the Shadhili or Tijani orders, or smaller with dozens or hundreds of followers.

Tawaf: Circumambulation of seven circuits around the Holy Kaaba, a ritual practice for Muslims visiting the Holy Mosque in Makkah, tracing back to the time of Abraham, and forming an essential part of the Greater and Lesser Pilgrimages (*Hajj* and *Umra*). The area surrounding the Ka'ba is called the *Mataf*, (literally, "the place of *Tawaf*").

Tawba: Repentance. Literally 'to turn' or 'return'

'Umra: The Lesser Pilgrimage, wherein the Muslim dons the *ihram* and performs the *tawaf* and *sa'ee*. '*Umra* is an integral part of the Hajj.

Wajd: Usually translated as ecstasy. Al-Hujwiri wrote, "*Wajd* is a mystery between the seeker and the Sought, which only revelation can expound."

Wali'ullah (plural *Awliya'ullah*): Literally, Friend of God, signifying a man of deep spiritual knowledge and attainment – a Saint. In Islam saints are not canonized as in the Christian tradition, but "recognized" by other gnostics. Some, perhaps most, *Awliya'ullah* are completely hidden.

Wird (plural *Awrad*): A prescribed litany recited regularly. In explaining the wird in his book "Realities of Sufism", Shaykh Abdul Qadir 'Isa refers to the Arabic lexicon al-Misbah, which defines a *wird* as: "A daily regimen of reading…The Sufis employ this word to refer to the formulas of remembrance that a Shaykh orders his students to recite in the morning after the morning (*fajr*) prayer and the evening after the sunset (*maghrib*) prayer."

Wudhu: The act of ritual purification prescribed by the Prophet Muhammad, peace be upon him, to precede the act of ritual prayer.

Yom Kippur: The 'Day of Atonement' in Judaism, the final day of the Jewish High Holy Days celebrated on the 10th day of the 7th month in the Jewish Calendar. Yom Kippur is called 'The Sabbath of Sabbaths.'

Zawiya: literally "Corner": The gathering place for the *dhikr* of a Sufi order. (Also known in Persian and Turkish as *Tekke, Khanaqah,* or *Dargah.*)

Ziyara: a visit. In the Sufi context *ziyara* is a visit to a sacred place, which could be the grave of one of the saints or to a living saint or gathering of *fuqara*.

BIBLIOGRAPHY

Addas, Claude, Quest for the Red Sulphur: The Life of Ibn 'Arabi, translated from the French by Peter Kingsley, Islamic Texts Society Golden Palm Series, Cambridge, 1993.
Addas, Claude, The Voyage of No Return, translated from the French by David Streight, Islamic Texts Society, Cambridge, 2000.

al-'Alawi, Ahmad, Two Who Attained, translated by Leslie Cadavid, Fons Vitae, Louisville, KY, 2005.

Amin, W. Mohd Azam b. Mohd, PhD Thesis: An evaluation of the *Qut al-Qulub* of al-Makki with an annotated translation of his *Kitab al-Tawba*, University of Edinburgh, 1991.

Ansari, Khwaja Abdullah. Intimate Conversations (*Munajat*), translated by W.M. Thackston, Jr., Paulist Press, New York, 1978.
Ansari, Abdullah, Stations of the Sufi Path (The One Hundred Fields - *Sad Maydan*), translated by Nahid Angha, Archetype, Cambridge 2010.

'Attar, Farid Al-Din. Muslim Saints and Mystics (*Tadhkirat al-Auliya*), translated by A.J. Arberry. Arkana, London, 1990.

al-Badawi, Mostafa, Sufi Sage of 'Arabia, Fons Vitae, Louisville, KY, 2005.

al-Bayhaqi, Imam, The Seventy-Seven Branches of Faith, translated by Abdal Hakim Murad, The Quilliam Press Ltd., Dorton, Bucks., UK, 1990.

Chittick, William C., Me & Rumi: The Autobiography of Shamsi Tabriz (Me & Rumi), Fons Vitae, Louisville, KY, 2004
Chittick, William C., The Sufi Doctrine of Rumi, World Wisdom Inc.,

Bloomington, Indiana, 2005.
Chittick, William C., The Sufi Path of Love, State University of New York Press, Albany 1983.

Chodkiewicz, Michel, Seal of the Saints, translated from the French by Liadain Sherrard, Islamic Texts Society, Cambridge, 1993.
Chodkiewicz, Michel, The Spiritual Writings of 'Amir 'Abd al-Kader, State University of New York Press, Albany, New York, USA, 1995.

Chourief, Tayeb, Spiritual Teachings of the Prophet, translated by Edin Q. Lohja, Fons Vitae, Louisville, KY 2011.

Cornell, Vincent J., Realm of the Saint: Power and Authority in Moroccan Sufism, University of Texas Press, Austin, 1998.
Cornell, Vincent J., The Way of Abu Madyan: The Works of Abu Madyan Shu'ayb, Islamic Texts Society, Cambridge, 1996.

al-Darqawi, Al-'Arabi, Letters of a Sufi Master, translated by Titus Burckhardt. Fons Vitae, Louisville, KY, 1998.

Farid, A.H., Prayers of Muhammad, Taj Company, Delhi, 1983.

al-Ghazali, Abu Hamid Muhammad ibn Muhammad, The Book of Repentance (*kitab al-Tawbah*), translated by S.M. Stern, Imam al-Ghazali Institute and Dar al-Fiqh, 2010.
al-Ghazali, Abu Hamid Muhammad ibn Muhammad, The Duties of Brotherhood in Islam, translated by Muhtar Holland, The Islamic Foundation, Leicester UK, 1980.
al-Ghazali, Abu Hamid Muhammad ibn Muhammad, Invocations and Supplications (*Kitab al-adhkar wa'l-da'awat*), translated by K. Nakamura, Islamic Texts Society, Cambridge, UK, 1990.
al-Ghazali, Abu Hamid Muhammad ibn Muhammad, Letter to a Disciple (*Ayyuha'l-Walad*), translated by Tobias Mayer, Islamic Texts Society, Cambridge, 2005.
al-Ghazali, Abu Hamid Muhammad ibn Muhammad, On the Manners Relating to Eating (*Kitab adab al-akl*), translated by D. Johnson-Davies

MacDonald, Islamic Texts Society, Cambridge, 2000.

al-Ghazali, Abu Hamid Muhammad ibn Muhammad, The Ninety-Nine Beautiful Names of God (*al-Maqsad al-asna fi sharh asma Allah al-husna*), translated by David B. Burrel and Nazih Daher, Islamic Texts Society, Cambridge, 1992.

al-Ghazali, Abu Hamid Muhammad ibn Muhammad, The Marvels of the Heart (*Kitab sharh 'aja'ib al-qalb*), translated by Walter James Skellie, Fons Vitae, Louisville, KY 2010

al-Ghazali, Abu Hamid Muhammad ibn Muhammad, Deliverance from Error (*al-Munqidh min al-Dalal*), translated by R.J. McCarthy, Fons Vitae, Louisville, Kentucky, Original edition 1980.

al-Ghazali, Abu Hamid Muhammad ibn Muhammad, On Vigilance and Self Examination (*Kitab al-muraqaba wa'l muhasaba*), translated by Anthony F. Shaker, Islamic Texts Society, Cambridge, 2015.

al-Haddad, Imam 'Abdallah Ibn 'Alawi, Gifts for the Seeker, translated by Mostafa al-Badawi, Fons Vitae, Louisville, KY, 2003.

al-Haddad, Imam 'Abdallah Ibn 'Alawi, The Sublime Treasures, translated by Mostafa al-Badawi, Fons Vitae, Louisville, KY, 2008.

al-Haddad, Habib Ahmad Mashhur, Key to the Garden, translated by Mostafa al-Badawi, The Quilliam Press, London, 1990.

Hafiz-i Shirazi, Khwaja Shams ud-Din Muhammad, The Diwan (The Green Sea of Heaven: Fifty ghazals from the Diwan of Hafiz), translated by Elizabeth T. Gray, Jr. White Cloud Press, Ashland, Oregon, 1995.

Helminski, Camille Adams, Women of Sufism: A Hidden Treasure, Shambhala, Boston 2003.

Huddleston, Diane M., "The Beat Generation: They Were Hipsters Not Beatniks", (referencing Norman Mailer, "The White Negro: Superficial Reflections on the Hipster,") Dissent, 1957.

al-Hujwiri, Ali bin Uthman, *Kashf Al Mahjub*, translated by Reynold A. Nicholson. Taj Company, Delhi, 1982.

Ibn al 'Arabi, Muhyideen, Divine Sayings: 101 Hadith Qudsi: The *Mishkat al-Anwar* of Ibn 'Arabi, translated by Stephen Hirtenstein and Martin Notcutt, Al Anqa Publishing, Oxford, 2004.

Ibn al 'Arabi, Muhyideen, Sufis of Andalusia (*Ruh al-Quds* and *al-Durrat al-Fakhirah*), translated by R.W.J. Austin, Beshara Publications, Sherborne, Gloucestershire, 1988.

Ibn al-Habib, Muhammad, The Noble Litany, translated by Abdul Rahman Fitzgerald, Fouad Aresmouk and Abdelkebir al-Belghiti, Editorial Qasida, London, 2016.

Ibn al-Sabbagh, The Mystical Teachings of al-Shadhili (*Durrat al-Asrar wa Tuhfat al-Abrar*), translated by Elmer H. Douglas, State University of New York Press, Albany, NY, 1993.

'Isa, Shaykh Abd Al-Qadir, Realities of Sufism. Translated by Suraqah Abdul Aziz. Sunni Publications, The Netherlands, 2009.

al-Iskandari, Ibn Ata'illah, The Book of Wisdom (*Al-Hikam*), translated by Victor Danner, Paulist Press, New York, 1978.

al-Iskandari, Ibn Ata'illah. The Subtle Blessings in the Saintly Lives of Abu al-Abbas al-Mursi and His Master Abu Al-Hasan (*Kitab Lata'if al-Minan fi Manaqib Abi'l-Abbas al-Mursi wa Shaykhihi Abi'l-Hasan*), translated by Nancy Roberts. Fons Vitae, Louisville, Ky, 2005.

al-Iskandari, Ibn Ata'illah, The Book of Illumination (*Kitab al-Tanwir fi Isqat al-Tadbir*), translated by Scott Kugle, Fons Vitae, Louisville, KY, 2005.

al-Iskandari Ibn Ata'illah, The Key to Salvation (*Miftah al-Falah wa Misbah al-Arwah*), translated by Mary Ann Koury Danner, The Islamic Texts Society Golden Palm Series, Cambridge, 1996.

al-Ja'fari, Salih, Reassurance for the Seeker (*al-Faw'id al-Ja'fariyya*) translated by Samer Dajani, Fons Vitae, Louisville, KY, 2013.

al-Jawziyya, Ibn Qayyim. The Invocation of God (*al-Wabil al-Sayyib min al-Kalim al-Tayyib*), translated by Abdurrahman Fitzgerald and Moulay

Youssef Slitine. ITS, Cambridge, 2000.

al-Jerrahi, Sheikh Muzaffer Ozak, The Unveiling of Love, translated by Muhtar Holland, Inner Traditions, New York, 1981.
al-Jerrahi, Muzaffer Ozak, The Unveiling of Love, translated by Muhtar Holland, Inner Traditions International, New York, 1981.
al-Jilani, Abd al-Qadir, The Secret of Secrets, interpreted by Shaykh Tosun Bayrak al-Jerrahi al-Halveti, Islamic Texts Society, Cambridge, 1992.

al-Jilani, Abdul Qadir. Futuh al-Ghaib (Revelations of the Unseen), translated by M. Aftab-ud-Din Ahmad. Sh. Muhammad Ashraf, Lahore, 1986.

Lings, Martin, Sufi Poems: A Mediaeval Anthology, Islamic Texts Society, Cambridge 2004.
Lings, Martin, A Sufi Saint of the Twentieth Century: Shaikh Ahmad al-'Alawi – His Spiritual Heritage and Legacy, Islamic Text Society Golden Palm Series, Cambridge, 1993.

Maharshi, Bhagavan Sri Ramana, Gems from Bhagavan, compiled by A. Devaraja Mudaliar, Sri Ramanasramam, Tiruvannamalai, 2000.

al-Maliki, Sayyid Muhammad ibn 'Alawi, Muhammad, the Perfect Man, translated by Khalid Williams, Visions of Reality Books, 2016.

Matusow, Allen J., The Unraveling of America: A History of Liberalism in the 1960s, New York: Harper & Row Publishers, New York, 1984.

Maududi, Abul'Ala, Towards Understanding Islam, WAMY, Jeddah, 1986.

Moustafa, Ahmed and Sperl, Stefan, The Cosmic Script Vols. 1 & 2, Thames & Hudson, London, 2014.

Perry, Charles, 'The Lotus & The Toad', Rolling Stone Magazine,

February 21, 1970.

al-Qushayri, Abu'l Qasim Abd al-Karim, Principles of Sufism, translated by B.R. von Schlegell, Islamic Book Trust, Kuala Lumpur, 2004.

Renard, John, Tales of God's Friends, University of California Press, Berkeley, 2009.

Rizvi, Saiyid Athar Abbas, A History of Sufism in India, Volumes One and Two, Munshairam Manoharlal Publishers Pvt. Ltd., New Delhi, 1986.

Rumi, Jalaluddin, Signs of the Unseen (The Discourses), translated by W.M. Thackston, Jr., Shambhala Publications, Boston, 1994.

Sarbanes, Janet, A Community of Artists: Radical Pedagogy at CalArts, 1969-72, eastofborneo.org, June 5, 2014

Shu'ayb, Abu Madyan, The Way of Abu Madyan. Compiled and Translated by Vincent J. Cornell, Islamic Texts Society, Cambridge, 1996.

Stevens, Jay, Storming Heaven: LSD and the American Dream, Paladin Grafton Books, London, 1988.

al-Sulami, Abu 'Abd al-Rahman, A Collection of Sufi Rules of Conduct (*Jawami 'Adab al-Sufiyya*, translated by Elena Biagi, Islamic Texts Society, Cambridge, 2010.

Welsford, Enid, The Fool: His Social & Literary History, Faber and Faber, London, 1935.

Yusuf, Hamza, Purification of the Heart, Sandala, Inc. Mountain View, CA, 2012.

Photo by Peter Sanders

MICHAEL SUGICH IS a native of Santa Barbara, California. He studied at University of California at Los Angeles (UCLA) and the California Institute of the Arts. In 1972 he was initiated into a traditional Sufi order. Since that time he has studied Sufi doctrine and practice with spiritual masters across the Arab and Islamic world. He lived for 23 years in the precincts of the sacred city of Makkah al-Mukarrama where he kept company with many men of knowledge and illumination. He has also lived in London, Bristol, Cairo and Dubai and currently resides in Istanbul.

He is the author of 'Signs on the Horizons.'

His Muslim name is Haroon.

Printed in Great Britain
by Amazon

45163391R00209